Structures of Influence

UNC | COLLEGE OF ARTS AND SCIENCES
Germanic and Slavic Languages and Literatures

From 1949 to 2004, UNC Press and the UNC Department of Germanic & Slavic Languages and Literatures published the UNC Studies in the Germanic Languages and Literatures series. Monographs, anthologies, and critical editions in the series covered an array of topics including medieval and modern literature, theater, linguistics, philology, onomastics, and the history of ideas. Through the generous support of the National Endowment for the Humanities and the Andrew W. Mellon Foundation, books in the series have been reissued in new paperback and open access digital editions. For a complete list of books visit www.uncpress.org.

Structures of Influence
A Comparative Approach to August Strindberg

EDITED BY MARILYN JOHNS BLACKWELL

UNC Studies in the Germanic Languages and Literatures
Number 98

Copyright © 1981

This work is licensed under a Creative Commons CC BY-NC-ND license. To view a copy of the license, visit http://creativecommons.org/licenses.

Suggested citation: Blackwell, Marilyn. *Structures of Influence: A Comparative Approach to August Strindberg.* Chapel Hill: University of North Carolina Press, 1981. DOI: https://doi.org/10.5149/9781469657141_Blackwell

Library of Congress Cataloging-in-Publication Data

Names: Blackwell, Marilyn.
Title: Structures of influence : A comparative approach to August Strindberg / by Marilyn Blackwell.
Other titles: University of North Carolina studies in the Germanic languages and literatures ; no. 98.
Description: Chapel Hill : University of North Carolina Press, [1981] Series: University of North Carolina studies in the Germanic languages and literatures.
Identifiers: LCCN 80-29545 | ISBN 978-1-4696-5713-4 (pbk: alk. paper) | ISBN 978-1-4696-5714-1 (ebook)
Subjects: Strindberg, August, 1849-1912 — Influence — Addresses, essays, lectures. | Scandinavian literature — 20th century — History and criticism — Addresses, essays, lectures. | Johnson, Walter Gilbert, 1905-.
Classification: LCC PT9816 .S73 | DDC 839/.726

Contents

Preface ... ix

Tabula Gratulatoria ... xiii

PART I. STRINDBERG IN SCANDINAVIA

The Symbiosis of "Spirits" in *Inferno*:
Strindberg and Swedenborg
   Göran Stockenström ... 3

Strindberg and Karlfeldt
   Karl-Ivar Hildeman ... 38

The Chamber Plays and the Trilogy: A Revaluation
of the Case of Strindberg and Bergman
   Marilyn Johns Blackwell ... 49

Strindberg: The Man and the Myth as
Seen in the Mirror of Per Olov Enquist
   Ross Shideler ... 65

Questions without Answers:
On Strindberg's and Ibsen's Dialogue
   Gunnar Brandell ... 79

Art and Passion: The Relationship
between Strindberg and Munch
   Reidar Dittmann ... 92

Strindberg and Hamsun
   Harald Næss ... 121

Strindberg's *Ett drömspel* and Peder W. Cappelen's
Sverre. Berget og Ordet: Two Dreams of Love
   Henning K. Sehmsdorf ... 137

Strindberg in Denmark
   P. M. Mitchell ... 151

Edvard Brandes and August Strindberg:
Encounter between Critic and Artist
  Carl Reinhold Smedmark   165

Strindberg and Diktonius: A Second Chapter
  George C. Schoolfield   183

PART II. STRINDBERG ABROAD

Strindberg at the Opera
  Raymond Jarvi   203

Strindberg's *Ett drömspel* and Hofmannsthal's *Die Frau ohne Schatten*
  Rochelle Wright   211

From *lilla helvetet* to the Boxing Ring: Strindberg and Dürrenmatt
  Gerhard P. Knapp   226

Some Notes on Strindberg and Péladan
  Örjan Lindberger   245

August Strindberg in America, 1963–1979: A Bibliographical Assessment
  Birgitta Steene   256

Strindberg and O'Neill
  Egil Törnqvist   277

III. Bibliography of Professor Walter Johnson   293

IV. Index of Titles and Names   301

Preface

In response to an invitation to contribute to this *festskrift*, a prominent Strindberg scholar replied: "Where would we all be without Walter Johnson?" This is not as rhetorical a question as it might seem: surely no single individual in the history of Scandinavian studies in America has done more to promote the development of our profession than Professor Johnson. As a member of the editorial staffs of *Scandinavian Studies*, *Scandinavica*, and the *Swedish Pioneer Historical Quarterly* and the author of some seventeen books (see the complete bibliography at the end of the volume), he has exerted an unparalleled influence on the development and standards of American-Scandinavian scholarship; we think in particular of his twelve years as editor of *Scandinavian Studies*. As a scholar his credentials are impeccable; he is the author of the much lauded *August Strindberg* and translator and editor of the "Washington Strindberg," which now comprises thirty plays in nine volumes. He has also written another twenty-two articles and seventy-four book reviews on widely disparate topics and compiled twenty-seven bibliographies. As chairman of the largest Scandinavian department in the country and *Doktorvater* to a whole generation of scholars, he has shaped Scandinavian studies in America for decades to come.

Professor Johnson's national and international eminence has, however, never interfered with his vocation as a teacher and his kindness as a mentor. As a teacher Walter Johnson possessed the ability to inspire self-confidence: he could find and bring out the best in his academic charges. His graduate students would sometimes smile at that favorite expression of his, "God, man, and the universe," but years later we realize that he tried to impart to us an ineradicable sense of the ethical demands of our chosen discipline and the far-reaching responsibilities of our professional endeavors. Despite his extraordinarily heavy commitments to publishing, administrative, editorial, and committee duties, Professor Johnson not only found time for his students, but also sought them out and evinced a deep interest in their personal and professional lives, a generosity that was coupled with the greatest self-effacement and modesty.

It is not surprising then that neither the United States nor Sweden has been slow in acknowledging Walter Johnson's contributions to Scandinavian scholarship. In 1961 he received the Royal Swedish Order of the North Star; in 1963 he was awarded the Distinguished Alumnus Award at Augsburg College; in 1972 he received the degree of Honorary Doctorate from the University of Uppsala; in 1973 he was the recipient of the Swedish Academy's Gold Medal, and in 1979 he was granted the American-Scandinavian Foundation Gold Medal.

Now the time is nigh for Professor Johnson to receive some token of the respect and affection that we all as individuals bear him. This *festskrift* is presented to him in a Strindbergian effort to repay in part the enormous debt we all owe him. It is, of course, not surprising that a *festskrift* for Walter Johnson should take Strindberg as its subject, for the Swedish dramatist has been a lifelong passion of his; it is by virtue of his pioneering Strindberg studies that Professor Johnson first achieved international eminence. Strindberg remains to this day, along with Vilhelm Moberg, Professor Johnson's major research interest, as is evident from his continuing publication of new volumes of the "Washington Strindberg." And, as he always strove to place Scandinavian literature within a comparative context and to expand the boundaries of our perception of literature, I trust he will not disapprove of a comparative approach to "Sveriges största eld" ("Sweden's greatest fire").

The studies in this volume are all comparative in nature, some tracing influences on Strindberg, others delineating Strindberg's impact on subsequent literature, and still others operating outside the rubric of influence and yet within a comparative literary framework. The purpose of including such diverse essays is quite simply to provide an insight into Strindberg's seminal position in the development of both literary history and the dramatic genre itself. The volume directs itself especially to relatively virgin scholarly territory, topics that have not previously been treated or that have been given short shrift. The reader, therefore, will seek in vain for a study on Strindberg and the Theater of the Absurd or Strindberg's impact on Expressionism. Unless otherwise mentioned, all references to Strindberg in Swedish are from the John Landquist edition of his works, *Samlade Skrifter* (Stockholm: Bonniers, 1912–20). English translations are, where possible, from Walter Johnson's "Washington Strindberg." An attempt has been made to translate all titles and major quotations into English, be they from French or German or one of the Scandinavian languages; the title translations are given only once, usually immediately after the first citation, and the quotation translations are incorporated into the footnotes so that the volume might serve a wider community of scholars.

Lastly, I would like to thank various organizations and individuals for their participation in this endeavor: The Royal Academy of Letters, History, and Antiquities for a very generous grant, the University of Virginia for a Xeroxing grant, George Schoolfield for his intelligent advice and ever-gracious help in all stages of the project, Patricia Banton and Ruby Parrish for their typing of manuscripts, Michael Blackwell for his perspicacious comments and constant support, and Mrs. Ruth Ingeborg Johnson, without whose collaboration this volume would never have been possible. Ten years of friendship have taught me to appreciate and value her for her own native intelligence and generosity of spirit as well as for the inestimable role which she played in the fine achievement that is Walter Johnson's.

Marilyn Johns Blackwell
October 1980

Tabula Gratulatoria

Individuals

Samuel Abrahamson
Hans O. E. Andersson
Norman C. Bansen
Else and Hans Bekker-Nielsen
Marie Bergsagel and
   W. Fred DeWolf
Jeffrey B. Berlin
Beth Björklund
Michael L. Blackwell
Haskell M. Block
Harold H. Borland
Philip N. Bottman
Hedin Brønner
Peter Buchholz
Dolores Buttry
Ulla and Curt Carlbom
Sten Carlsson
James E. Cathey
John S. Chamberlain
Marlene Ciklamini
Ingrid Claréus
Patricia L. Conroy
Birgitta Dahlgren Knuttgen
Gunnar Eidevall
Arvid Ernvik
Rolf Fjelde
Penny and Kjetil Flatin
Syrene and Don Forsman
Mrs. James Fredricksen
Erik J. Friis
Elinor Fuchs
Birgitte Graeber
Finnbogi Guðmundsson
Ingvar Gullberg
Valerie C. Gustaveson
Katherine Hanson
Mildred B. Hanson
Glenn A. Harper
Nils Hasselmo
Eva and Einar Haugen
Carin and Folke Hedblom
Patsy Adams Hegstad
Anne and H. Matthias Heinrichs
Mona and Gustaf Hilleström
Sigvald V. Hjelmeland
Shaun F. D. Hughes
Lars Huldén
Lloyd Hustvedt
Barry Jacobs
Rudolf J. Jensen
Marianne E. Kalinke
Arne O. Lindberg
Raymond E. Lindgren
John Lingard
Torborg Lundell
Brian Magnusson
Marshall N. Matson
Margareta Mattsson
Inger and Bertil Molde
Gerard F. Mueller
Van H. Neher
Jens Nyholm
Otto Oberholzer
Allan Lake Rice

Marianne and Sven Rossel
Paul Schach
Franklin Scott
Larry Emil Scott
Monica Setterwall
Inger and Leif Sjöberg
Steven P. Sondrup
Evert M. Sprinchorn
Kathleen M. Stokker
Alan Swanson

Carla Waal
Erik Wahlgren
Lars G. Warme
Donald K. Weaver III
John M. Weinstock
Lorraine and Wesley Westerberg
Joseph B. Wilson
Fern and Robert Wright
Virpi Zuck

Organizations

American-Scandinavian Foundation
Emigrantinstitutet, Växjö
German Department, Moorhead State University
German Studies, Stanford University
Institut für Nordische Philologie, University of Köln
Nordische Abteilung, University of Bonn
Scandinavian Department, University of California, Berkeley
Scandinavian Department, University of Washington
Society for the Advancement of Scandinavian Studies
Svenska Institutet
Swedish Information Service
Swedish Pioneer Historical Society

Part I
Strindberg in Scandinavia

The Symbiosis of "Spirits" in *Inferno*: Strindberg and Swedenborg

Göran Stockenström
(Translated by Matthew Dion)

"Tog fram Swedenborgs Himmel och Helvete vid middagstid; när jag läst en stund om Helvetet och dess evighet, blef det kolmörkt i rummet så att jag icke såg mer att läsa. Detta upprepades en gång till. Himlen hade varit strålande klar hela dagen, och blef sedan så till aftonen. Straxt derpå såg jag i sofftygets blommiga mönster Swedenborgs ansigte. Han var enögd och ena halfvan af ansigtet var svart; invid syntes Klemming med en Tysk studentmössa."[1]

"—Har du läst Swedenborg?
—Man *läser* icke Swedenborg, man undfår honom, eller undfår honom icke. Man kan endast förstå honom, om man upplevat detsamma som han."[2]

"Feif: . . . Det är ju underligt, att konungen sista åren omgivit sig med enögda!
Swedenborg: Ånej!
Feif: Jovisst! Frölich, Müllern, Grothusen och Görtz se bara med ett öga!
Swedenborg: Det skulle vara löjligt, om icke det låge en dold mening under det!
Feif: Bah! Slumpar!
Swedenborg: Nej, Feif . . . men det fattar han aldrig. . . .
Feif: Drömmar, Swedenborg, fattar jag inte!"[3]

I

In the annals of Swedish science, Emanuel Swedenborg is exceeded only by Linné in the number of significant contributions to various fields of scientific inquiry. Swedenborg was a natural scientist, a theosopher, and a theologian, though, perhaps, above all else he was a poet who portrayed his visions of a supernatural realm with a gripping concreteness. For both Linné and Swedenborg, the rigorous language of natural science ultimately did not suffice to evoke the inner truth that was concealed beyond the visible forms of nature. Strindberg also entertained the twin ambitions of being a physical scientist and metaphysical poet, so it is not surprising that he should have compared himself to Linné and Swedenborg in letters written during 1896: "Swedenborg var mineralog, rotade i jordens innandömen men äfven i andeverldens!. . . ." "Jag är naturalist-occkultisten, som Linné, min store lärare. Först fysiken, så meta–. Jag vill se med mina utvertes ögon först och sedan med de invertes."[4]

Swedenborg's *Diarium spirituale*, Linné's *Nemesis divina*, and Strindberg's *En blå bok*—each document incorporates a similar shift from adherence to a scientific explanation of man and the world to an explanation apparently grounded in some manner of religious experience. In spite of the general parallels between Swedenborg, Linné, and Strindberg, the important differences in their individual processes of spiritual development cannot be overlooked. The task of describing these spiritual processes for each individual, let alone seeking mutual impact and influence, has caused tremendous problems for literary scholars. Strindberg offered the following description of his own altered viewpoint in a letter to Anders Eliasson dated 28 October 1896:

Tycker du ej, Elias, i alla fall att lifvet vid vår ålder börjar te sig på ett annat sätt, än förr, att en viss ingripande hand emellanåt röjes, och att bakom de s. k. naturliga förklaringarne äfven, derjemte (!) andra förefinnas.
Jag som fört dagbok (och nattbok öfver drömmarne) sedan snart ett år, och lagt märke till allt är blifven som Du vet "mystiker." De naturliga förklaringarne godkänner jag såsom exoteriska populärexplikationer, men bakom dessa ligga de esoteriska. . . .[5]

During the spring and fall of 1896, Swedenborg first began to play a meaningful role in the crucial period in Strindberg's life, which has been named the Inferno crisis after the novel of the same name. This essay is an examination of the relationship between Swedenborg and Strindberg, as well as the diverse critical judgments that have been made regarding the issue of influence.

II

The attempt to determine one author's influence on another author is an extraordinarily hazardous enterprise. When it concerns Strindberg and Swedenborg, the task certainly does not become any easier. The period of influence can be limited in time to the so called post-Inferno production (1896–1912). Swedenborg's importance for the later works of Strindberg can be supported by a host of the author's own statements found in letters, diaries, and the literary works themselves. The number of direct references to Swedenborg's theosophical doctrines in Strindberg's prose is strikingly large. In the literary portrayal of the author's conversion found in *Inferno* (1897), *Legender* (*Legends*) (1898), and *Jakob brottas* (*Jacob Wrestles*) (1898), it was Swedenborg who saved Strindberg from madness. In a highly idiosyncratic interpretation of Swedenborg's spiritual teachings, Strindberg imagined that he had found an explanation for all the horrors and scourges that had afflicted him as well as his brothers-in-misfortune in Lund and Paris. In *Ockulta dagboken* (*The Occult Diary*) (1896–1908) exceedingly diverse phenomena are interpreted as symbolic signs according to Swedenborg's doctrine of correspondences. In this way, all these fearful experiences could be given a "natural" explanation. The spirit world, which Swedenborg assigned to a supernatural sphere of existence, was for Strindberg transposed to the here and now.

In Strindberg's rich post-1900 production, *En blå bok* (*A Blue Book*) occupies a central position. The origins of the work extend back to studies in natural philosophy that the author began in the mid-1890s. His stated purpose then had been to investigate "det oändliga sammanhanget i den stora oredan" ("the infinite order in the great chaos"), while in 1907 his aim had become to prove "axiomet om Guds existens" ("the axiom of God's existence"). The plans to construct and write a work of occult natural philosophy—"Detta är Vesterländsk Hermetism och är afsedd annulera Mme. Blawatzkis Hemliga Lära"—were realized in 1903 as a projected sequel to "Världshistoriens mystik" ("The Mysticism of World History").[6] At this point, Strindberg applied his own "philosophy of history" to mankind and the world in a series of "Colloquier," with Martin Luther's *Colloquia* serving as the formal model.

In the relatively complete drafts of the following year, the syncretistic religious ideas have moved into the foreground. This work in progress now had the working title "Breviarium," the manuscript for which is quite close to the final version, which was published in 1907 under the title *En blå bok*.

In the finished work the breviary form has been outwardly abandoned and a certain amount of systematization has taken place. This is true primarily for the natural scientific materials, which have been combined into longer sections. The interesting manuscript of 1906 is described by Strindberg as a "Swedenborgsk fuga med preludier."[7] By this term the author was probably referring to the themes from the master, which are repeated and varied at regular intervals throughout the manuscript.[8] This radical formal principle was modified somewhat at the time of publication due to a request of the publisher. Both the reactions of his contemporaries and the findings of later research indicate that Strindberg's artistic intentions were not effective means for producing the desired goal. It scarcely helped that he later sought to defend "den trolska oordningen"[9] by referring to the example of "Swedenborgs 'stenbrottsböcker'" ("quarry-books").[10] The choice of a musical principle of form must be understood as a manifestation of his experimental interest in music. But such a form did not fit well for a work that Strindberg wanted to advertise as a revivalist tract for the people. To this end, Strindberg had offered to subsidize a popular edition at the rate of one crown per book, and he considered establishing a foundation of "kristna, teosofer, och Swedenborgare."[11] Although these plans were not realized, the book which was produced was characterized by the author now as "mitt lifs syntes," now as "mitt testamente till menniskorna." Afterwards, he referred all inquiries about his beliefs and world view to "Blå boken, der ämnet är slutbehandlat."[12]

Although it is not possible in this context to give a detailed account of the complex origins of *En blå bok*, a brief look at the genesis of the work will permit us to draw a few important conclusions. During the first decade of this century, Strindberg had time and again entertained plans to summarize his religious opinions in a more systematic form. The appearance of "Världshistoriens mystik," or "Gud i historien,"[13] as it was originally called, should be seen as a step in the same direction. The dedication of *En blå bok* reads, "Till Emmanuel Swedenborg / Läraren och Ledaren / Ägnas denna bok / av / Lärjungen."[14] In "Blå bokens historia," a supplement to *En blå bok*, Strindberg sought to interpret the genesis of the work in terms of divine election or a call that was analagous to Swedenborg's own self-understanding.[15] The sum of Strindberg's devotion to Swedenborg is gathered in *En blå bok* and therefore the work must be said to occupy a decisive position in any attempt to determine the influence between the two.

There has as yet been no systematic investigation of *En blå bok* or the author's post-1900 religious opinions. Although there is a striking sense of continuity in Strindberg's *interpretation* of many of Swedenborg's ideas, there are nevertheless important shifts in emphasis in his views, especially with regard to the problem of reconciliation or atonement. Nor has there been a coherent and complete survey of the material in *Ockulta dagboken*. Even if the author's complete picture of reality cannot be reconstructed on the basis of the diary, it is nonetheless evident that it has great importance for illuminating the author's interpretation of reality and thus indirectly his world view. Whether or not the term "world view" ("världsåskådning") with its implication of systematic thought is applicable at all in this case is a central problem that is extremely difficult to resolve. The scholarly descriptions of Strindberg's opinions during the nineties differ considerably, and the varying choice of terminology betrays important differences in points of departure.

In some reflections on Swedenborg as a source of literary inspiration, Inge Jonsson points out that no systematic study of Swedenborg's influence has yet been carried out.[16] Those studies that do exist are limited to certain specific periods or individual authorships, for example, Schelling, Goethe, Balzac, Baudelaire, Blake, Emerson, and Yeats. Among Swedish literary figures Atterbom, Almqvist, and Strindberg have received some critical attention, while authors like Ekelund, Lagerkvist, and Gyllensten are yet untreated. Just how different scholarly results can be, and the great extent to which they are determined by the scholar's point of departure itself, is illustrated by two modern studies of the literature and cultural milieu of France during the 1890s: Phillipe van Tieghems, *Les influences étrangéres sur la littérature française* (*Foreign Influences on French Literature*) (1961), and Anna Balakian, *The Symbolist Movement* (1967). In the former work Swedenborg is only incidentally mentioned in connection with Balzac, whereas in the latter study he becomes one of the more prominent figures of the period.

The same situation of contrary judgments prevails in the question of Swedenborg's influence on Strindberg. In this case the evaluations are clearly dependent on the points of departure. On the one hand, there are scholars who emphasize the continuity in Strindberg's authorship and consequently assume Swedenborg's influence to be of only secondary importance. This is especially true of scholars like Torsten Eklund, Gunnar Brandell, and G. Vogelweith who proceed from the viewpoint of an individualistic psychology of one type or another.[17] They tend to see the Inferno crisis primarily as one in a long line of similar crises extending all the way back to the author's youth. The author's early childhood experiences become crucially significant for an understanding of his subsequent development. On this basis the scholars proceed to describe a collection of ideas and impressions engendered by the experiences of recurring religious crises. In the eyes of this school, these ideas do not comprise a coherent outlook or philosophy of life. Moreover, the new literary production after the Inferno is regarded as the result of projections emanating from a mind suffering from neurotic anxiety.

On the other hand, Swedenborg is considered to be of primary significance by those scholars whose research stresses the novel elements that appear in the growth of a new systematic religious viewpoint during the last phase of the Inferno crisis. This is to a large extent true of scholars who approach the subject in terms of intellectual history, for example, Axel Herrlin, Martin Lamm, Karl-Åke Kärnell, and Göran Stockenström.[18] To varying degrees they accept the conclusion that the development of a systematic religious position did occur during these years. To be sure, these scholars recognize the roots of Strindberg's religious ideas in his past, but they believe the ideas were formulated differently than before. The new view of life is seen as the basis for the innovative aspects of the later authorship.

Each scholar cited above uses his own terminology. In reality it is a question of complementary approaches and one cannot speak of an absolute dialectical opposition. None of the scholars employs one or another methodology exclusively; rather it is as always a question of nuances and accents. We will have reason to return to the arguments sketched above. Irrespective of the answer to the question of Swedenborg's influence, several other equally difficult questions remain: how much of what we attribute to Swedenborg was really his own, and how much was in general intellectual circulation? For the period of the nineties, at least, we can speak of Strindberg's direct contact with Swedenborg's writings, as well as indirect influence via the spiritistic movement and a large number of the French occultists. How much in Strindberg's work is based on the reading of Swedenborg's writings? How much must be assigned to other sources contemporary with the Inferno crisis? How much is timebound interpretation? To what degree is it a question of older subjective reinterpretations? What is it that basically happens when one great mind is inspired by another? How shall we be able to determine and describe such a process scientifically?

III

The first known contact between Strindberg and the works of Swedenborg dates from the middle of the 1870s. Strindberg borrowed the compilation of Swedenborg's ideas entitled *Tankar och syner i andliga ämnen* (*Thoughts and Visions on Spiritual Subjects*) from the Royal Library in 1875 and again the following year. The book was actually a translation of Daillant de la Touche's *Abrégé des ouvrages d'Emanuel Swedenborg* (*Summary of the Works of Emanuel Swedenborg*), an extremely scattered, rambling summary of Swedenborg's system based mainly on *Vera religio christiana*.

The loan records from the Royal Library confirm that Strindberg pursued fairly comprehensive studies of occult literature during the seventies. He borrowed, among other things, Plancy's *Dictionnaire Infernal* (*Infernal Dictionary*), the Leymaire edition of *Procès des spirites* (*Trial of the Spirits*), and Maximilian Perty's *Die Realität magischer Kräfte* (*The Reality of Magic Powers*). The last work was borrowed no fewer than five times.[19] Strindberg's studies in this literature can be partially understood against the background of the time. Ever since the mid-1850s modern spiritism had spread out from America to Europe in wave after wave. By the 1870s the movement had found its way into Sweden, where one of its leading figures was Strindberg's supervisor and mentor at the Royal Library, Gustaf Edvard Klemming.

In the above cited vision from 1906, which occurred in connection with the beginning of the final manuscript for *En blå bok*, Strindberg had envisioned Klemming's spirit as well as Swedenborg's. The association was in and of itself quite natural, for it was Klemming who edited the first edition of *Swedenborgs drömmar 1744* (*Swedenborg's Dreams 1744*) in 1858. It is at least plausible to suspect that impulses from Klemming inspired Strindberg's first contact with Swedenborg. In both *Ockulta dagboken* and *En blå bok*, we catch glimpses of Klemming, who is described on several occasions as the author's benevolent guardian spirit. In an autobiographical note from 1909 Strindberg wrote of his former supervisor: "Klemming och hans inflytande på min bana, har jag (i förtäckta ordalag dock) behandlat flerstädes, med vördnad och tacksamhet!"[20] At his request, Strindberg wrote the article "Djefvul" in the first edition of *Nordisk familjebok* (*Nordic Family Book*), published in 1880. In that case, as well as in the letters of his youth and in his later authorship, it is striking how often he identifies himself wtih demonic representations.

According to Torsten Eklund, Strindberg formulated a neurotic attitude toward life in his early years and this in turn gave rise to a fatalistic belief "att han var en av försynens eller ödets utvalda, utsedd för en stor världsomfattande mission eller, ännu vanligare, dömd till att själv kastas ned och även dra andra med sig i ett exempellöst lidande, att bringa fördärv över sig själv och andra."[21]

In this manner, Strindberg's paranoia, megalomania, and superstition are explained for us. Eklund, like Lamm and even later like Brandell, wants to trace these and similar notions to the early years of the author's life. From the perspective of source criticism, however, the problem of documentation is extraordinarily complex. For the study of the early years researchers are almost totally dependent on Strindberg's autobiography, lacking supplementary corroborating materials.

Many of the elements of thought that were original and important in Strindberg's religious speculations of the seventies became current again in the cultural milieu of fin-de-siècle Paris. There is, therefore, no reason to attach much importance to Strindberg's critical judgments of Swedenborg from the eighties, as these only represent the author's rationalistic standpoint at that moment. In *Inferno*, when Strindberg wanted to summarize his view of Swedenborg at an earlier phase, he wrote: "en charlatan, en tok med lösaktig inbillning."[22] Strindberg's opinions from the mid-eighties were in accord with the negative and ironic critique of the visionary extending back to Kant's *Träume eines Geistersehers* (*Dreams of a Spiritualist*) (1766). This attitude had been manifested during the Swedish Enlightenment in the struggle for "sans och vett" ("sense and wit"). The classic expression of antagonism toward the seer from that period is found in Johan Henric Kellgren's poem "Man äger ej snille för det man är galen" ("One does not possess genius simply because one is crazy").

In May 1896 Strindberg wrote a letter to the theosophist Torsten Hedlund that reflects some of the moods and impressions from the two years he had lived in Paris: "Swedenborg är mycket uppe här, och räknas some den förste teosofen i ny tid, före Allan Kardec; och jag får ofta läsa att jag är från Swedenborgs land etc. Derför har jag läst Séraphita af Balzac, Hvad det är stort och underbart!"[23] In this case, Strindberg is alluding to an article in the March 1896 number of *L'Initiation* in which Paul Sédir had paid homage to Strindberg as a fellow countryman of Swedenborg and mentioned Balzac's "Swedenborgbook." Strindberg was himself a collaborator on *L'Initiation* and he described the *tendens* of the journal in a June 1896 letter to F. U. Wrangel: "vetenskaplig ockultism, fortsätter Charcot, Ribot, Du Prel, Crooke o. fl. Om G. E. Klemming lefvat skulle han ha bestått den åt K. B."[24]

The investigations of hypnotism and related phenomena conducted during the eighties became the most important breeding ground for the occult world of the nineties. With the support of the authorities mentioned above, a psychological point of view with markedly mystical features evolved in Strindberg's thinking during the closing years of the 1880s. If the Swedenborgianism and raising of spirits of the eighteenth century can in one way be seen as a reaction against a prevailing image of the rationalistic world, so can the stream of occult ideas in the 1890s be explained in part as a reaction against the scientistic positivism of the nineteenth century. In certain respects, however, it is probably a question of a surviving tradition. Strindberg himself has stressed the continuity in the evolution of ideas during the preceding decades that led to *Inferno*: "Mins Du huru vi borta i Kymmendögropen anteciperade hela den nu pågående fin-de-sièclismen och sogar Satanismen. Mins Du 'Strindbergs Religion' om Satan som verldsfursten! Ja, vi voro Buddhor födda deruppe; anade i ensamheten, kölden, punschosena hvad som skulle ske i verlden och—vi voro då ännu längre än Huysmans är nu."[25] Strindberg also alluded to this continuity in the play "De creatione et sententia vera mundi" included in *Efterspelet till Mäster Olof* ("The Epilogue to *Master Olof*") (1877). In revised form and with the new title "Coram Populo," this work was used to introduce the French edition of *Inferno* (1898). Before the French public, Strindberg found it necessary both to assert his priority relative to French occultists like Huysmans, and at the same time to point out the continuity in his personal evolution. With the same purpose in mind, Strindberg included in the text of *Inferno* several scientific studies of a mystical character in order to indicate the necessary stages from positivism via occultism to religion.

Swedenborg's works had been translated and circulated in France since the end of the eighteenth century. It was first under the auspices of the Swedenborg society of Avignon founded by Pernetty and later the Parisian branch of this group that the work of spreading Swedenborgian teachings was conducted. Strindberg visited the Paris society in May 1896:

Det fins ett Swedenborgs sällskap här med Kapell, bibliotek, läsesal och förlag. Jag besökte det häromdagen, och såg två porträtt af teosofen. Men det är bara fodral och porträtt säga ingenting, annat än att våra själar äro instuckna i hölster som icke passa, och derför vantrifvas vi också här på jorden som man gör i kläder som icke passa. . . . Derför har jag läst Séraphita af Balzac. Hvad det är stort och underbart! Spelar i Norge, handlar om en Svenska, afkomling af Swedenborg. Och denna Svenska är såsom Swedenborgs änglar—tvåkönad. Hon har uppenbarelser . . .[26]

Balzac was indeed among the number of Swedenborg devotés in France, and it was through him that a powerful current emanated that struck such innovative figures in modern literature as Baudelaire and Strindberg.

For the author of *Inferno*, who was haunted by a fear of persecution and constant anxiety, the story of Séraphita's transformation from an earthly creature to an angel served to illustrate the possibility of a redemption from suffering. It was this evangelical idea of reconciliation ("försoning") in the novel that gripped Strindberg so strongly. Furthermore, the author saw Balzac's hero as a translation of Nietzsche's Übermensch ideal into a Christian ideal of superman as mystic. Balzac, in fact, shaped the androgynous character of Séraphita-Séraphitus out of a very freely interpreted understanding of Swedenborg's dualistic psychology. Balzac ignores Swedenborg's central notion of the dynamic internal struggle between the forces of heaven and hell. From the outset of the story Séraphita is basically an "ésprit angelique" and hence she cultivates only one of the life-alternatives in the Swedenborgian pattern.

Strindberg encountered the same idea of reconciliation in *Louis Lambert* which he read at Christmas time, 1896. The novel is an idealized portrait of a precocious youth's growing up, with many features drawn from Balzac's own life. Louis incarnates an ideal of Christian superman and he professes his faith in Swedenborg's theosophy as the synthesis of all the religions of the world. The book was of great importance for the development of Strindberg's own religious syncretism and he began to plan a study in naturalistic mysticism with the following title: "Swedenborg, Nordens Buddha! tolkad av Balzac."[27] It was Balzac's reinterpretation that captivated Strindberg in 1896, and this version can scarcely be said to be identical to Swedenborg's actual system. However, it did bring about a new rationalization that allowed the author to evade a confrontation with the strong feelings of guilt that drove him to the brink of insanity.

A contrast in viewpoints is also strikingly apparent whenever Strindberg came into contact with Swedenborg's own texts. "Här föllo Swedenborgs skrifter i min hand för första gången. Det är underbara ting deri,"[28] wrote Strindberg in a letter to Torsten Hedlund in September 1896. At that time the author found himself in Austria, where he had gone in hope of a reunion with his wife and child. A period of relative calm had commenced after the flight from Paris and the stay with Dr. Eliasson in Lund. In Austria, his mother-in-law Marie Uhl and her twin sister Melanie Samek, whom Strindberg described as adherents of a religious occultism based on Catholicism and Swedenborgianism, presented him with a book entitled, *Emanuel Swedenborgs theologische Werke oder dessen Lehre von Gott, der Welt, dem Himmel, der Hölle, der Geisterwelt und dem zukünftigen Leben* (*Emanuel Swedenborg's Theological Works, or His Teachings on God, the World, Heaven, Hell, the World of Spirits, and the Life to Come*). It was once again a question of Daillant de la Touche's compilation of Swedenborg, which, moreover, also served as Balzac's primary source. This time the author's impressions were of a wholly different nature than before. This is attested to by the detailed excerpts in *Ockulta dagboken* (8/9/96) under the heading "Swedenborgs beskrifning af helvetet" ("Swedenborg's description of Hell"). In contrast to *Séraphita*, Strindberg had now discovered a depiction of the torments of the damned in multiple hells, at once fascinating and terrifying in its concreteness. When his fear of persecution was intensified anew in October and November, Strindberg summarized his impressions:

Den verldsåskådning som vuxit ut hos mig är närmast lik Pythagoras' och upptagen af Origines: Vi äro i Inferno för synder begångna i en föregående existens. Derför: bed ej om annat än resignation: och begär intet, platt intet af lifvet. Var glad, om möjligt, i olyckan, ty med hvarje olycka utstrykes en post i deficit./Swedenborgs beskrifning på Inferno är så noga jordelifvet utan att han menar det, så på pricken att jag är öfvertygad.[29]

This citation is an excellent illustration of a recurring dilemma in the comparative approach to the history of ideas. The idea that earth is really hell, that human beings are reincarnated creatures, and that suffering itself is atonement was seen by the author as the essence of a world view with its roots in Pythagoras and Origen. In the context of Strindberg's life, it is a reinterpretation that allows him to continue playing the game of hide-and-seek with his personal guilt. Even if Swedenborg's image of hell did serve as a new argument, Strindberg's interpretation itself cannot be supported by Swedenborg's doctrines. One of Strindberg's earlier masters, namely Schopenhauer, could more justifiaby be adduced as the source of this thought. In the latter's works the world is consistently described as the true hell, human beings as creatures of torment, and life as guilt.[30] There is no doubt that these conceptions are of central importance to Strindberg. They are among the most prominent elements of the world view that grew out of the Inferno crisis. In terms of the history of ideas, this complex of opinions can be traced back in Strindberg's life long before his acquaintance with Schopenhauer. What we have in all likelihood is a largely original personal conception of mankind and the world, which Strindberg later was able to confirm in the writing of numerous learned authorities.

The fear of persecution and anxiety retained its hold on Strindberg after his return to Lund at the end of 1896 and long into the following year. The belief that various people were trying to persecute him was still an urgent matter. An alternative view of his condition, which Strindberg considered, was that he was suffering from authentic paranoia, in other words, insanity. A third possibility was that he was being tortured through the agency of higher powers, though Strindberg did not know if they were good or evil. Under the circumstances, it seemed more likely to him that they were malignant: "Allein wieder bin ich; umgezogen in zwei Zimmer wo ich kein Laut höre, nur mein Herz klopfen. Mit Gott und Schicksal habe ich gekämpft. Habe den lieben Gott gesucht, und fand den bösen Feind. Was heisst das?"[31] Unable to resolve his dilemma, Strindberg began to keep scrupulous notes about the visitations in his diary. In this way he felt he could better study and understand their hidden meaning. He also sought guidance in renewed studies of occult literature during the first half of 1897. Swedenborg's works occupied a clearly dominant position in these studies. In attempting to determine the extent of Swedenborg's influence on Strindberg, we must distinguish between at least two areas where this influence could have had profound effects. On the one hand, there is the role that Swedenborg played directly in the course of the crisis itself, and thereby indirectly in the evolution of a religious orientation in the widest sense. On the other hand, there is the question of artistic impulses in the form of ideas and structures that the author successively assimilated and used in his own writing.

It was the mother of Bengt Lidforss, herself a Swedenborgian, who lent Strindberg the first four parts of the Swedish edition of *Arcana coelestia* and the complete Swedish edition of *Apocalypsis revelata*. *Arcana* and *Apocalypsis* contain Swedenborg's allegorical interpretation of the Pentateuch and Book of Revelations respectively. The *Arcana* moreover contains a running account of Swedenborg's visions and teachings. In February Strindberg purchased Klemming's edition of *Swedenborgs drömmar 1744* at Tullstorp's bookshop. In March he came across Abbé Pernetty's two-volume French translation of *De coelo et ejus mirabilibus* and *De telluribus in mundo nostri solari*. The former is among the most widespread of Swedenborg's works. It has had a tremendous impact on the spiritistic movement, the basic concepts of which can be traced back to that work. Swedenborg's dream diary and *De telluribus* became of special importance to Strindberg in connection with the so-called March experience. In May and June Strindberg was able, through Axel Herrlin, to borrow that remarkable work on marital love from Swedenborg's old age *De amore conjugiali*. In addition to these texts, Strindberg also read a number of adaptations, for example, the monographs on Swedenborg written by Beskow and Atterbom, the result of which is a relatively comprehensive, if unsystematic, reading of Swedenborg concentrated within the space of a few months.[32]

In connection with Strindberg's study of Swedenborg, Axel Herrlin deserves special mention. His significance in this matter is attested to by many letters in which Strindberg has written of their joint venture in "deschiffering av makternas kilskrifter" ("deciphering the cuneiform of the powers"). The author also pondered the possibility of leaving the unpublished *Ockulta dagboken* to Herrlin or Torsten Hedlund, who were the two who had been closest to him during the Inferno crisis: "Förklaringen på denna dagbok fins i bref till Torsten Hedlund och i samtal förda med Docenten Herrlin. Efter min död tillfaller denna dagbok Torsten Hedlund eller Docenten Axel Herrlin i Lund eller båda! De enda som förstå den."[33] Later, Strindberg suggested as a third alternative depositing the diary with the Swedenborgian congregation in Stockholm at Nya kyrkan.

Docent Herrlin later became a professor in psychology and pedagogy. In addition to articles on Swedenborg, he published the first two studies on the subconscious in Swedish, *Själslifvets underjordiska psykologi* (*The Subterranean Psychology of the Mind*) (1901) and *Snille och själssjukdom* (*Genius and Mental Illness*) (1903). In *Legender*, Strindberg described his friend's suffering at the hands of the Swedenborgian disciplinary spirits so candidly that Herrlin obtained the proofs from Gernandt's and vigorously revised the legend about "det brådmogna underbarnet."[34]

Herrlin has played an important role in Strindberg research because of his study of the Inferno crisis. He placed the crisis in the context of the metaphysical ideas and natural philosophy of the time. Herrlin chose Spencerian evolutionary theory as the point of departure and key to the dominant existential outlook of the eighties. Despite the fact that Strindberg disputed the idea that the universe conformed to laws, he had difficulty freeing himself from the Christian teleological concept of a purpose and an order in the universe. His goal became to discover the hidden order behind the apparent chaos of nature. Incorporating impulses from Swedenborg, the Christian doctrine of providence, and his perception of earlier religious crises, he developed a coherent world view during the last phases of the crisis. Herrlin saw a marked parallel to Swedenborg in Strindberg's exaggerated manner of interpreting various situations in everyday reality. Both Swedenborg and Strindberg perceived a reality controlled by invisible spirits and forces.

Herrlin's insights had the effect of bringing about a dramatic change in Martin Lamm's Strindberg research, notably in his study *Strindberg och makterna* (*Strindberg and the Powers*) (1936). In contrast to *Strindbergs dramer II* (1926), Lamm now showed a much greater understanding of the personal characteristics in Strindberg's crisis of religious conversion. In light of the author's inclination to trace uncanny relationships in everyday life, even Lamm had to compare him with Swedenborg and point to the parallel evolution in a mystical direction, which had been noticeable in Strindberg's scientific research ever since the end of the 1880s. Lamm also emphasized the vital importance of *Ockulta dagboken* and *En blå bok* for the later Strindberg's ideas, but he was not inclined to ascribe the character of a coherent system to a series of notions and impressions that originated in the personal religious crisis of the Inferno period.

All subsequent research on the Inferno crisis proceeds in one or another respect from Lamm's *Strindberg och makterna*. Herrlin's basic view is found in the research of Kärnell and Stockenström, whereas Eklund and Brandell proceed from John Landquist's criticism of Lamm's work. Lamm was sharply criticized in a review by Landquist (*Aftonbladet*, 15 May 1936) for underestimating the role of guilt feelings as the central component in the religious crisis. Moreover, according to Landquist, Lamm failed to pay sufficient attention to the importance of external factors, such as the author's isolation and poverty during the years in Paris. For Landquist the poetic value of Strindberg's later writing was incompatible with a thoroughgoing conversion to superstition. Instead, he interpreted it as a symbol for a deeper and more coherent process: ethical conversion.

It was above all Swedenborg's depictions of the spirit world and the multiple hells that captured Strindberg's attention. He interpreted this material in a highly personal way with direct reference to his own circumstances. In a letter to Marie Uhl he communicated his first impressions: "Lese jetzt Swedenborg Arcana Coelestia und bin erschrocken. Es scheint mir alles wahr, und doch zu grausam von einem Gott der Liebe. Da ist Séraphita mir lieber."[35] Strindberg's guilt feelings were still so strong that he could not accept the thought of guilt and punishment in any form. Consequently, he characterized Swedenborg's moralism as a personal scourge in which he almost dared not believe. In the face of the terrifying prospect, the idea of reconciliation ("försoning") from *Séraphita* and *Louis Lambert* was revived: "Und Grossmama soll Séraphita kommen als Medicin für Frida-Mama. Da die Erde uns verlasst so haben wir den Himmel übrig. Und wenn Sie Séraphita verschluckt kann Sie über Louis Lambert auch von Balzac grübeln.[36] In another letter we find Strindberg repeating the familiar ideas that had been engendered by his religious crisis: "Lies in Euren Swedenborg und schau wie Er die Hölle schildert. Ganz genau das Erdleben. Also wir sind schon da, und sollen uns an den Leiden freuen, denn Jedes Leiden ist ein Abzahlung auf der Schuld."[37]

The Swedenborgian hell is transposed to earthly life and transformed into a purgatory where crimes from the present or some past existence are expiated. In this Strindbergian reinterpretation any sense of personal guilt and responsibility is explained away, but this rationalization has no basis of support in Swedenborg's own teachings.

Swedenborgs drömmar 1744, in which Swedenborg recorded his dreams from March to October, had an even greater significance for the development of the author's crisis. Swedenborg's agitated state of mind during the critical period of transition prior to the onset of the real visions is reflected in this day-by-day account. A condition of severe anxiety, marked by a trembling and shuddering so violent that he was often thrown to the ground, portended nightly revelations by spirits to Swedenborg. This was naturally of great interest to Strindberg, who had experienced so many nocturnal anxiety attacks himself. Strindberg eventually described the course of the attacks in terms nearly identical to Swedenborg. Of special interest to the author was the dramatic account of the vision of Christ that occurred on Easter 1744. Strindberg was able to follow the course of a crisis analogous to his own in Swedenborg's dream diary. There he read how Swedenborg became ever more intensely aware of the existence of spirits and how, with the aid of the doctrine of correspondences, he could interpret their true meaning. The parallel to Strindberg's own situation was obvious, but in spite of that he did not think he had found a satisfying explanation for suffering.

The author continued his intensive investigations of the seer's writings in the hope of an answer that would deliver him from his wretched situation. He scrutinized one text after another until March when he began to read a work that would differ in important respects for him from his earlier reading of Swedenborg. The work in question is *De telluribus*, which depicts the philosopher's visits to the other planets of our solar system through a series of "interiors" that capture the imagination. Besides *De cultu et amore dei*, *De telluribus* is one of Swedenborg's most engaging works from a literary point of view. To a great extent this charm is dependent on the contrast between existence on the other planets and life in this world. When Swedenborg depicts the different societies of spirits, he applies the same system that he did earlier but with a decisive difference. The spirits represent different degrees of innocence that no longer exist elsewhere. The contrast between that world and earthly life logically concludes in a stinging criticism. Swedenborg tries to examine the origin of languages and the sciences from the same perspective. What fascinated Strindberg more than anything else was the graphic description of the spirits' daily life in the different societies, as well as their presence and intervention in human life. From his own experience, he imagined he recognized the pale teaching spirits, the sparking and smoldering spirits of contradiction, and the brown-clad chimney sweeps. Strindberg's fanciful associations are reflected in the diary, and he had long before proclaimed the existence of "menskliga former vilka äga realitet som hallucinationer, fantasier, och drömmar."[38]

As he read about the spirits on Jupiter, Strindberg had finally found a passage that seemed to offer an acceptable causal explanation for his own suffering. The passage involved a detailed description of how the disciplinary spirits torment the inhabitants of Jupiter for the sake of their moral improvement. The relatively long account was noted down in the author's diary accompanied by the following commentary:

Läste i dag och i går i Swedenborg om Andarne på Jupiter och blef deraf *upplyst om mycket underbart som händt mig sista året. Således om Esprits censeurs et correcteurs som plåga menniskan från det onda till det goda* genom att plåga i handen (NB! mina händers sjukdom) i foten (se den 19:e Mars) eller omkring epigaster (magkatarren 1883, 84). Outre la douleur vers le nombril comme causé par une *ceinture* piquante; des étouffements de poitrine de temps à autre (angina pectoris) poussés jusqu' aux *angoisses*: des *degoûts* pour tout autre aliment que le pain, pendant quelques jours (Stämmer alltsammans!)[39]

All of it seemed to agree point by point with his own suffering. The psoriasis on his hands had worsened during the last years and had led to a stay in St. Louis hospital in January 1895. The troubles were not yet over, as this note from his diary indicates: "OBS! Mina händer äro rifna och blod utgår ur porerna på ofvansidorna."[40] The diary entry for March 19 shows that another event could now be explained: "Såg en dödskalle med munkkapuchong i kakelugnselden, något stack mig i högra hälen när jag gick ut, så att jag måste draga af stöfveln."[41] Even the stomach pains of the *Giftas* (*Married*) prosecution period now appeared in their true light. The sharp stinging corset of pain led Strindberg's thoughts back to all the "electrical assassination attempts" that he believed he had been exposed to in the past. Feelings of suffocation and symptoms of paralysis were regular features of his own attacks of paranoia, nor was aversion to food unknown to him—"stämmer alltsammans!"

Despite these obvious points of identification, the explanation for Strindberg's insight and relief lies elsewhere. Rather, it was the confirmation of the existence of a benevolent providence that had a liberating effect on him. The notions that the disciplinary spirits were well meaning and, consequently, that suffering was an atonement had long loomed in the author's mind. Only now were these notions definitely confirmed for the first time in Swedenborg's own writings. Through the belief that the power of evil was relatively limited and the denial of eternal damnation, it became possible for Strindberg to hope that he could atone for himself by carefully policing his thoughts and actions from that time onward. As a motto for the frontispiece of the diary the author wrote "Ne fais plus cela!" ("Do that no more!"), the standard warning of the disciplinary spirits to the sinner. As earlier, however, Strindberg's interpretation does not have a basis of support in Swedenborg, because the ideal society of the innocent spirits on Jupiter can in no way be analogous to the human situation on earth. In the Swedenborgian texts that he had read previously, there was no possible basis for the type of liberal reinterpretation Strindberg desired. It was for that reason that Strindberg had earlier reacted in a consistently negative way: "Swedenborg ist so grausam, so alles ist mir übel daran. Ist nicht meine eigene Hölle genug? Sollen noch andere dazu?"[42]

The impulses toward a mystical interpretation of reality had long been present, but it now seemed that these tendencies could be legitimized by the Swedenborgian teachings about spirits and the spirit world. The older notions of a meaningful and coherent universe could be gathered around a new dramatic pattern. In spite of everything, he was not insane. The strange events of the preceding years were part of reality. They had been neither the handiwork of human persecutors nor of evil spirits. It was the Swedenborgian disciplinary spirits who had tortured the author on the orders of the Eternal One ("Den Evige").

On the psychological level, the implication of the March experience seems to be that the feelings of guilt were again pushed into the background. Strindberg repeated the same experience as before in a letter to Carlheim-Gyllensköld in April 1896.

Hvad menniskors skenbara oblida angår, har jag personligen resignerat och endast derigenom att jag på försök med Pythagoras antog preexistens och reinkarnation, och hvarpå jag nu tror sedan erfarenhet och observation bekräftat antagandet. Att mitt öde ställt sig så pinsamt för mig ligger nog i begångna brott i en förtid, och jag är så lifligt öfvertygad att vi befinna oss i Inferno, helst jag i Swedenborgs beskrifningar på helvetet, återfann jordelifvet i detalj skildradt.[43]

Thus it is evident that we cannot speak of an ethical conversion, which implies an acknowledgment of guilt.

In literary terms, the experience finally made it possible to articulate an interpretation of the events of recent years in *Inferno* (1897). It is first in *Inferno* that the author can be said to make an effort to recognize his own guilt and responsibility. Nevertheless, the symptoms of crisis had not ceased. Strindberg was still held in the grip of mental agitation and paranoia. If the situation is seen as a whole, it could most nearly be described as a successive abatement of the mental crisis distinguished by reversals and a condition of anxiety. During the summer Strindberg did subject himself to moral self-examination, and in *Inferno* we can trace the more reconciled frame of mind and greater measure of resignation that were the result: "Kann ich dagegen Trost und Seelenruhe schenken, da bin ich bereit, weil Hass und Rache nich mehr bei mir wohnt, wie früher, seitdem ich entdeckt dass der Mensch sein Schicksal nicht verschuldet, und dass unsere Sünden uns als Strafe zugetheilt sind."[44]

The importance of the March experience is confirmed by the simultaneous increase in the number of entries in the diary. The increased number of entries mainly involved mystical interpretations of reality and there developed a relatively firm pattern in the author's associations and interpretations. Sometimes the formulations are paraphrases of Swedenborg, as when he writes in one diary entry: "Mötte en gumma med dödningsansigte. Vandrade ner till Hospitalet; erfor denna klämmning om bröstkorgen som jag kallat elektriska gördeln," and in another: "Klockan 5 e. m. var Papus i mitt rum men osynlig. Troligen läser han mitt manuskript just nu. Olustkänsla; beklämning i bröstet; ibland snörningar i ryggen, ibland hetta ini bröstkorgen."[45] All physical ailments were construed as manifestations of the activity of spirits. From that time on Strindberg kept a record in *Ockulta dagboken* of the scourges the disciplinary spirits visited on himself and others. Visions and dreams assume an ever greater importance and sometimes reflect a genuine expectation of revelations on a par with those reported by Swedenborg. When he thought that he had recognized Frida Uhl on a street in Lund, a question made its appearance: "Var det en vision?" One morning in a state between dream and waking Strindberg suddenly saw Herrlin "såsom genom ett flor; svagt gulaktig mot hvitt; han såg allvarlig ut; hade pince-nez och litet emellan såg han åt mig, såsom om han satt och vaktade en sjuk. Klockan var 1/2 7 f.m. Detta är den första vision jag haft. Få nu se om det händt Herrlin något!!!"[46]

In order to describe the author's thought scholars have employed different conceptions according to their own particular points of departure. Herrlin, for example, spoke from a psychological viewpoint about "förtolkningar av verklighetssituationer" ("misinterpretations of everyday situations"), whereas Lamm spoke from a religious perspective about the relationship between Strindberg and "makterna" ("the powers"). This last term was Strindberg's favorite expression. It was used for the first time in the spring of 1897, in connection with the idea of the Eternal One and his disciplinary spirits as upholders of the moral order of the universe. The term "makterna," it should be noted, has a more neutral connotation than "andar" (spirits), which is the usual conceptual term found in the private diary entries. I have myself used the term "mystik-mysticism" but not in the conventional sense of *unio mystica*, that is, the experienced ascent and absorption into the Godhead. It is used instead in reference to the other main current within mysticism, namely the intellectual-speculative tradition, for which Swedenborg himself can serve as an exemplary representative.

IV

Greve Max explains in *Götiska rummen* that "one doesn't read Swedenborg, but one is receptive [*undfår*] to him and he can only be understood by those who have had the same experiences." This viewpoint became decisive for Strindberg's interpretation of the conversion motif in the autobiographical confessional writings and penitential dramas. If reality could have been defined earlier in positivistic terms, then it now seemed like "någonting halvverkligt, en serie visioner, frammanade av någon och i medvetet syfte."[47] If this half-reality was staged by spirits, then neither actions in the usual sense nor human relationships can be explained in terms of any logical, causal connections. The new writing, itself a creative force, should be understood first of all in light of the spiritistically inspired world view that was the result of the March experience. Within the framework of this world view, Strindberg could insert the ideas and structures of the Swedenborgian spirit world that had stimulated him as a writer. In order to incorporate this whole complex of ideas, Strindberg himself used the Swedenborgian term "ödeläggelsen" ("devastation"). The author intended by this his own subjective version of the course of events. The fact that this distinguishes him from Swedenborg scarcely needs to be pointed out. When the term "ödeläggelsen-devastation" is used below it is in the Strindbergian sense in order to describe a central motif complex in the later authorship.

To this complex belong motifs that already had a pronounced literary character when they were originally used by Swedenborg. A representative scene from *Arcana* follows:

> De, som under det lekamliga lifvet haft för ändamål idel förnöjelser och blott velat öfverlämna sig åt sin medfödda natur, samt lefva i prakt och herrlighet, vårdande sig om blott sig sjelfva och verlden, aktande det Gudomliga för ingenting, utan tro och menniskokärlek, införas efter döden först i ett lif, likt det de haft i verlden. Det är en ort framtill åt venster, något djupt ned, der det icke är annat än förlustelser, spel, dans, ruckel och glam; dit införas sådana, och då veta de icke annat, än att de äro i verlden: men scenen förändras; efter någon tids förlopp nedföras de till ett Helvete under sätet, hvilket är idelt träckartadt i andra lifvet; jag har sett dem där bära träck och jemra sig.[48]

By analogy with the Swedenborgian doctrine of correspondences, the inner life of human beings is projected in external reality. In this way the transformation becomes a vehicle for visualizing the difference between appearance and reality in the metaphysical sense. Strindberg's excerpts from Swedenborg are filled with notes: "De osaliga tåla ej dagsljus och ren luft. . . . Då det himmelska ljuset når de osaliga så far en isköld genom ådrorna och blodet stockas. De osaliga ser ut som passionerna."[49]

It was in this way that Strindberg learned to know "Swedenborgs korrespondenser," which he often cited as "nyckeln till min metod" ("the key to my method"). The authentic meaning of the doctrine of correspondences in the Swedenborgian system, where everything natural is a shadow image of something spiritual and spiritual reality only the reflected image of the original ideal in heaven, was something that did not overly concern Strindberg. To try to relate Strindberg's conception to the abstract speculation behind the doctrine of correspondences is futile. The connection between Baudelaire's "universal analogies" and Swedenborg's system is equally tenuous, although the doctrine of correspondences was a departure point. What remains of the doctrine after its transformation for poetic purposes by Strindberg and Baudelaire is the conviction that the world and humanity reflect spiritual reality. If Baudelaire's version in the sonnet "Correspondances" is stamped by poetic mysticism in the spirit of the fin-de-siècle, then Strindberg's version is even more concrete, and, thus, dramatically effective. Witness, for example, the following lines from the sketch "Huru man blir Swedenborgare":

... en stor man, nationens störste son, efter döden blir anmodad stiga in i tronsalen (afklädningsrummet). Iklädd sin doktorsfrack och iförd sina ordnar anmodas den nykomne intaga sin plats under tronhimmelen. Så kommer nationen och helsar med tal; den store klädes i en krona och mantel och vid trummor och trumpeters klang utropas han till konung. Så börjar scenen ändra sig. Kronan blir en kastrull, manteln ett hvitt lakan; kransen tas som lagerbärsblad till kallopsen, ordnarne blir kontramärken. Nationen dunstar bort, den Store sitter ensam i ett ensligt hus, och tronen är en furufjöl."[50]

The transformation scenes in the post-Inferno dramas became metaphysical unmaskings of a type previously unknown in literature. If we compare the dinner scene in *Lycko-Pers resa* (*Lucky Per's Journey*) with the alchemist's banquet in *Till Damaskus II* (*To Damascus II*), the contrast is striking indeed. The motif of unmasking occupies a pivotal position in the Swedenborgian spirit-world and Strindberg often used the expression "afklädningsrummet" ("the stripping room") to characterize the world of spirits. In *En blå bok* he wrote: "Swedenborg har i sitt helvete ett avklädningsrum, där de avlidne införas genast efter döden. Där avklädas de denna skrud, som de tvingats anlägga i samhället, umgänget och familjen."[51] As a title for the unmasking process itself, Strindberg preferred another term derived from Swedenborg, namely "ödëläggelsen," or devastation. He perceived devastation to be analogous to the scourges visited on him by the disciplinary spirits and therefore it was natural to transpose the scenes from the spirit world to the world of human beings.

Like many authors before and after him, Strindberg was fascinated by the scenes from Swedenborg's spirit world. According to Swedenborg's doctrine, the dead are gathered in a realm between heaven and hell, the so-called spirit world, where at the outset they retain their individuality and have no idea that they are dead. The souls have been freed through death from their material bodies, which are subsequently replaced with spiritual bodies. To that extent they continue to appear in human shape, and on the strength of the doctrine of correspondences Swedenborg could equip the world of spirits with the same profusion of concrete details as in earthly life. This fusion of natural and supernatural clearly facilitated the poetic transposition of spiritual reality to the world of the here and now.

According to these beliefs, human beings determine their own doom in this life depending on whether they choose good or evil. God does not damn anyone to hell, because the wicked ones themselves desire to go where they may freely cultivate their vices. Those who are thoroughly evil are dispatched to a hell that corresponds to their particular style of evil. Concomitantly, the righteous win entry to a heavenly society that corresponds to their particular degree and manner of goodness.

For the greater number of men, however, it is a different matter. They are neither thoroughly good, nor utterly evil, but evince various mixtures of the two essential tendencies. These different shadings are hardly noticed in life because human beings can disguise themselves —a capacity that is lost in the spirit world. According to Swedenborg, there are two heavenly angels and two satanic spirits constantly at work inside every person. These spirits are in turn influenced by other spirits and, finally, all of these "powers" ("makter") are ruled by God. In this way, a human being becomes a center for a host of angels and spirits who can directly affect an individual's thoughts and feelings. The idea of a fundamental conflict between opposed forces carries with it an inherently dualistic concept of personality by which the person is divided into inner and outer selves. The heavenly light penetrates into the former, whereas in the latter the desires and passions of the flesh exert their influences.

The sojourn in the spirit world serves to remove the disparity between the inner and outer selves, that is, between appearance and reality in the metaphysical sense. It is this process that Swedenborg called "ödeläggelsen." If the good outweighs the evil in a person, then the wicked element is "devastated" and replaced by truth. If the evil is preponderant, then the element of truth is devastated and replaced by falsehood. The final goal of this purgation is to have the good and the evil voluntarily join the society in heaven or hell which corresponds to their respective true selves.

By analogy with the optimistic theodicy of the March experience, Strindberg used the term "devastation" exclusively in the first sense mentioned, that is, as a stage in the process of moral purification, which he had been exposed to through the agency of the disciplinary spirits. Thus, in a note to a draft Strindberg equated devastation and awakening; "Ödeläggelsen = Väckelsen" ("Devastation = Awakening").[52]

Devastation in the spirit world could occur through a successive chain of events in which the deceased could no longer conceal their thoughts, and, correspondingly, their physical appearances became mirrors of their true selves. This could also occur through a more dramatic series of actions, as was especially the case for those who refused to acknowledge their crimes. The completely unrepentant were unmasked by angels who would scrutinize their eyes and read from the so-called Book of Life, where all thoughts and actions were inscribed from inner memory:

> Uppdagningarna varade några gånger timmar igenom. Det var en, som ansåg för ingenting att förtala andra; jag hörde förtalen upprepade i ordning, och jemvel hans smädelser med sjelfva orden, om hvilka personer, och inför hvilka de förekommit; hvilka alla saker frambringades och på ett lefvande sätt framställdes på en gång; och likväl voro alla enskilda ting med omsorg dolda af honom, när han lefde i verlden. En viss förekom, som beröfvat en frände hans arf under en svekfull förevändning; denne blef ock likaledes öfverbevisad och dömd, och hvad som var förunderligt, de bref och papperslappar, som vexlats emellan dem, lästes i min åhörö, och det sades att icke ett ord fattades. Densamme hade ock, nyss före sin död, hemligen dödat en granne med gift; detta blef på följande sätt upptäckt. Han sågs uppgräfva en grop under sina fötter, och då den var uppgräfd utgick derur en man liksom ur en graf, och han ropade till honom hvad har du gjort mig? Och då afslöjades allting, huruledes giftblandaren talat vänligt med honom och framräckt bägaren, äfvensom hvad han förut tänkt och hvad som sedermera hände. Sedan dessa saker blifvit upptäckta, dömdes han till helvetet. Med ett ord, alla ondskor, illgerningar, röfverier, konstgrepp, svek, uppdagas för hvarje ond ande, samt framtagas ur sjelfva deras minne, och de öfverbevisas; icke heller gifves rum att neka, emedan alla omständigheter synas på en gång.[53]

The preceding paragraph is summarized in the margin of the author's copy with the words "Lifvet drar förbi" ("Life draws past"). Strindberg had immediately associated it with the so-called "livsrevyn" ("the life review"), that is, the panoramic overview of the past that is observed in the moments prior to death. In Swedenborg this phenomenon is connected with the biblical "Doomsday Book." Strindberg has captured better than anyone else the intrinsic dramatic potential of these scenes by characterizing them as a "skamdefilering" ("procession of shame"). In the devastation scenes of the post-Inferno dramas, the procession, or defilement, of shame is among the most constant elements, occurring in many different forms. Perhaps the most spectacular variant of this dramatic phenomenon is the asylum scene in *Till Damaskus*. It can be used by way of conclusion to illustrate some of the problems presented by literary comparison.

The scene is played out in a cloister named "Den Goda Hjälpen" ("The Good Help"), which alludes to Christ's act of atonement. The motif is embodied in The Stranger's inability to accept even the slightest token of mercy. It is emphasized even prior to that through the news about The Stranger's attempt to tear down a cross of Christ. The religious meaning of the scene is allegorized by a painting representing Michael slaying the Evil One. Whenever The Stranger tries to avert his eyes from the horrifying images that pass before his face, his glance is ineluctably riveted to the face of the Archangel. The scene is described by the author's stage directions:

Vid ett långt matbord till vänster sitter DEN OKÄNDE i vit sjukdräkt, ensam vid sin skål. Vid bordet till höger sitta DE BRUNKLÄDDA från första akten; TIGGAREN; EN SORGKLÄDD KVINNA med två barn; EN KVINNA, som liknar Damen, men icke är Damen, och vilken virkar i stället för att äta; EN MAN, som liknar Läkaren, men icke är han; DÅRENS LIKNELSE; FADRENS och MODRENS LIKNELSE: BRODRENS D:o; FÖRÄLDRARNE till den 'förlorade sonen' m.fl. Alla klädda i vitt men däröver kostymer av flor i olika färger. Ansiktena vaxgula, likvita; och något spöklikt i hela väsendet och i gesterna.[54]

The Stranger mutely observes all of these specters from his past, both the dead and those still living. Strindberg uses a variety of theatrical devices to underscore that these "ghosts" are materializations of guilt from the protagonist's point of view. It is interesting to note in this respect the number of features in this scene that parallel the vision of Herrlin mentioned earlier. The Stranger imagines that he sees the figures as in a mirror, and when he asks if they are real ("riktiga"), the Abbess answers him: "Om ni menar verkliga, så äga de en förfärande realitet" ("If you mean really real, then they do possess a terrible reality"). It is this inner reality of crime and guilt that Strindberg fashioned into visual, concrete dramatic form. The unconscious anxiety and fear of the protagonist is expressed in scenic symbols that assume the characteristics of the dream. The magnificent thing about the asylum scene is the author's ability to coalesce all of the theater's separate means of expression in order to produce the configuration of an inner psychological process. Stylistically speaking, the asylum scene has a much more expressionistic stamp than the earlier scenes.

It becomes clearly evident in what follows that the asylum scene originated in Swedenborg's spirit world. The Confessor steps into the role of a disciplinary angel and reads aloud the voluminous content of The Stranger's Book of Sins. One after another, the guilt-laden images step forward and confront the impenitent sinner. The course of events is musically accompanied by the requiem "Dies irae, dies illa." In the chant the idea of the book of sins is introduced:

> Liber scriptus proferetur   Boken öppnas där står skrivet
> In quo totum continetur   Vad av alla är bedrivet
> Unde mundus judicetur.   I det flydda jordelivet.
> Judex ergo cum sedebit   Uppenbart blir allt som gömdes
> Quidquid latet apparebit   Avdömt allt
> Nil inultum remanebit.[55]   Som förr ej dömdes.

The scene culminates with the recitation of the Deuteronomic Curse, at which the chorus of The Stranger's victims repeat: "Förbannad!" ("Cursed shalt thou be!"). The dramatic unmasking concludes with the flight of the protagonist, but prior to that he has inquired for the first time about the possibility of salvation.

It is striking how closely Strindberg followed Swedenborg when, with a sovereign dramatic instinct, he sought to realize the artistic intentions of the prototype, and orchestrated image, character, movement, and word into a unified metaphor for the stage. The aesthetic structure of the "procession of shame" is built on the technique of repetition. The psychological point of departure is the function of pangs of conscience in consciousness. In Swedenborg the devastating course of events is shaped along metaphysical lines alone. In Strindberg's drama the protagonist's insight into his own evil becomes the beginning of his rebirth. This rebirth is effected through the Stranger's transformation from one who projects his evil and destructiveness onto the world about him into a religious seeker in the latter part of the play. The central position of the scene in the structure of the drama is stressed by the dramatist:

> ... handlingen rullar opp sig framåt mot Asylen; der törnar den mot udden och så spjernas det tillbaka, pilgrimsfärden, baklexan, oppätningarne; och så börjas på nytt på samma plats der leken slutar och der den började. Du kanske ej märkt huru scenerierna rulla opp sig baklänges från asylen som är ryggen i boken hvilken sluter sig och sluter in handlingen. Eller som en orm den der biter sig i stjerten.[56]

On the one hand, Strindberg asserted that the circular composition and the inversion of the scenes in the drama is an expression of the drama's central idea. On the other hand, he declared that the asylum scene holds a unique position in relation to the remaining scenes. In other words, does the Swedenborg-inspired pattern in the asylum scene also have implications for the drama's form and technique in a wider sense?

We can scarcely investigate this complicated relationship under the present circumstances, but raising this comparatively important question can lead to a few hypothetical reflections. In general terms, the asylum scene is without a doubt the point of departure for Strindberg's dramatization of the central religious experience alluded to in the title.[57] The asylum scene differs stylistically from the remaining scenes in the sense that Strindberg had indicated to the audience that the characters are materializations of the protagonist's guilt. The scene also functions as a summation of the scenes of the first half of the drama, because it has been indicated to the audience earlier that The Stranger bears a burden of guilt towards these ghosts from his past. The asylum scene follows the Swedenborgian pattern closely in so far as the protagonist's guilt is totally revealed. In the spirit world, situations and actions are resurrected to the slightest detail, whereas in Strindberg's play, The Confessor cites all the particulars of the accusations. The motivation behind this correlation is seen in the fact that Strindberg had already produced a corresponding dramatization of the guilt material in the individual scenes of the first half of the play. In terms of technique, each of these scenes has been constructed so as to repeat and dramatically represent the protagonist's guilt in the present. From this perspective, the figures of the drama are seen to function consciously or unconsciously as Doppelgänger in relation to The Stranger. This is true to an equal extent with respect to the reflection of physical reality; the notes from the funeral march, the withering Christmas rose, the sound from the deathwatch beetle and the rumbling mill, the cloud formations and the chilling winds, the profile of the werewolf in the flowers on the wallpaper, the pattern in the tablecloth, or the rocks in the ravine. The Stranger asks himself time and again: "Vad är detta? Vem förföljer mig? Ni försäkrar att er man är vänligt stämd mot mig; jag tror det, och likafullt kan han icke öppna sin mun utan att såra mig. Varje hans ord stack mig som en syl . . . och nu spelas denna sorgmarsch, den spelas verkligen . . . och där har jag julrosen igen.—Varför går allting igen . . . lik, och tiggare och dårar och människoöden och barndomsminnen. . . ."[58]

In the drama the asylum scene is the culmination of the devastation pattern that the writer develops scene by scene. The interaction of the scenes almost recalls a Chinese box, where the asylum scene encloses, so to speak, the lesser boxes. Even if it is only the asylum scene that is given a dreamlike quality for the stage by means of costume, make-up, and patterns of movement, it can nonetheless be asserted that the entire action of the play actually takes place inside the protagonist.

In the introductory scene The Stranger sits and draws in the sand with a cane. In the final scene he is sitting on the same bench and again drawing in the sand. The Lady asks: "Vad gör du?" The Stranger answers: "Jag skriver i sanden; *fortfarande*."[59] In the first scene of the drama the protagonist draws in the sand three times and each time a new Doppelgänger reflecting an inner conflict materializes before him.

The suggestion of a similar conception of time can also be found in *Till Damaskus II*. In this case the protagonist is sitting in the Rose Chamber waiting for a child about to be born. He is still sitting in the same place when he receives the newborn baby in the final scene. Everything that happens in the drama is placed inside the frame of this present time and from this perspective the protagonist's terrifying experiences appear to be anguished dreams.

Strindberg started with a similar scenic metaphor in an early version of *Carl XII*, in which the king was presented on a camp bed outside Fredriksten fortress watching the flames in a fire. The king was still staring into the fire in the final act, until he finally rose to set off on the fateful final tour of the trenches. Through this theatrical setting, the tableaus of the drama would be comprehended as dreamlike images passing before consciousness in the moment before it is extinguished in death. This bold formal stroke was never executed, although a few recollections of it do remain in the drama.

This technique was developed with sovereign skill in *Ett drömspel* (*A Dream Play*), where the frame symbol is the chyrsanthemum on the roof of the growing castle. At the outset the flower is on the verge of blooming, and this process develops fully only at the conclusion. The course of time between these moments is the present of the drama. The characterization of *Till Damaskus* as "Mitt förra drömspel" ("my earlier dream play") is more apt than comparison first seems to indicate. The point of departure is a conception of reality that lies at the heart of the action in *Till Damaskus* and that takes its aesthetic inspiration from the devastations of the Swedenborgian spirit world.

In this connection, the course of action in the earlier and later halves of *Till Damaskus* can be compared to their corresponding Swedenborgian prototypes. Swedenborg's devastation process consists of two distinct stages. First, the defilement of shame and annihilation of evil occurs, as in the first part of Strindberg's opus. The second state involves the reestablishment of truth and goodness in order to facilitate entry into a heavenly society. Here again there are a striking number of parallels between the author's works and the Swedenborgian prototype. The procession of shame in the asylum scene transforms the protagonist into a religious seeker. In Christian terms, this would be the moment of awakening. The "reborn" protagonist is tested in scene after scene in Strindberg's play. The testing scenes are constructed according to the same technique of reflection as in the first half, but now the intention is to confront the Stranger with his old and corrupt attitude toward life. With the repetition of the drama's scenes in inverted order, the author brings about an effective contrast between The Stranger's view of the world from the first to the second half of the play. The artistic gain with this mirror effect lies in the possibilities of contrasting damnation and rebirth. Together, the two sides of the process amount to devastation, or conversion. If people and things in the first half were projections of the protagonist's evil, the second half is marked by a successive harmonization analogous to the Stranger's conversion. The Mother is altered and assures everyone that now she "skall tala vackert" ("will speak nicely"). The Beggar steps into the role of Christ and The Stranger is reunited with The Lady. The Christian symbolism assumes an ever more prominent significance and the journey is concluded by the church door in expectation of "de nya sångerna" ("the new songs").

The Stranger's retracing of the steps of his journey to the asylum is analogous to the recapitulation of crime and guilt: "Min son! Du har lämnat Jerusalem, och du är på väg till Damaskus. Gå dit! samma väg du befarit hit; och plantera ett kors på varje station, men stanna på den sjunde; du har icke fjorton du, som Han!"[60] The conversion of Saul to Paul on the road from Jerusalem to Damascus is used to interpret the transformation of The Stranger's inner life. A structural analogy to the protagonist's transformation is found in the way in which the succession of scenes retraces the fourteen stations of the Cross. The circular composition and mirroring effect can be graphically depicted in the following figure:

$$1, 2, 3, 4, 5, 6, 7,$$
$$0 \qquad\qquad\qquad X$$
$$1, 2, 3, 4, 5, 6, 7,$$

For Strindberg, this compositional arrangement was a direct expression of the process of conversion, which was central to the drama and derived from the prototype of the Swedenborgian devastation pattern. The assumption is corroborated by the author's own description: "Ja, det är nog en dikt med en förfärande half-realitet bakom sig.

Konsten ligger i kompositionen, som symboliserar Gentagelsen."[61] When Strindberg used the concept of *Gentagelsen*, or repetition, to characterize the principle of composition in the drama, he was clearly referring to the motif of the recapitulation of guilt so central to the process of devastation. Although the Danicism "gentagelse" actually originates in Kierkegaard, it is usually used by Strindberg as a parallel term for devastation, for example, "Helvetet eller Paradiset: Ödeläggelsen = Gentagelsen: Weltmühle" ("Hell or Paradise: Devastation = Repetition: World Mill").[62] The last item in the equation refers to the mill in *Sólarljod* (*Song of the Sun*) that stands at the entrance to the kingdom of the damned and grinds the evil ones into bits of black matter. This concept of the world mill goes back to Viktor Rydberg's *Undersökningar i germansk mytologi* (*Investigations into Germanic Mythology*) and emerges for the first time in Strindberg in *Inferno*. There it functions as an alternative designation for devastation and it is associatively linked with the latter through the procession of shame.[63]

The concept of "half-realitet" is again a stylistic description employed to characterize "detta halfreela tillstånd som ej är vision eller hallucination, utan motsvarar hvad Swedenborg kallar föras af anden."[64] Behind the course of action in *Till Damaskus* there lies Strindberg's conviction that "the powers" have staged a reality of the same sort as the one he created as a dramatist. In a letter to Herrlin in the spring of 1898 he wrote: "Ja, hvad är detta? Hvem ger oss dessa iscensättningar, och i hvad avsigt? Ega de realitet? Fins ett helvete utom detta?"[65] Another time he stated: "Det är tydligt, att makterna bliva strängare ifråga om sedligheten. Och märk, så moderna de ha blivit. Inga drömmar, inga syner, eftersom folk icke fäster sig vid sådant. Nej, i stället hela iscensättningar av fulländad realism, saker utbredda till åskådande, och där man inte kommer långt med resonemang."[66] It was this sense of concreteness in Strindberg's understanding of reality, its fundamentally half-real nature notwithstanding, that distinguished him decisively from the German expressionists and others who succeeded him. The oft cited epigram from the Talmud expresses exactly the author's attitude: "Om du vill lära känna det osynliga, så iakttag med öppen blick det synliga."[67]

V

Strindberg's Swedenborg studies certainly continued after the spring of 1897, but from the perspective of his ideas these impulses are of limited interest. For example, he read Swedenborg's *Vera religio christiana* in a French edition in early 1898, but he was again repelled by the aspect of rigorous moralism. Subsequently, he always insisted that: "På visst sätt är jag Swedenborgare äfven, men icke enlight *Vera religio christiana*, der Teologien börjar igen."[68]

During his studies of occult natural philosophy, he consulted Swedenborg's scientific works on several different occasions.[69] In the following years he first read Swedenborg's allegorical commentary on a motif in the *Book of Revelation*, *Du cheval blanc*. He consulted *Diarium spirituale* in the preparation of *Gustav Adolf* and *Carl XII*,[70] and read Swedenborg's epic of creation, *De cultu et amore dei*, in 1904. The reading of Kardec, Maeterlinck, Goethe, and Emerson brought Swedenborg to the fore by various turns, and the same could be said for his theosophical studies after 1904. In the personal library Strindberg left behind, there is a large and often well-annotated collection of Swedenborgian texts and adaptions that he had purchased through the years.[71]

In conclusion, it can be asserted that despite his extensive reading, Strindberg's devotion to Swedenborg rested on a narrow and subjective basis of understanding. He never had the slightest sense for the system of Swedenborg's theosophy. Nonetheless, the encounter of the two "spirits" during the final phase of the Inferno crisis did lead to a symbiosis, which engendered rich literary fruits. Even in the spring of 1910 he could still confess to his friend Nils Andersson: "Det är bara Swedenborg och Bibeln, som ger mig modet: Hopplöst ser det ut här i Helvetet, som Origines anser skapadt till förargelse för de onda, hvilka skola pina hvarandra fram till korset, och derför kan det icke vara på annat sätt. Äfven derför att vi deporterade alltjemt rekryteras."[72] In his one literary representation of Swedenborg,[73] Strindberg had him appear as the dreamer and the seer, who knew best how to decipher the riddles of existence.

Notes

1. *Ockulta dagboken*, 25 June 1906, Nordiska Museets Strindbergssamling (hereafter *NMS*) in deposition at the Royal Library, Stockholm. Hereafter the manuscript will be referred to as *OD*. "Pulled out Swedenborg's *Heaven and Hell* at dinnertime; when I had read for a moment about Hell and its eternity, it became so pitch black in the room that I could no longer see to read. This was repeated once more. The sky had been radiantly clear the whole day, and remained so until evening. Immediately afterward I saw Swedenborg's face in the flowery pattern of the fabric on the sofa. He was one-eyed and half of the face was black; Klemming could be seen alongside wearing a German student cap."

2. August Strindberg, *Götiska rummen* in *Samlade Skrifter* (Stockholm: Bonniers, 1920–25), 40: 259. Hereafter *Samlade Skrifter* will be designated *SS*. "—Have you read Swedenborg?—You do not read Swedenborg, you are receptive [*undfår*] to him, or you are not receptive to him. You can only understand him if you have experienced the same as he."

3. *Carl XII* in *SS*, 35: 212. "FEIF: . . . It certainly is strange that the King has surrounded himself with one-eyed people these last few years! SWEDENBORG: Oh no! FEIF: Yes, indeed! Frölich, Müllern, Grothusen, and Görtz see only with one eye! SWEDENBORG: It would be amusing if there were not a hidden meaning in it! FEIF: Bah! Pure chance! SWEDENBORG: No Feif . . . but that you'll never understand. . . . FEIF: Dreams, Swedenborg, I don't understand!" *Charles XII*, trans. Walter Johnson (Seattle: University of Washington Press, 1955), pp. 159–60.

4. Letters to T. Hedlund, 15 February and 21 June 1896, *August Strindbergs brev*, ed. Torsten Eklund (Stockholm: Bonniers, 1948–), 11: 132, 219. (Hereafter cited as *Brev*). "Swedenborg was a mineralogist, rooted in the bowels of the earth, but also in the world of the spirit! . . . I am a naturalist-occultist, like my great teacher Linné. First physics, then metaphysics. I want to see with my outer eye first and then with the inner eye."

5. Letter to A. Eliasson, 28 October 1896, *Brev*, 11: 369. "In any case, Elias, don't you think that life at our age begins to appear otherwise than before; that a certain intervening hand is disclosed from time to time, and that even behind the so-called natural explanations, there are others to be found?

"For a year, I have taken note of everything and kept both a diary and a nocturnal book of dreams, and, as you know, I have become a mystic. I approve of the natural explanations as exoteric accounts for the public, but behind these lie the esoteric truths."

6. Letter to G. af Geijerstam, 4 December 1897, *Brev*, 12: 230. "This is an occidental hermeticism that is intended to annul Mme. Blawatzki's *Secret Doctrine*."

7. ". . . a Swedenborgian fugue with preludes."

8. Letter to E. Schering, 24 November 1906, Bonniers Archive, Stockholm (hereafter BA).

9. ". . . the magic chaos."

10. Letter to K. Börjesson, 14 September 1907, The Royal Library, Stockholm, (hereafter KB).

11. Letter to K. Börjesson, 2 September 1907, KB ". . . Christians, Theosophists, and Swedenborgians."
12. Letter to E. Schering, 25 June 1908, BA; cf. Letter to R. Bergh, 1 November 1907 and *OD*, 22 August 1906. ". . . my life's synthesis," ". . . my testament to mankind," ". . . *The Blue Book*, where the subject is treated conclusively."
13. "The Mysticism of World History," or "God in History."
14. "To Emanuel Swedenborg / Teacher and Leader / Is dedicated this Book / by the Disciple."
15. *SS*, 46: 404 ff.
16. Inge Jonsson and Olle Hjern, *Swedenborg, sökaren i naturens och andens världar: hans verk och efterföljd* (Stockholm: Proprius, 1976), pp. 81–102.
17. Cf. Torsten Eklund, *Tjänstekvinnans son: En psykologisk Strindbergsstudie* (Stockholm: Bonniers, 1948); Gunnar Brandell, *Strindbergs infernokris* (Stockholm: Bonniers, 1950); and Guy Vogelweith, *Le personnage et ses métamorphoses dans le théâtre de Strindberg I–II* (Paris, 1971).
18. Cf. Axel Herrlin, "Bengt Lidforss och August Strindberg: En studie över deras tankegemenskap och förhållande till samtida naturfilosofiska och metafysiska idéströmningar," in *Bengt Lidforss: En minneskrift*, ed. Einar Sjövall (Malmö: Framtiden, 1923), pp. 53–86. Martin Lamm, *Strindberg och makterna* (Stockholm and Uppsala: Svenska Kyrkans Diakonistyrelses Bokförlag: 1936); Karl-Åke Kärnell, "Metaforen som världsförklaring," in *Strindbergs bildspråk: En studie i prosastil* (Uppsala: Almqvist & Wiksell, 1962), pp. 242–87; and Göran Stockenström, *Ismael i öknen: Strindberg som mystiker* (Uppsala: Almqvist & Wiksell, 1972).
19. Cf. Hans Lindström, *Hjärnornas kamp; psykologiska idéer och motiv i Strindbergs åttiotalsdiktning* (Uppsala: Appelbergs, 1952), pp. 223–24.
20. *SS*, 54: 471. "I have treated the issue of Klemming and his influence on my career in several places, always with reverence and thankfulness, but in veiled terms."
21. Torsten Eklund, *Tjänstekvinnans son*, pp. 267–68. ". . . that he was one of those chosen by providence or fate for a great, global mission or, more often, a conviction that he was not only doomed to be cast down himself, but even to draw others with him into unparalleled suffering; condemned to bring ruin on himself and others."
22. *SS*, 28: 55; cf. *SS*, 7: 24 and *SS*, 8: 345–46 ". . . a charlatan, a fool with a dissolute imagination."
23. Letter to T. Hedlund, 15 May 1896, *Brev*, 11: 192. "Swedenborg is very big here. He is reckoned as the first theosophist in modern times, before Allan Kardec. I often get to read that I am from the homeland of Swedenborg, etc. Thus, I read Séraphita by Balzac. How great and wonderful it is!"
24. Letter to F. U. Wrangel, 7 June 1896, *Brev*, 11: 206. ". . . scientific occultism, continuing the work of Charcot, Ribot, DuPrel, Crooke, and others. If G. E. Klemming were alive, he would have procured it for the Royal Library."
25. Letter to L. Littmansson, 17 July 1894, *Brev*, 10: 140. "Do you remember how we anticipated all this current fin-de-sièclism and even Satanism out there on Kymmendö? Do you remember 'Strindberg's Religion' of Satan as the Prince of the World! We were Buddhas out there; experiencing amidst loneliness, cold, and punch-fumes premonitions of what would happen to the world, and we had gone much farther then than Huysmans has now."
26. Letter to T. Hedlund, 15 May 1896, *Brev*, 11: 192. "There is a Swedenborgian Society here with a chapel, a library, a reading room, and a publishing house. I visited there the other day and saw two portraits of the Theosopher. But they are only casings and tell me nothing, except that our souls are thrust into holsters that don't fit, and thus, we feel no more comfortable here on earth than we do in clothes that don't fit. . . . Therefore I have read Séraphita by Balzac. How great and wonderful it is! It is set in Norway, deals with a Swede, a descendant of Swedenborg. And this Swede is like Swedenborg's angels—androgynous. She has revelations. . . ."

27. Letter to K. Staff, 24 January 1897, *Brev*, 12: 47. "Swedenborg, the Buddha of the North, interpreted by Balzac."

28. Letter to T. Hedlund, 7 September 1896, *Brev*, 11: 317. "Here I have come into contact with Swedenborg's writings for the first time. There are wonderful things in them."

29. Letter to T. Hedlund, 31 October 1896, *Brev*, 11: 376. "The view of existence that has evolved in me is almost like that of Pythagoras, which Origen later adopted: We are in hell for sins committed in a previous existence. Therefore, do not pray for anything other than resignation! Desire nothing, absolutely nothing from life. If possible, be glad in adversity, for each misfortune that happens, an entry in the 'deficit column' is struck out. Swedenborg's description of the Inferno is close to earthly life without his having meant it, so exact that I am convinced."

30. Cf. Eklund, pp. 286 ff.; Brandell, p. 99.

31. Letter to M. Uhl, 5 February 1897, *Brev*, 12: 62. "I am alone again; moved into two rooms where I hear no sound, only my heart beating. I have struggled with God and Fate; have sought the dear Lord, and found the evil One. What does that mean?"

32. Cf. Stockenström, *Ismael i öknen*, pp. 63–95.

33. *OD* cover page, 1896; cf. Stockenström, pp. 72–73. "The explanation of this diary is found in letters to Torsten Hedlund and in conversations with Docent Herrlin. After my death this diary should go to Torsten Hedlund or Axel Herrlin or both. The only ones who understand it!"

34. Cf. Stockenström, pp. 228–29 ". . . the precocious prodigy."

35. Letter to M. Uhl, 17 December 1896, *Brev*, 12: 21. "Am now reading Swedenborg's *Arcane Coelestia* and am terrified. It all appears to be true to me, and still, too cruel from a God of love. So I prefer *Séraphita*."

36. Letter to K. Strindberg, 26 December 1896, *Brev*, 12: 28: "And Grandma should receive *Séraphita* as medicine for Mama Frida. Because the earth forsakes us we have heaven remaining. And when you have absorbed *Séraphita*, you can muse over *Louis Lambert* by Balzac as well."

37. Letter to M. Uhl, 14 January 1897, *Brev*, 12: 39. "Read your Swedenborg and behold how he depicts hell. Exactly like life on earth. So we are already there, and should delight in sorrow, for every sorrow is a partial payment for sin."

38. *SS*, 28: 45–46, 59–60. ". . . human shapes who possess reality in the form of hallucinations, fantasies, and dreams."

39. *OD*, 21 March 1897, emphases in the original; cf. Stockenström, pp. 86–109. "Yesterday and today I read in Swedenborg about the spirits on Jupiter, through which I was *enlightened about many marvels that have happened to me these last years*. Thus, about *Esprits censeurs et correcteurs* that torment people from evil unto goodness by torturing their hand (NB! the disease on my hands) and foot (see 19 March) or about the stomach (catarrh, 1883, 84). Aside from the pain in the limbs they use a painful constriction around the navel. As though caused by a stinging corset; pains in the chest from time to time (angina pectoris) to the point of anguish, disgust for any food other than bread, for several days at a time. (All of it agrees!)."

40. "NB: My hands are torn and blood seeps from the pores on the back of my hands."

41. "Saw a skull with a monk's hood in the stove fire, something stuck me in the right heel when I left, so that I had to take off my boot."

42. Letter to M. Uhl, 17 December 1896, *Brev*, 12: 21. "Swedenborg is so horrible that everything about him bothers me. Isn't my own hell enough? Should there be others as well?"

43. Letter to V. Carlheim-Gyllensköld, 12 April 1897, *Brev*, 12: 102. "As far as the apparent harshness of people is concerned, I have personally become resigned, but only through an attempt, like that of Pythagoras, to assume preexistence and reincarnation. I now believe that the assumption has since been confirmed by experience and

observation. The explanation that my own fate seems so painful to me lies without a doubt in crimes committed in preexistence. I am so keenly convinced that we find ourselves in the Inferno, especially after finding earthly life represented in detail in Swedenborg's descriptions of hell."

44. Letter to Marie Uhl, 25 July 1897, *Brev*, 12: 133–34. "If I can offer solace and peace of soul on the other hand, then I am ready, because hate and revenge do not live with me anymore, as earlier, ever since I discovered that man is not responsible for his fate and that our sins are assigned to us as punishment."

45. *OD*. The two entries are from 29 April and 28 August 1897 respectively. "Met an old woman with the face of death. Wandered down to the hospital; experienced that oppression in the chest that I've called 'the electric corset.'" "At 5 p.m. Papus was in my room, but invisible. He is probably reading my manuscript right now. Feelings of discomfort; constrained feeling in the chest; sometimes I feel the 'lacings' in my back, sometimes heat in my chest."

46. *OD*, 10 July and 29 June 1897. ". . . as though through gauze; slightly yellowish, almost white; he looked serious and wore pince-nez. He looked at me a bit, always as if he sat and watched over a sick man. It was 6:30 a.m. This is the first vision I've had. Now I have to see if anything has happened to Herrlin!!!"

47. *SS*, 28: 235. ". . . something half-real, a series of visions, conjured by someone and with a conscious purpose."

48. Emanuel Swedenborg, *Arcana coelestia*, §943; cf. Stockenström, pp. 154 ff. "Those who in the life of the body had for their end mere sensual pleasures, and loved only to indulge their propensity and to live in luxury and festivity, caring for themselves and the world alone, holding Divine things as of no account, being without faith and charity, are after death introduced first into a life similar to that which they lived in the world. There is a place in front, to the left, at some depth, where there is nothing but sensual pleasures, sports, dancing, feasting, and frivolous talk. Such spirits are brought to this place and then they do not know otherwise than that they are in the world. But the scene is changed; after some tarry here they are brought down into a hell under the buttocks which is merely excrementitious; for such pleasure, which is merely corporeal, is turned into what is excrementitious in the other life. I have seen them there bearing dung and bewailing their lot." The *Heavenly Arcana Disclosed*, Rotch Edition (Boston and New York: Houghton Mifflin, 1907), II: 96.

49. *OD*, 8 September 1896. "The damned cannot tolerate daylight or clean air. . . . When the heavenly light reaches the condemned, an icy chill moves through the veins and the blood coagulates. The damned look like the passions."

50. "Huru man blir Swedenborgare," Nordiska Museets Strindbergssamling, carton 11; cf. the references to Sven Hedin in Harry Järv, *Strindbergsfejden: 465 debattinlägg och kommentar* (Staffanstorp: Cavefors, 1968), I–II. ". . . a great man, the nation's greatest son, is instructed to step into the throne room (the stripping room [*afklädningsrummet*]). Dressed in his doctor's frock and bedecked with the medals of his orders, the newcomer is called upon to occupy his place under the throne-sky. Then the nation comes to greet him with speeches; the great one is invested with crown and mantle and with the sound of drums and trumpets he is proclaimed a king. Then the scene begins to transform. The crown becomes a saucepan, the royal mantle a white sheet; the laurel wreath is thrown in the beef stew like bay leaves, the orders become contrary signs. The nation evaporates before his eyes and the great one sits alone in a solitary house, his throne transformed into a pine closet."

51. *SS*, 44: 49; cf. Stockenström, pp. 370–72. "In his vision of hell, Swedenborg has a "stripping room," where the deceased are led immediately after death. There they are stripped of the garb that they were forced to put on in society, among friends and family."

52. "Swedenborg: alpha," *NMS*, carton 9; cf. Stockenström, pp. 83–84, 96–97, 143–44.

53. Emanuel Swedenborg, *De coelo et de inferno*, §462 and 463; cf. Stockenström, pp. 82–83. "These exposures were made as suddenly as when a scene bursts upon the sight, and sometimes continued for hours together. There was one who had made light of the evil of backbiting. I heard his backbitings and defamations recited word for word and the names of the persons about whom and before whom they were uttered; all this was reproduced to the very life, though everything had been studiously concealed by him while he lived in the world. Another person, who had deprived a relative of his inheritance by a fraudulent pretext, was judged and convicted in the same way, and, wonderful to relate, the letters and papers which had passed between them were read in my hearing, and I was told that not a word was wanting. The same person, also, shortly before his death, secretly murdered his neighbor by poison; and this crime was brought to light as follows. He was seen to dig a hole under his feet, out of which a man came forth like one coming out of a grave, and cried to him, "What has thou done to me?" Every detail was then revealed; how the murderer talked with him in a friendly manner and offered the cup; also what he thought beforehand, and what happened afterwards. After these disclosures he was condemned to hell. In a word, all evils, villainies, robberies, artifices, and deceits are so clearly exhibited to evil spirits, and brought forth from their own memory, that they stand convicted; nor is there any room for denial, because every detail is disclosed." *Heaven and Its Wonders and Hell*, trans. F. Bayley, (New York: Dutton, 1909), p. 239.

54. *SS*, 29: 89. Cf. Stockenström, pp. 243–348. "By a long dining table to the left THE STRANGER is sitting in white hospital garb, alone next to his bowl. At the table to the right sit: THE BROWN-CLAD mourners from Act I; The BEGGAR; a WOMAN in mourning with two children; a WOMAN who resembles The Lady but is not The Lady and who is crocheting instead of eating; a MAN who resembles The Doctor but is not he; a MAN resembling Caesar; PEOPLE resembling his mother and father; the PARENTS of the "prodigal son"; and others. All are dressed in white but covering the white garments are veils in different colors. The faces are waxen yellow, corpselike; there is something ghostlike about their beings and their gestures." *To Damaskus I* in *Plays of Confession and Therapy*, trans. Walter Johnson (Seattle: University of Washington Press, 1979), p. 64 (hereafter *TD*).

55. *SS*, 29: 93–94. (The Swedish version is taken from *Svenska Psalmboken* 609: 2–6).

56. Letter to G. af Geijerstam, 13 March 1898, *Brev*, 12: 279–80. ". . . the action unfolds forward toward the Asylum; there it strikes the point and kicks back, the pilgrimage, the repeated lessons, the constant finishing up. So the game begins anew in the same place where it ends and where it had begun. Perhaps you didn't notice how the scenes coil up backward from the asylum, which is the spine of the book that closes itself and encloses the action. Or like a serpent that bites itself in the tail."

57. Stockenström, p. 302.

58. *SS*, 29: 45. "What is this? Who's persecuting me? You assure me your husband is friendly toward me. I believe you, but all the same he can't open his mouth without hurting me. Every one of his words cuts me . . . and now the funeral march is being played; it's really being played . . . and there's the Christmas rose again.—Why does everything repeat itself . . . dead bodies and beggars and madmen and human destinies and childhood memories. . . ." *TD*, p. 40.

59. *SS*, 29: 133. "What are you doing?" "I am writing in the sand; *still*." *TD*, p. 88.

60. *SS*, 29: 110. "My son, you've left Jerusalem, and you're on the way to Damascus. Go there! the same way you came, and place a cross at each station but stop at the seventh. You don't have fourteen as He did!" *TD*, p. 76.

61. Letter to G. af Geijerstam, 17 March 1898, *Brev*, 12: 279–80. "Yes, it is no doubt a poem with a terrifying half-reality behind it. The art lies in the composition, which symbolizes the Repetition [*Gentagelsen*]."

62. "Légendes de ma vie," *NMS*, carton 9(3).

63. Cf. Stockenström, pp. 190–91, 96–97; and Nils Åke Sjöstedt, *Søren Kierkegaard*

och svensk litteratur: Från Frederika Bremer till Hjalmar Söderberg (Göteborg: Wettergren & Kerber, 1950), pp. 248 ff. Sjöstedt rejects any connection with the religious and ethical categories in Kierkegaard's concept of "Gjentagelse" and points, instead, to "'unfolding of the past,' which is what is specifically Strindbergian in the concept."

64. Letter to G. af Geijerstam, 15 November 1897, *Brev*, 12: 212. ". . . that half-real state that is not vision or hallucination, but corresponds to what Swedenborg calls 'transported by the spirit.'"

The concept "föras af anden," or "transported by the spirit," is taken from the characteristics of the Swedenborgian visionary state, that is, dream-wake, dreamlike visions, and cultivated visions. Strindberg's interest in these and similar occultist ideas such as theories about somnambulism, reincarnation, and the astral plane is well attested. The term coined by the writer, "hexscener" (witch-scenes), is an excellent evocation of the style of these scenes from the spirit world. Cf. *Arcana coelestia*, §1882–85.

65. Letter to A. Herrlin, 10 March 1898, *Brev*, 12: 273. "Yes, what is this? Who produces these strange stagings and with what intentions? Are they real? Is there a hell beyond this?"

66. *SS*, 28: 285. "It is evident that the powers are becoming stricter in questions of morality. And note how modern they have become. No dreams or visions, for people don't pay attention to such things. No, instead there are whole stage–productions of complete realism, things spread out for observation, and where you don't get very far with a discussion."

67. *OD*, "Dagbok från Februari 1896 till . . ." (Frontispiece). Cf. Stockenström, pp. 158–59. "If you would know the invisible, then observe the visible with open eyes."

68. Letter to C. W. Palmgren, 27 September 1910; cf. Stockenström, pp. 208–20, 256–58. "In certain ways, I am a Swedenborgian, but not according to *Vera christiana religio*, where the theology starts again."

69. Stockenström, p. 349. The writer borrowed the following works from the library of the University of Lund: *Opera philosophica et mineralia I–II; Principia or First Principle of Things; Regnum animale, anamotice, physice, et philosophice perlustratum*.

70. Cf. Göran Stockenström, "Strindberg och historiens Karl XII," *Meddelanden från Strindbergssällskapet* 47–48 1971), 15–37, esp. 35–36.

71. Cf. Hans Lindström, *Strindberg och böckerna* (Uppsala: Almqvist & Wiksell, 1977), pp. 84–85, 94, 96, 100–102, 104–105, 108, 118, 190–91, 195, 203.

72. Letter to N. Andersson, 23 May 1910, BA. "It is only Swedenborg and the Bible that give me courage. It seems hopeless here in hell. As Origen understood, the world was created for the mortification of the wicked, who should torment each other forward to the cross, and, therefore, life cannot be otherwise than it is. Therefore we deportees are still recruited."

73. See *Carl XII; SS*, 35; and *Charles XII*, trans. Walter Johnson (Seattle: University of Washington Press, 1955).

Strindberg and Karlfeldt
Karl-Ivar Hildeman

Despite his eminence within Swedish literature Strindberg never received a Nobel Prize from the Swedish Academy. The generation that succeeded him could, however, boast of three Nobel Prize winners, the last of whom was Erik Axel Karlfeldt (1864–1931). Just after his death in 1931 the prize was awarded to "the poetry of E. A. Karlfeldt"; at the time of his death he was poet laureate and had dominated the Swedish literary scene for many years by virtue of artistic talents quite different from those of Strindberg.

To his Swedish contemporaries Strindberg never ceased to be regarded as both the major proponent of Swedish naturalism and the literary leader of the 1880s. But in the nineties the symbolist movement emerged, emphasizing aestheticism, fantasy, and "the joy of life" as qualities integral to literary expression: the Swedish audience was apparently satiated with realistic novels and social criticism, and the nineties became the golden age of lyric poetry and imagination, a tendency that overshadowed Strindberg's works at a time when he was usually living abroad and his production was less prolific because of personal crises. The vanguards of this new movement were Verner von Heidenstam (1859–1940) and his learned friend Oscar Levertin (1862–1906). In 1891 Selma Lagerlöf (1858–1940) and Per Hallström (1866–1960) also published their first works in accordance with this new trend, as did the most popular and most genuinely lyric poet of that generation, Gustaf Fröding (1860–1911). Karlfeldt did not really appear on the literary scene until 1895, with his breakthrough coming three years later with his second collection, *Fridolins visor* (*Fridolin's Songs*). He strengthened his position with *Fridolins lustgård* (*Fridolin's Pleasure Garden*) in 1901, and in 1904 he became a member of the Swedish Academy, the first representative of the younger generation. Until then the new literati had systematically been rejected by the dictatorial secretary of the Academy, Carl David af Wirsén, who did battle with the schools of the eighties and of the nineties with equal energy and contempt. At that time Strindberg had returned home and enjoyed a unique position because of his extensive literary output and his international reputation. But in many respects he did not seem to fit in with the pattern of current Swedish literature. The old warrior occasionally renewed his attacks on the establishment, as in *Svarta fanor* (*Black Banners*), with the same cannibal appetite that once had almost made him an outlaw within these circles. And although he was admired for his talent as an author, his aggressiveness made him very controversial to large, influential segments of the Swedish audience.

Karlfeldt's position was quite the opposite: he was unobtrusive and sensitive, quick to take offense, and disliked public quarrels, all of which led him to refuse to participate in the kind of literary feuds in which Strindberg seemed to bask. During a journey to Italy in 1901 Karlfeldt wrote for instance to a friend of his: "Vänlig hälsning från Rom. Jag kom först i går tillbaka hit . . . och strax grep mig lifvets allvar och bitterhet på nytt. Jag fann här två bref—det ena uppfordrar mig att ge mig med i en litterär fejd, som ej alls rör mig . . . Idyllen förbi."[1] Karlfeldt was not interested in political–literary parties and programs, and his works were not concerned with social, political, or even literary topics, but were quite simply lyric poetry of emotion and mood evocation. His production did not challenge any powerful group, and he was respected as an independent artist. Karlfeldt was sixteen years younger than Strindberg and it was only during a twelve-year period, 1900–1912, that they could possibly have met as equals. But one wonders to what extent they really did meet or know each other?

Few written sources can help us with this problem. Evidently they knew each other and had some close mutual friends, in particular Albert Engström, artist and writer. In his biography of Karlfeldt written in 1931, C. Mangård states that "mellan Karlfeldt och Strindberg rådde ett mycket gott förhållande trots olikheten i livssyn och temperament. Då de träffades, samspråkade de kordialt om också med någon spydighet å båda hållen."[2] Apparently Mangård has his information from Karlfeldt's friend Otto Silfwerskiöld, who tells us about several situations when Strindberg and Karlfeldt accidently met, and Karlfeldt's wording indicates a rather intimate attitude, incidents that may well be the entire basis for this statement. Mrs. Gerda Karlfeldt, ninety-six years old, recalled that they were not intimate friends: "de tyckte inte om varandra."[3] Her point of view is Karlfeldt's, of course, but he himself never confirmed this attitude (or any other) in print. On Strindberg as an author he has just one comment in all his production: in his book on the romantic poet C. F. Dahlgren, he praises Dahlgren's concrete metaphors and realistic style as "en stil-konst, som får sin glans i svensk litteratur genom Strindberg."[4] But he never comments on him as an individual. According to the register of letters preserved at Karlfeldt's home, Sångs in Sjugare, Leksand, there are no records of Strindberg.[5] In the rather limited collection of books at Sångs, Strindberg is represented by one drama, *Stora landsvägen* (*The Great Highway*), and four prose works, among them *Svarta fanor*, but by no lyric works (moreover, there are no dedications by Strindberg in any of the volumes at Sångs).

But what, one may ask, was Strindberg's attitude towards Karlfeldt? Professor Walter Behrendson's register of names in Strindberg's production is to be found in the Royal Library in Stockholm, where there is no mention of Karlfeldt. His name does not appear in Strindberg's letters, preserved in the same library,[6] and none of Karlfeldt's works have been found in Strindberg's library.[7] Relatives who had close contacts with him at that time do not recall that he had anything to say about Karlfeldt,[8] a fact that may be traced to his lack of enthusiasm for Karlfeldt's genre. Gunnar Ollén has pointed out that Strindberg despised lyric poetry: "Någon poesinjutare tycks han inte ha varit."[9] Harriet Bosse, his third wife, has verified that "om han någon gång tittade i en lyrikbok, så gick läsningen med svindlande fart."[10] It is furthermore doubtful that Strindberg paid much attention to the development of Swedish lyric poetry during his last years, when he was occupied mainly with theater, with, however, one important exception: the Strindberg Feud.

In the spring of 1910 Strindberg launched his last and most direct attack on the establishment, mainly the literary establishment, or those he regarded as his competitors as leaders of Swedish literature. Strindberg's target was the generation of the nineties, represented by the program writers—among them Heidenstam and the late Levertin—because they enjoyed a wide reputation that could rival Strindberg's. Strindberg was of the opinion that he had anticipated their program and that their laurels for the literary rebellion against gloomy naturalism in fact belonged to him. The country was divided in two parties, for and against, as were the newspapers, which quoted Strindberg's articles with applause or scorn. On the whole, rather few of the participants in the debate disputed Strindberg's literary importance, but even fewer approved of the way he treated his opponents. Levertin was dead and Heidenstam kept silent for almost one year in spite of Strindberg's repeated and insulting attacks. Until then Hallström was the only one of the poets of the nineties who made counterattacks and defended his school,[11] even though his name had never been directly mentioned by Strindberg. Nor had Karlfeldt's, but the mere absence of Karlfeldt's name does not necessarily indicate that Strindberg was not concerned with him and his role in Swedish literature. Certainly Karlfeldt was unobtrusive, and he was no intimate friend of the men whom Strindberg initially attacked, Heidenstam and Levertin. One of Karlfeldt's closest friends was Fröding, and everyone in the battles of the nineties treated him as an exception because of the quality of his poetry, the popular themes in his works, and his gentle and human genius—a heritage to which Karlfeldt was regarded as successor. Fröding had been legally prosecuted for immoral writing (like Strindberg) and thus could hardly be accused of ties with the establishment, even by the suspicious Strindberg.

But Karlfeldt could: he was more or less accepted by both sides, except that he was a member of the Swedish Academy. At that time the Academy was detested by the authors of the eighties and of the nineties alike; Wirsén, the secretary, accepted neither Strindberg nor Heidenstam. But in 1904 Karlfeldt was elected a member of the Academy as the first "modern poet," apparently because he ostensibly did not belong to any particular group and thus was not controversial from Wirsén's point of view. Wirsén's acceptance almost assured Strindberg's rejection. Strindberg started his literary feud by attacking the Academy as a part of the royal establishment. Nobody was mentioned by name, nor was anybody excepted. But at least one sentence seemed to have certain implications: "Och man märker strax, *även på de modigaste*, så snart de inträtt i Sv.A., *om också i föregiven avsikt att reformera*, att där råder en atmosfär och hovluft, som kväver, och fruktan att skriva om någonting driver den nödställde att öva 'konsten att säga någonting vackert om ingenting.'"[12] Karlfeldt's entrance into the Academy was interpreted as a sign: he was expected to break down barriers and introduce a new generation into the formerly closed circle. In 1910, six years later, little had happened to justify those expectations. Hallström had been accepted by the Academy in 1908, but Wirsén stubbornly continued to reject Heidenstam; Strindberg was out of the question as even more "immoral," and not until Wirsén's death in 1912 was Karlfeldt, as his successor, able to reform the policy of the Academy, by which time Strindberg was also dead.

From Strindberg's comment about "reformers" we cannot conclude whether his attack was aimed at Karlfeldt in particular or at him and some of his other colleagues. But we can notice the way at least part of the contemporary audience interpreted this passage and others. A poet with close contacts with both the school of the nineties and the labor movement (which largely supported Strindberg wholeheartedly) was K. E. Forsslund. He criticized Strindberg in the social-democratic periodical *Fram* and objected "att i en tidning intas en hånfull, groft okunnig artikel mot andliga stormän, sådana som Levertin och Karlfeldt (åtminstone åsyftad, såvitt jag förstått rätt)."[13] Another author, the young Lubbe Nordström, used other tactics in defending Karlfeldt and tried to separate him from the rest of the Academy: "Funnes mer rättvisa i världen borde Karlfeldt befrias ur denna samling (Sv.A.), ty jämte Fröding och Strindberg hör han till det levande folket. . . ."[14] Strindberg did not renew his attack on the "reformers" of the Academy. Other participants in the quarrel, who were numerous and frequently as violent as Strindberg, expanded the front and included several of the other poets of the nineties, but Karlfeldt remained uninvolved. As the debate concerning the nineties continued, both sides made a distinction between Heidenstam and Levertin on one hand and Fröding and Karlfeldt on the other. Heidenstam and Levertin were regarded as too sophisticated; Fröding and especially Karlfeldt as more simple, popular, genuine, and "Swedish." Therefore, they did not fit in with "the School" of the nineties. Even a moderate critic like Hj. Haralds could put it this way: "Huru sjuklig, osund och dekadensmättad står icke Heidenstams och Levertins diktning mot Karlfeldts, Fridolins diktare!"[15]

The leftists in particular were eager to recruit Karlfeldt as a member of the Strindberg group. The Strindberg Feud was not only a literary battle; it had also a political and social basis. Strindberg identified himself with the radicals and the workers; Heidenstam with his aristocratic roots and Levertin with his academic background were regarded as rightists, accepted by the establishment as its representatives. From that point of view Karlfeldt was more of a representative of the people. He came from a farmer's family and he emphasized the fact in his poetry, which was concerned with rural life. When Karlfeldt published his first collections he used the modest term "visor" instead of poems (i.e., popular songs in a less sophisticated manner than the traditional academic style), and partly because of his lack of pretension they actually became popular and were often described as "genuine" by the critics. Among the Strindberg defenders who strove to enlist Karlfeldt in their ranks, the most militant was Professor Bengt Lidforss. He used the Strindberg Feud for a personal war on Levertin and accused him of unfair treatment of Strindberg. "Även den konsekventa tystnad, som Levertin ständigt intagit gentemot Karlfeldt, är påtagligen ett utslag av hans antipati mot allt som är svenskt i djupare mening."[16] Levertin was a Jew, and Lidforss an anti-Semite; Levertin had not reviewed Karlfeldt's collections but acknowledged him as "a genuine poet." Karlfeldt disliked the decadent trend in Levertin's poetry but was nevertheless attracted and influenced by it. This influence was, however, never discussed by either

Karlfeldt or his contemporaries, perhaps because he was supposed to be "Swedish in a more profound meaning," as was Strindberg, according to Lidforss and his faction.

The attitude of Strindberg's proponents may have convinced him, if he were not already convinced, that he could find better targets for his attack on the nineties and on the Swedish Academy. It can hardly be doubted that he knew how Karlfeldt had come to be included in the Academy, for it was no secret at that time. Count Snoilsky, the old poet and a friend of the king, had been rather intimate friends with Karlfeldt, for he was the director of the Royal Library where Karlfeldt was employed. It was well known that he liked Karlfeldt's poetry and wanted him as his successor in the Swedish Academy. Snoilsky's opinion was important to the king and to Wirsén, who also felt that in the long run he could not prevent a younger generation from entering the Academy. But when Karlfeldt was offered a seat in the Academy, he refused, compelling Wirsén to make a futile trip to Dalarna in an attempt to persuade him. At least this was Wirsén's official version—in fact, he favored a different candidate.[17] There were also rumors that Karlfeldt had rejected the seat because of pressure from Heidenstam's supporters, who wanted their leader to be chosen instead.[18] The following year another seat was open, and this time Karlfeldt was elected by the Academy without being asked in advance, and he could show his independence only by turning down the royal order that at that time was given to members of the Academy. Thus everyone could clearly see that Karlfeldt dissented from the rest of the assembly.

Strindberg may have noticed this protestation, but the main reason that he never attacked Karlfeldt directly was probably that Karlfeldt "aldrig uppträtt med några pretentioner på att vara andlig förare, och hans dikt har dessutom en manlig öppenhet och blygsamhet, som ställer honom vid sidan av klicken (kring Heidenstam)," as one of Strindberg's supporters put it.[19] In fact, Karlfeldt had rebelled against Wirsén already in 1906, but this was hardly known outside the Academy.[20] During the entire Strindberg debate Karlfeldt himself kept silent; nor did he ever subsequently mention the feud.

Whatever personal relations may be, authors usually influence each other by their works. In this case it is *a priori* not very likely that Karlfeldt's poetry was of any importance to Strindberg's. Gunnar Ollén, however, thinks that there are some indications of such an influence in Strindberg's lyric collection *Ordalek och småkonst* (*Word Play and Minor Art*) of 1905. In the poem "Vargarna tjuta" ("The Wolves Howl") "diktaren ger sig tid med ett par bilder, 'Högt Orion svärdet svänger, Karlavagnen står på stup,' vilka har något av de Karlfeldtska *Dal-*

målningarnas festliga livfullhet."[21] Celestial constellations of this type are used by Karlfeldt in his "poetic transcription" of rural wall paintings with biblical motifs from his home province Dalarna. He uses them as metaphors; the constellations become active persons, animals, and facts in accordance with their names. In this case it is Karlfeldt's poem "Elie himmelsfärd" ("Elijah's Journey to Heaven") that is relevant. In that poem Elijah travels in his chariot through the sky surrounded by the Scorpion, the Bears, the Dog, the Lion, and the Snake—all Swedish names for constellations, like Karlavagnen ("Charles's Wain") and Orion in Strindberg's work. Ollén also indicates that Strindberg's second part of the poem "Holländarn" ("The Dutchman"), which has the microcosm motif in common with Karlfeldt's poem "Mikrokosmos," may point in a similar direction.[22] The two Karlfeldt poems are to be found in *Fridolins lustgård* (1901), but the parallels are hardly obvious, and Ollén's caution is certainly justified. In his book *August Strindberg* (1979), Olof Lagercrantz asserts that Strindberg has used Karlfeldt's poem "Häxorna" ("The Witches") for one of his last dramas, *Den siste riddaren* (*The Last of the Knights*). The parallels are, however, hardly evident enough to prove such a claim.[23]

One would rather expect Strindberg to be of importance to Karlfeldt and his poetry, and on a certain level the inheritance is clear. Karlfeldt has a taste for bold realistic metaphors that has often been admired. Some of them have been quoted so often that they are classics in the Swedish tradition—"höstmånens röda kastrull" ("the red saucepan of the autumn moon") and others. The only time Karlfeldt comments on Strindberg's function in Swedish literature he applauds the same tendency. As far as their linguistic tools are concerned, the poets of the nineties continued to be naturalists, drastic and daring. Many authors continue to this day to be indebted to Strindberg, for the modern Swedish language really starts with him and his vigorous prose. Apparently Karlfeldt was aware of his impact, accepted it, and tried to follow suit. Many of his metaphors in the bold realistic style that were once so admired appear doubtful today, and his copper saucepan is artificial compared with Strindberg's linguistic paintings. (This is the case with many of Karlfeldt's metaphors but certainly not all of them.)

Likewise, there is little evidence that Strindberg's lyric works were of any importance to Karlfeldt. As far as temperament and poetic technique are concerned, they were totally different as lyric poets. Nor are Strindberg's novels and short stories reflected in Karlfeldt's production in other ways than that mentioned above, although Strindberg's openness to nature should have attracted Karlfeldt. All of this leads us to investigate Karlfeldt's interest in Strindberg's dramatic works. Karlfeldt's interest in the theater seems to have been slight. Mrs. Karlfeldt recalled that he went there "sometimes." "På teatern gick han endast två eller tre gånger om året, utan att därför på minsta sätt underskatta den sceniska konsten," says Mangård.[24] Karlfeldt comments critically on a drama by C. F. Dahlgren from the 1820s, but he finds that "jämnt ett hundra år efteråt lyssnar man kväll efter kväll till likartade men dummare dialoger på landets främsta teater."[25] Evidently he had been to the theater often enough to form an opinion of his own. We do not know how many of Strindberg's plays Karlfeldt may have seen or read, but there are indications that at least one of them made a lasting impression, Folkungasagan (*The Saga of the Folkungs*) from 1899.

Karlfeldt wrote his last great poem in 1930, the year before he died. It is called "Vallfärd" ("Pilgrimage").[26] It deals once again with a recurring motif in Karlfeldt's poetry, the concept of sexuality. But here it is not a problem of guilt or lust as it often had been before, for Karlfeldt had encountered Freud, and the power of sexuality ("the mountain storm") is no longer a threat from evil forces. The background of the poem is medieval: a plague forces the people to set out for a pilgrimage to the monastery of Gudsberga in Dalarna, where one of the residents is Staffan, who is considered to be a saint and a seer (as a matter of fact he seems to have existed historically, and Karlfeldt uses certain local legends for part of his poem). The pilgrimage concludes in a religious and sexual ecstasy: "Syntes ock kvinnor, häxor lika, som ryckte sitt hår, flängde sin hud med spö, så lemmarna dröpo av sår."[27]

Karlfeldt alludes to the medieval scourgers, the flagellants, who also appear in Folkungasagan. Strindberg's drama has a similar background; a plague in the Middle Ages compels the people to penance. Here we encounter flagellants, "halfnakna människor, som deltaga i Litanian och gissla sig under ett slags högtidlig dans," according to Strindberg's instructions in the drama.[28] In this connection he has used a song out of popular Swedish tradition from olden times as a recurrent theme; it is intoned already in the first act and is echoed repeatedly later on. It is a kind of prophecy in rhyme, called "Stenen i grönan dal" ("The Stone in the Green Valley"). According to popular tradition it was attributed to Staffan in Gudsberga, which Strindberg may or may not have known, for the song and the tradition are not widespread and Staffan is not mentioned by name in his drama. But we can be sure that Karlfeldt knew this background because we can date a visit he made to Gudsberga where he was informed of its history, including that of a stone called Staffan's Stone, which we meet both in the song and in the poem.²⁹ The flagellants and the song in particular are not common material and I know of no other source where they are to be found in combination except in Strindberg's drama. So it seems probable that *Folkungasagan* contributed to Karlfeldt's image of the Middle Ages, as it is reflected in "Vallfärd."

Already in his third collection, *Fridolins lustgård*, which, we recall, was published in 1901, Karlfeldt has another pastiche from the Middle Ages or the Renaissance, called *I kungalunden* (*In the Royal Grove*). It is written in quite a different mood, as an elegant courtly poem, depicting a royal wedding long ago. A princess from "Vendens land," northern Germany, arrives at a castle in Sweden and is welcomed by the prince and the king. The poem is pure pastiche: Karlfeldt has amused himself by painting a milieu without any other function. There is just one historical situation that coincides with the plot (a Swedish crown prince who married a princess from northern Germany in the Middle Ages): the marriage of King Magnus Eriksson's oldest son, Erik, to Beatrix of Brandenburg in 1356. This is not an incident to which the history books pay much attention, but in Strindberg's *Folkungasagan* King Magnus is the main character and the young couple play a touching part as innocent victims of a retributive family guilt. A Swedish audience of today is aware of their existence only because of Strindberg's play, and Karlfeldt may well have belonged to that audience. *Folkungasagan* was published in 1899 and was performed for the first time in January 1901. Karlfeldt's poem was published in the spring that same year and the author's attitude to the young couple is strikingly similar to that of Strindberg. Indeed, to plead coincidence here would be to deny Strindberg his due.

The result of this investigation is almost as negative as one might have predicted. Scanty exceptions cannot eliminate the main impression of distance between the dominating dramatist and the leading lyric poet in early twentieth-century Sweden. Their domains, temperaments, and interests were so different that they effected a mutual lack of interest and also a lack of competition. Nevertheless, there are indications that even Karlfeldt could not withstand the omnipresent impact of Strindberg.

Notes

1. Ernst Malmberg's collection of mss, Uppsala University Library, (Uppsala, December 1901). "Best regards from Rome. I didn't come back here until yesterday . . . and immediately the seriousness and bitterness of life caught me again. I found two letters here . . . one of them urging me to join a literary feud which does not concern me at all. . . . The idyll lost."
2. *En bok om Karlfeldt* (Stockholm, 1931), p. 116. "K. and S. were on very friendly terms in spite of different temperaments and views of life. When they met they chatted cordially although with some malice from both sides."
3. "They did not like each other."
4. *Carl Fredrik Dahlgren* (Stockholm, 1924), p. 136. ". . . a kind of artistic style that achieves its splendor in Swedish literature through Strindberg."
5. The collection is now to be found in the Royal Library, Stockholm, and will become available in 1981.
6. Strindberg's letters from his last years are not yet published; the last volume, 15, was printed by Strindbergssällskapet (The Strindberg Society) (Stockholm, 1976) and covers the years 1904–1907.
7. Cf. Hans Lindström, *Strindberg och böckerna* (Stockholm, 1977). Cf. Göran Söderström, *Strindberg och bildkonsten* (Stockholm, 1972).
8. His niece Märta, n. von Philp, and her husband, Hugo Fröding. We discussed the matter on several occasions in the 1950s.
9. *Strindbergs 1900-talslyrik* (Stockholm, 1941), p. 30. "He does not seem to have enjoyed poetry."
10. Ibid., p. 30. "If he sometime happened to look in a book of poetry, he read at a breakneck speed."
11. Strindberg collected his articles in *Tal till svenska nationen* (*Speeches to the Swedish Nation*). Now all the contributions to the Strindberg Feud have been brought together by Harry Järv, *Strindbergsfejden I–II* (Uddevalla, 1968), (quot. *Strindbergsfejden*). Hallström's articles are in volume 1: 383, 664.
12. "And one notices immediately, *even when the bravest are concerned,* as soon as they have entered the Swedish Academy—*even with the official intention to reform it*—that there is an atmosphere that chokes, and fear of writing something forces the distressed (author) to resort to the art of saying something nice about nothing." (The italics are mine.)
13. *Strindbergsfejden II*, 795. ". . . that in a newspaper a scorning, deeply ignorant article has been published against champions of the spirit like L. and K. (at least alluded to, if I understood correctly)."
14. *Strindbergsfejden II*, 882; article in the radical newspaper *Afton-Tidningen*, 1 March 1911. "If there were more justice in the world K. ought to be released from this assembly (Sw. A.), for together with Fröding and S. he belongs to the living people. . . ."
15. *Strindbergsfejden I*, 485. Article in *Göteborgs Aftonblad*, 6 August 1910. "How sickly, unhealthy, and decadent are not Heidenstam's and Levertin's poetry in comparison with that of Karlfeldt, the poet of Fridolin!"
16. *Strindbergsfejden I*, 363; article in *Arbetet*, 30 July 1910. "Also the consequent silence

that L. has always used against K. is obviously a manifestation of his antipathy toward everything Swedish in a more profound sense."

17. Cf. G. Michanek, *Skaldens konung* (Lund, 1979), pp. 351–67.

18. Cf. letters to E. N. Söderberg from F. Vetterlund, poet and docent, in 1903. Both were friends of Karlfeldt but Vetterlund did not approve of Heidenstam. In the Strindberg Feud he joined the anti-Strindberg wing as a knight of Romanticism. The letters belong to the Rev. H. G. Söderberg, Torpa, Annerstad.

19. E. Håkansson in *Fram*, 11 November 1910. *Strindbergsfejden II*, 808. K. has "never acted with pretensions to be a spiritual leader, and, besides, his poetry has a manly openness and modesty that separate him from the clique (around Heidenstam)."

20. Cf. Michanek, pp. 379–83.

21. Ollén, *Strindbergs 1900-talslyrik* (Stockholm, 1941), p. 301. "The poet allows himself some metaphors, 'High Orion swings his sword, Charles's Wain leans down,' which have something of the gay liveliness of Karlfeldt's Dalarna paintings."

22. Ibid., p. 255.

23. Ibid., p. 424.

24. *En bok om Karlfeldt* (Stockholm, 1931), p. 204. "He went to the theater only two or three times a year without, however, underrating the scenic art in the least."

25. *Carl Fredrik Dahlgren* (Stockholm, 1924), p. 86. "Exactly one hundred years later we listen, night after night, to similar but sillier dialogues at the country's foremost theater."

26. *Den svenska lyriken: Erik Axel Karlfeldts Dikter* (Stockholm, 1953), pp. 418–22.

27. "One could also see women like witches who tore their hair, scourged their skin so that their limbs dripped with wounds."

28. August Strindberg, *Folkungasagan* in *Samlade Skrifter*, 35, ed. John Landquist (Stockholm: Bonniers, 1915), p. 89. ". . . half naked people who participate in the litany and scourge themselves while performing a sort of ceremonial dance."

29. For the background of the poem see Hildeman, *Sub luna* (Stockholm, 1966), pp. 152–86.

The Chamber Plays and the Trilogy: A Revaluation of the Case of Strindberg and Bergman

Marilyn Johns Blackwell

I

Even the most ardent detractor of biographical criticism would be hard put to explain away as mere coincidence the similarities in Strindberg's and Bergman's artistic concerns: the individual's struggle against God and against himself; his failure to communicate effectively with his fellow man; and, by extension, sexual strife, which begins in relatively clear-cut male-female conflicts and then becomes internalized to a sense of self-loathing and sexual blockage or illness. These affinities are especially apparent in the case of Strindberg's chamber plays and Bergman's trilogy.

The group of films that comprise the trilogy—*Såsom i en spegel (Through a Glass Darkly), Nattvardsgästerna (Winter Light),* and *Tystnaden (The Silence),* from 1961, 1962, and 1963 respectively—represents a major shift in Ingmar Bergman's aesthetics. There occurs at this time a fundamental transformation of the artistic ideals that had guided him throughout the fifties—a transformation that was to determine the nature of his entire subsequent artistry. This change in focus has ramifications for both the form and the content of his artistic endeavor and is founded in the innovations that Strindberg introduced into his dramaturgy during 1907 and that resulted in four of the dramas the author called chamber plays—*Oväder (Stormy Weather), Brända tomten (The Burned House), Spöksonaten (The Ghost Sonata),* and *Pelikanen (The Pelican).*[1] Bergman takes certain themes and techniques from his literary mentor and transposes them onto film, onto a new medium. In the course of examining a given theatrical technique through its effect upon the viewer and ascertaining how one can achieve the same effect on screen with a different method, we must grapple with the vastly different natures of the media and, concomitantly, try to discover what properties are inherent to each. In approaching influence studies and cross-genre comparative studies in film, various questions immediately surface as to the viability of traditional generic definitions; yet it is just this problem of genre that is the most important part of any influence study. By investigating the kinds of motifs and stylistic techniques that Bergman inherits from Strindberg, the use he makes of them, and the disparity in effect that they produce, we arrive at some, it is to be hoped, interesting insights into their respective genres.

II

Both artists are concerned with the investigation of the nature and quality of metaphysical faith, only to arrive at vastly disparate conclusions. If one may simplistically state that Strindberg's failure to find an answer to the questions of existence in humankind during his pre-Inferno period led him to search for them in a divine figure after his crisis, exactly the opposite may be said of Bergman. After exhaustively examining, prior to 1961, his Lutheran God as both one of mercy and one of wrath, the three chamber films convince him that he must seek the answers to his queries in individual human beings and their relationships. But for both of them, the path to increased understanding of the human dilemma lies not in intellectual analysis but rather in an almost Kiekegaardian leap of faith in which man surrenders himself to the absurd and offers up his life to a nonepistemological existence. *Såsom i en spegel, Nattvardsgästerna,* and *Tystnaden* represent for Bergman the collapse of a Christian ideology, which is replaced by a sense of human commitment and communication on a nonintellectual, nonverbal level. While making *Nattvardsgästerna,* Bergman comments on the necessity of emotional cognition: "Men det är en väldig skillnad på att inse något intellektuellt och att känslomässigt komma på det; först när man känslomässigt kommer på något, är det som luften går ur problemmet."²

This preoccupation is reflected in the major theme running through both the chamber plays and the trilogy: communication and the lack of it. The distinction between reality and appearance, communication and silence gives rise in both artists to a contrapuntal pattern of characterization and theme development. The cold, harshly empirical, scientific mind is set up in opposition to that individual who perceives the flux of life in an intuitive, phenomenological manner. The old man Hummel in *Spöksonaten* and the Mother in *Pelikanen* share a refusal to admit their own fallibility, to recognize the subliminal contents of their lives, just as David, Tomas, and Ester in the Bergman films cannot come to grips with their very deep-seated emotional needs and reject those who would remind them of their nonintellectual impulses. In contrast to such characters, Strindberg places variations on the "Sunday child," that individual who is capable of perceiving supernatural phenomena, of divining the truth, and of stripping away the facades of lies and deceits that other characters encase themselves in. The Stranger in *Brända tomten*, The Student in *Spöksonaten*, and, to a certain extent, Frederick in *Pelikanen* are such Sunday children and function, as do Karin, Märta, and Johan in the three films, to excoriate layers of lies and falsehoods and intellectual and social pretensions that surround their fellow man.

Language, therefore, takes on a new dimension and a new importance in Bergman, as it does in Strindberg. Words cover up our fear and hide reality—they are a smokescreen that the intellectual throws up to prevent the world from knowing him, a bulwark against reality.[3] Göran Persson in his seminal article on the trilogy discusses this problem: "Deras [Annas och Esters] ord i uppgörelsen är inte kontaktmedel, orden användes för att definiera en oförenlighet: två livsattityder som inte kan försonas, men väl skrämma varandra, ge varandra djupa sår. . . . Ord är farliga ting. I enkla sammanhang är de onödiga, i mer komplicerade blir de lätt lögner, därför är tystnaden att föredra."[4] The extent to which Bergman's and Strindberg's characters use words to insulate themselves against an unpleasant reality is also evident in the artists' use of role-playing to define life situations. Strindberg uses the illusion of theater to represent the illusion of life.[5] The Stranger in *Brända tomten* comments upon the way in which people go through life like theater directors giving other people parts to play. Hummel in *Spöksonaten* further tells the Colonel that he must keep calm so that everyone can go back to playing the same old roles again; indeed, all the major characters in the chamber plays act out self-imposed roles in order to shield themselves from painful reality.

The same defensive supposition of a false persona occurs in Bergman's characters. David of *Såsom i en spegel* feels called upon to act as a loving father, bestowing gifts upon his children, a pose that is not at all in accordance with his emotional coldness towards them. Tomas in *Nattvardsgästerna* also feels that it is his duty to try to comfort his spiritually needy parishioners, despite the fact that his own spiritual poverty prevents him from doing so effectively.

But this role-playing, be it the result of external social or internal psychological imperatives, is ultimately a falsification and each individual must come to a traumatic reckoning with his soul and his past in order to dispel the aura of introspective self-pity in which he wallows. The terror of Karin's vision of the spider god forces David to reconsider the role that he has played in his children's lives, in much the same agonizing way that Märta is compelled to confront Tomas's contempt for her by his shocking brutality in the schoolroom; and Tomas, his spiritual ineffectuality by Jonas Persson's suicide. The two sisters in *Tystnaden* also torment each other forward to a realization of their emotional emptiness, a technique that may well derive from Strindberg's use of psychological excoriation to unmask the people who populate his chamber plays. Like The Gentleman in *Oväder*, the inhabitants of the ghost house in *Spöksonaten*, and The Stranger in *Brända tomten*, Bergman's characters are compelled forward to a confrontation with their essential loneliness.[6]

But once the characters come to a true realization of the paucity of emotional commitment that characterizes their lives, few can withstand the horror of this truth. The moment of this truth is the moment of death, for both Strindberg and Bergman, because, as The Stranger in *Brända tomten* tells us: "När man ser sig själv, så dör man." ("When one sees oneself, one dies.") An acquiescence to the truth also kills The Young Lady in *Spöksonaten* and the Brother and Sister in *Pelikanen*, just as the reality of the spider god removes Karin to a land of the living dead in an insane asylum, and the awareness of their desolation invalidates any attempt to move outside their circumscribed lives for Anna and Ester.

Bergman and Strindberg are also committed to the idea that only after truly recognizing and accepting the abyss within our souls can one hope to restructure this life. For Strindberg, this restructuring takes the form of resigned acceptance of our divinely ordered lot in life—an acquiescence to the World Weaver and our Karma. But for Bergman the restructuring is of a singularly social nature: man must commend himself to humanity, to a sense of emotional sharing with his fellow man. It is this fellowship of love that we perceive in David's proclamation to Minus in *Såsom i en spegel* that God is love, in the final shots of *Nattvardsgästerna*, in which we hear Märta praying for Tomas and herself, and in Johan's attempt to learn the words for hand and face in the foreign language in *Tystnaden*. Bergman perceives a great hope in "gemenskapsglädjens läkande kraft" ("the healing power of the joy of togetherness") and would even use his medium to effect this transformation in the audience: "Behovet att få människor att lyssna, att korrespondera, att leva i värmen av en gemenskap kvarstod. Det blev allt starkare ju mer ensamhetens fängelse slöt sig omkring mig."[7]

The themes of communication and the expansion of the boundaries of self are also reflected in Strindberg's and Bergman's use of the relationship between character and setting. As early as the dramatic fragment *Holländaren* (*The Dutchman*), Strindberg had given expression to the thought that houses and rooms to a certain extent decide the fates of their inhabitants. Sven Rinman tells us in *Ny illustrerad svensk litteraturhistoria* that houses, not people, are the central characters in Strindberg's chamber plays.[8] One is not, however, exclusive of the other, for houses, in both Strindberg and Bergman, are metaphors for the total individual, the life that he has built around him, and the evil or good that he has done. The houses in *Spöksonaten*, *Oväder*, *Brända tomten*, and *Pelikanen* have gathered into themselves the past, memories, and associations. They are very much alive.[9]

The same reciprocal relationship between the individual and his environment is evident in the Bergman film as well. The filmmaker no longer uses settings in a historical-allegorical fashion, in which a landscape may function as a clear-cut equation with a character's state of mind, but rather makes his character an integral part of his environment, participating in it, rather than outlined against it. The sets Bergman chooses for the trilogy all serve to define the mental states of those who inhabit them. As in Strindberg, they are reflections of the personal and spiritual desolation within the characters. The barren rocky island in the middle of the Baltic is an accurate metaphor for the emotional no-man's-land in which David of *Såsom i en spegel* lives; just as the frozen Norrland landscape in *Nattvardsgästerna* speaks to Tomas's more spiritual stagnation and rigidity. The abundance of baroque detail in *Tystnaden* also functions to circumscribe the lives of those who inhabit the film's environment, in that the overwhelming and imprisoning sensuality of their surroundings points up all the more the emotional, spiritual, and sexual atrophy that defines these characters' existences. The degree to which an individual is in harmony with his surroundings is dictated by the extent to which he is capable of communicating with his fellow man and the extent to which he is conscious of the subliminal dictates of his life.

Human inadequacy, as it is manifested in an overpowering sense of loneliness, is described by both Strindberg and Bergman in terms of physical metaphors. Extremes of heat and cold are used as a metaphor for an emotionally tense situation in *Nattvardsgästerna* and *Tystnaden*, just as they are in *Oväder* and *Brända tomten*. This emotional tension is about to erupt into violent manifestations, which are foreshadowed by thunder and lightning on the part of both authors. The rains that descend on *Tystnaden* and *Såsom i en spegel* are waters of purification like those in *Oväder* and the fire that tears open the house in *Brända tomten*.

But the transference from emotion to sensation, as Karl-Åke Kärnell puts it, also exists on another level. There is in both Strindberg and Bergman a desire for, and a fear of, contact and the accompanying responsibility. In an effort to escape this, characters regress into a sense of physical self-loathing, a denial of self. Like Indra's Daughter in *Ett drömspel* (*A Dream Play*), Karin in *Såsom i en spegel*, Tomas and Märta in *Nattvardsgästerna*, and Anna and Ester in *Tystnaden* must all try to sublimate their physical being in order to transcend to a more spiritual, less earthbound level of existence. The desperation of these characters' psychic lives is so great that it is metaphorized onto their physical sense of well-being: the individual's state of health denotes his emotional or moral condition and the characters' many illnesses become metaphors for their emotional and/or physical depravity. Like The Young Lady in *Spöksonaten* who is afflicted with cancer of the womb, Bergman's characters are also "sjuka i livets källa." Karin is a schizophrenic, Tomas is suffering from a bad winter cold, Märta from eczema, and Ester from an unspecified respiratory disease. Leif Leifer points out that the illness that afflicts the Young Lady in *Spöksonaten* is a symbol for Original Sin,[10] an interpretation that might also be applied to Bergman's characters, who suffer as a result of sinning against the moral code.

Concomitantly, there is no healthy sexuality in Bergman's world: the filmmaker seems to have come to Strindberg's realization that sexuality is strife, that only by fixing our eyes on something beyond the physical can we hope to reach some kind of either secular or religious salvation. Sex has been reduced to a perverse and ugly animalistic copulation performed in the balcony of the theater and in the hotel room, to autoeroticism, incest, and implicit lesbianism. The negative connotations that sex assumes in Bergman's world may well be based upon a similar experiencing of sexuality in Strindberg's. In *Brända tomten*, *Spöksonaten*, and *Pelikanen*, sexuality has likewise become perverse and incestuous, serving to underline the degrading and disgusting substratum of the characters' lives.

In view of the fact that words are no longer sufficient to communicate our commitment, one must look elsewhere for a medium to serve this purpose. For Bergman, this medium becomes touch. Physicality is degrading and disgusting only insofar as it is a reflection of spiritual and emotional isolation, but in true communication touch becomes sanctified. As is always the case with the filmmaker, hands play the primary role in effecting this new communication or reflecting an absence of it. As William Alexander has noted,[11] the trilogy is suffused with images of hands withdrawing—Tomas's from the vestry desk, David's hand on Karin's blanket in *Såsom i en spegel*.[12] Indeed, the bankruptcy of verbal communication leads to an exploration of new communication techniques within both the narrative framework and artistic mode.

III

The revolutionary quality of these dramatic experiments is delineated in Strindberg's definition of the chamber play in his *Öppna brev till Intima teatern* (*Open Letters to the Intimate Theater*):

Kammarmusikens idé överförd på dramat. Det intima förfarandet, det betydelsefulla motivet, den soignerade behandlingen. . . . Om man nu frågar vad en Intim teater vill och vad som åsyftas med Kammarspel, så kan jag svara så här: I dramat söka vi det starka betydelsefulla motivet, men med begränsning. I behandlingen undvika vi all flärd, alla beräknade effekter, applådställen, solonummer. Ingen bestämd form skall binda författaren, ty motivet betingar formen. Alltså frihet i behandlingen, endast bunden av konceptionens enhet och stilkänslan.[13]

One observes in Bergman's trilogy the same attempt to impose upon his medium the concept of chamber music: "Såsom i en spegel och Nattvardsgästerna och Tystnaden och Persona har jag kallat kammarspel. Det är kammarmusik. Det är när man renodlar ett antal motiv över ett ytterst begränsad antal röster och figurer. Man extraherar bakgrunderna. Man lägger dem i en sorts paradis. Man gör ett distillat."[14] But Bergman's application of the term "chamber play" to the three films that compose his trilogy is a logical consequence of his aesthetic conviction that the film medium possesses very close affinities with the realm of music.

Immediately after completing the trilogy, Bergman called film "ett språk som gick förbi ordet,"[15] and went on in an English interview to maintain: "I find it easier to compare film, not to theater or the novel, but to music. In fact, I think of film and music as equals of a sort. In pure film and pure music there is a feeling that goes directly to some deeper level of the listener or viewer, and only afterward is it possible to analyze the experience."[16] The kinship of music and film is further clarified in Bergman's statement: "Men musiken är genom sitt sätt att verka direkt på publiken till sitt väsen starkt besläktad med filmen, även rytmiskt—en lång serie in- och utandningar—och jag avser att påverka publiken emotionellt. Det är konstnärens legitima rätt att gå direkt på medmänniskornas nerver."[17]

It is natural then that in all three of the chamber films he attempts to model the structure of the work on a musical form. *Såsom i en spegel* is based upon the pattern of the sonata; *Nattvardsgästerna*, inspired by Stravinsky, consists of three melodic movements followed by a coda; and *Tystnaden* is derivative of Bartok's mood and is characterized by a given leitmotif with variations.

Obviously, both authors in their use of musical format are attempting to expand the generic boundaries of their media, to impart an extra dimension of subliminal involvement to their art. By modifying traditional narrative presentational structure they are struggling to add depth to their works, striving for greater concentration, and the extent to which they succeed is dependent upon the natures of their genres. As in Strindberg's chamber plays, thematic content is subordinated to an evocation of mood; plot continuity and external action are subordinated to the portrayal of psychic states. The film makes sense not according to what happens, but according to how it happens. Agents serve to provoke characters to certain quintessential routines through which we see their lives circumscribed. This preoccupation with mood and atmosphere is also reflected in Strindberg's and Bergman's emphasis in their chamber work on an emotional mode of perception as opposed to the traditional analytic mode, which, to a certain extent, characterized Strindberg's pre-Inferno and Bergman's pre-trilogy production. This is not to say that their later artistic styles represent a complete about-face in their literary concerns, for one can indeed trace much of this insistence upon an emotional and psychological analysis of reality to their earlier productions. But it is only after Strindberg's Inferno crisis and Bergman's trilogy that these impulses come to dominate the artists.

But the major manifestation of Strindberg's influence on Bergman's cinematic structure in the trilogy is evident in the matter of concentration. Strindberg wanted to abolish regular sets and replace them with a kind of architectonic frame that would represent any set depending upon how it was lighted and what kind of props were used. He was striving for stylization, for scenic simplification instead of naturalism of technique. Bergman too is seeking to use his medium as an architectonic space within which individuals move and against which they react. Nils Petter Sundgren comments upon this tendency in Bergman's trilogy: "I de tidiga sextiotalsfilmerna avstår Bergman helt från sin egen virtuositet. Han håller tillbaka alla spektakulära effekter, koncentrerar sig på det mänskliga ansiktet i långa närbilder där kameran tränger in bakom ansiktet."[18] His style has become much more ascetic and severe, as exemplified in the scene from *Nattvardsgästerna* in which Märta reads aloud her letter to Tomas in a long, bold, austere close-up looking directly into the camera. It is his goal to move ever closer in toward the center of the individual. As Stanley Kauffmann would have it: "He is anatomizing narrower and narrower circles of material; and the emphasis is on the dissection rather than on the revelation."[19]

One of the reasons for both Strindberg and Bergman to remove the elaborate theatrical set-up that had previously characterized certain of their works is their desire for the audience to communicate in a very real and close way with the actors before them. Strindberg mentions this need for actor-audience involvement on several occasions in his *Öppna brev till Intima teatern* and Bergman makes the same point in his statement in a German interview: "Film ist für mich eine Kommunikation zwischen mir und den Menschen."[20]

This striving toward a closer audience identification that is inherent in the film is also the underlying factor for Bergman's changing concept of characterization. As is the case in the chamber plays, there is no longer simply one major figure toward whom all of our attention is directed, but rather the artists choose several characters to carry equally important themes and leitmotifs. For Strindberg, this means deemphasizing what might be called traditional dramatic depth psychology; for Bergman, a renewed concentration on a more intense investigation of character. With the trilogy, characters become more individualized. Bergman begins to focus on interpersonal relationships rather than on concepts. And although Strindberg is less concerned with profound psychological analysis, he too is dealing with the ways in which characters relate to one another and the distortions that their minds impose upon reality about them. Only by abolishing a single central character can the two artists achieve the social breadth that will in turn engender psychological depth—a depth of personality for Bergman and of metaphysical perspective for Strindberg.

But of equal, if not greater, importance in the matter of Strindberg's influence on Bergman in the chamber films is the director's changing style and structure. Bergman still makes use of the journey format, as he did in his films from the fifties, but traveling becomes much more claustrophobic and frustrating. Very little real progress is made in these journeys—from one small country church to another in Norrland, to the seething yet desolate Baltic city in the throes of war. The travels are less from one given philosophical stance to a new, enlightened one than through the twistings of the human mind. This sense of moving farther and farther into a psychic state of being may derive from Strindberg. Egil Törnqvist mentions this movement in his study of Bergman's latest production of *Spöksonaten*: "Om Studenten kan man snarare säga att han *instiger* i helvete: hans väg inåt från gatan (Akt I) genom runda salongen (Akt II) till hyacintrummet (Akt III) är en vandring från Paradisio via Purgatorio till Inferno."[21] The other three chamber plays possess the same type of structure, in which the observer sees layer after layer of falsehood removed and moves closer and closer toward the ugly truth. This same ever-inward movement is evident in Bergman's films from this period. We follow the major characters deeper into the recesses of their minds and souls to the point where they finally confront subconscious materials and must come to terms with them.

Yet another major facet of Strindberg's impact on the Bergman trilogy in the matter of concentration is the filmmaker's emphasis on close-ups. In an interview with Hollis Alpert shortly after completing *Såsom i en spegel*, Bergman says: "Our work in films must begin with the human face. We can certainly become completely absorbed in the esthetics of montage; we can bring objects and still life into wonderful rhythm; we can make nature studies of astonishing beauty, but the approach to the human face is without a doubt the hallmark and distinguishing feature of the film medium."[22]

Bergman had, of course, used close-ups prior to the making of the chamber films, but in the fifties they served chiefly to reinforce dramatic speeches, whereas now they function to register emotion. In an effort to concentrate all his attention, and consequently that of the spectator as well, upon the human face and the emotions that emanate from it, Bergman employs very few cuts, holds shots for an inordinately long time, and directs his actors towards more restrained and less "theatrical" acting, an admonition that Strindberg also gave to his actors at Intima teatern.

All these changes in cinematic style are brought about out of a concern for dramatic distillation, for setting up and maintaining a particular mood.

IV

But, upon viewing the trilogy, the question arises as to whether or not Bergman's efforts are not in conflict with his very medium, for while the films are emotionally powerful at many points, they also seem curiously flat at times. It may well be then that the filmic concentration is not synonymous with theatrical concentration. Clearly, theater and film share a greater or lesser dependence upon verbal expression and dialogue—the articulated word—and operate, at least traditionally, with a strong narrative line and clearly ordered aesthetic structure. They are predicated upon the presence of a directing intelligence behind the work (an implicit or explicit authorial persona), and differ from prose in their dimensionality and dynamism. Both force us to accept them at their own pace: we have no control over how rapidly we absorb, or perhaps do not absorb, the visual event before us. It is in these same two qualities, however, that the similarities between theater and film end. Film may be distinguished from theater (and perhaps linked back to prose) by the still greater degree of fluidity of movement it achieves through editing. Even a stylized stage such as that of Strindberg's intimate theater cannot make the immediate and radical changes of setting that film can; multiple stages or even stages that envelop the audience cannot give the spectator film's rapid movements from close-up to long shot, which permits of focusing in on a human eye or a panorama. It is because of this unique mobility that film is surely the most flexible aesthetic medium at our disposal today; on its surface we can perceive individual phenomena with unparalleled realism, and, when film is in the hands of a gifted director-editor, we can see in the movement from shot to shot an emotion-stirring force and a visual language that demands a unique critical apparatus, only part of which is grounded in traditional literary critical methods.

The film medium must inevitably use dimensionality differently than does theater, a difference that becomes apparent when we examine the spectator perception of, first, the theatrical proscenium and, then, the filmic frame. When we see a theatrical performance, the proscenium (even the imaginary proscenium we automatically erect around an arena stage) cuts the play off from the real world around us. This necessitates Coleridge's "willing suspension of disbelief," and results in a poetic creation that partakes directly neither of truth nor of falsehood because, as a world of its own, it creates its own laws and shapes our perceptions according to them. This world is, of course, three-dimensional in its use of space, and the willing suspension of disbelief is aided by the fact that we are, after all, dealing with real space. Strindberg's intimate theater demonstrates this, achieving much concentration and spectator involvement by condensing that space so that the spectator can take in the whole stage —actors and their movements and complementary expressionistic settings—with very little shifting of field-of-vision. The whole spectacle seems a piece—and a very effective piece.

Film's frame operates in a completely different manner. Rather than creating a world by exclusion, it invokes an implicit extension of the imagination beyond the circumscribed limits of the frame, in an extended breadth of reality past the edges of the medium. For like the human eye the camera selects what we eventually will see but in a square much narrower than the potential field of human vision, and thus it includes some things and excludes others in a way that we cannot help but notice. The frame further compounds this selection by directing our attention towards its center, causing us to make a selection of the selection. The result is that we are constantly aware that we are not seeing real space. Rather we see what was originally real space as it is reflected by another eye. We do not lend film the same immediate credence that we give theater as a world, at least not spatially, a refusal that is bolstered by the fact that film possesses two dimensions that are striving towards, and pretending to be, three. A constant tension arises between surface and depth. And it is in this regard that the much used term "uncinematic" begins to take on meaning, for films that ignore this tension and opt for a presentation of "real" theatrical space (and lack of camera mobility) are simply ineffective on screen.

If film is to engender the necessary "willing suspension of disbelief" and involve the spectator emotionally, then it must not try to achieve theater's direct presentation of space, but try instead to find some other way to capture theater's sense of a world-within-a-world. This would seem to require a return to the dynamism that is its forte, to the lively free-moving camera. For the free-moving camera, in its progression from shot to shot, negates the ineffective theatrical use of space. We move from panorama to detail, from action to reaction, and in the movement experience a mosaic sequence that adds up to a sense of the real. Through such dynamism and through careful editing, the director removes his film from the presentation of real space into his own convincing filmic version of time and space, thereby creating a cinematic kind of poetic reality. It is true that film remains framed and two-dimensional, but these factors now work for the film and not against it; for the director now accepts rather than struggles against the limits of his frame and uses it to make us see in a cinematically effective fashion. In a way, film becomes even more effective in the presentation of space than theater, not simply because we can see more detail in the shots, not even because we can see more shots more quickly, but because the director can control our perceptions by compelling us to see through mobile vantage points. Film, therefore, possesses an extra element of narrative structure. This seems a confirmation of Bergman's idea that film is similar to music, in that the transition from sequence to sequence, as from note to note and movement to movement, can be profoundly emotionally effective. Clearly, however, we are a long way from Strindberg's simplicity of presentation in the intimate theater: it begins to appear that the only way in which film can achieve concentration is, paradoxically enough, through complexity.

Bergman's choice of a chamber drama form in his trilogy is, in many respects, valid, but perhaps he errs in his presentation of this form. The trilogy possesses several affinities with the theatrical: the fragmentation of the world into expressionistic sets, the shrinking of nature into claustrophobic interiors that reflect the characters' mental states, the collapsing of time into an equation between real time and playing time, the deemphasis of cinematic framing in favor of stage settings, and the elimination of high and low angle photography in favor of straight-on angles. The first two tendencies can effectively serve, just as they do in an intimate theater, to unite disparate elements in the film. Bergman has made use of the same tendencies in earlier films; the alternation between harsh, rocky landscapes and beautiful pastoral scenes functions in *Det sjunde inseglet* not only as a beautiful individual element, but also to reflect two different character clusters. The latter three tendencies are, however, less felicitous. The abandonment of cinematic framing and the elimination of high and low angle photography (mobile camera) lead Bergman directly away from what we have seen to be a fundamental aspect of film aesthetics. No longer do we have the powerful emotions generated by the camera's machinations in earlier films, such as the conflicting light and dark tones of *Det sjunde inseglet* or the long, syntactically fluid (cinematically speaking) sequences of *Smultronstället*. If the films from the trilogy are effective, it is only because of their scripts. They present chamber-dramalike relationships beyond the use of the camera rather than in conjunction with it. Therefore, the trilogy can seem very frustrating to the spectator, as he observes Bergman struggling to establish theater's three-dimensional reality and Strindberg's simplicity of spatial presentation in a medium not suited to it.

This is not to say that posttrilogy Bergman is a complete cinematic failure. On the contrary, *Persona* is probably the most sophisticated film in his entire oeuvre precisely because it takes the problems of viewer-work and artist-work relationships and raises them to a very subtle and profound statement about the tension between the cinematic surface of film and what (and how) the viewer reconstructs from the apparent phenomenal surface. Through its alternation of cinematic narration and devices that destroy its own self-created illusion of reality, this work explores better than perhaps any other film what may be the most influential question facing contemporary artists and critics alike: the self-reflexivity of art. Although not quite so self-aware or critically subtle as *Persona*, *Viskningar och rop* fulfills many of the promises made by the trilogy, for its more dynamic use of the camera and its relativistic exploration of a chamber-type relationship through the eyes of the members of the relationship (one chamber voice for each movement in the piece) provide for an effective filmic example of the concentration and emotional power achieved by Strindberg in his verbal-visual creations based on musical form. But Bergman has seldom reached the heights of these two films in his other late works. Instead he has chosen to dwell in his own personal regions of dramatic, or not so dramatic, familial relationships, never allowing us to forget that he has discovered Freud. This is, it seems, an unfortunate choice and one that, it is devoutly to be hoped, he will revaluate in the near future.

Notes

1. By the time Ingmar Bergman was twelve years old he had already read *Spöksonaten* and was to see it on stage along with the other famous Olof Molander productions. "Först var det drömspelet. Jag stod kväll efter kväll i kulissen och lipade och visste inte riktigt varför. Sen kom Damaskus, Folkungasagan, och Spöksonaten. Det är sånt man aldrig glömmer och aldrig kommer ifrån, särskilt om man råkat bli regissör och allra minst om man som sådan sätter iscen ett strindberg-drama." ("First there was *A Dream Play*. I stood evening after evening in the wings and sobbed without really knowing why. Then came *Damascus, The Saga of the Folkungs,* and *The Ghost Sonata.* It is the kind of thing one never forgets and never escapes, especially if one happens to become a director and even less if as a director, one stages a Strindberg drama.") Bergman has further called *Spöksonaten* "den märkligaste pjäsen nånsin skrivits på svenska" ("the most remarkable play ever written in Swedish"), and has further evinced his interest in this body of drama by directing *Pelikanen* once and *Spöksonaten* three times during his career as a stage director.
2. Vilgot Sjöman, *L 136* (Stockholm: Norstedts, 1963), p. 127. "But there is a great difference between perceiving something intellectually and emotionally realizing it; only when one emotionally realizes something is the whole problem deflated."
3. Birgitta Steene, "Images and Words in Ingmar Bergman's Films," *Cinema Journal* 10, No. 1, p. 33.
4. Göran Persson, "Bergmans trilogi," *Chaplin,* 40 (October 1963). "Their words in the transaction are not means of contact, words are used to define an incompatibility: two life attitudes that cannot be reconciled, but instead frighten each other, wound each other deeply. . . . Words are dangerous things. In simple circumstances they are unnecessary, in more complicated ones they easily become lies, therefore silence is preferable."
5. Cf. Brian Rothwell, "The Chamber Plays," in *Essays on Strindberg,* ed. Carl Reinhold Smedmark (Stockholm: J. Beckman, 1966).
6. Bergman has said on the subject of the lack of interpersonal communication: "Så löper vi i en stor fälla där vi står och bräcker om vår ensamhet utan att lyssna på varandra eller ens upptäcka att vi håller på att klämma varandra till döds." ("Det att göra film," *Filmnyheter,* 19–20 [1954].) ("We are running to and fro in a large pen where we cry out our loneliness without listening to each other or even noticing that we are squeezing one another to death.")
7. Ingmar Bergman, "Den fria, skamlösa, oansvariga konsten," *Expressen,* 1 August 1965. "The need remained to make people listen, correspond, live in the warmth of a sense of community. It became even stronger the more the prison of loneliness closed in on me."
8. Sven Rinman, "August Strindberg," in *Ny illustrerad svensk litteraturhistoria,* 4 (Stockholm: Natur och Kultur, 1967), 30–144.
9. Cf. Birgitta Steene, *The Greatest Fire* (Carbondale: Southern Illinois University Press, 1973), p. 107.
10. Leif Leifer, "Den lutrende ild," *Samlaren,* 81 (1960).
11. William Alexander, "Devils in the Cathedral: Bergman's Trilogy," *Cinema Journal,* 2 (Spring 1974).

12. Märta's hands are diseased and the hand on the crucifix is hacked off in *Nattvardsgästerna*. The first foreign word Ester learns is hand—she then reaches out to touch her nephew with her own hand and later uses it for masturbation. Hands, too, beckon the boy Johan: his mother erotically, enticingly shimmers her hands as she crosses the floor, gesturing to him, then massaging his body. The hand of the old waiter draws Johan into his world and the dwarves' hands, reminiscent of Anna's, fuss about him and clothe him in a girl's dress. Traditional verbal means have, then, failed to create a new vocabulary by which we can communicate with our fellow man.

13. August Strindberg, *Samlade Skrifter*, ed. John Landquist (Stockholm: Bonniers, 1912–1920), 50: 118. "The concept of chamber music transferred to drama. The intimate action, the highly significant motif, the sophisticated treatment. . . . If anyone asks what it is an intimate theater wants to achieve and what is meant by chamber plays, I can answer like this: in drama we seek the strong, highly significant motif, but with limitations. We try to avoid in the treatment all frivolity, all calculated effects, places for applause, star roles, solo numbers. No predetermined form is to limit the author, because the motif determines the form. Consequently: freedom in treatment, which is limited only by the unity of the concept and the feeling for style." (Translation by Walter Johnson, *Open Letters to the Intimate Theater* [Seattle: University of Washington Press, 1966].)

14. Stig Björkman, ed., *Bergman om Bergman* (Stockholm: Norstedts, 1978), p. 127. "*Through a Glass Darkly* and *Winter Light* and *The Silence* and *Persona* I have called chamber plays. It is chamber music. It is when one cultivates a number of motifs with an extremely limited number of voices and figures. One extracts the backgrounds. One places them in a kind of paradise. One creates a distillate."

15. Ingmar Bergman, "Den fria skamlösa, oansvariga konsten," *Expressen*, 1 August 1965: ". . . a language that went beyond the word."

16. Hollis Alpert, "Style is the Director," *Saturday Review*, 23 December 1961, p. 41.

17. Frithiof Billquist, *Ingmar Bergman—Teatermannen och Filmskaparen* (Stockholm: Natur och Kultur, 1960), p. 265. "But by working directly on the public, music is by its nature closely related to film, also rhythmically—a long series of breathings in and out—and I intend to affect the public emotionally. It is the artist's legitimate right to go directly for people's nerves."

18. Nils Petter Sundgren, "Från raseri till frusen förtvivlan," *Veckojournalen* (December 1968). "In the films from the early sixties, Bergman completely relinquishes his own virtuosity. He holds back all spectacular effects, concentrates on the human face in long close-ups where the camera penetrates behind the face."

19. Stanley Kauffmann, *A World on Film* (New York: Dell, 1967), p. 287.

20. "Begegnung mit Ingmar Bergman," Television interview broadcast on Westdeutsche Rundfunk 6 August 1964. "Film is for me a communication between me and people."

21. Egil Törnqvist, *Bergman och Strindberg* (Stockholm: Prisma, 1963), p. 37. "One can rather say of the student that he *steps into* hell: his path inward from the street (Act I) through the round room (Act II) to the hyacinth room (Act III) is a journey from Paradisio by way of Purgatorio to Inferno."

22. Hollis Alpert, *op. cit.*, p. 41.

Strindberg: The Man and the Myth as Seen in the Mirror of Per Olov Enquist

Ross Shideler

To suggest a comparison of any Swedish author with Strindberg burdens both author and critic with an impossible task. Given that truism, however, the major contemporary novelist and playwright, Per Olov Enquist has created an extraordinarily interesting area for speculation by writing the play *Tribadernas natt* (*The Night of the Tribades*) (1975), in which he depicts Strindberg. *Tribadernas natt* may be the most important play written by a Swede in the past three decades, as its remarkable successes in Europe and its productions both on and off Broadway in the United States verify. However, the play created a great deal of controversy in Sweden over whether or not its supposedly realistic portrayal of Strindberg was accurate. Egil Törnqvist has presented the most effective summary and resolution of that debate and we shall take up his paper later on, but first we might ask: does August Strindberg have a major influence on Enquist's writing before *Tribadernas natt*, and, why did Enquist choose Strindberg as the subject of his drama?

Although one must remain admittedly tentative, we can assume that every Swedish author after Strindberg came to terms with his presence in the theater. He is, after all, virtually the only Swedish writer to attain and sustain worldwide recognition. In a general sense, Strindberg serves as "the master" for all modern Swedish authors. In "9 byggstenar till *Tribadernas natt*" ("9 Buildingblocks for *The Night of the Tribades*") Enquist quotes Stig Dagerman:

Det privata: pojken i manskostymen. 'Den Strindberg jag älskade var ynglingen Strindberg, den ensamme, smalaxlade, frysande . . . denne yngling förstod jag och älskade som bara en yngling kan förstå och älska en annan yngling.' Stig Dagerman i ett citat från 1949. Jo, det är ganska bra, ganska nära min egen Strindbergsbild (och vi håller oss ju nästan alla med en privat sådan bild, som vi energiskt bevakar och försvarar.[1]

This quotation tends to support the significance of Strindberg to Swedish authors in general and to Enquist in particular. The problem, however, is to define specific areas in which Strindberg's influence may be identified. In an interview, Enquist shied away from any comparison between Strindberg and himself as well as from any specific influences.[2] Like most Swedish school children, as a boy he read only a few of the traditional works by Strindberg, *Fröken Julie*, (*Miss Julie*), *Hemsöborna*, (*The Natives of Hemsö*), but these held little importance for him at the time.

One may, nonetheless, theorize about possible parallels between the two Swedish authors, and then pursue them into specific applications. First, if we assume that any young Swedish author has a sense of the figure, the myth, and the man Strindberg, such as the one proposed by Dagerman, what are some of the obvious characteristics likely to be of importance? There is the legend of the irascible genius, the folk historian, the public debater, and the social activist, and there is the literature, the innovation of realism, the use of colorful language, the introduction of naturalism, the great Strindbergian themes. Although his literary accomplishments sometimes seem neglected in favor of the legend, Strindberg's writing often uses historical events blended with his own version of such themes as survival of the fittest, the battle of the sexes, the wanderer and religious seeker.

If one grants these generalizations, a surprising number of parallels between Enquist and Strindberg emerge, although we may assume most of them are accidental. Nevertheless, for the purposes of establishing the kind of affinity or rapport that led Enquist to write *Tribadernas natt*, some parallels might be specifically mentioned. Strindberg, like Enquist, was a journalist as well as an author and an active participant in the public life of his times. Indeed, the one area where Enquist feels that Strindberg clearly influenced all modern Swedish writers and journalists was his use of the personal position within his writing. Strindberg's political and social activism established a tradition for all Swedish writers: the subjective writer, the writer who speaks out for his beliefs, became a precedent that stands to this day. Enquist's own role in Sweden as a highly involved journalist follows in this tradition.

Strindberg's unique use of history is related to his political activism. In the 1880s with *Svenska folket i helg och söcken* (*Swedish People on Holy Day and Every Day*) and the perhaps better known *Svenska öden och äventyr* (*Swedish Destinies and Adventures*), Strindberg brought a new perspective to Swedish history. These histories represented an early socialist view of the history of the Swedish people and brought him into considerable conflict with the established historians of his age.

While his histories depict the role of the people, as opposed to that of the kings and nobles in the making of history, Strindberg's historical dramas blend fact and fiction. He was accused of distorting history, of misrepresenting characters such as Master Olof or Queen Christina. These historical dramas, although a commonplace within literature and in Strindberg's case derived directly from Shakespeare, anticipate the modern docudrama and modern documentary fiction in general.[3] Enquist represents the foremost exponent of this form of writing in Sweden, and his use of history, with the clear intention of illuminating modern times, dominates such works as *Magnetisörens femte vinter* (*The Fifth Winter of the Magnetizer*) (1964), *Hess* (1966), *Legionärerna* (*The Legionnaires*) (1968), *Sekonden* (*The Second*) (1971), and *Tribadernas natt*. Not surprisingly, the critical reception of *Tribadernas natt* with its uproar about historical accuracy resembles the attacks against Strindberg's histories and historical dramas.

If Strindberg's subjective use of history and his strong statement of personal opinion constitute fundamental similarities or possible sources of affinity for Enquist, what other concerns do they share? Possibly one might include diversity of creative ability and a tendency toward public debate, if not scandal itself. Strindberg wrote novels, plays, short stories, essays, histories, and criticism. Not altogether uncommon in Swedish literature, other authors past and present have mastered several genres. Nevertheless, Enquist's success as columnist, critic, short story writer, novelist, and dramatist stands out even within this group. In this multiplicity of genres, Enquist has experimented, like Strindberg, with markedly different styles. His earlier works are in the mainstream of the "art of fiction": he uses sophisticated literary devices, stream of consciousness, and techniques of the "nouveau roman." After exploring the documentary novel, and historical and political forms of fiction, he turned to playwriting and has used diverse techniques within that form.

Similarly, Enquist's own role in the public life of Sweden has not been one-dimensional or free of debate. Whether berating the prime minister in print for not following a specific policy, or exposing in true Strindbergian fashion the weaknesses of the Swedish press in his coauthored *Chez Nous* (1976), Enquist remains a prominent figure in Swedish news. *Chez Nous* led to a major public debate, as at times did Enquist's columns on Vietnam and Cambodia, and, finally, he resigned, in print, from the evening newspaper *Expressen*. Such events in Enquist's life could be further enumerated, but would serve only to establish a sense of temperamental kinship, however limited, between him and Strindberg.

Given these general parallels, can any specific Strindberg influences or closely related themes be identified? While Enquist's first novel, *Kristallögat* (*The Crystal Eye*) (1961) offers little at first glance that reminds one of Strindberg, his second novel, *Färdvägen* (*The Route*) (1963) suggests a number of implicit and explicit comparisons. First, the title itself recalls to the reader a prominent Strindbergian theme, that of the road of life and the wanderer.

The book deals with a narrator who remains anonymous, though we eventually learn that he is a young Swede who goes on a trip to free himself from his introverted, self-preoccupied world and to discover reality. The reader discovers that the narrator has been driven into his introversion, because he feels guilty about the death of a young girl in a car accident in which he was the driver. The road to salvation takes the narrator through a series of unnamed cities and countries back to Sweden. The primary stops seem to be Germany, Switzerland, the Côte d'Azur, and Paris. The journey and the people he meets on the road constitute the novel, all of which sounds Strindbergian enough, but in Paris the narrator undergoes a crisis in which he degrades the people around him, parodies religious rituals, and tries to challenge God by standing on a fountain in pouring rain and gesturing to the sky.

In an interview with Karl Erik Lagerlöf, Enquist discusses the detailed construction of the book, its pyramidal structure, and its dependence on various authors such as Thomas Mann and Ernest Hemingway whom he consciously imitated.

Man kan också tala om Färdvägen som en religiös roman, fortsätter Enquist. Grundkonceptionen är Strindbergs *Till Damaskus*. Den avgörande scenen i min bok är en motsvarighet till asylscenen där. Boken börjar med en skissering av en lugn, sluten värld, det kristna alternativet, och den slutar med att huvudpersonen nöjer sig med en mycket liten lycka. Den avgörande upplevelsen i mitten, det yttersta försöket att utmana Gud att ge sig till känna —till den har jag lånat ytterkonturen från en episod i Strindbergs liv. Han hade en åskledare till sin bostad på Kymmendö och höll i den under ett åskväder i ett slags trots mot Gud. Trots är också ett slags tro.[4]

Enquist's comment provides not only a specific example of a consciously created Strindbergian moment within his writing, but it identifies one of the central themes that, surprisingly, they share. It is immediately apparent that the structure of the book and its anonymous narrator are strikingly similar to *Till Damaskus*; more subtle, however, is the theme of religion and salvation. Because of his active public life and his, in American terms, radical politics, Enquist tends to be considered primarily as an outspoken political writer. Yet, from his first book to his last, the problem of belief, of finding some way to deal with man's need for salvation remains central to Enquist's writing.

In his interview from 1965, Lagerlöf illuminates another aspect of this theme that explains how Enquist tries to deal with the problem of man's faith. The theme, repeated in *Tribadernas natt*, appears in *Färdvägen* in the scene modeled upon Strindberg's challenge to the heavens. Lagerlöf defines the attempt and then quotes from *Färdvägen*:

> Centralpartiet i Färdvägen berättar om ett försök att nå fram till något yttersta, en slutpunkt, ett centrum. Inte bara så att dess huvudperson kräver ett "metafysiskt" svar utan också på det sättet att han slutgiltigt vill veta vem han är. Dessa frågor är sammankopplade:
> > Mina ögon är igenmurade av regnet som blåser snett in mot oss. Och eftersom denna natt är slut och ingenting har förändrats, – – –eftersom mina förbannelser varken uppkallat vrede eller hämnd, bara likgiltighet, eftersom de linjer i mitt ansikte som skulle ha pekat på en utvecklad karaktär, antytt en linje, pekat på ett centrum, eftersom dessa nu bara verkar förvirrande och illa dragna, utmanar jag det som skulle finnas i mitt tänkta centrum.
> Och han hoppar upp på stenbalustraden runt torgets brunn, håller i åskvädret pekfingret högt upp och vänder ansiktet mot himlen. "Ingenting händer. Jag visste ju att ingenting skulle hända."[5]

The religious need for salvation dovetails with the need for a sense of identity and a "center," a sense of significance or purpose. The search for identity and purpose, symbolized here and in *Tribadernas natt* by a center, continues throughout Enquist's writing and *Färdvägen* suggests this thematic connection with Strindberg. In *Magnetisörens femte vinter*, Enquist focuses an entire novel on the theme of belief.

This book was Enquist's breakthrough novel and established him as one of the important young writers of Sweden. Based on the life and times of Franz Anton Mesmer, *Magnetisörens femte vinter* confronts man's emotional need for faith and a sense of significance with his aesthetic and rational needs and capabilities. The main character, Meisner, resembles the legendary Mesmer and combines personal willpower and strength with violence and hypocrisy. Meisner rises to power in the novel by using people's need to believe in something, to feel themselves a part of something. Other motifs, fantasy and reality, the journey, communication, might be compared to similar themes in Strindberg, but most strikingly Meisner combines, for his own fraudulent purposes, an almost Darwinian struggle to survive with the philosophical need to be a part of something, to believe.

While *Hess* employs some of these devices, it is too complicated a novel to refer to in this context. The novel that follows it, *Legionärerna* won the *Nordiska Pris* (Nordic Prize) for Enquist and stands as perhaps the finest documentary novel in Scandinavian literature. Both of these novels employ techniques and themes potentially related to Strindberg, but for the purposes of this paper, *Sekonden* most clearly combines the basis of historical fact with the themes of identity, political and religious faith, and what one might think of as a reply to Strindberg's view of the pitifulness of humanity. If many of Strindberg's later characters have a profound need for salvation and forgiveness within a religious framework, so too does Enquist's noble and pathetic fallen athletic hero. Whereas Strindberg had some difficulty in finding a resolution to that need, Enquist offers it in the vein of Lars Ahlin's "agape," forgiveness without the need for penance or absolution.[6] The narrator of *Sekonden* finally sees the answers for himself within a primarily political and economical religion, but for his victimized father he hopes for mercy and salvation in whatever terms the old man might use them. Enquist's recognition of man's need to belong, to have the possibility of a "salvation," involves not only religion and politics in *Sekonden*, but an ironic utopia.

An additional insight into the affinity between Enquist and Strindberg is provided by the utopia outlined by the narrator of *Sekonden*. He thinks of the utopia because of his father's belief in "improving the record" or bettering the result of one's effort, whether or not that record or result has any positive significance. The narrator fantasizes about a society in which different industrialized sections of the world could be drugged and returned to a period one or two hundred years earlier in their history. The basis for this return in history is "utveckling," that is, for Enquist, evolution, development, or progress: "Utveckling, sa man, är nyttig bara man inte definierar utvecklingens mål. Utvecklingen är lika med sig själv, utvecklingen är sitt eget mål. Utvecklingens rörelse är lycka. En tioprocentig utveckling innebär alltid samma mått av lycka, oavsett på uttvecklingsnivå utvecklingen försiggår."[7]

Although the word "utveckling" has slightly different connotations, Strindberg has a passage in the preface to his *Utopier i verkligheten* (*Utopias in Reality*) where the irony, the intellectual challenge to the concept of progress, and the basic content are remarkably similar. One assumes that this similarity rests on artistic kinship and not on any direct influence: "Utvecklingsteoriens anhängare hava i utvecklingen genom naturligt urval och ärvda ändamålsenligheter endast sett ett framåtskridande mot ett bättre. Men utveckling är icke alltid framåtskridande mot ett bättre. Ty en sjukdom utvecklar sig mot kris och död, ett sjukligt anlag utvecklar sig till sjukdom."[8] The resemblance of imagery, theme, even language is remarkable. Yet this likeness comes from the material itself, from an exploration of the sociopolitical problems of man as well as of the innermost core of man's philosophical striving. Strindberg's work has always been known for its dynamic blend of the sociological and philosophical. As for Enquist, even in his most recent novel, *Musikanternas uttåg* (*The Exodus of the Musicians*) (1978), this particular union of the social, political, and religious produces some of the best and most profound passages in his writing.

No one would try to claim that the presence of these themes in Enquist's works represents a direct Strindberg influence, but just as Strindberg provided an almost archetypal identity of the involved sociopolitical writer (one must always admit the powerful presence of C. J. L. Almqvist preceding Strindberg in such areas), he also laid the groundwork for the tradition of combining religion, philosophy, and art, a tradition that ranges in the twentieth century from Pär Lagerkvist to Lars Ahlin, Ingmar Bergman, and Lars Gyllensten. Thus, the social activist and the religious and philosophical writer, although familiar in authors such as Rousseau, Sartre, and Camus, represents a norm in Sweden typified by Strindberg and continued by Enquist.

In referring to *Musikanternas uttåg*, one should also note the continuation of additional Strindberg-related themes and devices. The partially autobiographical novel might well be construed as a careful brewing of the ingredients of *Hemsöborna* and *Tjänstekvinnans son* (*Son of a Servant*). *Musikanternas uttåg* has placed Enquist in the role of a worker's writer, a man in close contact with his own heritage among the workers in the mills and forests of Northern Sweden. The language of this novel provides the opportunity to turn to one final link between the two authors. Enquist uses colorful, earthy language and regional dialects in a sophisticated display of his own literary indebtedness to the naturalist writers following Zola and Strindberg.

Enquist himself refers to Thorsten Jonsson, Hemingway, and Dagerman as writers whose language influenced him. Yet, when one reads *Musikanterna*, one is immediately reminded of Strindberg's great contributions to Sweden's language and literature. One recalls that Strindberg was familiar with Zola's novels as well as his theories about theater. It is useful to remember that *Hemsöborna* and the naturalist plays *Fröken Julie* and *Fadren*, (*The Father*) were written during approximately the same period.

In summary, Enquist can be connected at least tentatively to Strindberg in the following ways: Strindberg as political activist, subjective author, experimenter in various genres, and as an author with themes ranging from the folk tradition and politics to the wanderer in search of answers to his religious and philosophical needs. Too, Strindberg's innovations in language, specifically his development of the language of naturalism in such works as *Fröken Julie, Fadren, Tjänstekvinnans son* and *Hemsöborna* is related to Enquist's own use of language in his plays and novels.

In what way does this information serve to illuminate Enquist's use of Strindberg in *Tribadernas natt*? First, it puts into context the accident that led to the play, Enquist's teaching of a course on Strindberg at the University of California, Los Angeles, in the spring of 1973. Enquist has dated the origin of the play to that period and identified the classroom discussions pertaining to Strindberg's views of the family and women, which, along with some visits to feminist meetings on the UCLA campus, motivated him to write the play.[9] Enquist himself said that when he first received word that he would have to teach a course on Strindberg he set about reading the works, because he felt unprepared and actually had devoted little time prior to this to studying Strindberg.[10] On the conscious level, Enquist's statement must be accepted, and there is little doubt that the play originated in the classroom situation described by Enquist. What the previous pages suggest, however, is that the idea was already present in his mind and he only needed conscious work with Strindberg to provide an impetus for the creation of *Tribadernas natt*. But how well does the play fit into the themes and patterns suggested above?

First, *Tribadernas natt* builds on elements connected with Strindberg in many ways. The obvious Strindbergian qualities are the characters, names, dates, and places. Yet, in developing these elements, Enquist uses a form often employed by Strindberg, the historical drama, in which the historical context illuminates our own era. Whereas Enquist's technique is more sophisticated, the concept was familiar to Strindberg, whose critics claimed that his historical dramas said more about Strindberg than about his characters.

One of the major themes of *Tribadernas natt* is the frustrated search for meaning, for a way in which the sense of purposelessness felt by each of the main characters can be overcome. His wife, Siri, accuses Strindberg of being terrified when not in the middle, the center of attention. The phrase recurs several times in the play, and the final tableau forms as the photographer moves Strindberg so that he stands in the middle, between the two women. This fear of being misplaced, having no purpose or function in life, first seen in *Färdvägen*, represents the same search undertaken by Siri and its failure is sadly portrayed in the life of Marie David's displaced mother. The struggle by Siri and Marie David, the two female characters in the play, to give their lives meaning, to stand in their own light rather than in the shadow of a man, allows Enquist to make obvious parallels with the feminist movement of the 1970s.

The battle of the sexes more obviously dominates the content of the play. Enquist here takes up one of Strindberg's major themes and uses it in a fashion that Strindberg, during one of his more liberal activist periods, would have appreciated. The play reflects not only the universal theme of the hostility between the sexes, but shows how the theme relates to the social and economic conditions of human beings in Strindberg's and Enquist's own lifetimes. Such a demonstration seems "naturalistic," in line with Zola and Strindberg. Finally, the play's language reflects that naturalistic tradition: earthy, vulgar, associative, illogical; it attempts to mirror the reality of the education and the social roles of the characters, the way people actually speak and think rather than the smooth and often beautiful styles common to so-called realistic writing. Since much of Strindberg's writing concerned itself with the problems that developed from economic pressures, Enquist's probing of the economic and social histories of the characters, although it seems uniquely twentieth-century in import, resembles Strindberg's histories and utopias.

The question that concerned the Swedish press to such an extent may be used to illuminate further Enquist's own technique and his use of Strindberg. Egil Törnqvist has lucidly discussed the relationship between Enquist's docudrama and the reality of Strindberg. Törnqvist quotes a number of critics, all of whom assume that Enquist wanted to give a realistic portrayal of Strindberg. "Lagercrantz utgår som en självklarhet ifrån att Enquist velat ge ett autentiskt Strindbergsporträtt. Utifrån den premissen blir hans bedömning negativ: 'Kan man överhuvud tänka sig att Strindberg någonsin, ens en enda dag av sitt liv, uppträdde och verkade så som han gör på Dramaten nu? Man kan det inte!'"[11] Törnqvist also quotes Torsten Ekbom, who admits there were exceptions to Strindberg's normal behavior: "Strindberg sällan eller aldrig uppträdde offentligt som han gör i Enquists pjäs. Han kunde vara misstänksam, snarstucken, någon gång i vredesmod bryta upp från en middag eller i berusat tillstånd ställa till en scen."[12]

Having defined the critics' hostility toward Enquist's version of Strindberg, Törnqvist turns to his own thesis: "'Med en sådan figur,' påpekar Ekbom, 'gör man inget drama.' Med andra ord: när den autentiska verkligheten kommer i konflikt med vitala konstnärliga intressen, måste man ge avkall på autenticiteten. *Tribadernas natt* är i första hand ett drama och måste fungera som sådant."[13]

Törnqvist establishes that Enquist portrays another Strindberg, an expressionistic one who might not have publicly acted as he does in the play, but could have written this way. Törnqvist also points out that Lagercrantz himself criticized Strindberg's *Mäster Olof* because it portrays not Master Olof but Strindberg. Similarly, he notes that some of Strindberg's own historical dramas use characters almost contemporary with him. Thus, Enquist uses a technique already developed by Strindberg. Törnqvist's final point derives from his interview with Enquist in which Enquist points out his wish to use the "myth" of Strindberg as a means of portraying contemporary man. Törnqvist concludes by quoting Leif Zern:

> I en utomordentligt insiktsfull artikel (DN 28.10.75) har Leif Zern framhållit att Strindberg i *Tribadernas natt* i kraft av sitt könsrollstänkande, sitt kvinnohat, sin rädsla, sin längtan efter gemenskap fungerar som ett identifikationsobjekt "med vars hjälp Enquist kan föra en ideologisk diskussion som bryter sig ut ur den historiska ramen och öppnar sig mot vår tid."[14]

Within the wider framework of Strindberg's own life and writing, we see here that Enquist's accomplishment is Strindbergian in the best sense. He uses literary, historical, political, and personal devices employed by Strindberg in order to wage an intellectual and ideological battle—an endeavor that Strindberg would have understood and perhaps even have admired.

One final attack against Enquist relates to Törnqvist's point about the aesthetic needs of the play dominating the historical facts. Asta Ekenwall attacked the principle of the modern documentary novel or play with its use of direct quotes from authors.[15] Specifically, she refers to Enquist's citations from Strindberg. For her, much of the value of *Tribadernas natt* comes from its language and she quotes a number of critics who also praise the play's language. However, her complaint is that nowhere does Enquist state exactly how much material he borrowed directly from Strindberg. She concludes by asking *Göteborgs-Posten* to offer a prize for the person who can find the most Strindberg quotations in *Tribadernas natt*.

Margareta Zetterström replies to Asta Ekenwall, but in her reply she returns to the debate about whether or not Strindberg is fairly represented.

> Strindberg må haft en småborgerlig livsföring och varit allmänt oförstående till frågan om jämlikhet mellan könen. Hans betydelse ligger ändå på ett annat plan. I den svenska litteraturhistorien är Strindberg framför allt den trotsige radikalen, som utmanade sin tids överhet med enastående kritisk skärpa och satirisk udd. Han är det moderna genombrottets store man, en författare som modigt gick till storms mot all humbug i samhället och som därför också ådrog sig etablissemangets hat.[16]

Many of the paradoxical qualities attributed to Strindberg in this quotation may one day be applied to Enquist, if they are not already. The modern stormy radical counters the preceding two articles by speaking to the myth as well as the man Strindberg, a point that Törnqvist takes up in his article. Enquist's reply gives an additional example of his own view of Strindberg and then defines Strindberg's role in the creation of *Tribadernas natt*. First, he states that he thinks Margareta Zetterström's belief that we should not look at the parts of Strindberg we do not like is either nonsense or censorship.

Också jag sympatiserar mycket mer med den tidige och sene Strindberg: samhällskritikern och socialisten. Men jag tycker inte man skall blunda för Strindberg i den ideologiska återvändsgränden. Han är nämligen inte placerad där av några metafysiska krafter, hans privata egenheter är inte privata, utan uttryck för det samhälle i vilket han levde—som betänkligt liknar det samhälle vi själva lever i. Detta är inte att reducera Strindberg. Det är att ta honom på allvar. Jag menar att "Tribaderna" både visar vägen in och vägen ut ur den återvändsgränden.[17]

Enquist then takes up his own use of Strindberg's writing within the play itself. He points out that the direct quotes from *Den Starkare* (*The Stronger*) are placed within quotation marks, yet notes that the quotations are to be read in a manner directly contrary to Strindberg's intention in the play. The most direct additional documentary material comes from a well-known letter from Strindberg to Pehr Staaff (21 August 1887). Enquist adds:

Men med risk att såra någon Strindbergälskare skulle jag vilja påpeka: detta berömda brev är ju faktiskt inte teater. Det är ett förtvivlat, otäckt eller gripande brev som diskuterats i alla tider, men *i sig* inte är teater och *i sig* inte fungerar på en scen.
Men bryter man upp texten, bryter man sönder entydigheten, då kan den fungera. . . .
Poängen är att jag här står i djup tacksamhetsskuld till Strindberg men inte för hans **ord** (man kan säkert förbättra också den autentiska brevmonologen på många sätt) men för en **teaterrytm**. Sättet att helt oförmedlat lägga helt motstridande känslor intill varandra, utan förmedling och utan att höja på ögonbrynen, är något mycket märkligt hos honom: det mer än orden är jag tacksam för.[18]

After this extraordinary insight into both himself and Strindberg, Enquist proceeds to discuss some of the citations he takes from Strindberg and shows how he had used them in ways quite different from Strindberg's context. He also mentions that some of the dialogue comes directly from his own writing, and suggests that much less direct quotation of Strindberg exists than Asta Ekenwall suspects. He initially estimates that, of all Strindberg's dialogue within the play, twenty percent might have some origin in Strindberg's own writing. However, in an addendum to the article, he adds that he went back through the play and discovered that of the 245 pieces of dialogue spoken by Strindberg, only 23 are either direct or revised Strindberg quotations; thus, excluding quotes from *Den Starkare*, only nine percent of the dialogue can be directly traced to Strindberg.

Enquist admits willingly that he borrowed pieces of Strindberg's life.

> "Poängen i allt detta är *inte* att jag påstår mig sakna tacksamhetsskuld till Strindberg. Tvärtom. Min tacksamhet är stor: jag har använt Strindbergs liv, hans biografi, jag har använt mig både av honom själv och myten om honom själv. Med hjälp av denna myt kan vi, i mytens och historiens spegel, titta oss själva i nacken."[19]

In conclusion, Enquist points out that the language of *Tribadernas natt* reflects the Swedish of the 1970s. Although he took the risk of writing about Strindberg, and could therefore use the man and his myth, the language, the dialogue of the play did not come to him in large blocks to be inserted easily into his play. Enquist's article returns us to Törnqvist's paper. Enquist used, revised, distorted, created the Strindberg of *Tribadernas natt* for his own personal artistic and intellectual purposes.

One might claim that Strindberg's myth and themes, outlined briefly in the beginning of this paper, were present in Enquist's creative consciousness long before he came to UCLA to teach the Strindberg course. The course and the feminist movement suddenly joined in Enquist's mind to give him an insight into the similarities of the 1880s and the 1970s. The play's subtitle, *Ett skådespel från 1889* (*A Drama from 1889*), defines Enquist's historical intention. This intention, along with all of the previously suggested parallels of politics, religion, language, and genre-experimentation, makes Enquist's "discovery" of Strindberg in 1973 less surprising, and it helps to reveal both their artistic kinship and Strindberg's modernity.

Finally, one may ask: does *Tribadernas natt* constitute the end of Strindberg's role in Enquist's writing? As I have already suggested, one can find parallels between the two authors continuing up to the present. *Musikanternas uttåg* clearly fits within the Strindbergian tradition outlined. In Enquist's latest play, *Mannen på trottoaren* (*The Man on the Sidewalk*) (1979), coauthored with Anders Ehnmark and premiered at Dramaten in the fall of 1979, one finds hints of Strindberg's chamber plays. In one scene a character is wound slowly in white gauze and the reader immediately thinks of the Mummy in *Spöksonaten* (*The Ghost Sonata*). When asked about the possible parallel, Enquist looks amazed at first, and then admits that at this point in his life Strindberg lives in a certain inner part of his consciousness. One of Enquist's major projects right now is a series of scripts for Swedish television—about Strindberg.

Notes

1. *Dramaten*, 47 (1975/76), 6. "The private: the boy in a man's suit. 'The Strindberg I loved was the youth Strindberg, the solitary, narrow-shouldered, shivering . . . that youth I understood and loved as only one youth can understand and love another youth.' Stig Dagerman in a quote from 1949. Yes, that is quite good, quite near my own Strindberg image (and nearly all of us have such a private image that we energetically guard and defend)."

2. An unrecorded interview held on 24 July 1979 in Stockholm. Other references in the paper paraphrasing Enquist's comments or ideas come from this interview.

3. Bo Nilsson, "Strindberg och den officiella historieskrivningen," *Dramaten*, 47 (1975/76), 14–17, and Per Nyström, "Överklassens svenska historia och folkets," *Dramaten*, 48 (1975/76), 3–6, discuss Strindberg's historical writings.

4. Karl Erik Lagerlöf, "Mellan tro och misstro," in his *Samtal med 60-talister* (Stockholm: Bonniers, 1965), p. 113. " 'One can also speak of *The Route* as a religious novel,' continues Enquist. 'The basic idea is from Strindberg's *To Damascus*. The decisive scene in my book corresponds to the asylum scene in it. The book begins with a sketch of a calm, enclosed world, the Christian alternative, and it finishes with the main character satisfying himself with a very small success. The decisive experience in the middle, the extreme attempt to challenge God to make himself known—I borrow the external contours of it from an episode in Strindberg's life. He had a lightning conductor in his house on Kymmend island and held it during a thunderstorm in a kind of scorn against God. Scorn is also a kind of belief.' "

5. Lagerlöf, *Samtal med 60-talister*, pp. 113–14. "The central part of *The Route* tells of an attempt to reach forward to something ultimate, a conclusion, a center. Not only in that its main character seeks a 'metaphysical' answer but in the way that he finally wants to know who he is. These questions are joined together:

My eyes are sealed closed by the rain that blows diagonally down on us. And because the night is over and nothing has changed—because my curses brought forth neither anger nor revenge, only indifference, because those lines on my face that should have pointed toward an evolved character, suggested a line, pointed toward a center, because these now seemed only confusing and poorly drawn, I challenge that which should exist in my imagined center.

And he jumps up on the stone balustrade around the square's fountain, holds his forefinger up into the thunderstorm and turns his face toward the sky. 'Nothing happens. I knew that nothing would happen.' "

6. Torborg Lundell discusses the tradition of "agape" in her book *Lars Ahlin* (Boston: Twayne, 1977).

7. *Sekonden* (Stockholm: Pan/Norstedts, 1972), p. 248. "Progress, they said, is useful only if one does not define the goal of progress. Progress is identical with itself; progress is its own goal. The motion of progress is happiness. A ten percent development always means the same degree of happiness, no matter at what stage of development the development proceeds."

8. August Strindberg, Förord till *Utopier i verkligheten* in *Samlade Skrifter* 15, ed. John Landquist (Stockholm: Bonniers, 1913), p. 5. "The supporters of the theory of evolution have only seen in evolution by natural selection and inherited abilities a progression toward something better. But evolution is not always progress toward something better.

For a sickness progresses into a crisis and death, an unhealthy tendency progresses into a sickness."

9. "9 byggstenar," *Dramaten*, 47: 8.

10. Interview, 24 July 1979.

11. Egil Törnqvist, "Scenens Strindberg och verklighetens. Per Olov Enquists Tribadernas natt (1975) som dokumentärt drama," in *Literature and Reality. Creatio versus Mimesis. Problems of Realism in Modern Nordic Literature*, ed. Alex Bolckmans (Ghent: Scandinavian Institute, University of Ghent, 1977), p. 200. "Lagercrantz takes as self-evident that Enquist wanted to give an authentic Strindberg portrait. On this premise his judgment is negative: 'Can one in general imagine that Strindberg ever, even one day of his life, behaved and appeared as he does at the Dramaten now? One can not!'"

12. Törnqvist, p. 201. "Strindberg rarely or never behaved publicly as he does in Enquist's play. He could be suspicious, short-tempered, sometimes in anger leave a dinner or while drunk create a scene."

13. Törnqvist, p. 202. "'With such a figure,' Ekbom points out, 'you cannot create drama.' In other words: when the authentic reality comes into conflict with vital artistic interests, authenticity must be left behind. *The Night of the Tribades* is first a drama and must function as such."

14. Törnqvist, p. 210. "In an extraordinarily insightful article (*Dagens Nyheter*, 28 October 1975) Leif Zern has emphasized that Strindberg in *The Night of the Tribades*, on the basis of his attitudes about sex, his misogyny, his fear, his longing for friendship, functions as an object for identification 'with whose help Enquist can lead an ideological discussion that breaks free of its historical framework and opens toward our own time.'"

15. "En August Strindbergs like?" *Göteborgs-Posten*, 10 March 1977.

16. Margareta Zetterström, "Enquist sviker Strindberg," *Göteborgs-Posten*, 23 March 1977. "Strindberg may have led the life of a petit bourgeois and in general misunderstood the question of equality between the sexes. But his importance lies on another level. In Swedish literature Strindberg is above all else the scornful radical who challenged the established authorities of his generation with unique critical accuracy and satirical bite. He is the great man of the modern breakthrough, an author who courageously fought against all the humbug in society and who, therefore, brought upon himself the hatred of the establishment."

17. Enquist, "Strindberg inte ensam på scenen," *Göteborgs-Posten*, 3 April 1977. "I, too, sympathize more with the early and the late Strindberg: critic of society and socialist. But I do not think you should close your eyes to Strindberg at an ideological dead end. After all, he was not placed there by metaphysical powers; his personal pecularities are not personal, but rather expressions for the society in which he lived—which curiously resembles the society we ourselves live in. This is not to reduce Strindberg. It is to take him seriously. I mean to say that *Tribades* shows both the way in and the way out of the dead end."

18. Enquist, *Göteborgs-Posten*, 3 April 1977. "Taking the risk of hurting those who love Strindberg, I would like to point out: this letter is actually not theater. It is a despairing, nasty, or emotionally gripping letter that has been widely discussed, but *in itself* it is not theater and *in itself* does not work on stage.

But if one breaks up the text, breaks apart the unequivocal, then it can work. . . .

*The point is that I owe Strindberg a deep debt of gratitude here, but not for his **words** (one can surely improve the authentic letter's monologue in many ways) but for a **theater rhythm**. The way in which completely unexpected and opposing emotions are placed beside each other, without warning and without a raising of the eyebrows, is something quite unique in him, **that** more than the words I am grateful for.*"

19. Ibid. "The point in all this is not that I deny indebtedness to Strindberg. On the contrary. My indebtedness is great: I have used Strindberg's life, his biography, I have used both Strindberg himself and his myth. With the help of that myth, in the mirror of myth and history, we can see the back of our heads."

Questions without Answers: On Strindberg's and Ibsen's Dialogue

Gunnar Brandell
(Translated by Marilyn Johns Blackwell)

"Vad dialogen slutligen angår, har jag brutit med traditionen något, i det jag icke gjort mina personer till kateketer som sitta och fråga dumt för att framkalla en kvick replik. Jag har undvikit det symmetriska, matematiska i den franska konstruerade dialogen och låtit hjärnorna arbeta oregelbundet, såsom de göra i verkligheten, där i ett samtal ju intet ämne tömmes i botten, utan den ena hjärnan av den andra får en kugg på måfå att gripa in i. Och därför irrar också dialogen, förser sig i de första scenerna med ett material som sedan bearbetas, tages upp, repeteras, utvikes, lägges på, såsom temat i en musikkomposition."[1]

Strindberg's only attempt to formulate a theory of good modern dialogue—quoted above from the preface to *Fröken Julie* (*Miss Julie*)—has to a great extent influenced our perception of his own artistic use of dialogue. One often hears the judgment that Strindberg's dialogue is more "irregular" than that of the French or of Ibsen but nonetheless more natural and more lively, this opinion often coming from actors who have tried to deliver his dialogue. But this is a simplistic assessment and contains several points that are not at all clear. In what way is a French dialogue "logical" and "symmetrical," and what does it really mean when Strindberg maintains that instead he would create a dialogue that is "musical"?

In at least one respect, he is distinctly lucid, namely in his point of departure. In Strindberg's dialogue we are confronted with "a conversation," an interaction in which one mind seizes what has been created by the other. During this period Strindberg constructed upon this concept of two mental entities that "seize" or "slip into" each other an entire theory of human life that also served as a formula for modern drama and applied to it the catchword "the battle of the brains." This idea in its aggressive Darwinian formulation eventually lost validity for him, but there is nothing to indicate that he deserted a conception of dialogue as an interaction between souls. The correlate of this idea, that of the individual's relative lack of character, he maintained at least as late as *En blå bok* (*A Blue Book*).

The purpose of this study is to attempt to discover how this type of dialogue—let us summarily call it "haphazard dialogue"—functions as a dramatic text. In the center I would place question-and-answer dialogue, a frequent variant in Strindberg's works and, of course, a basic form of dialogue in all dramatic works. For the purposes of demonstration, I have chosen an extreme form of haphazard dialogue, that which appears in the first act of *Spöksonaten* (*The Ghost Sonata*). For the sake of reference I have assigned the numbers 1 through 183, with one line being equivalent to each unit in the text that is to be delivered by a single actor and that is introduced with an identification of the speaker.[2] In order to demonstrate the "French," "realistic," or "well-made" type of dialogue, I have chosen the first act of Ibsen's *Gengangere* (*Ghosts*).[3] There are two reasons for the latter choice. First of all, there is a general similarity of motif in the two plays, and, secondly, one would expect that differences in presentational technique would manifest themselves in a comparison between a typical bourgeois realistic drama and a pre-expressionist piece such as *Spöksonaten*. In anticipation of the results of this investigation, I believe that these differences, if one wishes to express them in a formularized fashion, are to a great extent a question of what I call "dramatic information strategy."

If we initially ignore the fact that there are many different types of questions and answers—a problem which will be discussed later—and simply summarize those pieces of dialogue that correspond superficially to the question-and-answer form, it develops that Strindberg is ahead in the statistics. In the first act of *Spöksonaten*, this form occupies approximately a third of the dialogue, whereas in *Gengangere* it occupies one-fourth. In the first act of Chekhov's *The Cherry Orchard*, to involve yet another play with a related subject matter, it constitutes less than one-fifth of the dialogue.

This development appears quite natural when viewed against the background of Strindberg's ideas about dialogue. Question marks and exclamation points—in any event when they occur after an exclamation—mark extraordinarily clearly those points in the text where one speaker "slips into" the other's thought processes, in the former case by demanding an answer and in the latter by soliciting response or obedience. The answers indicate the other speaker's reaction, somewhere on the scale between subjugation and opposition. If Strindberg places priority on questions, answers, and exclamations at the cost of statements and declamations, it is precisely the result one would have expected from his preface to *Fröken Julie*.

Usually one thinks of questions and answers as a mode of information gathering. I ask and you answer, that is to say, you give me the information that I wish, expressed in textual linguistic terms: I designate a theme and you append a rheme. The same holds true within drama: questions and answers are a way to enlighten simultaneously the interlocutor and the audience about a relationship that may be meaningful in the future. Chekhov's *The Cherry Orchard* begins with just such a question-answer set: What time is it? Almost four. Like all information-yielding question-answer sets, both parts can easily be joined to yield a single statement: It is almost four o'clock. Chomsky as well maintains, in *Theory of Syntax*, that questions in this case are a transformation of statements.

In order that an informative process of this kind might function, the question and answer must both have a high degree of precision. The question must indicate what kind of answer is expected, which, of course, is always the case with yes-and-no questions and with many so-called w-questions, for example, that from *The Cherry Orchard*, where the answer can be any hour at all, but it must be an hour.

Such questions with an obvious informational purpose are more prominent in Ibsen than in Strindberg. When Pastor Manders first enters the house, he meets Regina and puts to her a long series of questions in order to orient himself as to the domestic situation: *And is everything going well out here? Rather busy though, I expect, getting ready for tomorrow? Mrs. Alving is at home I hope? I heard that Oswald should be here?*—all of which are properly answered. As audience we know that Oswald has come home and that Manders is rather particular about keeping tabs on this family, all of which is information that we shall need later in the play.

Such questions and answers appear also in Strindberg. Mr. Hummel, for instance, asks The Student about his circumstances and receives regulation answers: *Are you a medical student? —No, I'm studying languages, but as far as that goes, I don't know what I'm going to be. —Well, Well! Do you know mathematics? —Yes, pretty well. —That's good! Would you want a job perhaps? —Yes, why not?* (responses 46–51) and finally several lines down: *Are you a sportsman?—Yes, that is my misfortune.* (56–57)

Throughout we are dealing with questions and answers that can be transformed into statements and contain concrete information. But the questions come suddenly and impress one as capricious; if Hummel finds out what he wishes to know, the audience does not really receive a context into which it can place this information and does not know what information will be valuable later in the play. It might all have to do with The Student's past, for instance, his work at the fire—medical student, sportsman—or it might have to do with Hummel's plans. But if Hummel intended to give him work that would require knowledge of math, why does he speak shortly thereafter as though the only task that he requires of The Student is that he ingratiate himself with The Colonel's family—and then asks if he is a sportsman? None of these pieces of information plays any apparent role in the continuation of the play.

The preface to *Fröken Julie* is suffused with references to the irrational nature of man's mental processes, but as Strindberg grew older and underwent his Inferno crisis, he came to doubt all the more the value of information *per se* in its most general meaning. This is most obvious in *En blå bok*, which takes as its fundamental premise how thoroughly permeated the world is with "misunderstanding and lies," how one cannot rely upon anything, not upon what we read in school books nor upon what we learned under an oath of secrecy. If this were one of the points that Strindberg wished to make in *Spöksonaten*—and I believe this to be the case—it is only natural that he should also doubt the value of that information he imparts to the audience of his drama.

In the first act of *Spöksonaten* there is a suite of questions and answers that are directly associated with a common theme of *En blå bok*. "It is strange," says The Student, "how stories can be told in two such contrary ways." (33) and thereby states an opinion that Strindberg repeated many times in *En blå bok*. This occurs after Hummel, in three yes-or-no questions, all of which have been confirmed by The Student, has guessed what The Student's family might have said about him: *You've often heard my name mentioned in your family, have you? And perhaps mentioned with a certain disapproval? I suppose they said that I was the one who ruined your father?* (29, 31, 32). Against this, Strindberg places Hummel's own version of what transpired, according to which he "saved" old Arkenholz from "disaster" by offering him his savings of 17,000 crowns. But before the dialogue is completed, both these ranges of information have been placed within parentheses; we know that Hummel and Arkenholz did business together, but we do not know who was responsible for the bankruptcy. In other words, we share The Student's opinion that perhaps both variants may be true in their own disparate ways.

This vagueness of understanding that Strindberg implants in the audience is strengthened by the fact that the dialogue "slides" in a manner that is not at all uncommon in Strindberg but that one very seldom finds, for instance, in Ibsen. In Hummel's central response, he says: "Everyone who brings on his ruin by stupid speculation believes he was ruined by the one he couldn't fool. (Pause) The fact is your father made me lose 17,000 crowns, my total savings at the time" (32). Has he not, then, in some sense been cheated? Further on in the text, the contradiction is elaborated upon by a new version of the story (38). Here Hummel has not been "cheated" or "destroyed" but rather: "I saved your father from disaster, and he repaid me with all the terrible hatred gratitude causes." According to this version Arkenholz hates Hummel not because he could not deceive him but because he owes him a debt of gratitude. But in what way? Arkenholz's bankruptcy is an established fact within the play and it is this that we, like The Student, have considered to be his "disaster." But now some other disaster is posited, perhaps prison, which Arkenholz through Hummel's intervention has escaped, but we do not receive any information about this situation.

The Swedish Strindberg actor Lars Hansson was in the habit of saying that "it rains in" in Strindberg's dialogues and perhaps the preceding is an example of what he meant: unincluded or imperfect information, subtle contradictions in the information that is given, questions and answers that almost, but not quite, hang together. Strindberg even allows himself nonsense responses, as when Hummel responds to The Student's protestation that his father did not lie: "That's very true—a father never lies . . . but I'm a father, too, so . . ." (36). What The Student means of course is that a father, his father, did not lie to his son rather than that an individual who is a father is incapable of lying.

As a reader or viewer one can naturally write off these contradictions by interpreting them psychologically and maintaining that Hummel wants to appear simultaneously as the shrewd businessman who did not allow himself to be cheated and also as the unselfish doer of good deeds. This interpretation is in keeping with Hummel's character in the rest of the play and with Strindberg's technique of character development in general. But it merely serves to emphasize the parentheses around our information. Actually at this juncture we must give up and admit that no one can ever really know what truly happened—undoubtedly the impression that Strindberg, in keeping with the philosophy of *En blå bok*, wished to convey.

Even questions and answers that appear at first glance to be relatively precise can in Strindberg's dialogue be stripped of their information value so that, figuratively speaking, only the question mark remains. But there is another type of question that is more adaptable to the construction of free dialogue. The logicians Belnap and Steel call them "unclear questions" and maintain that they cannot really be formulated because possible answers cannot be deduced from them. As an example of such questions whose true contents are "Please relieve my vague puzzlement," Belnap and Steel mention "Who is that man living next door?" and "What is the relation between thought and language?"

By ignoring "unclear questions," Belnap and Steel exclude from their presentation (*The Logic of Questions and Answers*, New Haven: Yale University Press, 1976) much of the dialogue that appears in everyday life and—perhaps even more plentifully—in literature. Unclear questions about thought and language or, as is usually the case in Strindberg, about life and humanity are commonplace in literature and even if, from a purely formal and logical point of view, they can be answered in any way whatsoever, we would not want to dispense with the kind of answers that abound, for instance, in *Ett drömspel* (*A Dream Play*). In the first act of *Spöksonaten*, the section in which Hummel describes the inhabitants of the house is nothing more than answers to articulated or unarticulated questions from The Student—questions whose true content could very easily be described by the phrase "Please relieve my vague puzzlement" and formulated after the pattern of "Who is that man living next door?"

Questions such as "Who's the dark lady talking with the caretaker's wife?" and "Who was he?" and "But who was the dead man, then?" (79, 81, 99) contain no anticipation whatsoever of the answer that is to be forthcoming, and their true function is to direct our attention in a new direction, to accomplish what might be called an ongoing modification of focus in the dialogue. The same thing can be accomplished by an exclamation to the interlocutor ("Look at the old woman in the window!") or by a simple change of scene, as when The Caretaker's Wife comes out of the house and attracts the attention of the speakers. But whether or not he participates in the progress of the conversation, The Student adopts the same attitude of "puzzled bewilderment."

This striking passage in *Spöksonaten*—let us call it the "presentational passage"—becomes by virtue of its ongoing question-and-answer structure an especially clear example of the "haphazard" dialogue, which Strindberg wanted to introduce as early as *Fröken Julie*. The passage, which contains 48 lines (66–113), also includes two "intermezzos," the first about The Student's experiences and the second about Hummel's plans and approaching death. The "presentation" concerns numerous characters—The Colonel, The Mummy, The Daughter, The Dead Man, The Dark Lady, and The Caretaker's Wife—and in several cases the presentation is broken off only to be taken up again later. The changes of focus in the conversation can be illustrated in the following manner, with line numbers within parentheses:

1. Hummel's introductory line "All of them . . ." (66–67)
2. The Colonel (68–70)
3. The Mummy (71–77)
4. The Daughter (78)
5. The Dark Lady (79–80)
6. The Dead Man (80–82)
7. Intermezzo about The Student (83–92)
8. The Mummy (92–95)
9. The Caretaker's Wife (96–98)
10. The Dead Man (99–104)
11. Intermezzo about Hummel (104–107)
12. The Daughter (107–113)

The passage can therefore be divided into no fewer than twelve distinctly different sections of lengths varying from two to ten lines, each of which has its own theme. A comparison with a corresponding passage in Ibsen's *Gengangere* is also informative in this regard. The section in question is the long passage in which Pastor Manders and Mrs. Alving discuss her dead husband, in all some dozen pages and a hundred lines, where the dialogue centers around the same theme the entire time. There is no parallel here to Strindberg's constant alteration and modification of focus, and the presentation occurs with pedagogical clarity: first the pastor's unctuous paean of praise to Chamberlain Alving, a general repetition of ceremonial speeches to be heard the following day, and thereafter Mrs. Alving's revealing and contrasting portrait of her husband's moral corruption. Even in Strindberg there occurs a thematically related "funeral speech" with two variants, one negative and one positive, but in this case the speeches are disposed of in two short-line exchanges. From the first we learn that "What was most obvious was his vanity" (82); and from the second, that "he was a charitable man" (101)—sometimes. But which of the two pictures we are to believe remains an unsolved dilemma.

The articulated or unarticulated questions upon which dialogue is based are in both Ibsen's and Strindberg's cases what Belnap and Steel call "unclear questions" of the type "Who is the man who lives next door?" but whereas the answers in Ibsen are precise and, as we must assume, exhaustive, in Strindberg they are suspended, evasive, and distinctly fragmentary. In the first act of *Spöksonaten* there is only one place in which the author gives us precise information of the kind that could be a point of departure for an intrigue drama. It occurs in line 96: "The caretaker's wife!—Well, the dark lady over there is her daughter by the dead man, and that's why her husband got his job as caretaker . . . but the dark lady has a lover, who's aristocratic and expects to get rich; he's in the midst of getting a divorce from his wife, who's giving him a stone house to get rid of him, you see. The aristocratic lover is the son-in-law of the dead man and you can see his bed clothes being aired out on the balcony up there. . . ."

As theater-goers accustomed to the conventions of the drama, perhaps we think: "We must remember this, in case it should play an important role in the continuation of the play." But, as though it were not enough that it is completely irrelevant to our understanding of the rest of the play, whether we remember it or not, Strindberg also organizes the line in such a way as to make it almost useless as information. The question concerns The Caretaker's Wife, but after a very brief comment about her relationship with The Dead Man, we receive quick bits of information about, in turn, The Dark Lady, The Caretaker, The Dark Lady's suitor, the suitor's wife and so on. As in the dialogue as a whole, the focus is continually displaced. With textual-linguistic terminology perhaps one can maintain that new themes are introduced here at an unacceptably fast pace or that the line functions within too large a semantic field for it to serve an informational purpose. The Student expresses the viewer's natural reaction when he bursts out: "That's terribly complicated!"

Theater convention prescribes that in the first act, especially if it takes the form of a question-and-answer dialogue, we should receive reliable information about the drama's reality and prerequisites in a so-called exposition. This can be likened to an agreement on the rules of the game that will follow. The author provides certain facts about the drama's reality and implicitly promises that as the play continues he will confine himself solely to these prerequisites, whereas the audience accepts these prerequisites and adopts for the duration of the play "the willing suspension of disbelief." It is for this reason that Mikhail Bakhtin, one of the few literary critics who has interested himself in dialogue, has spoken of the drama in his *La Poétique de Dostoevski* as a "monolithic" art form: "Les personnages se rejoignent en dialoguant, dans la vision unique de l'auteur, du metteur en scène, du spectateur, sur un fond net et homogène."[4]

This is a formulation that is eminently adaptable to Ibsen and the type of well-made realistic drama to which *Gengangere* belongs. Ibsen has decided what we shall think about the dead Chamberlain. If he were, in the process of the drama, to abandon the portrait that he has provided of him and substitute another for it, he would betray the expectations of his audience; if the audience, on the other hand, were to imagine him other than Mrs. Alving has described him, it would be forsaking its implicit agreement with the author and placing itself outside the play.

In the first act of *Spöksonaten*, however, things are different. Initially it appears to be a typical expository act with its questions and answers, but Strindberg constantly sabotages our expectations—insofar as they desire straightforward information about the characters who are going to appear in the drama—sometimes by informing us in a vague and contradictory fashion, sometimes by making the facts too "tight," but primarily through organizing them in a rhapsodical and whimsical fashion. Strindberg does not construct for us a central perspective that would allow us to decide what is more or less important in what we hear, and therefore no agreement is reached as to what we shall and shall not believe. If, in spite of everything, we imagine that we have come to know something of import for the development of the drama, Strindberg reminds us after lines 146–178 that all the information we have in our possession comes from Hummel, an obviously not very reliable narrator who has his own hidden motives.

By way of a summary: "haphazard" dialogue, which is directed by the associations of both interlocutors, with many abrupt changes or gliding transitions between short segments, provided Strindberg with a formula as early as the preface to *Fröken Julie*. There can be no doubt that this type of dialogue, which is really unparalleled in other dramatists, is one of Strindberg's greatest resources as a dramatic author. If one adds to this—from a different point of view than I have maintained here—that this dialogue, precisely because of its "free" and capricious nature, is coordinated with the action on stage and the visual elements of the production, as occurs throughout the first act of *Spöksonaten*, one begins to understand why Strindberg's plays are so theatrically effective.

Strindberg gradually developed this type of dialogue into an art, for instance in *Dödsdansen*, the introductory sequence of which is the subject of a sound and interesting study by Egil Törnqvist in *Svensk Litteraturtidskrift* (3/1978). But from the very beginning of Strindberg's career, his dialogue is moving in this direction, for instance in *Mäster Olof* (*Master Olof*), and one may well assume that this tendency is rooted in his own artistic personality rather than in a learned or acquired theory, a supposition that is born out by the great movement and wealth of associations in his prose. An anecdote recounts that as a student in Uppsala Strindberg quarreled with his teacher Carl Rupert Nyblom about Dante. Nyblom maintained Dante was fair not only in placing his own enemies in hell but also in putting several of his friends there. He received a typical Strindberg answer in response: Is it fair to place one's friends in hell? Different unarticulated assumptions give these words different meanings—in this case the word "fair"—when in dialogue they are transferred from one interlocutor to another, as is the case in Hummel's line: "I am also a father. . . ."

The structure of "haphazard" dialogue in Strindberg might well be illuminated even more exactly than has hitherto been the case by employing the methods of the ever-developing school of textual linguistics. But a great deal of work is yet to be done in this field. As a layman, one would consider there to be too great a distance between Strindberg's dialogue and the logically organized presentation that linguists, as a rule, have in mind when they attempt to state what is linguistically "acceptable" and what is not.

Somewhat more problematic is the principle that I have called "unclear questions-unclear answers," that is to say when, through a question-and-answer dialogue, Strindberg awakens certain expectations about information that is then a "cul-de-sac," or floods us with so many facts that the effect on the spectator is the same. Both are techniques that can be traced back through Strindberg's dramaturgy. It is a matter of excluded "cul-de-sac" information when in *Fadren* (*The Father*) we never discover the daughter's true parentage and are left in doubt as to the true mental condition of The Captain. In this way, various major conventions of bourgeois drama, to which genre the play rightfully belongs, are subverted. The other important technique—to provide redundant information—is mentioned by Strindberg on several occasions and termed "abortive intention," in other words a method of fixing the audience's attention on something that is not then developed within the scope of the play. Both of these methods, of course, imply a radical departure from the principles that govern information strategy in the well-made play.

But these new, or reversed, principles for information strategy in the drama are not always cultivated. The first act of *Spöksonaten* is an extreme case. In *Fadren*, on the other hand, these principles are never taken so far as to shatter the realistic framework of the play. Despite a deep uncertainty as to what the action is really about, we find ourselves in a bourgeois home and witness a battle between two dueling parties; this battle constitutes in some sense the dramatic reality of the play. It is, however, especially enlightening to effect a comparison with the introductory dialogue in *Dödsdansen* as it is analyzed by Törnqvist. The similarities are many: not merely the "haphazard" dialogue but also cases of redundant information and what Törnqvist calls "false exposition," a concept that, were it extended, might be adapted for the entire first act of *Spöksonaten*. But the differences are also great. As the study shows, the dialogue in *Dödsdansen*, with all its deviations and digressions, centers around a matrix of motifs: the marriage between The Captain and Laura, the approaching silver anniversary, and Kurt's arrival. Therefore, in spite of all else, the drama has a kind of realistic substratum, the audience knows what it ought to be interested in, what the drama is about. In *Spöksonaten*, on the other hand, the entire exposition is false in the sense that we do not receive the necessary directions for interpretation. Throughout the play, information is fragmentary and doubtful, and the matrix of motifs never indicated. When the act is finished we might well imagine that the play would continue to concern the dead consul—especially if we were thinking of the kinds of dramatic assumptions exercised in *Gengangere*—or else Baron Skanskorg and his marital affairs—neither of which, of course, is the case.

On the other hand, one can correctly speak of a thematic center to the play. Together with the supernatural elements, the "haphazard" dialogue combined with an equally omnipresent negative information strategy gives the impression that life is incomprehensible confusion, full of threatening but never comprehensible secrets. It was this experience of existence, especially strong in his depressed periods, that Strindberg expressed in the phrase "life is a dream"; because dreams are disconnected, we experience in them a multitude of scenes and events but never really receive the key to them, lacking the information that would make the occurrences comprehensible. This is the dreamer's experience of "puzzled bewilderment" that Strindberg experienced in the face of life in general; and it was natural for him in the well-known preface to *Ett drömspel* to point out the formal similarities between dream material and the contents of his play.

As we know, there exists an earlier, unprinted preface to *Ett drömspel* in which Strindberg speaks not of dream form but rather of musical form, just as the concept of chamber drama implies an analogy with music. In what does this analogy consist? And what does Strindberg really mean: is it dream or music that we should think of as the dominant compositional principle? The answer must obviously be that both analogies allude to the same concept and are equally useful. Whereas traditional realistic dialogue is organized according to informational value, music, like dream, lacks organized informative contents. The same is true, at least in a relative sense, of Strindberg's dream plays, where "haphazard" dialogue allows him, with a freedom like that of either music or dream, to repeat, return to, and vary motifs or themes: the house symbolism, The Milkmaid, the motif of mercy.

A convenient comparison casts further light on the differences between Ibsen's *Gengangere* and Strindberg's *Spöksonaten*. At approximately the same time that these plays were written, Freud was asking his patients to recount their dreams and associate outwards from them —a question as in Ibsen and Strindberg of reconstructing the past and banishing spirits and ghosts from the mental world of the patient. This process has two stages: in the first, which is reminiscent of Strindberg's dream plays, the material lies in front of the patient and doctor in a chaotic condition with, however, certain stubbornly recurring motifs, and refuses to yield useful information. But after analysis and interpretation, one evolves a comprehensible picture of the patient's early history, an exposition for the psychological treatment that is more reminiscent of Ibsen's dramatic presentations. It is but a short step from this knowledge to an attempt to create order in Strindberg's dream plays, and one method is to subject them to the same treatment as Freudian analysis. It is a relatively easy task, and by accomplishing it, the clarity that was previously lacking is restored. But Strindberg's dramatic "point" lies precisely in the fact that explanation and analysis are excluded.

Finally, an encroaching question: is it not by studying, in this or preferably some more exact way, questions and answers in Strindberg's dialogue that we can better understand what a dream play is and what realism is in Strindberg's work, better understand how Strindberg, as a dramatic realist, is different from the Ibsen of the 1880s, and why we can experience something of a dream atmosphere even in a bourgeois drama like *Fadren* but feel the same dream atmosphere so much more strongly in *Spöksonaten* or *Dödsdansen*? Such a study would perhaps provide new answers to a number of old questions that have often been put forward by Strindberg scholars.

Up to now, Strindberg's dreamplay technique has been regarded as an expression of the special mysticism to which he devoted himself during the Inferno crisis. But without contesting the importance of the crisis for the spirit that suffuses the chamber plays and *En blå bok*, one can still wonder whether or not another aspect of the matter is even more important. If one replaces the notoriously vague word "mysticism" with the considerably more precise "mystification," the result is not only a useful formula for the dramatic technique that I have attempted to describe—"information" is replaced by "mystification"—but also a concept that points to Strindberg's continuity as a dramatist. He did not become a "mystic" until the Inferno crisis—if even then—but long before that he was overwhelmed by the feeling that life might be one great mystification, threatening for the most part, but sometimes also consoling, or better yet a drama, staged by unknown powers on Strindberg's behalf and with many more dark secrets than revealed truths. This one reads in *Ockulta dagboken*—and in a letter from 1887: "Faller ljus in i detta mörker så dimper jag ned krossad!"[5]

Notes

1. August Strindberg, *Samlade Skrifter*, 23 (Stockholm: Bonniers, 1914), p. 108. "As far as the dialogue goes, I have broken with tradition somewhat in not making my characters catechists who ask stupid questions in order to elicit clever replies. I have avoided the symmetrical, mathematical artificiality of French dialogue and have let my characters' brains work irregularly as they do in real life, in which a conversational topic is never exhausted but in which one brain gets from another a cog to slip into at random. For that reason my dialogue rambles, too, presents material in the first scenes that is later reworked, taken up, repeated, expanded, and developed like a theme in a musical composition," (trans. Walter Johnson, *The Pre-Inferno Plays* [New York: Norton, 1976], p. 81).

2. For the sake of readability, all the quotations from *Spöksonaten* have been rendered in English and are from Walter Johnson's translation *A Dream Play and Four Chamber Plays* (New York: Norton, 1975).

3. All quotations from *Gengangere* are from the Peter Watts translation *Ghosts and Other Plays* (London: Penguin, 1964).

4. *La Poétique de Dostoevski* (Paris, 1970), p. 172. "The characters meet in speech in a vision unique to the author, the director, the spectator, on a clear and homogenous basis."

5. Letter to Axel Lundegård, 12 November 1887. *August Strindbergs brev* 5, ed. Torsten Eklund (Stockholm: Bonniers, 1958), p. 298. "If light falls into this darkness, I would collapse shattered."

Art and Passion: The Relationship Between Strindberg and Munch
Reidar Dittmann

I

In the early fall of 1883, while Edvard Munch, not quite twenty years old, was rejoicing in his very first token of recognition when his painting *På morgenkvisten* (*Early Morning*) was accepted for showing in that year's State Autumn Exhibition in Oslo, August Strindberg, ailing, depressed, and bitter, was on the threshold of what he considered to be his final departure from "ett otacksamt fädernesland,"[1] determined to continue his creative career in more appreciative surroundings.

The Oslo event was, of course, a public affair, although Munch's contribution to it was generally ignored, the only encouraging word coming from Christian Krohg, who called the unpretentious canvas "superb."[2] Considering Krohg's distinguished position in Norwegian art, however, such criticism had a most soothing effect on the young debutant.

Strindberg's decision to leave Sweden was deliberately a hush-hush matter, each preparatory step carefully concealed to keep creditors at bay. Having spent the summer in his beloved Stockholm archipelago nursing his health while keeping up both writing and correspondence in an attempt to establish the necessary contacts at home and abroad, he was finally ready to pull up stakes early in September. By then he was so eager to get away that he stopped in the capital city only long enough to change from steamer to train. As he confided to a friend: "För öfrigt går jag som en rök genom Stockholm och försvinner spårlöst."[3]

These two episodes—Munch's unobtrusive debut and Strindberg's precipitous departure—on the surface entirely unrelated, may in a broader perspective be viewed as the first steps on separate paths that would ultimately merge, bringing these two central artistic figures in late nineteenth-century Scandinavia together. For already at that early stage there was a link between them: the commanding figure of Christian Krohg, whose companionship Strindberg would be enjoying that same fall while riding out the storm in a shelter provided by Carl Larsson and several other artists in their tranquil French haven Grez-sur-Loing on the southern edge of the Fontainebleau Forest. And in view of Strindberg's deep personal interest in painting and the nature of the group gathered in Grez, it is rather reasonable to assume that conversations around the punch bowl at the local inn those leisurely evenings would frequently turn to art and artists, at which time Krohg, an untiring advocate of new ideas, would have had ample occasion to bring up the name of his most promising protégé, Edvard Munch.[4] Therefore, the lot of this young Norwegian, also confined by an oppressive provincial establishment, must have become known to Strindberg even then. Similarly Munch, an avid reader of Oslo's only liberal publication, *Verdens Gang*, may well have received his first impression of Strindberg's writings at approximately this time through that paper's late-October publication of the poem *Landsflykt II* (*Exile II*), a scathing attack not only on Swedish exploitation of a brother nation but also on the stifling creative climate in Norway's hopelessly provincial capital:

> Jag ser lagvrängare och lakejer
> ta upp trottoarerna
> medan du, husbonden,
> får trampa i modd
> på gatans kullerstenar,
> men jag ser icke dina store män
> som fått gå i landsflykt,
> män, så stora att de räckte till
> även för oss ofantliga svenskar.[5]

Ten years were to pass before Strindberg and Munch met face to face—ten turbulent and trying years during which each produced some of his most significant works, Strindberg *Hemsöborna* (*The Natives of Hemsö*), *Fadren* (*The Father*), and *Fröken Julie* (*Miss Julie*), and Munch *Syk pike* (*Sick Girl*), *Melankoli*, *Vår* (*Springtime*), and *Aften på Karl Johansgate* (*Evening at Karl Johansgate*). Although none of these found wide acceptance by either critics or the public, the two pioneers, undaunted, continued their separate probing of the human psyche, gradually moving ever closer in purpose, until at last they seemed to cross each other's threshold, Strindberg in his dramas merging the literary-visual into a new creative totality, and Munch seeking a similar synthesis in his radically new and vibrantly expressive canvases.

Such overlapping of interests actually extended far beyond a deliberate heightening of the effect of the visual on the part of Strindberg in his works for the stage and Munch's persistent attempt at incorporating specific literary-psychological elements into his pictures. In reality, each had serious ambitions in the direction of the other's principal medium, Strindberg at one time actively striving for recognition as a painter, and Munch harboring a sincere desire to express himself in the form of drama.[6] A telling, even if apocryphal, episode in this context is related by Rolf Stenersen in his intimate volume on Edvard Munch, where he describes an evening of revelry in Berlin during the first period of friendship between the painter and the dramatist:

"I am Scandinavia's greatest painter!" Strindberg cried.
"If so, I am Scandinavia's greatest dramatist!" Munch retorted. "Skål!"[7]

Strindberg's first extended stay abroad, from 1883 to 1889, did not result in a new and more profitable career, nor did it provide him with a more appreciative audience. However, surrounded by searching artists, first in Grez and later in Paris, he had ample opportunity to probe the subject of the visual arts in their varied aspects. These embraced works in progress observed in the studios to which he had access as well as the finished works shown in public and private galleries in this crucial decade of transition and transformation in the world of painting. As a result, his eyes were opened more than ever before to the expressive potential inherent in visual representation. He must have reached the conclusion that in the visual arts Realist-Naturalist tendencies were issues of the past, that it was no longer a question of simple representational images but of an uncompromising revelation of the artist's soul: "Man skulle måla sitt inre och icke gå och rita av stockar och stenar, som ju voro betydelselösa i sig själva, och endast genom att passera det förnimmande och kännande subjektets smältugn kunde få någon form."[8]

Two years later Munch considered the same issues in a small brochure, reaching this conclusion: "Det skulle ikke lenger males interiører, folk som leser og kvinner som strikker. Det skulle være levende mennesker som puster og føler, lider og elsker."[9] This, too, speaks of the end of one era and the beginning of another and bodes well for a future exchange of ideas between the two artists.

Strindberg's declaration, found in his autobiographically inspired *Tjänstekvinnans son* (*The Son of a Servant*) and stated by its principal character, Johan, at a time when the author would have been only twenty-three years old, expresses an attitude toward the visual arts reflected nowhere in his correspondence from that period nor in any other early writings. It therefore follows that this new and highly perceptive view of the purpose of visual creativity must reflect his thinking at the time when that particular portion of the autobiography was written, in 1886-87, in the immediate wake of his three years of experiences and exposures in France.

It was toward art and art criticism that the author directed his character in *Tjänstekvinnans son*, surrounding him with "mänskor, som sysslade med konsten."[10] Strindberg himself, on the other hand, when making these retrospective observations, had abandoned his Grez circle and returned to serious writing. In so doing he brought with him his new ideas, and already in *Fadren* (1887) and *Fröken Julie* (1888) it is possible to detect a greater emphasis on the visual aspects of emotional tension than in his earlier dramas. This feature becomes, however, much more pronounced in the novel *I havsbandet* (*By the Open Sea*) (1890), where nature descriptions, in particular, more often reflect an inner experience of the landscape than an external manifestation of its colors and forms. Thus, just as the sea rises and falls in slow, glossy swells or loudly crashing breakers, so too the spirit of the character undulates in an equally unpredictable flow, eliciting different reactions at different times:

Men naturen, hos vilken han förr sökt umgänge, blev nu död för honom, ty mellanledet, människan, saknades. Havet, som han dyrkat och vilket han sökte såsom det enda storslagna i hans tarvliga land med dess gnetiga, småaktiga sommarvillslandskap, började förefalla honom trångt, allt efter som hans jag svällde ut. Denna blåa, terpentingröna, gråa ring stängde honom som en fängelsegård, och det enformiga lilla landskapet medförde samma pina som lär vara straffcellens: bristen på intryck.[11]

This paragraph, so visually emotional, stands as a direct, though literary, response to the challenge in *Tjänstekvinnans son*: "Man skulle måla sitt inre. . . ," ("One should paint one's interior. . . ."). So rich is Strindberg's verbal palette throughout the novel that certain of his painter friends—Richard Bergh and Karl Nordström among them—enthusiastically professed their indebtedness to him in their own approach to depicting seaside landscapes.

Strindberg's ambition in the direction of a career in painting was not limited to his youth, as might be inferred from the quoted portion of *Tjänstekvinnans son*. At regular intervals throughout his life, often when material and emotional pressures approached the unbearable, his interest was reignited. This was the case in the period following the completion of *I havsbandet*, when marital problems and related conflicts raced toward their inevitable conclusion. Then, tramping the rocks and the beaches of the archipelago with his easel and paint box, observing, sketching, and painting, he finally succeeded—or so he thought—in projecting his emotions onto the canvas—or rather a series of cardboard pieces of varying size. In 1892, greatly in need of funds, he chose eight out of a total of thirty paintings for a sales exhibit in a private gallery in Stockholm.

It was a modest show of little variety, his pictures all representing aspects of the archipelago. Characteristically, they were composed of brooding pigments applied with a palette knife in broad splashes or long arcs, sometimes also in turbulent spiral motions. From a thick initial application the surface was built up in layers, one color riding on the top of the other, from darker toward lighter hues, often resulting in a relief pattern. Space proportions in these and other Strindberg paintings tend to favor the sky, as in Dutch landscapes. It is frequently depicted in a state of turbulence, whipping the sea into a raging frenzy, with the horizon appearing as a serrated range of snow-capped mountain tops. The sky is invariably more skillfully manipulated than is the sea or any section of land that may be visible. A good case in point is the composition *Vita Märrn* (*The White Sailing Mark*), a relatively large painting, eighteen by twenty-four inches, featured in his 1892 exhibit. Somber grayish-green colors contrast with half-tones of chalky white as an impetuous sky hurls itself in broad masses of parallel diagonal streaks onto the stormy surface of the sea, which flays a rocky promontory. There, unaffected by the hostile onslaught, stands the rigidly unyielding sailing mark: clearly a symbol of Strindberg's own stubborn defiance of the turbulent elements in his life.

Two major books and a number of articles have been written on the subject of Strindberg and the visual arts.[12] However, his towering prominence in literature makes it very difficult to arrive at an unbiased evaluation of his achievement as a painter. Whether his talent was sufficient to have earned him a place in the annals of European art is really a moot question. Whereas Göran Söderström claims that Strindberg deserves full and unqualified recognition as a painter, Jean Cassou assumes a more neutral stance, choosing to view the paintings within the framework of the totality of Strindberg's multifaceted creative strivings: "Här placerar vi oss inte i det moderna måleriets historia utan i den mikrokosm som kallas Strindberg. August Strindbergs snille kan inte liknas vid någonting annat, inte heller hans uppsyn, inte heller hans öde. Så kom den stund då denne mycket egenartade August Strindberg kände behovet att måla. Det vill säga han kände med sig att det i måleriet stod honom ännu ett medel tillbuds med vilket han kunde ge uttryck åt sin oförytterliga personlighet."[13]

In the present context it is particularly significant that Strindberg's first serious attempt at entering the ranks of the professionals in the visual arts occurred on the threshold of his 1892 departure for Berlin, where he was destined to meet, among many others in the northern avant-garde, Edvard Munch, who in record time had succeeded in making himself the center of a raging art controversy.

Strindberg's debut as a painter preceded by a few weeks Munch's boldly conceived second retrospective, mounted in Oslo in the late summer of 1892. It was that exhibition that would pave the way for his imminent appearance in Berlin. Munch's reception in Oslo was no more favorable than Strindberg's in Stockholm. Indeed, in both cases critical reaction took the form of scorn and hilarity rather than professional evaluation. Only two reviews of the Strindberg presentation appeared. One was written by a personal friend lacking any insight in the arts, who found the pictures intriguing: ". . . åtskilliga förfela ingalunda att på åskådaren göra samma intryck, som de imponerande scener, hvilka han sökt skildra, gjort på den som skapat dem." ("Some of them by no means fail to elicit the same response that the powerful scenes that he has tried to depict first made on the man who created them.") The polar opposite, however, was the assessment of a professional who, abandoning any attempt at sincerity, produced little more than an accumulation of vulgarisms, strikingly similar to those that would be in store for Munch. Beginning with a lengthy comparison between Strindberg and the artist portrayed in Murger's *Scènes de la vie de Bohême* (*Scenes from the Life of Bohemia*), who hauls his masterpiece from one gallery to the next because no one can agree on what it seems to represent, the critic goes on to say:

Jag skulle nästan vara färdig att tro att den skalken Strindberg då han satte dessa små "studier" i breda förgylda ramar och skickade dem till uställning som "taflor" endast haft för afsikt att skämta med publiken och se huru långt den "tål kallt stål" i fråga om konst. Om jag undantager den bit som kallas "Stiltje på hafvet" och som verkligan visar en glimt av målaretalang hos sin mästare, trotsar jag någon att kunna säga hvad de andra taflorna föreställa—, så framt man toge bort rubriklapparne. Om "Snötjocka på hafvet" skall föreställa ett smutsigt lakan, upphängt till torkning, eller vara prof på ett nytt sätt att måla ladugårdsdörrar är omöjligt att säga, likasom om "Packis" skall vara en tallrik margarinsmörgåsar eller ett fat griljerade kalffötter med hjärnsås.
"Slätprick" skulle man kunna taga för en gammal smörkärna färdig att skänkas till Nordiska museet, och "Ruskprick" för ett "Stilleben" med motiv från renhållningsbolagets gård.[14]

Included in Munch's 1892 retrospective were fifty paintings, among them *Syk pike*, *Vår*, *Aftenstemning* (*Evening Mood*), *Fortvivelse* (*Despair*), several scenes from Karl Johansgate, and, remarkably, *Pubertet* (*Puberty*) and *Dagen derpå* (*The Day Thereafter*), both destroyed in a fire in 1891 and repainted expressly for the show.

Pubertet may be Munch's first attempt to go beyond direct appearances by intensifying the expressive potential of a living model, for it is inconceivable that the young person posing could have displayed an inner anguish as profound as that exuding from this canvas. It is a visual representation of the inexpressible fear of reaching sexual maturity, of stepping from innocence to awareness, articulated in color and structure and with a compassion perhaps deeper than many would expect of a man. The model's gauntly yellow flesh tones, the starkly plain wall and the greenish-white bed give the viewer an instant chill turning into a shudder at the sight of the huge, foreboding shape hovering on the wall—a monstrous phallus rather than a reasonable rendition of the shadow of the frail creature portrayed. She, within her cell-like space, sits tautly on the edge of the bed, legs tightly pressed together, arms instinctively attempting to cover her nudity, her wide-set eyes livid with fear. Every muscle, every fiber in her body set for flight, she is inescapably imprisoned in the fate inherent in her lot as a woman.

Dagen derpå, in a similar vein, inspired not by any social or moral concern but by the same deep awareness of a biologically motivated destiny, may be interpreted as the justification of the child-woman's dire apprehension. Even a casual glance at the setting is sufficient to reveal the same spatial confinement—the wall, the bed, even the same hovering shadow. And a closer scrutiny shows the face in both paintings to be the same, only with a sensuous, mature beauty added in *Dagen derpå*.

No such discovery of purpose was made by the critics in provincial Oslo in the 1890s. Many of the paintings had been shown earlier, either in his first retrospective in 1889 or in the various State Autumn Exhibitions where Munch had been represented, and had received their usual negative treatment in the press. This second showing prompted no recantations, nor did his new works bring him any paeans. *Aftenposten*'s reviewer speaks in terms similar to those applied by Strindberg's critic: "Han maler sin berømmelige gule båd . . . og plaserer nu i forgrunden noget der nærmest tager sig ud som fleskeskinker og blodpølser—en hel slagterbutikk! Han maler med blodige fingrer—og det kaller han 'Aftenstemning.' "[15]

Two other Scandinavians, both better known than Munch, happened to be exhibiting in Oslo at the same time. One was Adelsteen Normann, a Norwegian genre painter strategically residing in Berlin where, capitalizing on a prevailing German sentiment for things

Nordic, he had made a name for himself depicting rugged west Norwegian landscapes and robust Hardanger-costumed maidens. The other was the Dane, J. F. Willumsen, back from Pont-Aven, Paris, and his association with the French avant-garde. He and Munch, who met for the first time during those days, could take comfort in their mutual failure with the critics. It was *Aftenposten* again that brought a joint review of "de vidunderlige frembringelser som de to ovennevnte championer på den allermodernste malerkunsts område har præstert." Following that acid introduction the critic adds these warning words:

På de allerfleste har vel de to udstillinger ikke gjort annen virkning end at sætte deres lattermuskler i bevegelse. Men der har dog heller ikke manglet dem, som har taget det hele alvorligt og med andagt har sagt at finde en mening i dette skrækingydende Galematias av "Fremtidskunst." Naturligvis. Der gives ikke den skjønhed eller sandhed i verden, som ikke kan vrænges om til sin egen karikatur. Og der gives ikke den galskab og dårskab i verden som ikke en eller anden nar finder på at beundre.[16]

Such a fool was Adelsteen Normann, so full of admiration for Munch's *Galematias* (*Absurdity*) that he prevailed on the prestigious *Verein Berliner Künstler* to extend an invitation to the young Norwegian to exhibit in the new Round Room of the *Architektenhaus*. It was a double distinction, for it would mark both the opening of this attractive facility and the first time the association had sponsored a one-man show. It is impossible to explain how this unimaginative painter fifteen years Munch's senior and steeped in the rigidly conservative establishment of the Prussian capital happened to become Munch's first mentor abroad, except for the obvious fact that he was a much better critic than painter. At any rate, on 20 October 1892 the young Norwegian, with his entire retrospective as well as a few brand new canvases in the baggage car, set out for Berlin, hoping, as Strindberg had before him, for a more appreciative public in these much more sophisticated surroundings.

Strindberg's passing reference to "ett otacksamt fädernesland" on the eve of his departure in 1883 has its more elaborate parallel in one of Munch's newest works in the 1892 retrospective, the eerie *Aften på Karl Johansgate*—so different from the norm, even in Munchian terms, that it made critics and public question the artist's sanity. With this extraordinary canvas he may have had two specific, if unrelated, aims. First of all, through this strikingly new interpretation of a thoroughly familiar scene featured in several earlier works he may have wanted to proclaim an end to his Impressionist leanings, which up to that time had been rather pronounced. Secondly, he may have felt an urge to issue an indictment against his fellow citizens, those inflexible, unimaginative men and women whom Ibsen in *En folkefiende* (*An Enemy of the People*) had called "den kompakte majoritet ("the compact majority"), who had greeted all his efforts with hostile resistance or ridicule. Never has anyone by visual means so poignantly conveyed the meaning of the Ibsen phrase as Munch in *Aften på Karl Johansgate*, and this he accomplished without abandoning his primary purpose—to create a work of art. With a basic structure of acute diagonals—a row of houses, the street, the sidewalk—radiating from the center of the picture surface, he slices through the surging crowd, dissecting it by bringing some of its representatives up close, so that their vacuous stares are eye to eye with the viewer. And this spectral portrayal of randomly chosen individuals painted in glaring pigments contrasts sharply with the deep blue of the summer night, resulting in a color scheme so dissonant that it plunges the entire canvas into a shuddering representation of human conformity—against which one solitary individual moves without apparent concern.

Ever since the 1850s, but more specifically after the city had become the capital of the German Reich in 1871, Berlin had been a center of activity for young Scandinavians bent on widening their horizons by a stay abroad. Reflecting not so much a preference for Berlin over Paris or Rome, it was rather a natural gravitation toward a part of the Continent for which these artists and intellectuals were culturally and linguistically prepared. The serious student was attracted by the universities and music conservatories in Leipzig and Berlin. Among painters the migration to Germany had started out in the direction of Dresden, where the Norwegian Johan Christian Dahl was a professor of landscape art. Later Düsseldorf and Karlsruhe became popular, and finally Munich. But when all these young people from universities, conservatories, and academies had finished their formal education and wanted to sample a cosmopolitan life devoted to intellectual-creative activities, they often chose to begin their careers with an extended stay in the new German capital. Yet by the time Strindberg had embarked on his first extended journey abroad—to Grez and Paris in 1883—Berlin had already entered a period of temporary decline as a center for Scandinavians, so it was only natural that he would go elsewhere. More importantly, Strindberg was primarily Francophile in his leanings and in Grez and Paris groups of friends and supporters were eagerly waiting to welcome him. Munch too went first to France, convinced that the rigid German approach to art, which he felt had stifled the creative originality of his contemporaries, Krohg and Werenskjold among them, was far behind the times and that Paris was the only place where he personally would find it possible to grow and develop.

When it came to a second exile for these two they were both drawn to Berlin by special opportunities that beckoned: in Munch's case, the forthcoming exhibit; in Strindberg's, the recent Berlin success of two of his plays, the publication in German of several other works, and most of all the promising statements by his young countryman Ola Hansson, who wrote to Strindberg about theaters, admirers, and grand financial prospects. This was in the immediate aftermath of Strindberg's divorce from Siri von Essen, and he felt deeply in need of the support Hansson promised.

For a month or so after his arrival things seemed to be going well for him. Having settled in Friedrichshagen near the Hanssons, he had first paraphrased the name into Friedrichsruhe (Friedrich's Peace), expressing his satisfaction in a letter to a friend: "Är Du nöjd med din verld och går det dig efter önskan? Mig synes Ödet för stunden ha ledsnat på att förfölja."[17] Yet only a few days had passed when in a note to the Swedo-Finnish writer Adolf Paul he had changed the name of his place of residence, now calling it Friedrichshölle (Friedrich's Hell) not only because he was suffering a momentary hangover but because he was beginning to feel exploited by the Hanssons.

The opening of the Munch exhibition on 5 November 1892 marked not only a significant event in the Scandinavian community in Berlin but would later be recalled as crucial in the development of German art. For it led to the now famous Berlin Secession, which split the German capital's art community apart—not in support of or opposition to the works of Edvard Munch but in a drive by the progressives aimed at drawing a clear line of distinction between a liberal and a conservative, academic approach to painting. *Aftenposten*'s Berlin correspondent was really quite wrong when he gleefully reported back to Norway that Munch's pictures were hardly important enough to have set such passions in motion. Regardless of their relative merit at that time, it was their presence in Berlin and the controversy surrounding the closing of his exhibit that provided the spark that ignited an already explosive situation.

Strindberg, busy with his own publishing and theatrical projects— of primary concern was a proposed staging of *Fröken Julie* in Paris— and a hasty love affair with a young Norwegian woman, seems to have missed both the grand opening in the *Architektenhaus* and its sensational closing "in the name of decency and proper art" a week later, for none of this figures in his correspondence. And on 16 November, referring to a projected book on himself to be edited by Ola

Hansson, he suggests that Richard Bergh be asked to provide a suitable portrait—which implies that he was unaware of Munch's presence or at least as yet had not begun posing for him.

By the end of the month, anxious to extricate himself from his current love affair, Strindberg hurriedly left for Weimar, intending to continue to Dresden, possibly also to Vienna and Prague. He got no farther than Goethe's and Schiller's city, where he remained for two weeks, short of funds but initially enjoying himself all the same because of the appearance on the scene of the Tavaststjerna couple, he a Finnish poet and long-suffering Strindberg admirer, she a beautiful young actress whose favors Strindberg sought without the slightest consideration for the feelings of her doting husband. When the Tavaststjernas left, Weimar became unbearable; Strindberg felt confined to his hotel room "som i en tortyrkammare" and had to cable Berlin for help.[18] To his rescue came Adolf Paul with the Polish poet, musician, and art critic Stanislaus Przybyszewski. They succeeded in collecting enough money to bail him out of his Weimar hotel.

It must have been immediately after his return to Berlin, and most likely through Przybyszewski, whose professional interest must have kept him close to the current art controversy, that Strindberg and Munch finally met. Perhaps it was Przybyszewski too who suggested that Strindberg pose for a portrait. At any rate, a notice of 10 December in *Dagbladet*, an Oslo daily pursuing Munch's career with modest interest, reported that the painter had rented a studio in Berlin and was in the process of painting August Strindberg. By that time the Munch exhibit and its aftermath were no longer front-page news. Even so, Strindberg must have heard a great deal about it, first from the artist himself as he posed for him in his studio, secondly from his own friends and followers as he resumed his daily routines, part of which included extended stays in his favorite café, *Zum schwarzen Ferkel* (*The Black Piglet*). Here Strindberg presided over a court of avant-garde poets, painters, musicians, and others, and Munch quickly became one of the more prominent members of the coterie. As for the portrait, it must have been completed in record time, for it was ready to be included in his next Berlin exhibit. Norwegian sources give 27 December as the opening date of this event, while a Strindberg letter, dated 23 December, contains this triumphant note: "I dag öppnar Munch sin utställning ånyo för att slå nya slag för den Skandinaviska Renässansen."[19]

To call the combined contribution of the Scandinavian creative community in Berlin a Renaissance was not as presumptuous as it might seem. Hermann Sudermann, the distinguished German playwright, professed his indebtedness to the Scandinavians in an afterdinner speech a month later, declaring: "Vom Norden her kommt uns das Licht!" ("The light comes to us from the north!") And in the Ferkel circle were a great many, in addition to Strindberg and Munch, who contributed to that light. There was Holger Drachmann, Danish poet and painter, who was tall, blond, with chiseled features. And there were Gunnar Heiberg, Norwegian playwright and iconoclast, his countryman Knut Hamsun, whose *Sult* (*Hunger*) and *Mysterier* (*Mysteries*) had been received with equal enthusiasm in Scandinavia and Germany. Among the painters there were Christian Krohg and Severin Segelcke, Norwegians, both in the process of doing Strindberg's portrait, and the Finn, Axel Gallén-Kallela, who produced a particularly sensitive likeness of Munch. There were German participants in the group, the poets Richard Dehmel and Max Dauthendey, the writer and theater man Otto Erich Hartleben, two literary physicians, Carl Ludwig Schleich and Max Asch, and on rarer occasions the painter Hermann Schlittgen.

Munch's second Berlin exhibit, following the first by five weeks, during which the paintings had been shown in several art centers throughout the Reich, was mounted in a private gallery in the heart of the city, a huge Norwegian flag—without, however, the union insignia—marking the spot. The press gave reasonable coverage of the event; *Berliner Tageblatt* expressed its pleasure that the citizens had been given another chance to evaluate the controversial works and pointing out that a few new paintings had been added, among them a portrait of "dem norwegischen [sic] Dichter Strindberg."[20]

Jens Thiis, Norwegian art historian, in Berlin at the time and a frequent visitor to the exhibit, was standing in front of the Strindberg portrait one day when artist and model entered the room:

Det var Munch og Strindberg. Munch forestilte mig for ham. . . . På mig virket Strindberg avgjort sympatisk. Det var en viss stilig svensk grandezza over hans måte å føre sig på, som var nokså forskjellig fra Munchs umiddelbare norske vesen, men de to trivdes utmerket sammen og der var sikkert ikke liten idéutveksling mellem dem allerede fra denne første Berlinertid.[21]

A clear indication of Munch's respect for his fellow Scandinavian and his pride in having had him as a model is the fact that at this exhibit the Strindberg portrait was placed between his own favorite canvases, *Syk pike* and *Vår*. The portrait, now in Stockholm's Nationalmuseum, is a somewhat stylized yet powerful representation with head and torso emerging vividly from a warm background, suggesting an impetuous temperament and perhaps a touch of superiority. As for

Strindberg himself, he was far from pleased. "Jag ger sju i likheten," he is reported to have said. "Det får lov att vara ett stiliserat diktarporträtt! Som Goethes porträtter! Det borde Munch ha begripit!"[22]

It is likely that he looked askance at other pictures as well. After all, the exploitation of woman by man as implied in *Pubertet* and *Dagen derpå* would never have struck a consonant chord in him, and at that particular time his divorce and its aftermath had brought him into one of his most pronounced misogynist phases. On the other hand, it so happened that he too was painting just then and may have been scrutinizing Munch's canvases with greater interest and objectivity than would otherwise have been the case, recalling how he had once decided that to paint was to visualize one's own inner emotions. He could not have failed to respect and appreciate Munch's creative effort, for in the principal works on view all superficial attention to traditional realism had been eliminated in favor of the expressive intent. And Strindberg, hypersensitive and impressionable, must have experienced with Munch his profound grief in *Syk pike* and *Vår*. At the sight of *Kysset* (*The Kiss*) and *Aftenstemning*—one representing the sacrifice of the self on the altar of love, the other the inconstancy of the female heart—he may have felt both nostalgic regret and scornful resentment. And in the throbbing turbulence engulfing the solitary figure in *Fortvivelse* he may have been looking at a reflection of his own emotional wilderness.

The exchange of ideas between the two must have had its beginning in the difference between their respective points of view on women, Strindberg's as relentlessly negative as Munch's was compassionately positive. Although there is no reason to believe that they associated on any other than an equal level, it is nonetheless evident from a sudden change of tenor in Munch's works which of the two held sway. Only a few weeks following their initial meeting Munch wrote to his sister: "Udstillingen min slutter nu om noen dage, hvilket jeg er vel fornøiet med for du kan tænke jeg er kje av billedene mine."[23] It is, in fact, impossible to imagine any such thing, for so much a part of him were Munch's paintings that he felt dismembered when they were not within immediate reach. Therefore, this abrupt change of attitude must have been promoted by a radically revised frame of mind in regard to the validity of a key section of his artistic program, that dealing with the portrayal of the relationship between man and woman. Strindberg, older, more experienced and persuasive, may already at that stage have succeeded in enlisting Munch and his exceptional talent on the male side in the ongoing battle of the sexes.

The evolvement of Munch's thoughts on the painting now known as *Vampyren* (*The Vampire*) tends to bear this out. An ink sketch from 1889 showing a man kneeling before a woman, his head in her lap and her lips caressing his hair, seems to be its germinal idea. A version no longer extant, painted sometime in 1892, was exhibited in Munch's controversial Berlin show under the title *Erotisch*. The painting presently in the Munch Museum was completed in the spring of 1893 and shown in Berlin in December of that year; entitled *Liebe und Schmerz* (*Love and Pain*) and grouped with certain others under the collective designation *Liebe*, it suggests the beginning of the somewhat nebulous, never quite defined concept referred to as *Livsfrisen* (*The Frieze of Life*). It shows man prostrate at woman's breast, seeking simultaneously the protective warmth of the mother and the passionate fire of the lover, a dualism stressed and symbolized on the one hand in the all-consuming embrace under the flaming veil of her cascading hair, on the other by the distinct presence of an all-encompassing ovate mass suggestive of the womb.

In a written observation most likely dating from the time the ink sketch was made, Munch speaks of a need to press "sitt trætte hode mod en øm kvinnes bryst, ånde ind hendes duft og høre hendes bankende hjerteslag. . . . Da vilde hun ømt stryke hans hår."[24] But later, having readily adjusted to the prevailing misogynist interpretation of his works, in which the same painting had been seen as "a broken man, on his neck a biting vampire"[25]—Przybyszewski's Strindbergian description that led to the picture's current title—Munch recalls the same experience in an entirely different vein: "Og han lagde sitt hode mot hendes bryst, følte blodet bruse gjennem hendes årer. Han lyttet til hende hjerte. Og da han skjulte sitt ansikt i hendes bryst følte han to brennende leber mot sin nakke—det sendte en gysning gjennem ham."[26]

As Munch's own interpretation of this particular pre-Berlin subject changed, so his approach to subsequent topics of an erotic nature appears quite different once he had become part of Strindberg's entourage in Berlin. A chilling manifestation of this was found in his second major Berlin exhibit held in December of 1893. Among the pictures on view were some of the most pessimistic visions ever committed to the canvas—not allegorical extravaganzas but awesome visual commentaries relying on readily identifiable imagery rooted in basic experiences and in repressed human emotions laid bare: the ghastly, nearly monochrome *Feber* (*Fever*) recapitulating *Døden i sykeværelset* (*Death in the Sickroom*), only stripped of all but its vacuous horror; the nightmarish *Døden* (*Death*), a variation on Max Klinger's Böcklin-inspired *Der Tod und die Mutter* (*Death and the Mother*); the shudderingly Gothic *Døden og piken* (*Death and the Maiden*), with its revealing Symbolist frame of fetuses and sperms; and above all, the painting that more than any other would point the way toward twentieth-century Expressionism, the radically synthesized, vertiginously distorted, nearly audible canvas *Skriket* (*The Shriek*).

II

Following the premiere of a Sudermann play at Berlin's *Residenztheater* early in January 1893, a carriage brought a young woman to one of the city's most sophisticated neighborhoods, where she entered a brightly lighted home just as the hostess bid three gentlemen goodbye. One was the painter Hermann Schlittgen; the other, ". . . en mycket smärt man, en efeb, förandligad, blond, ett smalt, blekt ansikte med härliga blåa ögon, en som är blyg i sitt liv och som i sin konst vågar allt: Edvard Munch, målaren som jag hade velat träffa för länge sedan så gärna som jag ville leva." Yet the recognition of this much admired personality was completely overshadowed by the magic exerted upon the impressionable young woman by the presence of the third gentleman, half hidden behind the others: "En mörkgrå regnkrage har han över skuldrorna. Som en skrovlig grå klippa står han där. Stengrå är kappan, stengrått håret, som av grå sten är det mäktiga huvudet, grå irrande ögon, grå de ihåliga kinderna."[27]

The moonstruck hero-worshiper was Frida Uhl, sent to Berlin from Vienna as cultural correspondent for her father's conservative daily, *Wiener Zeitung*. That evening she was introduced to Strindberg twice and succeeded—so she claims—in changing his mind about leaving the party. Whatever did happen at this first encounter, there can be little doubt that Strindberg was flattered and intrigued by the interest this elegant young lady, twenty-three years his junior, showed in him. Yet there are indications that at the outset he intended to cultivate her only as an attractive friend, not as a lover, let alone a potential wife. Moreover, his thoughts of her as reported in *The Cloister*, the autobiographical novel based on his Berlin experiences, evoked the image of his own sister, consequently, "anything of an erotic nature— if such there had been—was eliminated, and his only memory was of a good female friend."[28]

This temporary sister fixation may have been prompted by his close association with Munch and his familiarity with the items in the Berlin exhibit, for among them were no less than six major works featuring Munch's sisters, one of them, a full-length portrait of Inger at age twenty-one, showing a taut, apprehensive figure not unlike that in *Pubertet*. Through such persistent preoccupation with the physical features of the one in his family with whom he had the closest relationship, Munch—as perhaps also Strindberg—seems to have built up a shield against erotic involvements that would, in his view, lead inevitably to guilt and shame.

Despite a conscious or subconscious effort to remain aloof, however, both Munch and Strindberg experienced during those early months of 1893, parallel with Strindberg's infatuation with Frida Uhl, a strange relationship with one and the same woman, Dagny Juell, whose presence in their midst threatened not only the tenuous equilibrium of these two but of other members of the *Ferkel* group as well.

Dagny Juell—bold, progressive, and devastatingly attractive—was a product not only of the prevailing drive for women's emancipation but also of the broader quest for individual freedom expressed in the unorthodox lifestyles of intellectual-artistic groups gathering in various European centers at that time, such as the Bohêmes in Oslo to which Munch had belonged, and Strindberg's own circle in Berlin.

Born and raised in an upper middle-class family in provincial Kongsvinger in Norway, she had come to Germany to prepare for a career as a concert pianist but was equally at home in literature and the visual arts. She must have found it easy as well as challenging to create a place for herself within the group gathering at *Zum schwarzen Ferkel*—easy because of her own uninhibited social manner, challenging because so many of these men, professed radicals, still maintained a traditional, reactionary view on the position of women. To Strindberg, their chief spokesman, the emancipation movement posed the ominous threat of the wholesale suppression of the male sex and the creation of a ruling female class of androgynes. This specter, together with composite feelings of guilt and his ultimate rejection by Dagny, may well account for his vicious attacks on this otherwise so greatly admired woman. These began in his correspondence immediately following the termination of the relationship and were kept up with passionate vengeance for more than a year. In letter after letter he expounds on her flagrant promiscuity, writing to people as widely apart on this issue as the young Swedish scientist Bengt Lidforrs, who was himself deeply in love with Dagny, and Georg Brandes, who, having been totally unaware of her existence and never expressing the slightest interest in Strindberg's erotic escapades, had learned that this allegedly insatiable woman had allowed herself to have "fyra folkslag öfver sig på trettio dagar," Sweden having been ably represented by Strindberg himself, who had simply done his patriotic duty and retired from the field.[29]

In the autobiographical novel *The Cloister* (the title is derived from the original name of *Zum schwarzen Ferkel*), based on his Berlin experiences but written five years after the facts, Dagny appears as Aspasia —named for a Greek courtesan—and Munch as The Danish Painter. It is reported that The Danish Painter had deliberately stayed away from their gathering place because he was entertaining a young lady from Norway whom he feared to bring within sight of The Swede, Strindberg. However, when learning of The Swede's imminent engagement to a distinguished Austrian lady—Frida Uhl—he considered the danger past and brought the visitor around. The Swede, contrary to expectation, lavished upon the newcomer all the pent-up passion the formal circumstances of his courtship had compelled him to repress, and the young Norwegian, promptly abandoning her long-time friend, submitted to the bold Swede.

Transposing these events from fiction to facts, we learn from Strindberg's correspondence that his rapidly growing passion was accompanied by a steadily growing feeling of guilt at the thought of Frida, who had gone to Vienna to obtain her father's permission to marry. Deeply disturbed by his own deceit he wrote: "Komme her und hüte mich . . . sonst ist Alles verkehrt. Böses Gewissen, schlechte Notizen von Stockholm, Unruhe treiben mich in das Schwarze Ferkel." A confession followed (in his next letter): "Ich habe Angst for mir! Ich habe so viele Verbrechen diesen letzen Tage, seitdem Du verreist bist. . . ."[30] In this state of mind he began to look at the "other woman" through eyes dimmed by a hatred generated by his own guilt and found her "ugly and badly dressed, and there were moments when the idea that he might be taken for her wooer made him feel ashamed."[31]

Strindberg's portrayal of Munch, The Danish Painter, as a rejected lover is difficult to accept in light of Munch's paintings and personal notes from that period. To be sure, the *Sjalusi* (*Jealousy*) series is rooted in his Berlin experiences, but the triangle that is represented, invariably showing Dagny and the unmistakable Przybyszewski, her future husband, with his pointed beard and drooping mustache, never includes a third person with iconographic features resembling those Munch applied when portraying himself. They are closer to those of his friend Jappe Nilsen, who found Dagny impressively regal and "achingly desirable,"[32] or the young Bengt Lidforrs, the Swedish scientist who had met her in Lund and followed her to Berlin in the hope of restoring their relationship, only to find himself totally upstaged by Strindberg.

As for Munch himself, he showed throughout his life that his art towered above all other considerations. Therefore, although no doubt happy to welcome Dagny to Berlin, he had no intention of cultivating a friendship that would interfere with his creative activities. Consequently, he may have kept her "to himself" only for as long as he needed the kind of intimacy and inspiration the situation provided, and then, deliberately and by no means fearfully, brought her to his friends at the *Ferkel*. This is not to say that Dagny Juell's role in Munch's life was not important. On the contrary, she is the only woman whose influence is directly and repeatedly reflected in his significant works of the 1890s, most dramatically in the series conceived already in the 1880s but not begun in earnest until the summer of 1892, when he first met the mature Dagny—the so-called *Livsfrisen*.

Among the many direct and imagined visions of her is the one his most recent biographer has called his "Apotheosis of Woman,"[33] *Madonna*, completed in 1893. Originally it is a painting antithetical to the Strindbergian misogynist point of view. Its consummate quality of transfigured beauty speaks movingly of man's adoration of woman: "En Madonnas bleke skjønnhet. Hun oplever det øieblikk da nytt liv bruser gjennem henne, når kjeden knyttes fra tusener av år tilbake. Liv fødes for å fødes påny og for å dø. . . ."[34] Also from 1893, but of earlier origin, is a preparatory study for *Madonna*, a painting entitled *Hendene* (*The Hands*). This work, more programmatic and hence much less subtle, shows Dagny upright, naked, and haughtily challenging, surrounded by an arabesque of hands greedily reaching for her femininity.

It has been pointed out that *Pubertet* and *Dagen derpå*, two of Munch's most important paintings, were destroyed in a fire in 1890 but repainted before the Berlin exhibit. Except for a passing reference to the first versions in a press notice of the Norwegian State Exhibition in 1886, there exists no contemporary description of compositional details or features of the women portrayed. Yet it is highly unlikely that facial characteristics in the first versions had much in common with those in the 1892 replicas, for a careful scrutiny of the latter clearly reveals that the faces are those of Dagny as shown in *Hendene*, *Madonna*, and in the formal portrait Munch painted in 1893.

It is the latter portrait, incidentally, that gives us a clue to Strindberg's less biased opinion of Dagny. For when asked by Frida to describe this particular painting that he had just seen in Munch's studio he seemed suddenly reignited by the model's unique personality: "Modernaste typ, späd och fin, en andlig förförerska mer än en kroppslig. En själsvampyr med längtan efter det högre och full av den finaste differentiering. . . . Hennes ansikte är egendomligt, aristokratiskt, sympatiskt livfullt."[35] Such a characterization appears far more valid than the vindictive picture drawn of Dagny in *The Cloister* and the correspondence, and it is very much in tune with Frida Uhl's own impression of her when for an instant she stood face to face with the controversial woman: "En vacker figur; lång och smärt. Klädd i förnämt färglöst grått. Lockigt blond hår över ögonbrynen. Där nedanför springer en fin grekisk näsa fram. Läpparna äro smala och rörliga, tänderna vita."

Though certainly justified in her particular situation in disliking and denouncing Dagny, her recent rival, and undoubtedly preconditioned toward such a reaction by Strindberg, Frida, recalling the meeting, chose instead to look deeper, beyond the immediate issue, and found herself in a state of puzzled admiration and secret compassion: "Ur den färglösa sommarklänningen har en mörk skugga krupit ut över oss, den tynger honom som en mara, och jag kan inte jaga bort den.... Jag kan inte annat än undra över vrångbilden av kvinnan, som i verkligheten är så annorlunda mot hur mannen ser henne."[36]

More than a year later, when married to Frida, Strindberg had occasion to return to Berlin very briefly when he spent an evening at a gathering in the home of the newly married Przybyszewskis. He must have shared the experience with Frida, for it is only from her we know of his reaction. This time the mellowness of her attitude toward Dagny has given way to bitter satire:

Aspasias salong bestod visserligen bara av ett enda hyrt rum, som var tämligen fattigt möblerat men förstugan fylldes av Przybyszewskis ståtliga bibliotek. Det fanns bara ett bord, och mittemot det stodo husets båda stolar under lampan, vilken bar en urblekt röd skärm. Dessa stolar voro egentligen ur räkningen, emedan de äldsta vännerna i huset, Munch och Lidforss, i allmänhet lade beslag på dem, drickande och tysta. . . .
Strindberg skulle helst med våld velat befria Munch, som han högaktade, och den dåraktige polacken, som alltmer drunknade i alkohol, och den ännu dåraktigare Bengt Lidforss ur denna luft. Men de voro hemfallna åt kärleken.[37]

This appears to be the last time the Przybyszewskis and Strindberg met face to face, and obviously it was not a pleasant occasion. In his year of absence Berlin had definitely lost its previous charm. The *Ferkel* group had dissolved and been replaced by a somewhat different coterie gathering in Dagny's salon. Strindberg felt ignored. "Ich habe nicht angenehme Tage allein hier und in Noth,"[38] he wrote to Frida the day after his arrival.

This meeting with certain members of his old group, in particular the Przybyszewskis, Munch, and Lidforss, may also have reawakened his old guilt feeling, and it is in that spirit that most future references to his "högaktade" ("esteemed") friend, his "själsvampyr" ("vampire of the soul"), and her husband are made. Within that context all three would be playing key roles in his autobiographical novel *Inferno*, based on his stay in Paris in the mid-1890s, a period more difficult than any he had previously experienced and in the course of which he learned to say with Jeremiah: "I have forgotten what happiness was."

When Munch arrived in Paris at the end of February 1896 and took a studio in Rue de Santé, Strindberg had just moved into the hotel that would figure so prominently in *Inferno*, the dismal Orfila in Montparnasse. Munch makes no mention of a first meeting between them, but the British composer Frederick Delius in his memoirs, written twenty-five years later, seems to take credit for bringing them together again: "Edvard Munch had just arrived in Paris and came to see me in my flat in Rue Ducouedic. I asked him to join me for a visit to Strindberg. We found him pouring over his retorts, stirring strange evil-smelling liquids, and after chattering for five or ten minutes we left in a most friendly manner."[39]

Considering that Munch's friendship with Strindberg was already well established and that there is no evidence to suggest that there had been a break in it, this version of their first Paris meeting seems less convincing than Strindberg's in *Inferno*, where Munch, The Danish Painter, appears at a time when Strindberg was beginning to experience the world as a vale of tears. It was springtime, but as in Munch's painting of that title the regenerative season had no effect on the prevailing mood: "Jag är bedrövad till döden. . . . Min levnad förrinner och ålderdomen nalkas . . . höst inne, vår därute."[40]

Munch's own spirits were rather low just then, for his only brother, Andreas, had succumbed to pneumonia a few weeks earlier. Had Strindberg known this, he might not have drawn such negative conclusions from their first accidental meeting: "Denne man, som förr stått på vänskaplig fot med mig, hade kommit till Paris för sex veckor sedan, och då jag mötte honom på gatan hade han hälsat på ett främmande, nästan ovänligt sätt. Antagligen för att överskyla detta besökte han mig dagen därpå och inbjöd mig till sin ateljé, i det han sade mig artigheter alltför granna för att icke kvarlämna intrycket av en falsk vän."[41] Munch, by nature shy and deeply burdened by the new tragedy in his family, may have wanted to spend some time by himself. Moreover, aware of Strindberg's strained circumstances he may have decided not to impose himself upon him. Then, having reacted with understandable embarassment at their unexpected encounter in the street, he was anxious to make amends and called on Strindberg the very next day.

Much later, in a letter dated July, Munch mentions that he has finished a lithograph of Strindberg, implying that the two must have been seeing each other with some regularity prior to that. As

Stringberg approached his mental crisis, however, his association with Munch, a constant reminder of Berlin and of Dagny and Przybyszewski, the latter now his principal adversary, became in his mind an ever-present threat. To Munch, who relished and needed the artistic opportunities offered in Paris, a steady contact with Strindberg seemed no longer as inspiring as it had once been. "Jeg er av og til med Strindberg der nu er nokså gammel," ("Every now and then I see Strindberg, who is rather old now,") he says in a letter. The lithograph is the now famous arabesqued portrait with the subject's name misspelled "Stindberg." Widely acknowledged to be the most meaningful visual interpretation of the controversial genius, it is certainly a far more appropriate *diktarporträtt* than the Goethe-like interpretation Strindberg had his heart set on when first posing for Munch in Berlin three years earlier.

The preceding year Munch had pictured himself in a lithograph featuring a skeletal arm extending across the lower edge of the print, thereby stressing his own peculiar preoccupation with death. He had also portrayed Przybyszewski with a similar skeletal addendum, inspired, perhaps, by the Pole's principal work, *Totenmesse* (*Mass of the Dead*). It is that portrait that plays such an important role in Strindberg's approaching Inferno crisis: "I danskens ateljé . . . stå vi och betrakta ett porträtt af Popoffsky [Przybyszewski], målat för två år sedan. Det är endast huvudet, med en sky nedanför, och därunder ett par korslagda benknotor som på gravskrifter. Det avskurna huvudet kommer oss att rysa, och den dröm jag hade den 14 maj dyker upp för mig likt ett spöke."[42] This eerie picture, as well as Munch's self-portrait, have much in common with the Strindberg lithograph. The apparently peripheral commentaries in all three cases constitute significant interpretative attempts on the part of the artist.

That the Strindberg portrait and its serpentine frame have been conceived of as a single composition is clearly borne out by the way the principal subject, posed slightly to the left of the center, seems drawn toward the elongated nude of the frame to provide complete pictorial balance. The woman's hair rising as through the effect of magnetic currents is not a new feature in Munch's iconography, for it occurs already in paintings completed in 1893, among them *Vampyren*, *Sjalusi*, and *Løsrivelse* (*Separation*). Rather than being an influence from William Blake, as has been suggested,[43] this notion may derive from Strindberg himself and his pseudo-scientific investigations into the phenomenon of energy, physical and psychic, which so occupied him both in Berlin and in Paris. In *Inferno*, walking between two people, the main character experiences a feeling of discomfort, as of a thread between them. In the Strindberg portrait this feeling has been made much more drastic, for there it is no longer a question of a thread between two people, but of one of them, woman, enclosing man within her irresistible power.

Although this juxtaposition of the male and the female no doubt constitutes a deeply sincere attempt at interpretative portraiture, the artist's conspicuous misspelling of his model's name may be an example of Munch's relatively infrequent use of satire, perhaps a commentary similar to the remark, "Strindberg der nu er nokså gammel." It is possible, though only remotely, that this interesting detail may have come about accidentally. But if so, why was it not corrected as soon as the first proof appeared? Because this did not happen, the omission of the letter r in the name, making it read "Stindberg," calls for another explanation.

It happened that the portrait was in the making simultaneously with a lithograph commissioned by Lugné-Poë in preparation for the Parisian premiere of *Peer Gynt*. Munch, deeply engrossed in Ibsen's strident dramatic poem, could easily have detected something vaguely familiar in Peer's musing on the inscrutable Memnon statue:

> Han, Memnon, faldt det mig bagefter ind,
> lignet de såkaldte Dovregubber,
> slig som han sad der stiv og stind.
> med enden plantet på søjlestubber.[44]

In that staid, self-centered—*stind*—Egyptian colossus that sings only when caressed in a certain way by the rays of the sun, Munch may have seen an image of the temporarily silent poet posing for him that early summer.

In letters to friends and associates Strindberg bemoans his cruel destiny, saying in one letter: "Mig äro alla djeflar efter som vanligt och förfölja."[45] The principal figures in this persecution are Popoffsky— the novel's name for Przybyszewski—and Przybyszewski's closest friend, Edvard Munch, to whom Strindberg confides that "ryssens hat gör ont i mig likasom strömmen från en elektricitetsmaskin."[46] Rumors in Paris had it that Popoffsky had been arrested in Berlin, suspected of having murdered his common-law wife and two children. "Hans vän dansken börjar bestrida sannolikheten av att han begått brottet, åberopande att rannsakningen icke har bestyrkt anklagelsen. . . ." And finally, "Ryssen har släppts fri ur fängslet av brist på bevis; hans vän dansken har blivit min fiende."[47]

Munch's commentaries follow in a letter home early in August: "Strindberg er reist hjem til Sverige—han er vist under lægebehandling for sindsygdom—han havde så mange rare ideer—lavet guld, og fandt ud at jorden var flad og at stjernene var huller i himmelvælvingen. Han havde forfölgelsesmani og troede engang at jeg vilde forgive ham med gas."[48] A prelude to this observation by Munch may be found in a short note to him from Strindberg, dated 19 July: "Sist jag såg Dig, tyckte jag du såg ut som en mördare—eller åtminstone en handtlangare."[49]

III

Two years elapsed between this and the next and final contact between the two. Indirectly and through an intermediary it came about in June of 1898 when Emil Schering, editor of the avant-garde periodical *Quickborn*, suggested in a letter to Strindberg the publication of a special issue devoted to Strindberg's writings illustrated by Munch. He must have discussed the matter with Munch in advance and received his promise to participate—Munch perhaps hoping in this way to bring about a reconciliation with his old friend. Strindberg, on the other hand, had serious misgivings: "Hvad Munch beträffar, som är min fiende, erfar jag en olust att gå tillsammans med honom, i synnerhet som jag är säker han ej skall försumma sticka mig med en förgiftad knif."[50]

Nevertheless, the issue did become a reality and contained prose pieces, some poems, and a one-act drama by Strindberg. Munch's contribution was entirely without poisonous stabs and featured a series of pictures reflecting the text material only in the most general way. An exception was a sketch illustrating a prose piece entitled "Auf zur Sonne" ("Up to the Sun"), where Munch in an art nouveau manner showers a range of Alpine peaks with a flood of sunshine.

Although he went so far as to include the lithographed Strindberg portrait without its telling arabesque and misspelled name, Munch failed to bring about the hoped-for reconciliation. Quite the contrary. Strindberg's reaction implied an intensification of the feeling of hostility he had developed toward the artist he had once proudly hailed as a key figure in the "Scandinavian Renaissance": "Sänder imorgon Munchs sista rysliga mästerverk, dem jag föraktar. På sju år har han inte fått en ny intention, inte ens upptäckt ett nytt föremål att karrikeras."[51]

As for Munch, he apparently never ceased to admire Strindberg. "Når talen falt på Strindberg," Inger Alver Gløersen recalls, "—og det var ikke så sjelden—ble Munchs ansikt så preget av lidelse, at det var lett å skjønne, tapet av Strindbergs omgang var av de store sorger livet gave ham."[52] A similar impression is conveyed by Torsten Svedfelt. Recounting a conversation with Munch in the late 1930s, he felt particularly moved by the artist's reminiscences about his association with Strindberg. Svedfelt remembered that there was no trace of animosity or betrayal in Munch's recollection, though perhaps a nostalgic puzzlement quickly shrugged off by a decisive, "Han var allikevel et storartet menneske."[53]

Although the unique friendship between these two extraordinary members of the Scandinavian creative community in the 1890s extended over a mere four years, with the actual direct contact between them limited to a few troubled months in Berlin and Paris, its effect is clearly reflected by many of the most significant works of each artist. This is primarily true of those produced during and immediately following their months together, but also in efforts of much later date. Strindberg's autobiographical writings, in which this often problematic relationship plays a considerable role, led to dramas so different they were destined to revitalize that entire medium of expression: *Till Damaskus* (*To Damascus*)—all three parts—and *Ett drömspel* (*A Dream Play*). A step beyond these are his highly concentrated, visually synthesized Chamber Plays, one of which (*Spöksonaten* [*The Ghost Sonata*])—despite its cadence of a tremulous harp tune lingering through a vision of Böcklin's otherwordly *Toteninsel*—rings dissonantly as an echo of the decadence, sickness, and death so agonizingly woven into Munch's early canvases.

On Munch's side the Strindberg spirit is evident in a great many of his post-1892 works, most palpably in the *Sjalusi* series, *Marats død* (*The Death of Marat*) and *Døden og piken* (*Death and the Maiden*) with their unmistakable misogynist messages, but also in *Kvinnen i tre stadier* (*Woman in Three Stages*), *Livsdansen* (*The Dance of Life*) and the recapitulation of these and previous subjects in their starkly synthesized graphic versions—Munch's equivalent of Strindberg's Chamber Plays—all profoundly pessimistic in their representation of the human condition. On the opposite side of the coin, however, is the possibility that Munch's monumental manifestation of his slowly, painfully gained belief in a positive force behind all human striving, his university mural *Soloppgang* (*The Rising Sun*), may have been inspired by Strindberg's prose piece in *Quickborn*, "Auf zur Sonne."

It is perhaps disturbing that Strindberg's last published words on Munch are those referring to him as a murderer, an enemy, and an artist whose works he despises. Yet these words, conceived in frustration and anger, should, of course, not be taken at face value. "Man går jorden rundt, och kommer igen till samma punkt," Strindberg wrote to Carl Larsson, who was also destined to become a victim of his countryman's wrath. "Men man är icke densamme, ty man har sett så mycket på vägen, och det är det bästa!"[54]

A similar mellowing of spirit is implied in a partly documented exchange between our two principal subjects, in all likelihood having taken place on the occasion of Strindberg's sixtieth birthday. Munch must have sent a congratulatory greeting of which no record exists. However, an inconspicuous postcard in the archives of the Munch Museum, dated January 1909, contains a single word above Strindberg's signature: "Tack" ("Thank you").

Notes

1. *August Strindbergs brev*, ed. Torsten Eklund (Stockholm: Bonniers, 1948–74), 3: 274 (hereafter *Strindbergs brev*). ". . . an ungrateful fatherland."
2. *Edvard Munchs brev* (Oslo, Tanum, 1949), p. 56 (hereafter *Munchs brev*).
3. *Strindbergs brev*, 3: 296. "Besides, I will move through Stockholm like a streak and disappear without a trace."
4. Although Munch found it difficult to acknowledge his indebtedness to Krohg, the evidence of such influence is very obvious in Munch's early work.
5. August Strindberg, *Samlade Skrifter*, ed. John Landquist (Stockholm: Bonniers, 1912–20), 13: 135 (hereafter *SS*). "I see law breakers and lackeys / crowd your sidewalks / while you, the master / wearily tramp / the cobblestoned streets, / but nowhere do I see / your great men / forced into exile, / men, great enough to have been sufficient / even for us immense Swedes."
6. A play, *Fra den fri kjaerligheds by*, exists in manuscript in the Munch Museum archives.
7. Rolf Stenersen, *Edvard Munch: Close-up of a Genius* (Oslo: Gyldendal, 1969), p. 25.
8. *SS*, 19: 9. "One should paint one's inner emotions and not keep copying sticks and stones that in themselves are insignificant and could attain proper meaning only by passing through and being molded by the individual's perception."
9. Document in the Munch Museum archives: "It should no longer be a question of interiors, people reading and women knitting. It should be living human beings who breathe and feel, suffer and love."
10. *SS*, 19: 17. ". . . people occupied with art."
11. Ibid., 24: 224. "But nature, with which he had always sought to communicate, now appeared dead to him, for the intermediary, man, was missing. The sea, which he worshiped and had sought as the only grand feature in his paltry country with its frugal, trivial summer cottage landscapes, now began to seem confining in the same degree that his own self seemed to expand. This blue, turpentine-green, gray circle closed in on him like a prison compound, and the monotonous little landscape evoked the same anguish as that of a prison cell with its total lack of new impressions."
12. Göran Söderström, *Strindberg och bildkonsten* (Stockholm: Forum, 1972) and Torsten Måtte Schmidt, ed., *Strindbergs måleri* (Malmö, Alhems förlag, 1972).
13. *Strindbergs måleri*, p. 14. "Here we do not find ourselves in the history of modern painting but in that microcosm that bears the name Strindberg. Strindberg's genius cannot be compared to anything else any more than his appearance or his destiny can. The moment came, then, when this singular Strindberg felt the need to paint. That is to say, he felt that in painting he had at his disposal another means whereby he might express his own inalienable personality."
14. Söderström, p. 181. "I'm almost ready to believe that that rascal Strindberg, when putting these small 'studies' in gold frames and hoisting them up for exhibit as paintings, did so with only one purpose in mind: to poke fun at the public and see how far it can tolerate 'cold steel' when it comes to art. If I exclude the piece entitled 'Calm Ocean,' which actually shows a flicker of talent in its master, I dare anyone to tell me what the other canvases represent—if one removed the title cards. Whether 'Snow-

storm at Sea' is meant to be a dirty sheet hanging up to dry or a new method of painting barn doors is impossible to tell. Just as it is whether 'Pack Ice' is a plateful of margarine sandwiches or a platter of calf's feet with brain sauce. 'Sailing Mark' might as well be an old butter churn ready for donation to the Nordic Museum, whereas 'Storm Mark' might be a still life based on a motif from the storage shed of the department of sanitation."

15. *Aftenposten*, 9 October 1892. "He paints his notorious yellow boat . . . now placing in the foreground something that most closely resembles hams or blood sausages—a veritable butcher shop! He paints with bloody fingers—and this he calls 'Evening Mood!' "

16. Ibid. ". . . the monstrous achievements which have been made by the two above-mentioned champions of the most modern field of art. . . . At most these two exhibits have had no other effect than to set their laughter muscles in motion. On the other hand, those have not been wanting who have taken all this seriously and have solemnly declared themselves to have made sense of this horrendous absurdity of 'the art of the future.' Of course. There is not a beauty or a truth in this world that cannot be turned into its own caricature. And there is no craziness or inanity in the world that some fool or other will not decide to admire."

17. *Strindbergs brev*, 9: 76. "Are you satisfied with your world and does it go according to your wishes? Destiny, for the moment, seems to have wearied of persecuting me."

18. Ibid., p. 95. ". . . as in a torture chamber."

19. Ibid., p. 104. "Today Munch opens his exhibit once more to strike a blow for the Scandinavian Renaissance."

20. Jens Thiis, *Edvard Munch og hans samtid* (Oslo: Gyldendal, 1933), p. 205.

21. Ibid. "It was Munch and Strindberg. Munch introduced me to him. . . . On me he made a very favorable impression. There was a certain grandiosely Swedish stylishness about him, so different from Munch's straight-foward Norwegian ways, but the two seemed to get along well together, and already during this first period in Berlin there must have been quite an exchange of ideas between them."

22. Adolf Paul, *Min Strindbergsbok* (Stockholm: Norstedt, 1930), p. 52. "I don't give a damn about the likeness. . . . It was supposed to have been a stylized portrait of a poet! Like those of Goethe! Munch ought to have known as much!"

23. *Munchs brev*, p. 124. "My exhibit closes in a few days, which pleases me, for you can imagine how tired I am of my pictures."

24. Munch Museum archives. ". . . his head against a gentle woman's breast, inhale her aroma and listen to her beating heart . . . Then she would tenderly stroke his hair."

25. Stanislaus Przybyszewski, *Erinnerungen an das literarische Berlin* (Munich: Winkler, 1965), p. 225.

26. Munch Museum archives. "And he put his head against her breast, felt the blood surge through her veins. He listened to her heart. And when he buried his face in her bosom he felt two burning lips against his neck—it made him shudder."

27. Frida Strindberg, *Strindberg och hans andra hustru*, 1 (Stockholm: Bonniers, 1933), 21. ". . . an elegant man, spirited, blond, a narrow, pale face with wonderful eyes, one who is shy in his daily life but in his art dares all: Edvard Munch, whom I long ago had wanted to meet as ardently as I want to live." "A dark rain cape over his shoulders. Like a huge gray rock does he stand there. Stone gray is his cape, stone gray the hair. As though chiseled from gray stone is his powerful head, gray and searching eyes, gray his hollow cheeks."

28. August Strindberg, *The Cloister*, ed C. G. Bjurström, translated and with commentary and notes by Mary Sandbach (New York: Hill and Wang, 1969), p. 33. Due to the inaccessibility of the original, which is in reality a composite of two separate manuscripts, necessity dictates that this text be cited in translation.

29. *Strindbergs brev*, 10: 107–108. ". . . four nationalities over her in thirty days."
30. Ibid., 9: 153–54. "Come and protect me . . . otherwise everything is wrong. A bad conscience, poor notices from Stockholm, and restlessness drive me to *Zum schwarzen Ferkel*. . . . I am afraid of myself. I have done so much wrong these last days since you have been gone. . . ."
31. *The Cloister*, p. 47.
32. Thiis, p. 211.
33. Ragna Stang, *Edvard Munch, mennesket og kunstneren* (Oslo: Aschehoug, 1979), p. 109.
34. Munch Museum archives. "The pale beauty of a Madonna. She is experiencing the moment when new life rushes through her, when the link is tied from thousands of years in the past. Life is born to be born anew and to die. . . ."
35. Frida Strindberg, 1: 181. "A most modern type, delicate and refined, a spiritual rather than a physical seducer. A vampire of the soul striving for higher things and full of the finest differentiations. . . . Her face is unique, aristocratic, sympathetically alive."
36. Ibid., 1: 316, 318. "A beautiful figure. Tall and sophisticated. Dressed in dignified colorless gray. Curly blond hair above her brows. Down below a fine grecian nose. Her lips are narrow and sensual, her teeth white." "Out of her colorless summer outfit a dark shadow has fallen upon us. It weighs him down like a nightmare, and I cannot chase it away. I cannot help wondering about the reverse side of the picture of this woman, who in reality seems so different from the way man sees her."
37. Ibid., 2: 203. "Aspasia's salon consisted of only one single rented room, rather poorly furnished but with the entry full of Przybyszewski's stately library. There was only one table, and by it stood the salon's only two chairs under a lamp with a faded red shade. Actually, the chairs were out of circulation, for they were permanently occupied by the oldest friends of the house, Munch and Lidforss, who sat there in silence, drinking. . . . Strindberg would have liked to rescue Munch, whom he respected highly, and the crazy Pole, who was about to drown in alcohol, and the even more crazy Bengt Lidforss—take them out of this atmosphere. But they were addicted to love."
38. *Strindbergs brev*, 10: 39. "I am not having very pleasant days here, alone and in need."
39. John Bolton Smith, "Edvard Munch and Frederick Delius," *Kunst og Kultur*, 48, No. 3, p. 140.
40. *SS*, 28: 63. "I am sorrowful unto death. . . . My life withers away and old age approaches . . . autumn within, springtime without."
41. Ibid., p. 65. "This man, before on friendly terms with me, had arrived in Paris six weeks ago, and when I had met him in the street he greeted me in a strange, nearly unfriendly manner. Perhaps to compensate for this, he visited me the day after and invited me to his studio, while saying niceties too shallow not to leave the impression of a false friend."
42. Ibid., p. 76. "In the studio of the Dane . . . we are looking at a portrait of Popoffsky painted two years earlier. It is only the head with a cloud beneath, and under that a pair of crossed bones as on gravestones. The decapitated head makes us shudder, and the dream I had on 14 May comes back to haunt me like a ghost."
43. Gösta Svenaeus, "Strindberg och Munch i Inferno," *Kunst og Kultur* 50: 1–28.
44. *Peer Gynt*, Act IV, Scene XII, Archer translation. "That Memnon, it afterward crossed my mind, / Was like the Old Man of the Dovre, so called, / Just as he sat there, stiff and stark, / Planted on end on the stumps of pillars."
45. *Strindbergs brev*, 11: 227. "As usual, all devils are out to persecute me."
46. *SS*, 28: 77. "The Russian's hatred hurts me like currents from an electric generator."
47. Ibid., p. 78. "His friend the Dane begins to question whether he has committed

the crime, basing it on the fact that the search did not strengthen the indictment. . . . The Russian has been freed from his prison for lack of evidence; his friend the Dane has become my enemy."

48. *Munchs brev*, p. 160. "Strindberg has returned to Sweden—he is supposed to be under treatment for insanity—he had so many strange ideas—made gold and found out the earth was flat and that the stars were holes in the firmament. He had a persecution complex and believed at one time that I was going to poison him."

49. *Strindbergs brev*, 11: 277. "The last time I saw you, I thought you looked like a murderer—or at least his helper."

50. Ibid., 12: 319. "As for Munch, who is my enemy, I feel unwilling to cooperate with him, in particular because I am certain he will not miss an opportunity of sticking me with a poisoned knife."

51. Ibid., 13: 86. "Will send you tomorrow Munch's latest masterpieces, which I despise. In seven years, he has not had a new idea, has not even discovered anything new to caricature."

52. Inger Alver Gløersen, *Den Munch jeg møtte* (Oslo: Gyldendal, 1965), p. 91. "When the talk came around to Strindberg—which was not infrequently—Munch's face became so marked by suffering, that it was easy to tell that the loss of Strindberg's companionship was one of the greatest sorrows that life had dealt him."

53. Torsten Svedfeldt, "Strindberg, Munch, och *Quickborn*," *Bokvännen*, 24 (1969), 51–56. "He was, in any event, a great man."

54. *Strindbergs brev*, 14: 341. "One travels around the world and returns to the same point. But one is not the same, for one has seen so much on the way, and that is the best of it."

Strindberg and Hamsun
Harald Næss

The articles contained in *En bok om Strindberg* (*A Book about Strindberg*) —which was finally printed in 1894 in Karlstad after no reputable publisher would touch it—were not particularly up to date. Justin M'Carthy's original article in the *Fortnightly Review*, the first English presentation of the subject according to *Poole's Index*, was from 1892; Arne Garborg's was written in 1891; and Knut Hamsun's in 1889. Actually Hamsun's contribution was based upon a still older article published in 1888 in the journal *America* (Chicago), making it the first treatment of Strindberg in the English language. Whereas Garborg concentrated his discussion on *I havsbandet* (*By the Open Sea*) (1890), and M'Carthy on *Fröken Julie* (*Miss Julie*) (1888), Hamsun's analysis was based on *Sömngångarnätter* (*Sleepwalking Nights*) (1884) and other early works. The readers were warned of its timeworn quality already in the title, "Et Overblik. Skrevet for mange Aar siden" ("A Survey. Written Many Years Ago").

Tore Hamsun and other biographers tell us that Hamsun lectured on Strindberg as early as 1881, during his time as a road worker at Toten, Norway.[1] As Olaf Øyslebø has shown, the date is wrong, and there is little likelihood that Hamsun knew Strindberg before his first stay in America from 1882 until 1884.[2] At that time he lectured on a number of subjects, including literary figures like Ibsen and Bjørnson, but it is not reported that he showed any interest in Strindberg.[3] It is reasonable to think, though, that Hamsun made the acquaintance of the Swedish dramatist during and immediately after his first America years: not only do we know that Kristofer Janson, in whose house Hamsun lived, had several works by Strindberg in his library, but Hamsun subscribed to *Nyt Tidsskrift*, in which Strindberg was introduced to a Norwegian audience in two articles by Artur Bendixson and Georg Nordensvan in the winter of 1884–85.[4] It must have been during his stay in Norway from 1885 until 1886, then, that Hamsun first lectured on Strindberg. The place was indeed Toten (Gjøvik), the time was Saturday evening, 8 May 1886, and the lecture, according to one of the five people present—when he thought of it almost forty years later—was "mættet av eksplosive, flammende billeder, heftige utfald og varsom, kjærtegnende lyrik."[5] Back in America, after first working one year there as a streetcar conductor and farm laborer, Hamsun continued his literary series during the months from December 1887 to February 1888, treating a new author every Sunday afternoon: Balzac, Flaubert, Zola, Bjørnson, Ibsen, Lie, Janson, Kielland, and, on 29 January 1888, August Strindberg. Interest in literature was not particularly strong among Norwegians in Minneapolis, but some thirty people turned out to be assured by Hamsun that Strindberg "trots all sin bitterhet och båtskhet (vore) en stor och verklig filantrop; bak hans oförsonligaste utfall och smädelser hör den lyssnande en barmhärtig samaritan, som gråter."[6] The line "a Samaritan is heard sobbing behind this rude force," is repeated in the article on Strindberg that Hamsun wrote the same spring and that John G. O. Hansen helped him translate and place in the Chicago weekly *America* in the 20 December 1888 issue. Unfortunately, as Hamsun wrote to Victor Nilsson, it appeared "i en styg, forvansket Form. Der er strøget og sat til, saa Artiklen er ikke til at kende igen." But he sent it to Strindberg on 13 January 1889, even at the risk of being taken to task for its contents.[7]

Hamsun's first prolonged stay in Copenhagen coincided with Strindberg's last winter in this city (1888–89), and Hamsun could not help marveling at the productivity of the man he had first learned to admire in distant America. He wrote to Victor Nilsson:

Det er forresten galt med Strindberg. Brandes fortalte mig at han gaar i en stadig Frygt for at blive gal. Han er ofte oppe hos Brandes og klager sig. Han har dog den samme storartede Arbejdsævne. Gud bevare os vel, hvor den Mand arbejder. "Frøken Julie" er et mærkeligt Arbejde—Hundrefold bedre, genialere end Ibsens "Fruen fra Havet." Brandes fortalte at Strindberg har 22 Skuespil liggende i sin Skuffe—tænk det, trods alle de Bøger han udgiver. I 1888 har han udgivet 5 Arbejder. Han er saa kolossalt produktiv, at han gør Balzac til en Dværg. Foruden de Bøger han udgiver, skriver han jo ogsaa i alle Nordeuropas Tidsskrifter. Det er Gud evig straffe mig den største skrivende Arbejdskraft, som har gaat paa Jorden!

Han skriver naturligvis ogsaa fejlfulde bøger, endog daarlige Bøger, men ogsaa i sine daarlige Bøger slynger han nu og da—plutselig som en Lynstraale i Natten, en Aabenbaring—en genial Tanke, et luende Genistrejf ind i Teksten —og hele Arbejdet er reddet! Hans allersidste Bog "Blomstermaalningar" har jeg endnu ikke læst, men Brandes beundret den, sagde han; den var saa fin, sagde Brandes.

Naturally Hamsun wanted to meet him, but as he writes in the same letter to Nilsson: "Det var jo ingen Grund for mig at gaa til den Mand bare under Paaskud af at ville hilse paa ham. Store Mænd vil jeg jo holde mig borte fra til jeg har fortjent at blive lukket ind til dem. Jeg er stolt, jeg holder ikke af at levere mit Kort og derpaa faa den Besked at vedkommende ikke er hjemme (for mig). Nej, saa venter jeg heller." He also mentions that he has been invited to a party where Strindberg was supposed to be present, but that he (Hamsun) did not go—"jeg er nu lidt stolt paa min Maade."[7]

During the following five years Strindberg's and Hamsun's ways parted. Hamsun was busy writing—*Fra det moderne Amerikas Aandsliv* (*The Cultural Life of Modern America*), *Sult* (*Hunger*), *Mysterier* (*Mysteries*), *Redaktør Lynge* (*Editor Lynge*), *Ny Jord* (*Shallow Soil*) in addition to articles—and moving from place to place: Copenhagen, Sweden, Lillesand, Samsø—before settling in Paris in the fall of 1893. By this time his book on America had been mentioned favorably by Strindberg in a letter to Georg Brandes,[8] and from one of Strindberg's letters to Birger Mörner (16 January 1893), we understand that Mörner had met Hamsun in Copenhagen and decided to go to Berlin with him and visit their mutual friend Strindberg there.[9] Hamsun, however, did not get to Berlin and never was part of the famous circle around Strindberg at *Zum schwarzen Ferkel*. But two years later in the spring of 1895 he played a part in Strindberg's life, as is well known from most biographies of the two men.

In an article in *Nya Pressen* in 1899,[10] Hamsun claimed he never knew Strindberg well personally; however, he did finally meet him in 1894 after he had developed his moustache (*sans* goatee) to simulate the master,[11] and, if we are to believe Johan Bojer, discussed many a topic with him. Bojer writes about the Scandinavians at *Café de la Regence*: "Der kom gjerne henimot midnat en statelig skikkelse i graa dress, graa hat og hvit vest med blaat kunstnerslips under haken. Det var August Strindberg. Naar han tok hatten av kom der tilsyne en høi pande under en endnu høiere haarmanke. Hamsun og han sat ofte sammen, og fik man adgang til deres bord kom man til at opleve en duel av paradokser. Det var lyn i lyn."[12]

When Strindberg's situation deteriorated, it seems that Hamsun remained one of his few companions.[13] In an oft quoted letter of 19 March 1895 to Adolf Paul, Hamsun related how one winter evening he had gone to a restaurant with Strindberg, who had nothing to wear but his light summer suit (see Bojer above) and therefore wanted to find a dark room where he would not be observed. At one place he exclaimed: "Nei, her er for lyst for mig, her er for dyrt—lad os gaa til et andet Sted." And Hamsun adds: "Men Maaden hvorpaa han sagde: her er for lyst for mig, greb mig voldsomt. Han sagde det ikke med nogen klagende Stemme, men ganske som et Faktum. Her er for lyst for mig. Og saa var det dog August Strindberg. . . ."[14]

It was Hamsun who first conceived the idea of a collection to improve Strindberg's financial situation. He composed a call for help, which was also signed by Jonas Lie, Allan Østerlind, Sven Lange, Albert Edelfelt, and Anders Zorn, and which was published in a number of Scandinavian newspapers in March of 1895. Hamsun recalls that when Strindberg heard what these friends and colleagues had done for him, he thanked Hamsun very warmly and asked that he especially greet Jonas Lie from him. However, when Strindberg personally began to receive money gifts (which should have gone to the newspapers), he found it undignified, wrote the Scandinavian papers that a collection had been taken up without his knowledge, and asked that whatever money might come in be sent to his children in Finland. But since the children did not need the money as badly as Strindberg himself, Hamsun interpreted Strindberg's attitude as an attempt on his part to thwart and frustrate his friends. In his March 19 letter to Adolf Paul, Hamsun indicated that Strindberg no longer favored his presence the way he used to—Strindberg had told him directly that he found Hamsun's personality too strong for his taste— and his misgivings were not mistaken. In a letter to Jonas Lie dated 17 April 1895, he tells how Strindberg, whom he had last seen on 26 March, suddenly and without explanation had cut off all connections with him. On 6 April, after he had tried to deliver a sum of money at Strindberg's door, he had received a card saying "Behåll de trettio silfverpengarna och låt oss vara färdiga med hvarann för hela lifvet." All attempts to secure an audience with the man after that had been in vain.[15]

As possible reasons for Strindberg's sudden animosity, Hamsun gives Strindberg's paranoia—that Strindberg may have thought an unfriendly article in *Le Journal* was written by Hamsun, or else that he (Strindberg) had had repeated to him Hamsun's description of Strindberg's deplorable state in an earlier letter to Lie. Jonas Lie, who remained, miraculously, on speaking terms with Strindberg throughout this period, criticized his friend for lack of gratitude, and Strindberg replied that he had not refused the help, but that he had shown Hamsun the door because he exploited Strindberg's predicament, "för att utsätta mig för moralisk misshandel."[16] In May Strindberg again thanked Jonas Lie for his loyalty, adding, "var öfvertygad att jag ej är okänslig derför äfven om min skygghet för stad och menniskor håller mig från ett besök."[17] But to Birger Mörner he wrote: "Det afskyvärda tiggaruppropet var ej välbetänkt och ej välment of någon annan än Lie och Österlind (under lågo mycket tarfliga motiv.)"[18] In a letter to Count F. U. Wrangel (18 April 1895), Jonas Lie describes Strindberg's case: "Hvad han øiensynlig er mest saarbar og ømfindtlig for er enhver personlig Tilnærmelse, hvori han tror at kunne føle noget slags Indblanding eller paavirkende Formynderskab. . . . Jeg er mindre tillbøjelig til at tro ham 'sindssyg' end lidende under et overanstrengt Nervesystem."[19] But Albert Edelfelt, one of Hamsun's signatories, is more direct in his assessment, writing to his mother that "Lie sade mig, unter uns (det samma försäkrade Ville Vallgren, Spada och Sven Lange) att Strindberg redan är galen, lider av fixa ideer, förföljelsemani o.d. Hans otacksamhet och hat känna nu ingen gräns, och just de som varit vänliga mot honom få lida mest."[20]

After being treated like a Judas, Hamsun sent Strindberg a card saying, in effect, that a man who has suddenly become rich enough to throw away thirty pieces of silver ought first and foremost to pay his debts. And he reminded Strindberg that he had borrowed money from as poor a person as Hamsun himself.[21] However, even though he was disappointed and annoyed, there was not on Hamsun's part any "break with Strindberg." Unlike others whom Strindberg had treated in the same manner, Hamsun continued to admire the man and to review his work favorably. Frida Uhl recalls how, on Strindberg's last birthday, when Norwegian authors asked Hamsun how they could best celebrate the Swedish dramatist, he had answered "Köp blommor och gör musik, något annat behövs inte nu för att göra August Strindberg odödlig. Han är och förblir våra dagars stora otämda mysterium. Köp blommor för hela livräntan, alla rosor från Stockholm till Nizza; gör honom till Millionär i tulpaner, och—lämna honom i fred!"[22] On 2 May 1912, six days after Strindberg's death, *Dagbladet* (Oslo) carried the following obituary by Knut Hamsun:

> Han var som ingen anden, og vi hadde den fordel at være hans samtidige. Eftertiden vil let faa øie paa hans karakter, vi derimot oplevet daglig hans overordentlige rigdom ogsaa i det smaa. En gigant i arbeide og omfang, et barn i indtryksømhet og i saarbarhet, den store neurose.
>
> Mine personlige minder om Strindberg skriver sig fra tre aar i Paris. Trods en og anden uoverensstemmelse den gang bevarer jeg en inderlig tilfredsstillelse ved at ha lært ham at kjende.[23]

Of this person who always admired Strindberg one would expect that he had read and reread most of the master's central works. Hamsun's articles on Strindberg, however, show no signs of systematic reading; indeed, Kristofer Janson's description of Hamsun's reading habits in America—how he flicked carelessly through the pages of a book, yet seemed always to catch the gist of the argument—also characterizes his study of Strindberg's work.[24] Rather than *development* he is looking for what he considers to be the *essential* in Strindberg— "denna oregerliga ande med det brinnande upprorssinnet och den stora poetiska begåfningen"[25]—and finds it more often in the early "realistic" than in the later "romantic" works. Thus, in his review of *Till Damaskus* (*To Damascus*) he does not appreciate Strindberg's new use of "characterless characters" or his mixture of fantasy and reality: "Vid brunnen finns en uppträdande sköldpadda . . . men på taflan står skrifvit Tiggeri förbjudet. . . . Det er som att komma från det sällsamaste sagoland och falla ned i närheten af Berlin."[26] Strindberg is said to have been particularly proud of *Till Damaskus*, sufficiently so for him to send a copy of the play to Henrik Ibsen. Hamsun, however, describes it as "en bok, hopkommen i en hast, som icke är af det godo. . . . Den hade icke bort blifva tryckt sådan den nu är."[27] Similarly, in his review of *Den romantiska klockaren på Rånö* (*The Romantic Sacristan of Rånö*) Hamsun has no understanding of the way in which the story anticipates the new romantic trends of the 1890s, what Strindberg termed "Pepitaattentattet och Byronska snobbskolans återkomst."[28] He describes it as "Rids, Rids til alle Kanter, skjødesløse, uomhyggelige Rids. Der er hverken Kunst eller Psychologi i denne Beretning. . . ." and he uses the rest of his space to ridicule, à la Mark Twain, the structure of the story (typically, the review was written in the same year as the hilarious *Fra det moderne Amerikas Aandsliv*).[29] *Bland franska bönder* (*Among French Farmers*), on the other hand, Hamsun finds valuable. It contains "en Rigdom af Iagttagelser, som er af største Interesse. Den er en liden Kulturhistorie . . . saa indtrengende og dygtigt udarbejdet, at den overgaar Strindberg's øvrige Afhandlinger."[30] This unusual enthusiasm for Strindberg's "Afhandlinger" explains why Hamsun rarely quotes moving scenes or colorful descriptions in Strindberg, but rather the author's private views, interjected in his texts in the form of paradoxical or otherwise provocative pronouncements and profusely illustrated with curious examples from cultural history or the natural sciences. On the basis of numerous such examples—grape aphids (phylloxera), tree-climbing fish, the study of Shakespeare at Uppsala during the 1860s, and many others—it is possible to show that, in writing his first article about Strindberg (*America*, 1888), Hamsun had been mainly inspired by *Sömngångarnätter* and by the prefaces to *Utopier i verkligheten* (*Utopias in Reality*) and *Giftas I* (*Married I*), as well as by the first pages of *Jäsningstiden* (*The Time of Ferment*). In the expanded *Dagbladet* article one year later, *I röda rummet* (*In the Red Room*) otherwise known as *Tjänstekvinnans son II* (*The Son of a Servant II*) and the prefaces to *Giftas II* and, particularly, to *Fröken Julie* have been explored.[31]

In his letter of 13 January 1889 to Victor Nilsson in Minneapolis, Hamsun complained that the *America* article had been cut. Because we don't have the original manuscript, we do not know what has been left out, only that the much longer *Dagbladet* article (1889) contains, in addition to the ideas expressed in *America*, a treatment of Strindberg's attitude to women, his view of the modern theater, and his indebtedness to the German philosopher Eduard von Hartmann. The *America* article (1888) asks why women should want to study Cicero, but does not, like the *Dagbladet* article (1889), go on to say that women should concentrate their efforts on bringing up children, that women are inferior to men, that there are no great philosophers, statesmen, inventors, discoverers among them, that they can prepare food but not become chefs, or clean floors but not invent a mechanical floor sweeper; furthermore, that this is not so because of lack of opportunity, for during the matriarchy women had ample time to prove what they were good for, and so on. If Hamsun had hoped to defend this kind of reasoning in his first article on Strindberg, the editors of *America* apparently did not want to include it. Strindberg's revolutionary ideas of the theater, which Hamsun had studied in the preface of *Fröken Julie*, are also not mentioned in the earlier version, one reason being that *Fröken Julie* was not available in Minneapolis when Hamsun wrote the article. Finally, the earlier article does not include Hamsun's analysis of the relationship between Strindberg and Eduard von Hartmann, though in this case it could have: during his last stay in America Hamsun had looked in vain for Hartmann's works in the Minneapolis Atheneum, no doubt after reading Strindberg's treatment of the German philosopher in *Tjänstekvinnans son*.[32]

Sömngångarnätter, the major inspiration for Hamsun's first article on the Swedish dramatist, was dedicated to Strindberg's two Norwegian friends, Bjørnstjerne Bjørnson and Jonas Lie, who reacted very differently to this volume of poetry: to Bjørnson it was a "hastverksarbejde," whereas to Jonas Lie it showed "tidsaanden blæsende indover os fra et varmt, til grunds oprørt og bevæget hjærte."[33] Hamsun must have been attracted to what Henry Olsson describes as "ögonblickartad . . . passionerad och febrilt spörjande" in *Sömngångarnätter*.[34] In his first article he says of Strindberg: "I have found in no literature such a velocity as Strindberg's. It is no tempest; it is a hurricane. He does not speak; he does not say his opinions; he *explodes* them."[35] Hamsun, then, like Lie, was fascinated by the enthusiasm and topicality of the poems, but his article does not otherwise tell us much about the man Strindberg. Mostly it is simply a presentation— using the author's own curious illustrations—of Strindberg's radical Rousseauism: the attack on the church, on the religion of beauty, and on the modern belief in the powers of natural science. Central in the discussion is Strindberg's contention that culture destroys nature, with the result that modern man has lost his natural health. Strindberg, according to Hamsun, has "cultural-enmity in his blood" (actually Strindberg's own expression in *Jäsningstiden*). He explains this fact from Strindberg's personal background (which Hamsun had studied in *Tjänstekvinnans son*), describing his temperament as that of a "brutish rebel who overthrows temples and strikes Philistines" but is at the same time "the tender, sensitive spirit who fights the evil principles in life."[36] This man has striven fearfully, he says, and found a harbor—nature—though Hamsun admits that Strindberg is also a product of culture who longs for "the happy society which he sees in his vision." It is interesting to note, then, that during the same spring when Georg Brandes made his volte face in Copenhagen and declared Nietzsche, rather than John Stuart Mill, to be the prophet of the times, Hamsun sat in Minneapolis and presented August Strindberg as the man of the future.[37]

Hamsun was temperamentally drawn to Strindberg, in whom he found the same androgyny ("brutish" and "tender") as in Bjørnson, Mark Twain, and presumably in himself. Both men were looked upon in their respective countries as *enfants terribles* who felt called upon to give their people some fundamental *Umwertung aller Werte*. If they were different in appearance—Hamsun big, handsome, outgoing, with an impressive voice; Strindberg a "small man, so slender-built, so nervous,"[38]—they shared a kind of nervousness (Hamsun speaks repeatedly of his neurasthenia) and above all a deep-seated sense of inferiority that manifested itself as superiority, mainly in the areas of sex and class. Both were misogynists; both wished to appear aristocratic, though they looked upon their own background as socially inferior and referred to themselves, respectively, as "son of a servant" and "farmer." On the other hand, there was a fundamental difference in their intellect and education. Whereas Hamsun was an autodidact who read little but well, Strindberg had academic training and remained a voracious reader with wide interests in the sciences and arts, and talents not only in all literary genres, but in music and painting as well. Even if Hamsun wished to follow Strindberg's back to nature program, he could never hope to acquire Strindberg's knowledge and interests, as demonstrated in, say, "Om pessimismen i den moderna trädgårdskonsten" ("On Pessimism in Modern Landscape Architecture") from *Blomstermålningar* (*Flower Paintings*), which Brandes had recommended for its beauty. But Hamsun must have felt that he could emulate the master in matters of literary style, and his own emphasis on form versus content constitutes another major difference between the two writers. In his second article Hamsun claims that Strindberg never shows himself to be a master of form, and quotes Strindberg's own statement that "min tanke betyder mer änn en versfot."[39] Hamsun, much as he wanted to be known as a thinker, was essentially the aesthete, painstakingly rewriting and polishing his sentences. But he did have a literary program, and he found its major tenets in the writings of August Strindberg.

In Hamsun's most important article from the 1890s, "Fra det ubevidste Sjæleliv," the main argument is directed against Taine's idea of the *faculté maîtresse*, which Hamsun remembered even sixty years later when he was examined at the Psychiatric Clinic in Oslo by Professor Langfeldt. He then claimed that he himself was neither good nor bad, but rather, like his created characters, more subtly differentiated, and he reminded his inquisitor that Dostoevsky and others had taught us all something new about man. Strangely, he did not refer to Strindberg, who was the first person he himself ever mentioned as a fighter against Taine's characterology. Hamsun most probably had his formulations from the preface of *Fröken Julie*, though the ideas appeared originally in *Tjänstekvinnans son*, where Strindberg writes as follows about character: "En s.k. karaktär är en mycket enkel mekanisk inrättning; han har bara en synpunkt på de så ytterst invecklade förhållandena i livet. . . . En karaktär måste följaktligen vara en tämligen vanlig människa och vara vad man kallar litet dum. Karaktär och automat tyckas något så när sammanfalla. Dickens' berömda karaktärer äro positivdockor. . . ."[40]

Hamsun, in his article from 1890 states his case more poetically:

Hvad om nu Literaturen i det hele taget begyndte at beskæftige sig lidt mere med sjælelige Tilstande, end med Forlovelser og Baller og Landture og Ulykkeshændelser som saadanne? Man maatte da ganske vist give Afkald paa at skrive "Typer,"—som allesammen er skrevne før—"Karakterer," som man træffer hver Dag paa Fisketorvet. Og forsaavidt vilde man maaske miste en Del af det Publikum, som læser forat se, om Helten og Heltinden faar hinanden. Men der blev til Gengæld flere *individuelle Tilfælder* i Bøgerne, og disse forsaavidt kanske mere svarende til det Sindsliv, som moderne Mennesker i Nutiden lever. Vi fik erfare lidt om de hemmelige Bevægelser som bedrives upaaagtet paa de afsides Steder i Sjælen, den Fornemmelsernes uberegnelige Uorden, det delikate Fantasiliv holdt under Luppen, disse Tankens og Følelsernes Vandringer i det blaa, skridtløse, sporløse Rejser med Hjærnen og Hjærtet, Blodets Hvisken, Benpibernes Bøn, hele det ubevidste Sjæleliv.[41]

The expressions "Blodets Hvisken, Benpibernes Bøn" probably could have appeared in a Strindberg text. As Olaf Øyslebø has shown,[42] Hamsun shared Strindberg's interest in the poetic use of, for example, the body, bodily functions, and disease, as in Strindberg's poems "Sårfeber" ("Septic Fever") and Hamsun's "Feberdigte" ("Fever Poems"). Hamsun's refined rhetoric in the above passage, however, is rather an "American" feature of his style, and his criticism of Whitman applies to himself: "Han kan ikke sige en Ting enkelt og rammende, han er ude af Stand til at *betegne*. Han siger en Ting fem Gange og altid paa samme storslagne, men betegnelsesløse Vis."⁴³

Hamsun's and Strindberg's sense of inferiority does not have the same effect in their attitude to workers. Hamsun, even though he was much closer to the common man, having worked on road construction and railway construction and having befriended his political leaders, soon turned against "inferior" races and classes: Blacks, Indians, Lapps, factory workers, and in his early books, even farmers. Strindberg, whose distance from these people was much greater, wrote socialist treatises, including his *Lilla katekes för underklassen* (*Little Catechism for the Lower Classes*), which would have been unthinkable in Hamsun's case, even during the early, somewhat liberal phase in his career.⁴⁴ In their attitude to women, the situation is again different. Strindberg, feeling he had always suffered in his relationship with the other sex, wrote about them with a fear and hatred that was alien to Hamsun. As a young man in America, Hamsun had to put up with the arrogance of certain women and came to look upon them as intellectually and morally inferior, but for all his jealousy and suspicion, he retained throughout his life the somewhat more enlightened standpoint of Strindberg's *Giftas I*, encouraging his wife to write, and hiring a woman lawyer.

Strindberg's major influence on Hamsun is the result of his role as a mediator of Rousseau's ideas—this despite the fact that Hamsun hated Switzerland as fervently as Strindberg praised it.⁴⁵ Strindberg's back-to-nature program is the central thesis in all Hamsun's articles about him and no doubt what first drew him to the Swedish writer. Already in the *America* article he quotes Strindberg's characterization of himself as "an animal longing for the woods," which corresponds to Hamsun's own "jeg hører skogene og ensomheten til."⁴⁶ However, in Hamsun's case the line is more convincing. Strindberg in the early 1880s, for all his passion and vehemence is, like his Swiss mentor, more the man of the eighteenth century: deep down there is something urbane, constructive, even optimistic about him. Though he is against the excesses of modern culture, he is not against culture as such. In his essay "Jaktminnen" ("Hunting Memoirs") from *Blomstermålningar*, which may well have been part of the inspiration for Hamsun's unusual novel *Pan*, Strindberg writes: "Naturen kan vara mycket älskvärd, men när den uppträder hotande, livsfarlig, känslolös, då är den ryslig. Och i dessa stunder kände jag den fasa, som efter naturguden Pan har fått namnet panik."⁴⁷

But in Hamsun's novel what Glahn seeks is exactly this kind of panic, and the author sympathizes with his protagonist, who finds enjoyment in natural catastrophes—catastrophe as a sign of supernatural force, something above and against culture. A case in point is the ending of *En Vandrer spiller med Sordin* (*The Wanderer 2: On Muted Strings*), where Hamsun's elated hero watches an avalanche at close quarters. (Leo Lowenthal has interpreted similar features in Hamsun's novels as a sign of latent fascism.)[48] But even if Glahn and other early protagonists are drawn more in the spirit of Nietzsche's Dionysus, in later works like *Markens Grøde* (*Growth of the Soil*), as well as in his personal life, Hamsun tried to realize Strindberg's farmer ideals.

Beyond the ideas he shared with the master, Hamsun admired above all Strindberg's unusual impressionability—his *Indtryksømhed*—and a refreshing recklessness, which made even his didacticism palatable. Hamsun wrote in his *America* article:

He is not the impartial thinker, he does not look forward methodically and solicitous—no he is an *ingenious mind* who receives suggestions, suspicions on the first hand. He is an observer, of the finest, the sharpest any age has ever produced. The manner in which he knows is just the manner in which he feels; he is the man of strong convictions—his heart is warmer than his head is cold. . . . What is called his "contradictions" seems to me psychologically consistent. He uses no deliberate planning, and not the method of positive criticism; he guesses his way, throws out ingenious forebodings, bold paradoxes, gives information about everything, outside-information, assertions. And here are constantly many chances for objections.[49]

Strindberg had the good fortune to overcome the monomania of his Inferno period and retain a youthful susceptibility to the end of his days. This was not the case with Hamsun, and part of the explanation, I think, can be found in his post-American doctrine that form matters more than content, beauty more than new ideas and social reform. Hamsun's early literary style shows a remarkable sense of refinement and innovation, but his general aesthetic was conventional, as can be seen in his simple artistic taste in all other areas than literature. Unlike Strindberg, Hamsun did not appreciate Munch's paintings or Beethoven's piano sonatas.[50] His favorite music was Yradier's "La Paloma," and his art collection at Nørholm proves a liking for the pretty-postcard painter E. Ulving. In furniture Hamsun loved the empire, or regency, style for its purity and pleasant beauty, and his ideal society corresponded to this predilection: a stratified community in which everybody—particularly women and factory workers—knew his or her right place. For this reason Hamsun came to appreciate less and less the social mobility of twentieth-century

Norwegian society and to long instead for the static beauty of feudal systems like those of Russia and Turkey, and—after World War I and the Weimar Republic—for the law and order of Nazi Germany. His gradual isolation in a social-democratic country like Norway was hastened by his arrogance and his cult of beauty. In 1935–36 he did not heed his colleagues in the Norwegian Authors' Union, who condemned his attack upon the German freedom fighter Carl von Ossietzky, and during World War II he disregarded the warning letters of well-meaning citizens, under the pretext that they were poorly written. In the summer of 1949 he closed the door on his last friend, Christian Gierløff, with the same heartless resolve Strindberg had shown him in Paris fifty-four years earlier. Like Strindberg's lust for power, Hamsun's cult of beauty led to a crisis, in Hamsun's case longer and more tragic than the Inferno, since it came at the end of his life.[51] Hamsun had time, though, to write *Paa gjengrodde Stier* (*On Overgrown Paths*), a less powerful book than *Till Damaskus*, but still a moving document, and like nearly all of Hamsun's work, beautiful, humorous, and charming. Today, thirty years after its appearance, it is possible to say that, if Hamsun's cult of the beautiful had destroyed his personal ties with his countrymen, it apparently had not tarnished his reputation as a writer, for his books are now read and discussed more than ever.[52]

In his review of *Konerne ved Vandposten* (*The Women at the Pump*), Thomas Mann singled out Hamsun's relationship to Dostoevsky and Nietzsche and claimed that neither artist had in his own country a disciple of Hamsun's stature.[53] He could have added Strindberg's name to the other two. Here is a remarkable parallelism of both life and thought, and even if Hamsun the dramatist did not turn out to be a man of Strindbergian proportions, as a novelist and fellow student of Rousseau he is a worthy follower of the author of *Hemsöborna* (*The Natives of Hemsö*).[54]

Notes

1. Tore Hamsun, *Knut Hamsun* (Oslo: Gyldendal, 1959), p. 61.
2. Olaf Øyslebø, "Om Hamsuns første litteraturforedrag," *Edda*, 63 (1963), p. 145.
3. Harald Næss, *Hamsun og Amerika* (Oslo: Gyldendal, 1969), p. 36–41.
4. At the home of Arne and Peggy Tveraas in New Lisbon, Wisconsin, Lawrence Berge has recently discovered nine Hamsun letters and four copies of *Nyt Tidsskrift* with Knut Hamsun's signature and the notation "Til velvillig Anmeldelse" ("Complimentary Review Copy"). The two articles referred to appeared in *Nyt Tidsskrift*, 3 (1884), p. 537 and 4 (1885), p. 159.
5. Johan Enger in *Nationen* (Oslo), 31 January 1925. ". . . saturated with explosive, fiery images, violent attacks and delicate, loving poetry."
6. Olaf Øyslebø, p. 154. ". . . despite all his bitterness and hatred [he] was a great and real philanthropist; behind his most implacable attacks and insults anyone listening would hear a merciful Samaritan weeping."
7. Letter to Victor Nilsson, 13 January 1889, in Tore Hamsun ed., *Knut Hamsun som han var* (Oslo: Gyldendal, 1956), pp. 57–58. ". . . in an ugly, garbled version. They have cut and added so that I cannot recognize the article." Other quoted passages read in translation:

"Things are not well with Strindberg. Brandes told me that he lives in constant fear of becoming insane. He often comes to Brandes to complain. Nevertheless he has the same magnificent ability to work. Good heavens, how that man works. *Miss Julie* is a remarkable work—a hundred times better and more ingenious than Ibsen's *Lady from the Sea*. Brandes told me that Strindberg has twenty-two plays lying in his drawer—think of that, despite all the books he is now publishing. In 1888 he has published five works. He is so fantastically productive that he turns even Balzac into a dwarf. In addition to the books he publishes, he also writes in all North European periodicals. I'll be damned if this is not the greatest writing force that ever walked this earth! Of course, he also writes books with imperfections, even bad books. But also in his bad books, he projects occasionally—like a bolt of lightning in the night, like an epiphany—an ingenious thought, a flaming stroke of genius onto the text, which then saves the whole work! His very last work, *Flower Paintings*, I still have not read, but Brandes said he admired it, it was such a fine book, Brandes said."

"There is no reason for me to go to this man simply under the pretext of wishing to say hello. Great men I want to keep away from until the time when I deserve to be let into them. I am proud, I don't like to leave my card and then be told that the person in question is not at home (for me). No—then I'll rather wait."

". . . after all, I am proud in my own way."

8. In Georg and Edvard Brandes, *Brevveksling med nordiske Forfattere og Videnskabsmænd*, 6 (Copenhagen: Gyldendal, 1939), p. 298.
9. *August Strindbergs brev*, 9, ed. Torsten Eklund (Stockholm: Bonniers, 1965), p. 118.
10. "Det Litterära Omslaget," *Nya Pressen* (Helsingfors), 11 July 1899.
11. See Victor Nilsson, "Min Hamsun," *Bonniers Litterära Magasin*, 2, No. 8 (1933), p. 51.
12. P. G. La Chenais, *Johan Bojer* (Oslo: Gyldendal, 1932), pp. 43–44. "Usually there would come toward midnight a stately character in a gray suit, gray hat and a white waistcoat with a blue artist's tie under his chin. It was August Strindberg. When he

took off his hat, there appeared a tall forehead under an even taller head of hair. Hamsun and he often sat together, and whoever was admitted to their table would experience a duel with paradoxes. It was like one bolt of lightning after another."

13. Erik Lie, *Erindringer fra et dikterhjem* (Oslo: Aschehoug, 1928), p. 142.

14. In Adolf Paul, *Strindberg-minnen och brev* (Stockholm: Bonniers, 1915), p. 197. "No, here it is too bright for me, too expensive—let us go to another place." And Hamsun adds: "But the way in which he said: here it is too bright for me, touched me immensely. He did not say it with a complaining voice, but in an entirely factual manner. Here it is too bright for me. After all, it was August Strindberg."

15. Letter to Jonas Lie, in Erik Lie, pp. 142–46. "Keep your thirty pieces of silver and let us be through with each other for the rest of our lives."

16. *Strindbergs brev*, 10: 399. ". . . in order to expose him to moral torture."

17. Ibid., 11: 6. ". . . please rest assured that I am not unappreciative even if my fear of the city and people keeps me from paying you a visit."

18. Ibid., 11: 10. "The repulsive beggar letter was not well thought out and, except by Jonas Lie and Österlind, not well intended (very base motives)."

19. In F. U. Wrangel, *Minnen* (Stockholm: Norstedt, 1925), p. 231. "Evidently what makes him most sensitive and vulnerable is any personal approach in which he senses some sort of interference or influencing guardianship. . . . I am inclined to think of him less as 'insane' than suffering from an overworked nervous system."

20. In Albert Edelfeldt, *Middagshöjd* (Stockholm: Holger Schildt, 1928), p. 183. "Lie told me confidentially (and Ville Vallgren, Spada, and Sven Lange assured me likewise) that Strindberg already *is* crazy, suffering from fixed ideas, persecution mania and the like."

21. Erik Lie, p. 143.

22. Frida Uhl, *Strindberg och hans andra hustru*, 2 (Stockholm: Bonniers, 1934), p. 425. "Buy flowers and play music, nothing else is needed to make August Strindberg immortal. He is and remains the great untamed mystery of our day. Buy flowers for the whole annuity, all the roses from Stockholm to Nice; make him a millionaire in tulips, and—leave him alone."

23. Reprint of article in *Nationaltidende* (Copenhagen), 19 May 1912. "He was like no one else, and we had the advantage of being his contemporaries. Posterity will soon be able to decipher his character; we, on the other hand, experienced daily his extraordinary riches also in little things. A giant in work and stature, a child in sensitivity and vulnerability, the great neurosis. My personal memories of Strindberg come from three years in Paris. Despite some disagreements at that time, I preserve the intense satisfaction of having learned to know him. No one was like him."

24. Kristofer Janson, *Hvad jeg har oplevet* (Kristiania: Gyldendal, 1913), p. 221.

25. In *Nya Pressen* (Helsingfors), 10 November 1898. ". . . this unruly spirit with a burning revolutionary mind and great poetic gifts."

26. Ibid. "By the well there is a performing tortoise . . . but the signpost has the legend Beggars Not Allowed. . . . It is like coming from the strangest fairytale land and then tumbling down in the vicinity of Berlin."

27. Ibid., ". . . a book written in a hurry, which is not a good thing. . . . It ought not to have been printed in its present state."

28. Martin Lamm, *August Strindberg* (Stockholm: Aldus/Bonniers, 1971), p. 210. ". . . the Pepita attack and the return of the Byronic school for snobs."

29. *Dagbladet* (Oslo), 26 January 1890. "Mere outlines, outlines all over, slovenly, careless outlines. There is neither artistry nor psychology in the story. . . ."

30. Ibid. "a wealth of observations, which are of the greatest interest. It is a little cultural history . . . so penetrating and skillfully worked out that it surpasses Strindberg's other dissertations."

31. The two articles in *Dagbladet* (Oslo), 10 and 11 December 1889, are published in

virtually the same form in *En bok om Strindberg* (Karlstad, 1894), as "lidt om Strindberg," a reprint of which is available in Knut Hamsun, *Artikler* (Oslo: Gyldendal, 1939), pp. 14–45.

32. Knut Hamsun, *Fra det moderne Amerikas Aandsliv* (Copenhagen: Philipsen, 1889), p. 59.

33. In Henry Olsson's article on *Sleepwalking Nights* (*Sömngångarnätter*) in *Nordisk Tidskrift*, 7 (1931), p. 350. ". . . a superficial job." ". . . the *Zeitgeist* streaming toward us from a warm, utterly provoked and impassioned heart."

34. Ibid., p. 329. ". . . impressionistic . . . impassioned and feverishly questioning."

35. *America* (Chicago), 20 December 1888, p. 31.

36. Ibid., p. 30.

37. See Harald Beyer, *Nietzsche og Norden*, 1, Universitetet i Bergen, *Årbok 1958*, p. 65. Beyer quotes Georg Brandes in a letter to his brother Edvard as saying, "Jeg er fra Englænderne vendt tilbage til Tyskerne i Filosofien. Den engelske Filosofi synes mig at have kulmineret. Men min Ven N. har fremtid for sig. Desuden bliver jeg mere radikal, mindre historisk, og stedse mere aristokratisk i æsthetiske og historiske Synsmader." ("From the English I have returned to the Germans in philosophy. It seems to me that English philosophy has reached its culmination. My friend N., however, has a future. In addition, I am becoming more radical, less historical, and continually more aristocratic in my aesthetic and historical views.").

38. *America*, p. 31.

39. *Artikler*, p. 39. ". . . my thought is more important than a foot [verse]."

40. August Strindberg, *Samlade Skrifter*, 18 (Stockholm: Bonniers, 1913), p. 212 (hereafter *SS*). "A so-called character is a very simple mechanical device; he has only one view of the extremely complicated conditions in life. . . . A character must therefore be a rather ordinary person and be what one describes as somewhat dumb. Character and automaton seem to be approximate synonyms. Dickens's famous characters are puppets. . . ."

41. In *Artikler*, pp. 60–61. "What if literature generally began concerning itself a little more with states of mind than with engagement parties and balls and picnics and accidents as such? True, one would then have to give up creating 'types'—all of which have been created before—'characters,' whom one meets every-day in the fish market. And to that extent one would lose that part of one's audience that reads in order to see if the hero and heroine are united in the end. But, in return, there would be more *individual cases* in the books, and these again more corresponding to the intellectual lives that modern people now lead. We would learn a little about the secret stirrings that go on unnoticed in the remote parts of the brain, the incalculable confusion of perceptions, the delicate life of imagination held under the magnifying glass, these wanderings of mind and emotions into the unknown, trackless, traceless journeys with the brain and the heart, the whisper of the blood, the prayer of the bone, the whole unconscious life of the mind."

42. Olaf Øyslebø, *Hamsun gjennom stilen* (Oslo: Gyldendal, 1963), p. 77.

43. Hamsun, *Fra det moderne Amerikas Aandsliv*, p. 84. "He cannot say something in a simple and striking manner, he is unable to *characterize*. He says something five times and always in the same grandiose but nondescript way."

44. *Hamsun og Amerika*, p. 83. During his last year in America, Hamsun seems to have leaned toward socialism and counted among his best friends some of the young socialist leaders in Minneapolis, for example, Krøger Johansen and Charles Douzette.

45. Hamsun on Switzerland: see, for example, Knut Hamsun, *Samlede verker*, 5 (Oslo: Gyldendal, 1954), p. 414.

46. *SS*, 18: 243. The Hamsun quotation "I belong to the forests and the solitude," is the last line of his novel *Pan* (1894). Similar sentiments are expressed by other characters in his novels and by himself.

47. *SS*, 22: 234. "Nature can be very charming, but when it behaves in a threatening, dangerous, or unfeeling fashion, then it is very frightening. And at such times I felt that terror that after the nature god Pan has received the name of panic."

48. Hamsun's hero watches an avalanche: *Samlede verker*, 5: 423. Leo Lowenthal in *Literature and the Image of Man* (Boston: Beacon Press, 1963), pp. 199–201.

49. *America*, pp. 30–31.

50. See Richard Vowles, "Strindberg and Beethoven," p. 163 in *Växelverkan mellan skönlitteraturen och de andra konstarterna* (Uppsala: Sixth International Study Conference on Scandinavian Literature, 12–16 August 1966), 1967.

51. Knut Hamsun's last years have been discussed in great detail (781 pp.) by Thorkild Hansen in *Prosessen mot Hamsun* (Oslo: Gyldendal, 1978).

52. Ranked according to entries in the *MLA International Bibliography* 1960–70, the major Scandinavian writers are: Ibsen (351), Strindberg (343), Kierkegaard (282), H. C. Andersen (143), Birger Sjöberg (99), Hamsun (73), Hjalmar Bergman (71). (The figure for Birger Sjöberg is probably misleading due to Birger Sjöberg Sällskapet's many publications during the decade in question).

53. In *Prager Presse*, 29 January 1922, reprinted in *Gesammelte Werke*, 10 (Berlin: Fischer, 1925), pp. 287–95.

54. Although it is probably not profitable to look for instances of direct borrowing from Strindberg in Hamsun's work, one can safely say that much of the sentiment of Hamsun's first-person novels *Pan*, *Under Høststjernen* (*Under the Autumn Star*), and *En Vandrer spiller med Sordin* (*The Wanderer 2: On Muted Strings*) is inspired by the Rousseauesque Strindberg. In *Markens Grøde* (*The Growth of the Soil*) idyllic nature is temporarily invaded by industry in the same way as in *Hemsöborna* (*The Natives of Hemsö*). And as Walter Berendsohn has indicated (*August Strindbergs skärgårds—och Stockholmskildringar* [Stockholm, 1962], p. 111), Hamsun's famous character August has much in common with Strindberg's Carlsson. On the whole, the spirit of *Hemsöborna*—in Sweden, Strindberg's most popular work—is present in all of Hamsun's "happy" novels: *Sværmere* (*Dreamers*), *Benoni*, *Rosa*, *Børn av Tiden* (*Children of the Age*), *Segelfoss By* (*Segelfoss Town*), *Markens Grøde*, and the August trilogy.

Strindberg's *Ett drömspel* and Peder W. Cappelen's *Sverre. Berget og Ordet*: Two Dreams of Love

Henning K. Sehmsdorf

I

One measure of the importance of Strindberg is the continued impact of his work on contemporary dramatists. The Norwegian Peder W. Cappelen, author of some twelve plays, is one example. In an unpublished letter (dated 17 April 1979) he acknowledges that Strindberg, next to Shakespeare, is the dramatist who has meant most to him in his own development as a playwright. In particular Cappelen mentions the influence of *Ett drömspel* (*A Dream Play*) on *Sverre. Berget og Ordet* (*Sverre. The Mountain and the Word*) (1977), an influence that is immediately apparent to the reader. Cappelen's drama, like Strindberg's, is a "dreamplay"—polyphonic in structure, steeped in mythological imagery, and focused on the theme of love. But the essential differences between the two plays are equally obvious. Whereas the mythological idiom of Strindberg's play derives mostly from Hindu sources, Cappelen's is largely Christian. Strindberg develops a profoundly pessimistic view of human existence in which matter tyrannizes spirit, and love is hopelessly doomed to failure; Cappelen adopts the view that spirit can, and indeed must, sanctify matter. Strindberg means by "love" mostly physical passion (eros), whereas Cappelen means compassion (agape). In Strindberg's drama mankind is seen as caught in a "dreamplay" initiated by the gods; in this dreamlike illusory existence man looks to woman for redemption but finds his spirit bound to the earth by physical attraction (Maya). In Cappelen's play, by contrast, dream is the source from which the hero derives strength to sustain his spiritual battle in the historical world of space and time. In *Ett drömspel* dream sequences are structured polyphonically to express a unifying theme. In *Sverre. Berget og Ordet* the dream sequences are focused in the central protagonist of the play. Here the unity of character is as important as the unity of theme. And, finally, Strindberg's protagonists are allegorical and symbolic throughout, whereas Cappelen makes use both of allegorical figures and of characters derived from history. The title figure of this play is one of the most famous kings of medieval Norway, Sverre the priest, whom some have thought of as a saint and others have reviled as a devil.

II

As Harry Carlson has pointed out in his study *Strindberg och myterna* (*Strindberg and Myths*), *Ett drömspel* constitutes "an incomparable synthesis of elements taken from many sources—Hindu, Greek and biblical mythology, Mahayana Buddhism, Gnosticism, courtly traditions, and the Tales of One-thousand and One Nights."[1] But the controlling mythological framework is clearly derived from Hinduism—a Hinduism, however, as perceived through the radically pessimistic reading of Indian metaphysics by Schopenhauer. Strindberg by and large shared the German philosopher's view of the world as "a place for atonement, a kind of penal colony."[2] Thus, in *Ett drömspel* Strindberg develops a mostly negative view of human existence as incapable of redemption through love. Agnes, the daughter of the god Indra, takes on human form in order to experience for herself the cause of human suffering. She attempts three relationships with three different men, but each founders on the irreducible polarity between body and spirit. Agnes eventually retreats to the higher regions from which she has descended, having learned from bitter experience to detach herself from the body and its passion.

Inasmuch as Agnes is able to achieve distance from that part of herself that craves "passionate" possession of the material world, she exemplifies the illumined soul Hindu myth speaks of. But in presenting her liberation as possible only through radical removal of the spirit from the physical self, this "klädnad . . . av blod och smuts" ("dress . . . of blood and filth"),[3] the dramatist gives expression to his own despair rather than to Hindu tradition. All higher religions envision an existence beyond the life of the body, but "illumination" ("grace" in the Christian context) is a function of a changed perspective rather than the shedding of the physical self (disembodiment). Hindu scripture speaks of a liberated individual as one able to live in the material world while maintaining his spiritual freedom. In the Upanishads we find the image of the swan that drinks the milk of the world, but ingests only the cream (the spiritual essence) and not the whey (illusory matter). Analogously, Christian thought makes the reference to the believer who is "in the world" but not "of the world."

Clearly, in Strindberg's play this religious perspective is not allowed for. Love for him is always a physical force engendering an experience of passion in the original Latin sense of the word (*passio* from *pati*, *passus*), meaning suffering. Love taken in this sense seduces men and women into believing in the possibility of happiness, into nurturing the dream of a partnership in marriage, of creating one being out of two, of achieving unity and security in a transient, manifold world. But in Strindberg's experience, the lofty ideal of love's poetry invariably fails before the prose of the everyday tyranny of the trivial. To speak in the language of Hindu myth, the veil of illusion (Maya) is always rent. It would thus appear that the suffering engendered by passionate love is also a teacher, a guide toward detachment from all material being. But again, while erotic love seems to instruct the soul to rise above matter, it paradoxically holds it fast in the round of creation at the same time. Suffering is balanced by desire. Characteristically, Strindberg seeks the cause for the fateful imprisonment of the human soul in this cycle among the gods themselves. Referring to the Hindu myth of creation, he relates how in the beginning of time Brahma permitted himself to be seduced by Maya, that is, by matter, thus creating the universe of space and time in which we exist. One conclusion Strindberg seems to draw from this is that the gods themselves are responsible for the "fall" of the spirit. "Detta det gudomliga urämnets beröring med jordämnet var *himlens* syndafall."[4]

Furthermore, whereas the descendants of the gods, the human race, may struggle to be freed of matter, they are held fast by the paradoxical power of physical love:

Men, för att befrias ur jordämnet, söker Bramas avkomlingar försakelsen och lidandet . . . Där har du lidandet såsom befriaren . . . Men denna trängtan till lidandet råkar i strid med begäret att njuta, eller kärleken . . . förstår du än vad kärleken är, med dess högsta fröjder i de största lidanden, det ljuvaste i det bittraste![5]

III

The mythological world we meet in Cappelen's play is essentially different from that found in *Ett drömspel*, not so much because it is mostly derived from a Christian context rather than Hindu, but because it is based on a radically different concept of love. Echoing the well-known passage from Paul's First Letter to the Corinthians, Chapter 13, the two children who throughout the play function as a mirror to Sverre's inner struggle, identify themselves with the very core of Christ's teaching.

Jenta: Vi er tro!
Gutten: Håp!
Begge: Kjærlighet!⁶

It is clear that love in this context does not mean *eros*, love born of physical desire, but *agape*, which is identified with the very essence of God. Christianity makes love of God the motive of obedience to His will; and its correlative, love toward men, or compassion, is made the basis of all ethics. An important difference between Christian belief and the Hindu myth is that in the context of the former, God is always conceived of as personal, a benevolent being who directly commands mankind to live by His law of love; Hindu myth conceives of the divine essence in its highest manifestation as pure spirit without personal form. For the Hindu, compassion arises not least from the sympathetic understanding of man's natural propensity to cling to the forms, rather than the essence, of reality. In Strindberg's play, the god-being Agnes feels pity for mankind clinging to the ecstasy and, no less, to the suffering engendered by erotic love; but there is almost no expression of compassion between the men and women holding each other captive with their desire and their hate.

For Sverre the problem of love is not primarily one of physical passion, but he is no stranger to the power of *eros* either. Consistent with the tradition of the historical king known from the saga, Cappelen introduces Sverre as a young man living happily on the Færoe Islands with his betrothed, a woman by the name of Astrid who bears him several children. Although we have no way of knowing whether the decision to forsake the love of his youth in order to pursue the crown of Norway required great personal sacrifice of Sverre, historians have noted that the king was rather atypical in refusing to compensate his loss by keeping mistresses. Lest this fact be taken as an indication of narrow-minded puritanism, it should also be mentioned that the saga shows that Sverre had complete sympathy for the common man who would rather make love to "den munnfagre Ingunn" ("Ingunn with the beautiful mouth") than fight the king's war.

Cappelen follows the saga closely in these matters, but in his interpretation, Sverre's decision to leave Astrid and their children becomes an important element in the king's moral and religious development. In the play, Astrid, though physically separated from Sverre, continues to represent what the king in his isolated position lacks the most: personal warmth, intimacy, and tenderness—everything that the dramatist renders with the untranslatable term "nærvær" (roughly "presence").[7] But Astrid also continually confronts the king with a challenge. In moments of reflection as well as of crisis, she appears to call on him not to lose sight of his capacity for human sympathy and gentleness in the face of brutality and indifference. In the final act of the play for example, where we find Sverre in his last and most difficult struggle to resist the urge to exact a justified revenge from the defeated enemy, Astrid returns in a dream vision to bring him his children. In keeping with the dramatic device of letting certain figures represent multiple characters (a device Cappelen derives from Strindberg), Sverre and Astrid's children are played by the same boy and girl who since the opening scenes of the play have functioned as a kind of mirror to Sverre's thoughts. Here the identification of these two children with Sverre's own may be taken to indicate that the king has learned to transmute the natural love he bears for his biological children into an all-encompassing sympathy so that his own children are in these returned to him. Thus, in contrast to Strindberg, Cappelen interprets erotic love as capable of guiding the individual to personal growth rather than enslaving him.

The secret of Sverre's ability not only to win his political fight, but also to grow in spirit, is his radical orientation to what he perceives to be the will of God. When the children ask him why he is no longer a priest, Sverre answers that perhaps God thought that he could serve Him better as king (46). The hypothetical "perhaps" in this answer goes to the heart of Sverre's quest. What is the will of God? Sverre is sufficiently certain of his divine command to exercise faith, hope, and charity: he is always committed "to choose the higher or harder path" (19). But how does he know that God wills the priest to cast off his vestments and "seek Him in Norway" in the role of warrior and king? Sverre's enemies accuse him of being an impostor. They reject the claim that he is a son of king Sigurd Munn and charge that his true ally is not God but Satan. Most historians, however, take at face value Sverre's own words reported in the king's saga and quoted almost verbatim by Cappelen:

> . . . skulle Sverre selge seg til djevelen
> For dette usle rikes skyld? Gi sjel
> Og sjelehjelp for å bli konge her?[8]

These are the words of a genuinely religious man for whom the spiritual significance of life is always the primary consideration. Sverre's quandary arises from the impossibility of knowing for certain whether it is God's will to unseat Magnus Erlingsson from power. Magnus saw himself as the vicar of Saint Olaf, *rex perpetuus Norvegiae*, and the founder of the Norwegian church. Magnus was the first

Scandinavian king to be crowned and annointed by a bishop and therefore looked upon his kingship as a sacrament. Hence Sverre's claim to the throne put him in opposition not only to the ruling king but also to the Church, for which the Pope excommunicated both him and all his supporters. Sverre based his claim on the law of St. Olaf that only heirs descended through the male line were entitled to the throne. Magnus, the son of Sigurd the Crusader's daughter Kristina, was thus, in Sverre's eyes, the real impostor, his rule illegal and offensive to God. But it appears that the personal power of Sverre's commitment derives not so much from legal claims but rather from a continuous dialogue with God in dream visions and, not least, in prayerful silence:

> Jenta: Hvordan kan du vite hva Gud virkelig vil?
> Sverre: Jeg lytter etter stemmen Hans.
> Jenta: Når hører du den?
> Sverre: Når alt
> Er taust. Guds røst er lav, den drukner lett
> I skrålet fra de tusen stemmer som
> Vil lokke deg på djev'lens vei.[9]

Cappelen makes use of three of Sverre's prophetic dreams recorded in the saga. The first dream occurs before Sverre's mother has revealed to him his royal birth. The young Sverre dreams of an eagle so great that it covers the whole of Norway and he intuits that the eagle is himself. The dramatist combines the other two dreams into a single terrifying vision. Sverre dreams that the prophet Samuel anoints his hands with the power of hate needed to defeat his enemies; but when Sverre begs Samuel to be anointed also with the power of love, he is denied and commanded instead to devour a human body:

Drømmeskikkelsen: Du skal ete, og du vil ete; for det vil Han som rår for alt.
Sverre: Jeg kan ikke!
Drømmeskikkelsen: Du må. Om du skall fylle det kall, som dine hender er salvet til. Du må, om du vil vinne fram.[10]

The horrible truth is that once Sverre eats as commanded, he can no longer control himself. He is possessed by a bestial desire to eat the whole body including the head, but the dream figure stops him. The dream expresses a profound conflict within Sverre: how to be obedient to God's will in restoring the rightful ruler to Norway's throne usurped by an impostor and at the same time be obedient to Christ's command to love even one's enemy. Sverre's quandary is manifested by various other images, for instance, the children enacting the fight of the Crusaders against the pagans holding sacred

Jerusalem captive. Their play makes amply clear that God's warrior can indeed be as godless in his violence as his pagan enemy (21,39). Another poignant expression for Sverre's struggle to find a synthesis for the various roles required of him is the inscription on his royal seal: "Suerus rex Magnus; ferus ut leo, mitis ut agnus" (28). The images of the furious lion and mild lamb are derived from the New Testament, where the former is identified with the battling, and the latter with the triumphant but merciful, Christ.

Historians generally agree that nowhere did Sverre demonstrate his humanity more fully than at the siege of Tunsberg, which gave the final blow to Sverre's opponents. The saga tells us that Sverre successfully appealed to his men not to kill the enemy forced by hunger and cold to abandon their mountain stronghold. The king personally nursed the enemy leader, Reidar Sendemann, back to health but could not himself recover from the enormous deprivations suffered under the siege. He died shortly thereafter. In Cappelen's play the king's impending death is adumbrated in the visionary promise of Astrid that they will soon be reunited in the forest of their youth:

> Hør Sverre, du er framme nå, og snart
> Er veien slutt. Da møtes vi påny.[11]

Cappelen has chosen Sverre's battle for the mountain at Tunsberg as the focal image of the play. Like the castle in *Ett drömspel* the mountain in Cappelen's play becomes a symbol of a larger reality. The castle and its accessory buildings (towers, prisons, fortifications) appear frequently in Strindberg's works. In *Ett drömspel* the image represents on one level the immaturity of The Officer being held captive; whereas on another, more general level, it symbolizes the world of matter imprisoning the human spirit. When Agnes gives up her body to return to the pure world of spirit, the castle burns while a great chrysanthemum bursts into bloom above it, echoing the Hindu myth that the universe flowers at the moment the illumined soul detaches itself from the transitory and forms of material being. But as is consistent with Strindberg's metaphysical pessimism, the god-being leaves humanity behind, unredeemed. The Officer, The Lawyer, The Poet, remain captives of the paradoxes of their existence. As the castle burns it lights up the ground to show "en vägg av människoansikten, frågande, sörjande, förtvivlade."[12]

In Cappelen's play the mountain has multiple meanings. On one hand, it is a physical place, the actual site of a decisive historical battle (A.D. 1201-1202) between King Sverre and the Bagler Party. On the other hand, the mountain symbolizes a spiritual battleground and as such represents an inner reality:

> Ved dette berg skal hver og én ta opp
> Sitt valg med Gud. Han ser det er et berg
> I deg: et berg av hat og vold og is;
> *Den* fienden vil Han du skal vinne på![13]

That mountain can grow, just like the castle in Strindberg's play, its increase in mass symbolizing violence, hate, and indifference feeding on itself. But once the mountain has been conquered, it takes on a different symbolic significance. It becomes a "mountain of joy," *mons gaudii*, or "Feginsbrekka," as it is called in the historical sources that refer to the slope from which the Crusaders caught the first glimpse of sacred Jerusalem lying before them. In Sverre's saga the term is used to name the hills (*Steinbergene*) outside of Nidaros from which Sverre beheld the shrine of St. Olaf on the day (A.D. 1179) of the first important battle in his struggle to win Norway's crown. In Cappelen's play "Feginsbrekka" is identified with the presence of God:

> Gud er nær,
> Og under deg er landet heilt i ro.[14]

Repeatedly throughout the play the children ask Sverre to take them to "Feginsbrekka," which he promises, praying that it will not "be washed away by blood" (61). But instead of bloodshed, the siege of Tunsberg ends in peace. The play concludes with Sverre taking the children to show them "the mountain of joy." Matter has been sanctified by the spirit of compassion.

IV

We must also consider briefly how in each play the idea of life as a dream is related to the dramatic structure. Gunnar Brandell and others have pointed out that the perception of life's illusory or dreamlike nature can be found in Strindberg's works as early as the 1880s. This perception was deepened by the so-called Inferno crisis and may well be the reason why Strindberg later referred to the first play he wrote after the crisis, *Till Damaskus* (*To Damascus*) (1898), as his "first dream play." But it is one thing to say that life is a dream, meaning that it is illusory or nightmarish, quite another to conceive of dramatic technique based on the alogical aesthetic of nocturnal dreams. In the note prefacing *Ett drömspel* Strindberg developed his concept of the dream on which he modeled the dramaturgy of his play. Dream images may appear incoherent, he says, but they express patterns of meaning. Ordinary space and time do not exist; past, present, future, different physical locations interfuse each other. Persons double, split, expand and contract. And, finally, dream experiences are focused in the "dreamer," who acts as a narrator but does not evaluate or interpret the dream.

The last statement is probably the most crucial and has caused considerable discussion and disagreement among interpreters of Strindberg. How is that unifying consciousness, the dreamer, actually represented in the play? Is it Strindberg's alter ego, The Poet? Is it Agnes? Or is it perhaps an abstract "bisexual psyche projecting its extended experience of life through a number of dramatis personae?"[15] In staging *Ett drömspel* in 1970, Ingmar Bergman opted for the first reading, locating the dream in the mind of The Poet, who remained seated at a table on stage during the entire play. It would seem that Bergman's interpretation is justified by what the play has to say on the relation of poetry to dream and reality:

Diktaren: . . . Vad är dikt?
Dottern: Ej verklighet, men mer än verklighet . . . ej dröm, men vakna drömmar. . . .[16]

But Carlson points out that Bergman's solution in effect "demythologizes" the play.[17] If we take seriously the metaphysical model given in *Ett drömspel* as an aesthetic representation of the dream nature of existence resulting from the seduction of the spiritual principle of creativity (Brahma) by the material principle (Maya), then we must conclude that the illusory dream is indeed the god's dream. The dream amounts to the illusory forms woven by the seductress before the eyes of the god held captive by her spell.[18] Furthermore, not only the god dreams, but the human personae populating the divine dream, dream of each other. In the play we are thus dealing not with a single (divine) consciousness in which all the dream sequences are made to focus, but with at least four others who project themselves and each other in their dreams, namely, Agnes, The Officer, The Lawyer, and The Poet.

In this metaphysical model effectively represented through the dramatic structure and technique of *Ett drömspel*, The Poet has a special role to play. On one hand, the ontological status of poetry, too, has been assimilated to that of the dream because The Poet, like all human beings, is a captive of Maya. And yet, by virtue of his heightened sensibility and the power of his imagination, The Poet is able to catch glimpses of the potential freedom of the soul. He is a dreamer but he dreams "vakna drömmar" ("wide-awake dreams"). And furthermore, although The Poet's visions cannot liberate the soul, at least they give comfort and encouragement to humanity:

Diktaren: Och mänskobarnen tro att vi diktare blott leka . . . hitta på och finna upp!
Dottern: Väl är det, min vän, ty eljes skulle världen läggas öde av brist på uppmuntran. Alla skulle ligga på rygg och titta åt himlen; ingen skulle ta i tu med plog och spade, hyvel eller hacka.[19]

Turning to *Sverre. Berget og Ordet*, we see that consistent with the different underlying *mythos*, dream finds another kind of expression in the dramatic structure of this play. It has been said of the historical Sverre that "his destiny was the realization of a dream."[20] The king was an intensely practical man who kept both feet firmly planted on the earth, but he was also a dreamer, a visionary, who just as firmly believed in the primacy of spirit over matter—and acted accordingly. The action of the play is thus unified thematically by Sverre's religious vision.

But the action also consists of dreams in the specific and concrete sense, and in contrast to *Ett drömspel*, there can be little doubt about who the dreamer is in this play. Possibly due to the influence of Bergman's stage version of Strindberg's drama, Cappelen locates the dream sequences comprising the action in the mind of Sverre, who is seen kneeling in prayer before a cross during most of the play. What Cappelen calls "drømmesyn" ("dream visions") are thus the images passing before the inner eye of the king as he responds to the spiritual challenge posed by the historical siege at Tunsberg.

As in *Ett drömspel*, ordinary space and time have been suspended in Sverre's "dream visions." The action takes place both before Tunsberg in the years 1201–1202 and 25 years earlier at Kirkubø on the Færoe Islands, as well as at various other times and different places in Norway and Sweden. The fact that Sverre is seen kneeling in prayer may be taken either to suggest his prayerful and meditative stance throughout the protracted struggle he fought with himself, not only during the long winter of 1201–1202, but during all the years since first raising his claim to the Norwegian throne; or it may be taken, more literally, to suggest that the action represents memories of past experiences, thoughts, and feelings flashing through Sverre's mind during an hour of decision.

Another important aspect of time in Cappelen's play is the passage of the seasons. In *Ett drömspel* hours, months, and years pass instantaneously. Trees sprout green leaves only to lose them but a moment later. Characters change from youth to old age in no time at all. On the other hand a minute may seem as long as a year. Altogether the imagery suggests that neither the actual seasons nor time measured by the clock corresponds meaningfully to human experience. In *Sverre. Berget og Ordet* by contrast, the imagery of the changing seasons serves as a primary vehicle to express the development of character.

When Sverre began the siege before Tunsberg he was in the fifty-first year of his life, but it was also his last year because he did not survive his victory for more than a few weeks. Consequently at the beginning of the play we find him in the prime of his life, symbolized by the seasonal correlative of summer. Decline and death are as yet held at bay:

> Jenta: Gå, gå høst og død
> Vi jager deg med sommergrein. . . . [21]

But as the siege lengthens into winter, the hardships suffered take their toll. Sverre's soldiers clamor for relief from hunger and the cold; they demand that Sverre lift the siege or take the mountain by force, sparing none of the enemy. In his despair Sverre's dream of Astrid for a moment turns into possessive jealousy. He envisions her with another man and calls her a bitch and a whore. And finally, giving in to his soldiers, the king condemns a deserter to death and, watching his execution, collapses in agony.

It is during this most difficult phase that two allegorical figures are introduced: "coldness," represented by Bishop Nikolas, the leader of Sverre's enemies; and "violence." Through these allegorical figures the season of winter is identified with indifference, hatred, and revenge. Yet the imagery also makes clear that beneath snow and ice there awaits new life. Christmas, the day of the birth of Christ, occurs during the darkest period of the year but it carries with it the promise that the light will return. And Sverre does win the struggle over himself and over his soldiers. When the enemy comes down from the mountain, Sverre offers peace and water from a spring identified with the name of St. Olaf. The year is reborn and so is hope. Astrid returns bearing green branches and bringing Sverre's children:

> Astrid: Tidshjulet snurrer Sverre, og nå har
> Det dreiet rundt. [22]

The image of the turning wheel of time, once more, suggests a number of possibilities. Most obviously it refers to the renewal of spring after the change of the seasons. The context also strongly suggests that the image of the wheel that has turned points to the completion of Sverre's life work. The burden will now be lifted from his shoulders and he will return to Kirkubø—in death. But finally, the turning wheel may refer to the hope, Sverre's dream, that the victory achieved at Tunsberg will usher in a new era, fulfilling the command of Christ to replace the law of an "eye for an eye" with a law of compassion.

Notes

1. (Stockholm: Författarförlaget, 1979), p. 183.
2. Carlson, p. 28.
3. August Strindberg, *Samlade Skrifter*, 36, ed. John Landquist (Stockholm: Bonniers, 1916), p. 304 (hereafter *SS*).
4. *SS*, p. 324; emphasis is mine. "This, the union of divine and earthly, was heaven's fall from grace." This and all subsequent translations from *Ett drömspel* are from Walter Johnson's *A Dream Play and Four Chamber Plays* (New York: Norton, 1975).
5. *SS*, p. 324. "But to free themselves from the earthly, Brahma's descendants seek self-denial and suffering. . . . There you have suffering as the savior. . . . But this longing for suffering is in conflict with the instinct to enjoy or love. . . . Do you yet understand what love is with its greatest pleasure in the greatest suffering, the most pleasant in the most bitter!"
6. (Oslo: Gyldendal norsk forlag, 1977), p. 68 (hereafter *Sv.*). "The Girl: We are Faith. The Boy: Hope. Both: Love."
7. For a fuller discussion of the term "nærvær" in Cappelen's authorship, see my forthcoming article "Folktale and Allegory in Peder W. Cappelen's 'Briar Rose, The Sleeping Beauty'," *Proceedings of the Pacific Northwest Council on Foreign Languages*, 1979.
8. *Sv.*, p. 27. "Would Sverre sell himself to the devil / For the sake of this wretched kingdom? Give soul, / And salvation to become king here?" Cp. Fredrik Paasche, *Kong Sverre* (Oslo: Aschehoug & Co., 1966), p. 231.
9. *Sv.*, p. 47. "The Girl: How can you know what God really wants? Sverre: I listen to His voice. The Girl: When do you hear it? Sverre: When everything / Is silent. God's voice is low, it is easily drowned out / By the din of the thousand voices who / Would tempt one to the ways of the devil."
10. *Sv.*, p. 39. "The Dream Figure: You shall eat, and you want to eat; for He who governs all wishes it so. Sverre: I cannot! The Dream Figure: You must. If you are to follow the call for which your hands are anointed. You must, if you would triumph."
11. *Sv.*, p. 67. "Sverre, you have arrived now, and soon / The path will end, Then we shall meet again."
12. *SS*, p. 330. ". . . a wall of human faces, questioning, sorrowing, despairing."
13. *Sv.*, pp. 69–70. "At this mountain, everyone shall take up / His choice with God. He sees there is a mountain / In you: a mountain of hate and violence and ice; / That enemy He wants you to defeat!"
14. *Sv.*, p. 25. "God is near, / And under you the country is at peace."
15. Birgitta Steene, *The Greatest Fire: A Study of August Strindberg* (Carbondale: Southern Illinois University Press, 1973), p. 99.
16. *SS*, p. 301. "The Poet: What is poetry? The Daughter: Not reality, but more than reality . . . not dreaming, but waking dreams. . . ."
17. Carlson, pp. 183–84.
18. It may be relevant to point out that this model is not consistent with the mainstream of Hindu philosophy. According to the Upanishads, Brahma is the spellbinder and Maya his creation: "He is the Magician, Maya His magic spell, the universe is the illusion projected by Him on Himself as the only substantial background." Swami

Nirvedananda, *Hinduism at a Glance*, 4th edition (Calcutta: Ramakrishna Mission, 1969), p. 173.

19. *SS*, p. 301–302. "The Poet: And the children of man think we poets only play . . . invent and make up! The Daughter: And that is good, my friend; otherwise the world would be laid waste for lack of encouragement. Everyone would lie on his back looking up at the sky; no one would put his hand to the plow and spade, plane or hoe."

20. Paasche, p. 216.

21. *Sv.*, p. 13. "Go, Go autumn and death / We chase you with summer boughs."

22. *Sv.*, p. 67. "The wheel of time is spinning, Sverre, and now / it has come round."

Strindberg in Denmark
P. M. Mitchell

Strindberg's association with Denmark is not a casual one. For nearly two years in the 1880s Strindberg was part of the literary scene in Denmark, placed his hopes on thespian developments in the Danish capital, and had experiences that were soon to be reflected in his work. From a pragmatic, positivistic standpoint, therefore, the literary historian can envisage a traditional study of "Strindberg in Denmark" that cannot be disregarded even by a modern critic who is wearied by positivistic and pragmatic argument. Ultimately the biographical facts, interesting as they may be *per se*, may or may not contribute to a deeper understanding of the effect and impact of a writer's ideas and formulations—or contributions toward the mutation of a genre.

To the student of literary psychology all biographical facts are nevertheless of potential importance, and insofar as literary phenomena are to be interpreted psychologically, we must be grateful for a delineation of events in the life of an imaginative writer who is himself something of a psychological phenomenon. In this sense the well-documented books by Harry Jacobsen, *Digteren og Fantasten* (*The Poet and the Visionary*) (1945), *Strindberg paa "Skovlyst"* (*Strindberg at "Skovlyst"*) (1946), and *Strindberg i Firsernes København* (*Strindberg in the Copenhagen of the Eighties*) (1948) are immeasurably helpful. Jacobsen has spared no pains to collect the facts pertaining to Strindberg's stays in Denmark and to Strindberg's attempt to establish an experimental theater there in 1887–89. What Strindberg has meant within the context of literature in Denmark, however, remains an unanswered question to which we await either a complex answer or several answers. Our purpose here is to provide an orientation that may be helpful when the history of Strindberg's role in Danish literary life is made to take on canonical form. It is safe to say that Strindberg's own experiences in Denmark contributed little to his being appreciated by Danish critics and authors as a dramatist and narrator. Not his biographical excesses but the intrinsic originality and force of his imaginative œuvre have created for him a role within Danish intellectual life, as is evidenced by the number and nature of his works that have been translated into Danish and by the Danish critics and writers who have been and are associated with his name. Particularly striking is the large number of Danish authors who have themselves engaged in producing Danish versions of works by Strindberg. They range from the Danish writer and publisher Peter Nansen in the 1880s to a leading Danish poet of today, Inger Christensen.

Strindberg had placed himself firmly at the forefront of contemporary Swedish literature with the publication of *Röda rummet* (*The Red Room*) in 1879 and the very next year he was corresponding with a would-be Danish translator of the work, the young journalist and aspiring writer Bertel Elmgaard (1861-94), whose own first volume of short stories was not published until 1883. Strindberg offered the rights to novel to Elmgaard for 250 Danish crowns.[1]

In an article by the Swedish critic Georg Nordensvan that appeared (in translation) in the prestigious critical periodical *Tilskueren* in 1885, the interested Danish reader could be apprised of *Röda rummet*: "Fra den Bog kan vi regne den unge Litteraturens Liv" as far as Sweden was concerned.[2] Strindberg was characterized "med hans voldsomme Optræden, hans geniale Paradokser, hans æggende Angreb"—an image that has not changed substantially in the last ninety-five years, although it has lost its force to intimidate or repel.

Even earlier the Danish thinker and critic H. S. Vodskov (1846–1910) had called attention to Strindberg in an article entitled "Carl Snoilsky og Strindberg" contained in the Christmas 1881 number of the popular journal *Illustreret Tidende*. Vodskov had great expectations for Strindberg's future as an imaginative writer and cultural critic and offered positive assessments of the works that Strindberg had issued so far, again with particular emphasis on *Röda rummet*, although the article actually was occasioned by the publication of Strindberg's *Gillets hemlighet* (*The Secret of the Guild*), a work that Vodskov considered (a bit incongruously, we might feel today) as worthy of "en Plads paa ethvert nordisk Julebord" ("a place on every Nordic Christmas table"). *Mäster Olof* he found "som historisk Drama et grundigt og dygtigt Arbejde" ("as a historical drama, a thorough and competent work"), but he doubted that the play would be a scenic success. Noteworthy is the fact that Strindberg already had submitted this drama to the Royal Theater in Copenhagen in 1878 and that it had been rejected. He did not soon give up hope of seeing his first important drama performed in the Danish capital, however, as is evidenced by a letter to Elmgaard in which he asks rhetorically, "Skulle icke Mäster Olof gå i Köpenhamn. . . ."[3]

Although a Danish version of *Röda rummet* was not issued until 1885 (as *Det røde Værelse*), a selection from the novel had been published as early as 1880 in the translation of the influential critic and editor Otto Borchsenius in his own widely distributed periodical *Ude og Hjemme*. Borchsenius had a keen sense of literary promise; his willingness to translate from *Röda rummet* is indicative of the impact the book had made upon publication and the guarantee of future success it seemed to contain. (Incidentally, within a year of his giving Strindberg a boost on the Danish literary scene, Borchsenius was the primus motor in having the future Nobel prize-winner Henrik Pontoppidan's first stories published.) Borchsenius's association with Strindberg, although somewhat disjointed, continued for many years. In 1884 he translated the first collection entitled *Svenska öden och äventyr* (*Swedish Fates and Adventures*). Before Strindberg knew who his translator was, he wrote to Borchsenius enraptured by the quality of the Danish version: "ju förträffligt öfversatta, så vidt jag förstår! Men hvem som gjort det vet jag ej!"[4] Having been apprised who the translator was, Strindberg observed that "en författare må skatta sig lycklig att råka i sådana händer."[5] And Borchsenius had not ended his stint as a translator. His Danish version of *Lycko-Pers resa* (*Lucky Per's Journey*) appeared in 1886. By this time considerable public interest had been aroused in Strindberg because of his *succès de scandale*, *Giftas* (*Married*), from the year 1884. Strindberg was skeptical of the reception of that work in Denmark were it to be translated and wrote to Borchsenius on 26 June 1884, "Kanske Danskarne äro för sedliga för mina noveller. . . ."[6] He based his fears on the difficulties that Herman Bang had experienced with the publication of the much less provocative *Haabløse Slægter* (*Hopeless Generations*). Although the original Swedish version of *Giftas* did indeed arouse much attention in Denmark, it did not become available in Danish translation until a quarter of a century had passed. Danes who would read it had had access only to the original until 1911–12, when Poul Uttenreiter's two-volume Danish version was published. In the interim, some twenty-six volumes of Strindberg's other works had appeared in Danish translation (including two different versions of *Röda rummet*, 1885 and 1886). *Skärkarlsliv* (*Life in the Skerries*), translated originally in 1888 by Viggo Adler as *Skærgaardsfolk*, was apparently the most successful of Strindberg's books on the Danish market, for it was reissued in 1909 and 1911, and again in 1919.

Strindberg's well-known tendency to paranoia led him in part to go to Denmark in 1887 at a time when a performance of *Fadren* (*The Father*) was being prepared for the Casino Theater in Copenhagen. He had written to Edvard Brandes in April 1887: "du tänker fortfarande på mig när alla mina landsmän öfverge mig!"[7] Nevertheless, he was not without suspicions towards Danish entrepreneurs and the very next year he was complaining to the publisher P. G. Philipsen that Philipsen was more interested in suppressing than in publishing his works, "under tryck af någon dam." In this same letter Strindberg evinces an ambivalent position toward his early Danish translators: he asks Philipsen to send proof, "ty de hittills utgifna skrifterna anses vara rysliga, mest af öfversättarens okentskap med Svenska språket."[8] It is not clear whether Strindberg was now including the translations of Borchsenius in his condemnation. Generally speaking, however, his complaint is not without basis. It should be borne in mind that not all the translations to which Strindberg may have been referring had been published, notably the version of *Mäster Olof* that the Royal Theater rejected in 1878.

If not a utopia in actuality, Denmark seemed in 1887 to be an enlightened and inviting place to Strindberg and in November of 1887 he established himself at Klampenborg north of Copenhagen while he entertained the idea of founding an experimental theater in the Danish capital. The move to the "Skovlyst" estate near Lyngby in May of 1888 has special significance in Strindberg's life, for the story of its degenerate, aristocratic owner was to become the nucleus of Strindberg's best-known naturalistic play, *Fröken Julie* (*Miss Julie*) and to provide the substance for his novel *Tschandala*. Incidentally, this novel enjoys a peculiar position in the history of Strindberg's texts, for the original Swedish manuscript was lost a matter of months after it was written—but not until it had been translated into Danish by the writer and publisher Peter Nansen. The Swedish version now included in the collection *Svenska öden och äventyr* is thus a retranslation from the Danish. Although Strindberg was given to hyperbole in his description of the "gypsy" baroness Ivanoff in his novel, the parallels and similarities are striking between her and the owner of the rundown "Skovlyst" estate, the self-anointed Countess de Frankenau, factual information about whom is to be found in Harry Jacobsen's above mentioned book about Strindberg's life at "Skovlyst."

Although Strindberg's Danish experimental theater, the forerunner of the later Intima Teatern, was in point of fact no success, it nevertheless came into brief being early in 1889, after an infinite number of false starts, emotional tugs of war, and clashes of personality and opinion in which Strindberg was involved for more than a year. Despite his tottering on the brink of catastrophe, in part as a result of his irrepressible optimism—in spite of real and imaginary misery—Strindberg never lost sight of his ideal of an intimate experimental theater that would champion the new drama and engage the public imagination. As early as May 1887 he was treating with a possible producer and with possible actors for the stage he envisaged, but it was not until 9 March 1889 that his "Forsöksteater" ("Experimental Theater") had its première—not on an independent stage, to be sure, but at the well known Dagmarteater in Copenhagen. The initial success here encouraged Strindberg to enquire of Nathalia Larsen three days later whether Bang would be "scene-instructör och regissör" for the new theater.[9]

In the interim, Strindberg's *Fadren* had already been played in Danish at the Casino Theater. The premiere on 14 November 1887 had evoked a sharply divided partisan reaction, with the Brandes camp applauding Strindberg's work. Strindberg took encouraging words more to heart than discouraging ones and he was not hesitant in trying to engage well-known writers and actors to support his proposed experimental theater. Although his enthusiasm and vision kept the project alive, that same enthusiasm led him into various misunderstandings with potential collaborators. An announcement that Henrik Pontoppidan, Herman Bang, and Gustav Wied all would be furnishing the nonexistent theater with new plays drew forth a flat public denial from Pontoppidan, who seems to have had no further association with Strindberg.

One might have expected some bitterness in Strindberg's attitude toward the Danish theater in general, for his experiences with the prestigious Royal Theater were negative. As mentioned above, *Mäster Olof* had been rejected outright. *Gillets hemlighet* was accepted by the theater but never performed; and *Herr Bengts hustru* (*Sir Bengt's Wife*) was also rejected. Moreover, *Fröken Julie* was considered by right-thinking burghers to be immoral, and the premiere scheduled in early March of 1889 was forbidden by the ministry of justice and prevented by the police. Strindberg's *Paria* was substituted for the more shocking play. Feelings about *Fröken Julie* ran so high that the Copenhagen newspaper *Avisen* agitated editorially against it (11 March 1889) and demanded that Strindberg be deported from Denmark. Like Ibsen's *Gengangere* (*Ghosts*) in Berlin, Strindberg's *Fröken Julie* was originally performed privately—in Strindberg's case at "Studentersamfundet" ("The Student Society") in Copenhagen on 14 and 15 March 1889, apparently through the mediation of the Danish playwright Gustav Wied.

Strindberg was also involved tangentially in the realm of Danish belles-lettres. He contributed to Carl Behrens' periodical *Ny Jord*, where Knut Hamsun first published part of *Sult* (*Hunger*), and to the two popular journals *Ude og Hjemme* and *Illustreret Tidende*. Even before he came to Denmark, "Den literære Reaktion i Sverige efter

1865," the Danish version of a lecture Strindberg had given 25 November 1885 in Paris, appeared in the journal *Tilskueren*.[10] Despite all the difficulties that Strindberg is perceived as having had during his prolonged sojourn in Denmark, he seemed for a time to prefer the Danish to the Swedish atmosphere. In a letter of 14 April 1888 to Verner von Heidenstam he could write, "Dansken är nya intelligensadeln, Svensken den döende soldat-adeln."[11] Such a radical assessment is accepted today as having limited validity in any analysis of Strindberg's conviction—as is his comment to one of his Danish translators, Gustav Wied's one-time fiancée Nathalia Larsen: "Jag sade också åt Georg Brandes sist att jag trodde mankönet vara öfverkultureradt och derför på retur, så att om man ville göra något man måste adjungera sig med qvinnorna som hafva barnatron och derför kraften."[12]

It was as if a grand balloon had been blown up only to suffer a rip in its fabric and lose its carrying capacity. Within a month Strindberg's attention was directed to other matters than the "Försöksteater." The gas was gone from the balloon and his Danish collaborators were left to extract themselves from the shreds. On 24 March he wrote to Nathalia Larsen and, after announcing prematurely that he was divorcing Siri von Essen, remarked that since "jag snart reser till Stockholm, må Ni se till att spela ihop Era pengar sjelfva. . . ."[13] And on 31 March he wrote Gustav Wied: "Bed henne [Nathalia Larsen] emellertid icka trötta ut mig med sitt bjebb och erinra henne artigare än jag kan skrifva det; att vid Strindbergs Försöksteater . . . fins endast en oumbärlig person, Strindberg sjelf!"[14] In the same letter he passed judgment on Wied's play *En Hjemkomst*, which he already had incorporated into the repertoire of the "Försöksteater": "jag finner ditt stycke dumt" ("I find your piece stupid"). For Strindberg there was apparently little milk and honey left in Freya's realm. Chapter one of "Strindberg and Denmark" was ended. Strindberg left Denmark for Stockholm during the second half of April 1889.

During the time that Strindberg was living in Denmark he was well represented on the book market. Six books by him had appeared in Danish—translated by Viggo Adler, Peter Nansen, and Nathalia Larsen. In the following nine years, however, Strindberg became literally and figuratively more distant and only two items in book form were issued in Copenhagen, both translated by Adler: *Ved Havbrynet* (*I havsbandet*) (*By the Open Sea*) in 1892 and *Helvede* (*Inferno*) in 1897. In 1899 interest in Strindberg took an upswing, for in that year three plays appeared, all again translated by Adler: *Erik XIV, Folkungerne* (*The Saga of the Folkungs*), and *Gustav Vasa*. Strindberg suddenly acquired a quite different cast than the radical iconoclast of the 1870s and 1880s. He was now a force to be reckoned with on the modern stage—a dramatist with numerous facets. Danish critics of various persuasions paid attention to him, although he remained clearly identified with the Brandesian circle, with whom he maintained a cordial relationship, as his many letters to Georg and to Edvard Brandes attest. By 1894 Georg Brandes wrote a twenty-page article assessing Strindberg's work for *Tilskueren*,[15] and four years later Johannes Jørgensen, who had been converted to Catholicism in 1896, sensed in Strindberg as the author of *Inferno* a contemporary who understood "Videnskabens Bankerot" ("the bankruptcy of science"), and who spoke "som en kristen, som en Katolik, ja som en Mystiker."[16]

During the 1893-94 season Strindberg had enjoyed a remarkable stage success: a Danish version of *Lycko-Pers resa* at Folketeatret had no fewer than thirty-six performances—more than any other play in that season's repertoire in the Danish capital. The tenor of Danish academic criticism indicated a recognition of Strindberg's genius. By the time of his death in 1912, his position on Parnassus was indisputable. Two Danish poets, Sophus Michaelis and Kai Hoffmann, published memorial poems in *Tilskueren* that year, and in the following issue of the periodical Ola Hansson edited "August Strindbergs Breve til mig fra Holte."[17] That is, Strindberg had suddenly become part of the literary establishment and an historical figure. By the beginning of World War I it was possible to speak of a Strindberg renaissance, as the critic Louis Levy indeed did in reporting on the guest performances of the Swedish Intima Teatern in Copenhagen in 1914.[18] In 1915 Strindberg's third wife, Harriet Bosse, visited Copenhagen. She was one of four distinguished actresses who played in dramas by Strindberg that year: the others were Johanne Dybwad, Manda Björling, and Betty Nansen.

"Atter en Strindberg-Forestilling! Det gaar unægtelig Slag i Slag," exclaimed Louis Levy in *Tilskueren* in early 1918. He continued, "Ja, det er det, vi oplever i vor dramatiske Kunst: Strindbergs Erobring af Teatret. Vore dramatiske Digtere dyrker Sjælfuldhed, Strindbergs Aand og Ild."[19] His remarks were induced by the spate of performances of plays by Strindberg in the years of World War I and in particular the visits of the Stockholm Intima Teatern in Copenhagen and the appearance of the Swedish actor-director August Falck on Danish stages. Worthy of particular note is the fact that the plays now given were no longer always the starkly naturalistic pieces that had exercised critical opinion and some public wrath in the 1880s but also some of Strindberg's historical and symbolistic works. The naturalistic plays were not pushed aside, however, for August Falck played in *Bandet* (*The Bond*). *Fadren* was revived at Betty Nansen's private theater, but with limited success, whereas *Påsk* (*Easter*) at the Royal Theater in early 1918 was labeled "en glimrende Agitationsforestilling for Talescenen" by Louis Levy, writing as usual in *Tilskueren*.[20] *Tordenluft* (the Danish version of *Oväder* [*Stormy Weather*]) given at the Royal Theater in 1917 was evidently a disappointment to the critics. In early 1916 the company of Intima Teatern had staged *Gustav III*; a year later *Ett drömspel* (*A Dream Play*) was given at Dagmarteatret.

The Royal Theater finally presented *Mäster Olof* (in Danish) in 1920, but this early work by Strindberg did not live up to critical expectations. Levy wrote: "Det er ikke den Strindberg, vi tørster efter. . . ." ("This is not the Strindberg we thirst for. . . .") Within the next two years, however, spiritual pablum was made available, albeit in a mixture of older and newer works. Max Reinhardt staged German versions of Strindberg's *Spöksonaten* (*The Ghost Sonata*) and *Oväder* at the Casino Theater in 1920 and gave the theater-going public insight into the imaginative modern theater that we associate with his name. Photographs of stage settings made under his direction suggest not only a new, dynamic interpretation of the Swedish dramatist, but mark the advent of a stimulating kind of staging that emphasized lighting effects. The Dagmarteater produced *Dödsdansen* (*The Dance of Death*) (in Danish, *Dödedansen*) the same year, although without the spectacular technique of Reinhardt's performances. Levy called it "en *fornem* Forestilling" ("a *distinguished* performance"), a characterization that was no doubt meant as a left-handed compliment, but Axel Broe identified the play as "Kunstens Triumf over Livets Tragedie."[21] Curiously enough, Reinhardt also put on his own German version of *Dödsdansen* at Dagmarteater in 1920, but despite the independent quality of his presentation, criticism favored the Danish performance, if we are to trust the judgment of Sten Neuman.[22]

The year after the Copenhagen public had enjoyed both Reinhardt's staging of Strindberg and a taste of the later Strindberg as well, Sven Lange's edition of Strindberg's works in seven volumes began publication. Instead of marking a new departure, however, this edition punctuated the second chapter of the saga of August Strindberg in Denmark. Rather than becoming a basis for renewed concern with the Swedish dramatist or the instigation for new performances, the edition served to put Strindberg into a retrospective historical focus and bestow on his work an historical patina. A younger generation was not encouraged to orientate itself on Strindberg in its own dramatic travail. And a new Danish drama was evolving.

The late 1920s and the 1930s were productive and many-faceted years for Danish drama. The living Strindberg tradition preserved the master's precepts, but it was not keyed to a changing world and did not permit the freedom of treatment and interpretation with which a classical dramatist eventually becomes endowed—and that Strindberg has achieved today in Denmark as elsewhere. In 1917 Otto Rung had written that "Strindberg bør indgaa som fast i enhver Tids aandelige Ernæring—saavel som Shakespeare og Holberg."[23] Although the statement may be considered a truism, Strindberg had to be liberated from his own theater in order to join Shakespeare and Holberg as a classic. When August Falck brought his company to the Danish Royal Theater in 1926 and gave *Fadren* and *Påsk*, he did not achieve a popular success. His was really a final act of the dramatic apostolic succession. Strindberg's brilliance was dimmed, although now and then there were revivals of the one play or another. During the years of the second World War, three of Strindberg's plays were given in Copenhagen: *Ett drömspel* at the Royal Theater in January 1940, *Fröken Julie* at Riddersalen (a theater that corresponded in size to Strindberg's concept of an intimate theater) in October 1941, and *Svanevit* (*Swanwhite*), also at Riddersalen, in November 1942. The first of these wartime performances was called "en Begivenhed" by the incisive Danish critic Fredrik Schyberg, but the last of the plays was, according to Schyberg, received "uden Varme" and Schyberg himself dismissed that play as a "Læsedrama." *Fröken Julie* was moderately successful, but, as Schyberg pointed out, was an especially difficult assignment since the play had become in retrospect a prototype of the naturalistic drama: "det farlige . . . ligger ja netop i dets Berømmelse."[24]

In the 1930s Denmark became preëminent in Scandinavia by virtue of its own drama. Kaj Munk, Kjeld Abell, and Soya, the three leading Danish dramatists of these years, could not help being familiar with Strindberg, but it is not easy to pin down elements of their work for which they are indebted to him. Indeed, although a few parallels might be drawn with some passages in Kaj Munk, both Abell and Soya are non-Strindbergian. There was much that was original in all three playwrights, and the inspiration from without that helped generate and form their works for the stage did not derive from Strindberg—not even via the independent interpretations of Max Reinhardt.

Not until forty years after Strindberg's death did his work begin to exert a dominant force in the Danish theater. By the late 1950s, the spell cast by Intima Teatern was broken and Strindberg's stature was fully recognized and heeded. The modernity of Strindberg was now felt and the possibilities that his plays offered were appreciated. He was no longer the author of *Röda rummet*—today read only by students of literary history—or even the author of *Giftas*, although that work is not banned merely to the realm of literary history. For Denmark, like the rest of the world, Strindberg is primarily a dramatist—and one of the eminent dramatists of the world. Nevertheless, a selection from *En blå bok* (*A Blue Book*) translated by Leif Leifer was issued in the popular series "Hasselbalchs Kultur-Bibliotek" in 1963 and a selection of Strindberg's poems edited by Erling Nielsen was published as a volume of "Gyldendals nordiske lyrikserie" in 1961.

With the aid of the annual *Teateraarbogen* edited by Svend Kragh-Jacobsen, it is easy to follow the history of performances on all Danish stages starting with 1955 and for a little more than a decade. As a consequence, Strindberg's fate in the Danish theater can be clearly plotted for these years.

During the 1955–56 season no Strindberg at all was played in Denmark, but the next year *Påsk* in the version by H. Jahn-Nielsen had ten performances at the Aarhus Theater and in addition *Fröken Julie* in the old translation of Sven Lange was shown on Danish television 12 December. The following season, 1957–58, *Fröken Julie* in a new translation by Povel Kern was played twenty times at the Royal Theater in Copenhagen, and a Swedish company (the municipal theater of Norrköping-Linköping) recalled the beginnings of Strindberg on the Danish stage in the late 1880s by giving two performances of *Paria, Den starkare* (*The Stronger*), and *Leka med elden* (*Playing with Fire*) at the provincial theater of Odense. In 1958–59 *Fröken Julie* again dominated the scene, but now as a ballet at the Royal Theater, with twenty-eight performances. The play itself was also broadcast once more on Danish television in February of 1959. *Den starkare* in a new translation by Einer Plesner was shown on television in June of the same year.

Radio and television found Strindberg to be useful and malleable. In 1959–60 Otto Borchsenius's nineteenth-century translation of *Bandet* —which previously had been broadcast in December of 1952—was transmitted by the Danish Radio Theater. In January 1960 *Oväder* was transmitted in Swedish from Stockholm over Danish television and in April television brought a performance of *Påsk* in Sven Lange's translation. The following season there was but a single performance of a play by Strindberg, Sven Lange's translation of *Oväder*, broadcast by the Radio Theater in September. The 1961–62 season, however, was a highpoint in the new appreciation of Strindberg, but with radio and television dominating. Sven Lange's Danish version of *Oväder* was repeated, and *Påsk* in the translation by H. Jahn-Nielsen, which first had been broadcast in 1954, was given in April 1962. The Radio Theater also broadcast Danish versions of *Den starkare, Ett drömspel,* and *Leka med elden* (the last two in Lange's translation). Somewhat more remarkable was the broadcast in February 1962 of a new translation of *Erik XIV*, for the translation was the work of one of Denmark's leading imaginative writers, Hans Christian Branner. There were also two performances in Swedish broadcast: one of *Fröken Julie* by radio in March, one of *Dödsdansen* by television in May of 1962. On the legitimate stage Strindberg was represented only at the Aarhus theater where a combined program of *Leka med elden* and *Paria* (in Lange's translations) played ten times and *Den starkare* played eight times.

In 1962–63 there was again but a single performance—of *Ett drömspel* transmitted by television from Stockholm (5 May 1963), but in the next season, 1963–64, Strindberg's popularity reached a new height. *Gustav III* in a new translation by Povel Kern played thirty-five times at the Royal Theater while a new troupe, "Det Danske Teater" played *Fröken Julie* on various stages no fewer than forty-four times. The theater at Aalborg performed both *Fröken Julie* and *Bandet* in the new Danish translations twenty-six times. In addition Danish versions of *Ett drömspel* and of *Påsk* were transmitted by the Radio Theater in July and in March respectively. The following season, 1964–65, *Gustav III* continued for seventeen more performances at the Royal Theater. The Radio Theater repeated the Danish version of *Bandet* that previously had been transmitted in 1952 and 1960, but also broadcast a new translation (by Hanne Dissing) of Strindberg's *Maradörer* (*Marauders*) on 12 January 1965. These statistics, although fifteen years old, suggest the position that Strindberg holds in the realm of Danish theater today. We might wish for more recent and more detailed statistics that would round out the story of Strindberg on the Danish stage. Such statistics could, to be sure, be worked out, but not by a scholar one ocean and many soybean fields removed from Kongens Nytorv.[25]

The lasting attraction of Strindberg is suggested by the many prominent literati who have taken the trouble to translate him into Danish. The prestige associated with his name today makes it the more understandable that Hans Christian Branner and, more recently, the poetess Inger Christensen and the opera singer Frans Lasson would use their energies to produce new Danish versions of works by Strindberg—*Brända tomten* (*The Burned House*) and *Drottning Kristina* (*Queen Christina*) respectively. The accuracy and quality of the many translations have never been examined and evaluated. That is a future task for an inquiring critic.[26]

A word remains to be said about Strindberg's image in Danish literary history and criticism. From being the wild man from the north, he has himself become a measuring stick and criterion—which is something else than being taken for granted. He is no longer a matter of dispute or even critical reassessment—unlike Ibsen. Danish literary journals since World War II have devoted very little space to any discussion of Strindberg, whereas newspapers have concerned themselves with criticism of the various aspects of the many performances of Strindberg's plays that have taken place on Danish stages. Strindberg has finally joined Shakespeare and Holberg, as Otto Rung wished that he might in 1917.

Notes

1. *August Strindbergs brev*, ed. Torsten Eklund, 2 (Stockholm: Bonniers, 1948), pp. 205–206 (hereafter *Brev*).
2. Georg Nordensvan, "De unge i Sveriges Literatur. En Oversigt," *Tilskueren*, 2 (1885), p. 651. Translation by N. Neergaard. "With this book commences the life of the new literature." ". . . with his violent manner, his brilliant paradoxes, his stirring attacks."
3. Letter to Bertel Elmgaard, 7 August 1882, *Brev*, 3: 64. "Wouldn't *Master Olof* go in Copenhagen?"
4. Letter to Otto Borchsenius, 8 April 1884, *Brev*, 4: 108. ". . . superbly translated, as far as I can understand. But as to who has done it, I do not know."
5. Letter to Otto Borchsenius, 24 May 1884, *Brev*, 4: 176. ". . . an author may count himself fortunate to be in such hands."
6. Letter to Otto Borchsenius, 26 June 1884, *Brev*, 4: 236. "Perhaps the Danes are too moral for my novellas. . . ."
7. Letter to Edvard Brandes, approximately 29 April 1887, *Brev*, 6: 194. "You are still thinking of me when all my countrymen abandon me."
8. Letter to P. G. Philipsen,' 19 April 1888. ". . . under the influence of some lady." ". . . for the pieces thus far published are considered dreadful, largely because of the translator's lack of familiarity with the Swedish language."
9. Letter to Nathalia Larsen, 12 March 1889, *Brev*, 7: 279. ". . . stage manager and director."
10. *Tilskueren*, 3 (1886), 388–99.
11. Letter to Verner von Heidenstam, 14 April 1888, *Brev*, 7: 73. "The Dane is the new aristocracy of intelligence, the Swede the dying soldier-aristocracy."
12. Letter to Nathalia Larsen, 20 December 1888, *Brev*, 7: 206. "I also told Georg Brandes recently that I thought the male sex is over-refined and therefore on the decline, so that if one wants to accomplish anything one must coopt the women who have childlike faith and therefore strength."
13. Letter to Nathalia Larsen, 24 March 1889, *Brev*, 7: 292. "I am shortly going to Stockholm; you will have to see to it yourselves that you recoup your money. . . ."
14. Letter to Gustav Wied, 31 March 1889, *Brev*, 7: 298. "Ask her [Nathalia Larsen], however, not to tire me out with her yapping and remind her more politely than I can write it that at Strindberg's 'Experimental Theater' . . . there is only one indispensable person, Strindberg himself!"
15. Georg Brandes, "August Strindberg," *Tilskueren*, 11 (1894), 341–62.
16. Johannes Jørgensen, "Strindbergs nye Bog," *Tilskueren*, 15 (1898), 153–72. ". . . as a Christian, as a Catholic, yes, as a mystic."
17. Sophus Michaëlis, "August Strindberg," *Tilskueren*, 1912/1: 527–28; Kai Hoffman, "Ved August Strindbergs Død," ibid., pp. 529–30; Ola Hansson, "August Strindbergs Breve til mig fra Holte," *Tilskueren*, 1912/2: 31–49.
18. Louis Levy, "Teater-Dagbog," *Tilskueren*, 1915/1: 108–112.
19. Louis Levy, "Strindberg og Teatret," *Tilskueren*, 1918/1: 176–80. "Again a Strindberg performance! It proceeds inexorably, without pause." "Yes, that is what we are

experiencing in our dramatic art: Strindberg's conquest of the theater. Our dramatic poets worship a plenitude of soul, Strindberg's spirit and fire."

20. Louis Levy, "Strindbergs 'Paaske'," ibid., p. 476. ". . . a glittering, stirring performance for the spoken stage."

21. Axel Broe, *Teatret*, 20 (1920), 26. ". . . the triumph of art over the tragedy of life."

22. Sten Neuman, "Dødedansen," *Teatret*, 20 (1920), 60.

23. Otto Rung, "Det kgl. Teaters Strindberg-Forestilling," *Teatret*, 17 (1917), 1–6. "Strindberg should be permanently included in the spiritual sustenance of every age—as are Shakespeare and Holberg."

24. Fredrik Schyberg, *Teatret i Krig: 1939–1948* (Copenhagen, 1948), ". . . an event" (26). ". . . without warmth" (27). ". . . closet drama" (57). "The dangerous aspect of the matter . . . lies precisely in its fame" (57).

25. Some information about the performances of Strindberg's plays in Sweden, Denmark, and elsewhere is to be found in reports printed annually in *Meddelanden från Strindbergssällskapet*. See No. 39 (May 1967) and following for the years 1966 ff.

26. An analytical—and damning—review of the Danish versions of *Hemsöborna* is to be found in *Meddelanden från Strindbergssällskapet*, No. 34 (March 1964), pp. 19–23.

Edvard Brandes and August Strindberg: Encounter between Critic and Artist

Carl Reinhold Smedmark
(Translated by Horace Engdahl)

The explosion of social and literary ideas in Scandinavia in the late 1870s and 1880s that we are accustomed to call "the modern breakthrough" brought the writers of the different Nordic countries into close contact with each other: they had a common enemy in political and cultural conservatism, and they encountered the same difficulties in winning acceptance for their views in the newspapers and periodicals. Neither before nor after has there been such a close relationship among the Nordic writers, and in many respects the literature of the Scandinavian countries formed a single movement.

Georg Brandes, whose slogan in *Hovedstrømninger i det nittende Aarhundredes Litteratur* (*Main Currents in Nineteenth-Century Literature*) about putting problems into debate through literature became a common program, also tried to assume the leadership of the new radical literature, in conjunction with his brother Edvard Brandes. Their activity effectively contributed to an increase of the contacts between writers. It is typical that Edvard immediately wrote to Strindberg when he had read *Röda rummet* (*The Red Room*), asking for information about Strindberg's other writings for an intended article. They had corresponded frequently about political and literary questions. In the letters Edvard Brandes is anxious to have Strindberg join "our little circle"—that is, J. P. Jacobsen, Alexander Kielland, and Edvard Brandes—but his admiration for *Röda rummet* did not stop him from making openly critical remarks. For the first time, but not the last, he charges Strindberg with using such exaggerations as would destroy the verisimilitude of fiction. This applies, for example, to the publisher Smith, and in Brandes's view the book is too careless in its aesthetic design, the composition is loose and the character portrayal lacks the necessary consistency. According to him, Falk, Rehnhjelm, and Sellén should have been fused into a single character: "Er de ikke den samme Karakter anbragt i forskellige Kunstfag?"[1]

In the letters they also discuss efforts to promote each other's books in their respective countries. Strindberg tried to interest Ludvig Josephson, manager of the New Theater in Stockholm, in Edvard Brandes's plays. But these endeavors were in vain. Initially Strindberg reaches for an outstretched hand, but one gets the feeling that whereas Edvard Brandes is anxious to secure him for his own party, Strindberg is not looking for any organized mode of cooperation and defends his artistic independence.[2]

The epistolary friendship with Edvard Brandes came to a sudden end because of Strindberg's chapter about the Jews in *Det nya riket* (*The New Kingdom*). Through Edvard Brandes he had, however, come into contact indirectly with J. P. Jacobsen, and directly with Alexander Kielland. Later, when Strindberg went to Paris in the autumn of 1883, he became personally acquainted with Bjørnstjerne Bjørnson and Jonas Lie, both of whom declared him to be a genius, and Bjørnson saw him as Scandinavia's greatest playwright, an opinion based solely on *Mäster Olof* and the plays of the early 1880s. Through the intervention of Jonas Lie, Edvard Brandes resumed his correspondence with Strindberg, taking as an excuse J. P. Jacobsen's death in 1885. By this time the literary and cultural situation in Denmark and Scandinavia had changed. Bjørnson's play *En hanske* (*A Gauntlet*), in which the writer insisted on the same degree of premarital chastity for men as for women, had complicated the question of emancipation for women. In the course of the so-called *sedlighetsfejden* ("morality controversy") that developed around this problem, the unity between the Nordic writers dissolved: the Brandes brothers were no longer the undisputed leaders of the movement. Their demands for a literature of "tendency" and for ideological solidarity caused many writers to revolt. The brothers now found themselves involved in a battle not only with Bjørnson but also with the feminist movement, in addition to which there were now Danish writers of considerable standing—Drachmann, for example—who dissociated themselves from the literary policy of the Brandes brothers.

Edvard Brandes, together with the politican Viggo Hörup, founded in 1884 a newspaper of his own, *Politiken*, and was therefore in need of a great radical writer as a contributor to the new paper. He wrote to Strindberg on 25 June 1885: "Du tror, vi er et Parti hertillands. Aa, Gud hjælpe os. Nej, vi er en tre, fire Stykker, som lige holder os oven Vande. Der gaves engang et literært Venstre, som var antiromantisk og antireligiöst—men det er forbi. Vi er blot Resterne tilbage."[3] The fact was that Strindberg in an earlier letter, had described his own situation as that of a complete loner, whereas in Denmark there was "a party."

At the same time, the trial centering around the short story collection *Giftas* (*Married*) in 1884 changed Strindberg's position with regard to the Swedish reading public, and the resistance against his works solidified. He needed a new market for his books, and accordingly, he promptly accepted Edvard Brandes's promise to give his works vigorous promotion in Denmark. But what were the conditions necessary for a successful cooperation between the two writers?

Brandes sympathized with Strindberg's revolutionary socialist views and with his recently developed atheism. Brandes emphasizes the importance of Strindberg's antireligious outlook. They also shared a critical attitude to the morality propounded in Bjørnson's *En hanske*. As a journalist, Edvard Brandes could also well understand Strindberg's utilitarian view of art, which made a clean sweep of belles-lettres, although he repudiated the pointed overstatements of Strindberg's aesthetics. He admired his prose style and his skill in writing dramatic dialogue, his extensive knowledge, and his wealth of detail in widely disparate areas. On the other hand, he did not appreciate the unrestrained subjectivity of Strindberg's personality and production, and he had a strongly critical opinion of the excesses of Strindberg's struggle against the feminist movement. In particular he rejected Strindberg's reactionary criticism of the feminist demand to be given access to the labor market, and took a negative view of his misogynist attitudes. Brandes had a very low opinion of Strindberg as a theoretical thinker: his ideas were not even worth "a bean." Brandes also pointed to inconsistencies in Strindberg's cultural criticism. Ironically, however, it would develop that Edvard and Georg Brandes's naturalistic view of art was far more limited than Strindberg's own. Edvard Brandes was far too quick in describing the strong effects of Strindberg's writings as melodramatic. Finally, the brothers showed themselves unable to appreciate the psychology that appears in Strindberg's naturalistic plays of the late 1880s and in "Hjärnornas kamp" ("The Battle of the Brains"), blinded as they were by the feminist problem. Nor was Edvard Brandes capable of understanding the radical dramatic form that Strindberg initiated with *Fröken Julie* (*Miss Julie*).

The relationship between Strindberg and Edvard Brandes developed very rapidly in 1885. Not more than a month after the first contacts were made, Edvard Brandes invited him to write for *Politiken*, and after another two months he wanted to become Strindberg's literary agent in Denmark. We read in a letter of September 1885:

"Endelig: vær saa venlig at betragte mig som Din Befuldmægtigede her i Danmark. Det vil sige, annuler alle gamle Aftaler og slut ingen nye uden gennem mig."[4] Edvard Brandes wanted complete control of Strindberg's Danish connections.

Thereby Strindberg found himself joined to the cultural campaign waged by the Brandes brothers. Edvard Brandes's view of literature is manifest in the following quotation from a letter to Strindberg on 8 July 1885: "Og om jeg dramatiserer min Avisartikel og kalder den for et Skuespil idet jag fingerer at mine Abstraktioner er virkelige Mennesker, hvad er Ulykken? Hvad det kommer an paa, er at finde de bedst mulige Midler til Agitation, Propaganda, Udspredning af Fornuft—jeg er lige glad, hvordan det sker, naar det blot nogenlunde kan lykkes."[5]

A corroboration of Edvard Brandes's opinion of Strindberg's writings can be found in an examination of his reviews and various statements in the letters. In this context one has to point out that in all probability not all of Brandes's letters to Strindberg have been preserved. There are many more letters from Strindberg, at least some of which ought to have been answered.

The first book to be reviewed by Edvard Brandes after the contact had been resumed was *Utopier i verkligheten* (*Utopias in Reality*), which Brandes himself translated, with the exception of the story "Samvetskval" ("Pangs of Conscience"). (Otto Borchsenius had published a translation of that story in *Ude og Hjemme* in 1884.) Already in a letter of September 1885 he characterizes the book as an important work and calls attention to "Återfall" ("Relapse") as being the best story,[6] but wanted to save his critical objections for a review article.

But when he presents *Utopier i verkligheten* in *Politiken* on 10 December 1885, he takes the opportunity to strike out at the conservative opinion in Scandinavia that had driven two of the foremost writers of the Nordic countries, Ibsen and Strindberg, into exile. Thus *Utopier i verkligheten* is used as a weapon in the cultural struggle and it is the stories inspired by socialism that receive praise. Strindberg is entirely a social critic, he is "paa en gang en Læge, der vil kurere, en Advokat, der vil forsvare, en Arkitekt, der vil bygge, en Profos, der vil eksekvere, en General, der vil føre."[7] The review calls attention to the struggle against social injustices, but refrains from mentioning Strindberg's cultural criticism, the inconsistencies of which Edvard Brandes had commented on in *Politiken* on 20 October 1884, then with reference to *Giftas*. His polemics are confined to objections against the merciless sentence that Strindberg passes upon belles-lettres in "Över molnen" ("Above the Clouds"). Most likely Brandes restrains his critical remarks on a work that, in the beginning of his article, he characterizes as the most important book to be published in Scandinavia in 1885. "Jeg vil berømme den (*Utopier*) af al Magt, naar den foreligger paa Dansk. Vi har fælles Fjender, saa vil vi ikke kriges," he writes in a letter to Strindberg on 23 September 1885.[8]

It is remarkable that the review completely fails to mention "Samvetskval," which we today tend to look upon as the most interesting story in the collection because of its harrowing description of von Bleichroden's mental breakdown. The review shows that Brandes focuses on the intellectual battles, and that seems to be the reason why he makes no reference to "Samvetskval" in spite of its psychological interest.

The next work that he came to consider was *Tjänstekvinnans son I* (*The Son of a Servant I*). "Den er betydelig og gavnlig og dybsindig og ærlig. Jeg skriver vist imorgen en Artikel om den—jeg har snart Vanen med at gøre Reklame for Dig."[9] On 15 November 1886 he reviewed the book, directing attention primarily to both the description of the child as deprived of legal protection as well as the inability of the grown-ups to mitigate the sufferings of the child because they have forgotten all about their childhood. In a moderate way he tries to temper the picture of the father and breadwinner as a martyr and the picture of the idle mother by pointing to her frequent childbirths. Strindberg also here falls victim to his own widely proclaimed antiaestheticism. Edvard is of the opinion that Strindberg puts too few artistic demands on himself, and he maintains that *Tjänstekvinnans son* contains repetitions and rather extensive digressions, but he gives no examples, and one is entitled to take a skeptical view of this criticism. It is uncertain if Brandes wholly appreciated the psychology of *Tjänstekvinnans son*. He talks about the vacillations of the style, "noget usammenhængende i Udviklingen,"[10] but perhaps this is only meant as a defense for the brutal sincerity of the book. In any event it may well indicate that the picture of Johan's personality did not quite appeal to him.

Giftas II was reviewed by Georg Brandes, the reason for which can hardly have been that he should have rated it superior in artistic value to Strindberg's other writings. As a matter of fact he turned his review of 25 December 1886 into a contribution to the campaign against woman's emancipation. After pointing out that Strindberg had more or less turned around on the question of women's rights since he wrote *Giftas I*, and had plunged himself with reckless subjective zeal into downright misogyny, and completely lost his good spirits in the process, Georg Brandes condemns the battle of the sexes, which he looks upon as a greater evil than war between states and races. But once he has made this reservation, he rushes to Strindberg's defense. The blame for starting the battle of the sexes did not lie with Strindberg, but with the emancipation movement itself. Brandes falls in with Strindberg's objections against the morality of *En hanske*, regretting at the same time that he damages his cause by exaggerations and thereby comes to resemble the extreme feminists. This, however, gives Brandes occasion for a lengthy digression about the man-hatred of the Norwegian writer Camilla Collet and her followers.

Georg Brandes shared his brother Edvard's opinion of Strindberg's utilitarian view of art. In *Giftas II* Strindberg abandons his reliable and effective artistic form in favor of an open expression of his views. But Brandes finds an excuse for this inclination by emphasizing the fact that Pontoppidan's *Mimoser* (*Mimosas*) and Garborg's *Mannfolk* (*Menfolk*) are written in a way so as to make possible an interpretation contrary to the one that the writers had actually intended.

Edvard Brandes is not necessarily of one mind with his brother Georg, but in a letter on 18 December 1886, speaking of the preface of *Giftas II*, he complains that the stories have been written without care, but he also agrees with the objections against the *Gauntlet* morality.[11]

To far too great an extent the judgment of Strindberg's plays came to be determined by the woman problem. Part of the blame for that must, no doubt, fall on Strindberg himself. The original version of *Kamraterna* (*Comrades*), which was called *Marodörer* (*Marauders*), is very similar to *Giftas* and is more concerned with the woman problem than is *Kamraterna*. In a letter Edvard Brandes praises this comedy because of its technique, a judgment that has not been confirmed by posterity. But, he posits, since Bertha is a villain and Axel an angel, the play becomes a "witty and ingenious pamphlet." Gaga is but vaguely drawn, and certain other characters are also too loosely delineated.[12] On 28 April 1888 *Kamraterna* was reviewed by Edvard Brandes, and this time the play was surprisingly enough censured for its composition. It is quite possible that the opinion of his brother Georg had influenced Edvard. In a letter of 2 April 1888 he reports that his brother had criticized the composition but gives no further details.[13] On the subject of the woman problem he condemns, as always, Strindberg's objections to women's struggle to win access to the labor market. He adopts Georg Brandes's tactics of contrasting Strindberg's idea of women with the romantic worship of women cherished by the feminist champions of emancipation and by some other writers. "Man bør da langt mindre betragte hans (Strindbergs) sidste Skuespil som *Reaktion* mod Ibsens eller Bjørnsons, end som *Supplement* til den."[14] Strindberg applies the same standards to women as we do to men. Axel's departure in the last act stands as a parallel to Nora's departure in *Et dukkehjem* (*A Doll's House*), and Brandes maintains that women of Bertha's kind do exist. For tactical reasons he thus suppresses his real opinion about Bertha and Axel, such as had found expression in the letter on *Marodörer* earlier that year.

On 21 May 1887 Strindberg arrived in Copenhagen,[15] where he wanted to investigate the possibilities of having his plays performed. On 26 July of the same year Edvard Brandes reported to Oscar Levertin: "Strindberg! Den arme Mand, et nedbrudt hallucineret Menneske, som trænger til Medgang, for hvem nu alle Sunde er spærrede. De kan umulig tænke Dem noget saa Tragi-Komisk som hans Kjøbenhavnerophold."[16] It is hard to determine whether Edvard Brandes's personal contacts with Strindberg in any way changed his attitude toward him. In any case it did not influence his judgment of *Fadren* (*The Father*). The day before Strindberg arrived Brandes expressed his admiration for the play, for the skillful dialogue and the dramatic crescendo.[17] But he objects to Laura's being a villain only because she is a woman. He thought that *Fadren*, too, was something of a diatribe against women. On the other hand he considers the story "Hjärnornas kamp" in *Vivisektioner* (*Vivisections*) as less significant. Thus, he still thinks of Strindberg's plays as merely a product of the struggle against the emancipation of women. He takes no notice of the new psychology of the play: in the review of 5 October 1887, speaking of Laura, he repeats the word "pamphlet." But Strindberg's exposition, with the problem of Nöjd's paternity, receives Brandes's unqualified praise, as does the gradual development towards the final collapse. But Brandes's ideological perspective seems curiously restricted when he finds nothing else worth mentioning in the brilliant scene between The Wet Nurse and The Captain in the last act than its strictures against Christianity. The Wet Nurse appears to him as a "Resumé af mange religiøse Disputer."[18] This is a superficial observation, for the interaction between The Wet Nurse/Mother and the child in The Captain, in its mixture of grotesque cruelty and tender affection, makes for one of the most shattering moments of the play. The ideology is of more interest to Brandes than Strindberg's view of human existence.

On 6 November 1887 Strindberg and his family arrived in Copenhagen again.[19] The immediate occasion was that *Fadren* was going to be performed in the Casino Theatre, with the actor Hunderup, an old admirer of Strindberg who had known the writer since a visit to Stockholm, acting the part of The Captain. Georg Brandes had taken it upon himself to rehearse the actors. The opening night was planned to take place on the birthday of Oehlenschläger, the national poet, a date that was chosen, according to Harry Jacobsen, because of its import in the cultural battle.[20] Strindberg was frequently in touch with the Brandes brothers during these winter months, but the necessary conditions of a more intimate contact did not exist. Strindberg did not even drop the formalities of address with Georg, and the letters to Edvard retain the same character as before their personal meeting. Already in the beginning of 1888 Strindberg withdrew and went to seek company elsewhere. In a letter to Oscar Levertin on 24 June 1888 Edvard Brandes complains about the lack of personal contact: "Strindberg ser jeg aldrig noget til. Han lever tæt herved i Lyngbye. Men allerede fra Januar maaned af søgte han mig ikke mer, naar han var i Kjøbenhavn." His letters are wholly taken up by business matters, he continues, "og han søger open langt hellere slet Selskap— daarlige Skuespiller og forfaldne Kontorister—end ordentlige Folk. Dels frygter han, vi stjæler hans Ideer, dels ser vi vist kritiske og altfor velklædte ud. . . . Han er altid lige vanvettig, genial og beklagelseværdig."[21] In the letter Edvard gives to understand that he had not found in Strindberg the supporter he had hoped for. It seems disquieting to read his conclusion that Strindberg does not "feel any solidarity with us." Lack of solidarity had often been the cause of breaches between Danish and Norwegian writers. The Brandes brothers demanded rigid unity around shared ideas, and many writers felt it was difficult to endure this pressure. When Strindberg finally comes to disagree with Edvard Brandes he points out that he is in good company: Ibsen, Bjørnson, Kielland, Drachmann were among those who had alienated themselves from the Brandes brothers. Strindberg probably felt this pressure when he came to Denmark and deliberately kept at a distance. But as long as Edvard Brandes was still of use to him, he tempered his disaffection.

The correspondence shows a long hiatus between 25 January and 16 March. We have eight letters from Strindberg, but only one from Edvard Brandes, dating from December 1887 to 16 March 1888, indicating that a number of Brandes's letters have been lost. Between 2 April and 4 September there is another interruption with no letters at all, an irregularity of correspondence that shows that their relationship lacked personal warmth.

Nevertheless Edvard Brandes continued to fight for Strindberg in his reviews and to attack cultural conservatism in Sweden. In the year 1888 he reviewed—besides *Kamraterna*—*Hemsöborna* (*The Natives of Hemsö*) and *Skärkarlsliv* (*Life in the Skerries*), and it was no great effort for him to praise these books. In a review of 15 April 1888 he stresses with obvious satisfaction that in *Hemsöborna* the author's attitude to the fictional characters has an objectivity that from a naturalistic point of view is most healthy. He does not have to trouble himself with Strindberg's "philosophy, doctrines, and pedagogy" as in the more subjectively conceived works. The treatment of human character bears the impress of nature and is free from the image of woman as a villain and man as a paragon of virtue, which was found, in part, in both *Fadren* and *Kamraterna*. That Edvard Brandes was not fond of stark artistic effects is shown by his strange reaction to the final scene of the novel, in which Carlsson dies. This magnificent scene "has a certain melodramatic touch" that does not appeal to him: "Carlsson lever sikkert endnu."[22] And Strindberg's style and expert handling of dialogue now as always come in for their share of praise. In his review of *Skärkarlsliv* on 1 October 1888 Edvard Brandes lauds the author for his extensive knowledge and his power to inflame the mind, and he describes the introduction about the archipelago of Stockholm as amazingly well informed. Otherwise, now as before, it is Strindberg the naturalist who is singled out for praise; the description of the organ, for instance, he calls magnificent "in the manner of Zola." He ranks "Den romantiska klockaren på Rånö" ("The Romantic Sacristan on Rånö") as the finest piece of the collection, and behind "Uppsyningsmannen" ("The Inspector") he is inclined to see Strindberg's own face.

The first serious conflicts with Edvard Brandes came as a result of Strindberg's plans to start the Scandinavian Experimental Theater. Edvard Brandes had no faith in Strindberg as a theater manager. Despite repeated reminders he stubbornly refused to contribute any of his own plays to the repertoire of the theatre, for this represented the limit beyond which he was not prepared to extend his practical support. When Henrik Pontoppidan later, in an article in *Politiken*, ironically denied Strindberg's allegation that he was to be among the contributors, Brandes refused to publish a sharp retort from Strindberg. This conflict took place in January 1889.[23] Yet it belongs to a later date than certain statements about *Fröken Julie* and *Fordringsägare* (*Creditors*) in the letters—statements that clearly show the limitations of Edvard Brandes's understanding of Strindberg's dramatic creations.

Edvard Brandes made no contributions to the Experimental Theater. *Politiken* made no mention of *Fröken Julie* when it was published as a book, which omission Strindberg, suspicious as always, immediately noticed.[24] As it turned out, Brandes's articles about the naturalistic plays and about the Experimental Theater were rather to work against Strindberg than to support him.

After the quarrel centering around Pontoppidan the correspondence ceased and was not to be resumed until Strindberg had returned to Sweden at the end of May 1889. One gets the impression that Strindberg no longer had any function to fulfill in the cultural campaign of the Brandes brothers. Edvard's true opinions and the limitations of his appreciation become ever more apparent.

The circumstances around Edvard Brandes's review of *Fröken Julie* and *Fordringsägare* on 3 March 1889 are rather strange, a fact that has already been pointed out by Harry Jacobsen.[25] The first performance of the Experimental Theater was originally announced to take place on 2 March, but due to interference by the censor the performance of *Fröken Julie* was prohibited, and the first night had to be postponed until 9 March. Nonetheless Brandes published his review article on 3 March. He began by making comparisons—unflattering to Strindberg —with Antoine and the Théâtre Libre. He relates how the latter spent two years in careful preparation for his theater, which he contrasts with the Scandinavian Experimental Theater, "sikkert ikke raadende over et sammenspillet Personale."[26] It seems as if Edvard Brandes took Strindberg's failure for granted and yet wanted to emphasize that Strindberg's reputation did not rest on his possible ability to manage a theater but rather on his writings.

However, this introduction was tactless in anticipating the course of events, and Strindberg took offense. Harry Jacobsen thinks that Edvard Brandes's attack in the Danish parliament on the privileges of the Royal Theater gave him a reason not to take part in the activities of the Experimental Theater.[27] He also may have felt wronged because he was not consulted more frequently, a supposition that Strindberg supports in a letter to Siri von Essen: "Edv. Br. kommer troligen att skälla ner allihop derför att han ej fått öfva in Er!"[28] He considered himself an expert in theater and had written a book on acting, all of which might explain the ironical tone of the review but hardly accounts for his lack of understanding of the psychology and the new dramatic technique in *Fröken Julie* and *Fadren*.

He begins with a sharply critical examination of Strindberg's view of women in *Fordringsägare*, to which he gives more space than to *Fröken Julie*. All tactical considerations that had induced him to defend Bertha in *Kamraterna* are now brushed aside. *Fordringsägare* is written along much the same lines as *Fadren* and *Kamraterna*, but in these two plays Strindberg, according to Brandes, expressed himself much better. Consequently Brandes is unable to see anything but the connection between the plays and Strindberg's polemics on the subject of the woman problem. He speaks ironically of Gustav and suggests that Tekla may be right when she calls her first husband an imbecile. Strindberg gives a "kadaver-tragisk" ("utterly tragic, absurdly tragic") description of the antagonism between man and woman, which compels Brandes completely to reject the subtitle "tragicomedy." The character portrayal is blurred and we have too little information about the characters: Gustav is an angel of vengeance and Adolf a dependent "milksop." Not even Tekla, who after all gets the mildest treatment, arouses any enthusiasm. But the masterly dialogue and the language are highly praised, as usual. A comparison between the review and the statements in the letter of 19 September 1888 shows that the criticism has been considerably sharpened. In the letter Edvard Brandes still looks upon Strindberg's image of woman as a counterimage to the idolization of women during the preceding decades. The dialogue is "often brilliant, psychologically subtle."[29] The strictures concern the vague delineation of Gustav's motives and Adolf's lack of independence.

Brandes returns to the subject of the weakness of *Fordringsägare* in his review in *Politiken* of the opening performance of the Experimental Theater on 10 March 1889, which shows even more clearly that Edvard Brandes is unable to accept Strindberg's art of psychological characterization and his technique of allowing dialogue to create dramatic tension by itself. Brandes maintains that the action is confused: "Tilskueren skal ikke sidde og spekulere over, hvorfor *det* Menneske taler og handler, som han gør."[30] Brandes also calls attention to the dramatic pattern and dismisses Strindberg's dramatic technique as inadequate: Strindberg falls short in the art of preparing for the decisive major scene of the play. Brandes adheres here to the technique of the French drama and, as we might expect, he makes reference to Dumas *père* and Dumas *fils*, as well as to Ibsen's *Fruen fra havet* (*The Lady from the Sea*). The appearance of Ibsen's sailor is foreshadowed admirably; the conversation between Gustav and Adolf, on the other hand, begins when Gustav suddenly turns up, without a word of explanation. Such an occurrence, says Brandes, has no real interest. *Paria* (*Pariah*) comes in for a share of the same kind of criticism. " 'Stykke' kan *Paria* kun kaldes med stort Forbehold: det er en Scene mellem to Personer, som vi ikke kender mere til end Katten."[31] It is a disconnected scene from a melodrama. In his review of *Tryckt och otryckt* (*Printed and Unprinted*) on 10 April 1890 Edvard Brandes, on the subject of *Paria*, expatiates on the art of preparation. He raises the same objections against *Den starkare* (*The Stronger*). "I ti Minuter fortæller den sin stumme Tilhørerinde en Mængde Sager, for hvilke de ganske uforberedte Tilskuere ikke kunde føle mindste Interesse. . . ."[32] It is obvious that Brandes had not been able to grasp Strindberg's method of basing his play exclusively on dialogue, and consequently he also fails to understand its new psychology.

On the other hand, two younger Scandinavian writers—Brandes's juniors by about ten years—the Swede Ola Hansson and the Norwegian Knut Hamsun, did understand the novelty of the naturalistic plays, because both had a deep interest in psychology. Ola Hansson, who had made Strindberg's acquaintance at the end of 1888, expresses genuine astonishment at Edvard Brandes's article of 3 March: ". . . hans kritik är periferisk alltigenom." And he goes on to state his own opinion, that the strong point of the play is "det skiftande spelet hos denna människa [Tekla] af dessa tvenne inflytanden [Gustavs och Adolfs] med dess skuggor och dagrar och alla de nyanserade mellantillstånden mellan båda."[33] He objects to Edvard Brandes's juxtaposition of Tekla with Laura and Bertha. *Fordringsägare* foreshadows a new technique for portraying women and not another contribution to the emancipation debate.

Knut Hamsun attended the first performance of the Experimental Theater and expressed his opinion of *Fordringsägare* in a newspaper article in *Dagbladet* (10 December 1889).[34] He returned to his quarters after the performance deeply moved by what he had seen. Hamsun thinks that the writing is exceptionally powerful, even if the play is no tragicomedy. He notices that the composition of *Fordringsägare* does not agree with what one expects and that the dialogue is completely predominant. But at the performance of the play all such objections are put to rest. Harry Jacobsen's supposition that the relative lack of appreciation in the reviews could ultimately have depended on the inability of the actors to do justice to the play is consequently open to discussion.[35]

Edvard Brandes's lack of understanding of the novelty of Strindberg's dramatic writings is also evident in the review of *Fröken Julie*. In a letter of 28 September 1888 he ranked the characters in the following order: Jean, Kristin, Julie. Julie is described as "less a novelty."[36] In the review of 3 March 1889 we read: "Maaske er Fröken Julie ikke ligesaa fast i Støbningen som de to andre. . . ."[37] This evaluation must seem astonishing to posterity. It is due to the fact that Brandes dwells primarily upon the social gap between the servant and the mistress. He defends this motif and the ruthlessness with which Jean's brutality is executed. He has failed to notice the deeper stratum of the play, Julie's death wish, and already in the letter of 1888 he objects to the suicide. In this case his opinion bears witness to a certain shallowness and lack of imagination, and to a narrowly naturalistic artistic creed of copying after nature. He does not believe in Julie's suicide. "Man slaar sig ikke hjel, naar der ingen Fare er paafærde, og her er ingen Fare. Maaske om 5 Maanader men ikke den Nat. Slutningen er Romantik og nødtvungen Ende paa Pjesen med Effekt."[38] We are asked by Brandes to imagine Miss Julie waiting for the pregnancy and then taking her life! In fact, Strindberg reacted sharply in a letter to Georg Brandes on 4 December 1888. He refutes the anticipated criticism of the suicide. He repeats the explanations given in the preface and points to Julie's death wish. "Sjelfmordet är motiveradt riktigt: olusten att lefva, längtan till slägtens slutande i den sista dåliga individen, adelskänslan af skam öfver tidelaget med en lägre art, närmare: suggestionerna af fogelns blod, rakknifvens närvaro, fruktan för stöldens upptäckande och den starkare viljans befallning."[39] Georg Brandes answered on 5 December that he was "almost" convinced: "A little something is lacking." The reservation was to remain with him. We have good reasons to believe that Georg shared the basic attitude of his brother. This view still finds an expression in *En bok om Strindberg* (*A Book About Strindberg*) (1894). Large parts of Georg Brandes's essay are devoted to Strindberg's contribution to the debate on the woman problem. Having dealt with *Giftas*, Georg Brandes continues with the plays of 1888–1892, which "all take the battle between the sexes as their subject. . . ." After *Fadren* there follows a "number of minor plays—*Kamraterna, Fordringsägare, Fröken Julie*." *Fröken Julie* is described as the most important of these dramas, but the only character in the play who receives mention is Jean, "en med uforligneligt Mesterskab tegnet Lakaj-Figur."[40] Not a word about Strindberg's new psychology or his new method of dramatic construction!

A far more accurate and far-sighted opinion was the one held by Knut Hamsun, whom we have already quoted in relation to *Fordringsägare*. Likewise in *En bok om Strindberg* (1894) he published an essay on Strindberg, which to a large extent uses material from two newspaper articles in *Dagbladet* of 1889. He begins with the following statement: "For mig er han sit Lands, maaske sin Tids mærkeligste Forfatterskikkelse; et overlegent Talent, en Hjærne tilhest, ridende sin egne Veje og efterladende de fleste andre langt bag sig."[41] Toward the end of the essay he lays particular stress on Strindberg's achievement in the field of psychology and points to *Vivisektioner* and the naturalistic plays:

. . . efter mit Skøn er Strindberg omtrent den eneste Forfatter i Norden, som har gjort alvorlige Tilløb til at levere moderne Psykologi. I en del dramatiske Arbejder og novellistiske Smaaskitser fra de senere Aar har han tilført Literaturen psykologiske Studier af ikke liden Værdi. . . . Strindberg fatter, fatter og erkender den nu herskende Karakterpsykologis Utilstrækkelighed til at skildre det splittede og disharmoniske Nutidsmenneske.[42]

When we return to Edvard Brandes's judgment of the same plays, it becomes even more obvious that he did not understand them, a fact that Strindberg well knew. On the day of the first performance he writes triumphantly to Ola Hansson: "Edv. B. är på efterkälken. . . . Din Paria går i afton! Den begriper han väl ej ett spår af."[43] In a review article on 15 May 1889 about Strindberg's early plays up to and including *Herr Bengts hustru* (*Herr Bengt's Wife*), Edvard Brandes extols *Mäster Olof* and *Gillets hemlighet* (*The Secret of the Guild*), and predicts a future for them as "the classical masterpieces of the Swedish stage." On 8 October 1893 there appeared a rather negative review of *Dramatik*, a volume containing all Strindberg's one-act plays from 1892 except for the best plays—*Bandet* (*The Bond*) and *Leka med elden* (*Playing With Fire*). Edvard Brandes finds them insignificant, although he notices the intense concentration of the composition and the dialogue. Misogyny rules in *Inför döden* (*Facing Death*), which "seems almost parodical." *Första varningen* (*The First Warning*) is seen in the light of *En dåres försvarstal* (*A Madman's Defense*), which due to its passionate, almost hallucinatory, intensity had made a strong impression on Brandes, but which, on account of its autobiographical background, does not do its author "much credit all the same." *Debet och Kredit* (*Debit and Credit*) is praised. On the other hand, he maintains, the most original play is *Moderskärlek* (*Mother Love*), where the set is an old actress's home and the conversation between the two half-sisters "possesses all the desirable flow and vigor."

One must agree with Hakon Stangerup when he describes Edvard Brandes's support for Strindberg as of vital importance.[44] On the other hand, it is impossible to fall in with his view that Brandes's reviews of Strindberg are "weighty reviews,"[45] for Brandes's analyses of Strindberg's plays reveal that he is hampered by an older theory of drama and by a limited view of human psychology. Nor had Strindberg any great respect for Brandes's dramatic production. Indeed, on 9 November 1889 he writes to Ola Hansson that Edvard Brandes "sank into 'Shoemaker realism' in his plays."[46]

The correspondence ceased when Edvard Brandes and Strindberg ceased to be of use to each other. The relationship with Georg Brandes was different. It is Georg Brandes who introduced Strindberg to Nietzsche, and it is to Georg Brandes that he turns in order to solicit support for his *Antibarbarus*. And finally, it is to Georg Brandes that he confides his Inferno experiences when they meet in Copenhagen in 1896.

When Strindberg in an article in *Politiken* (22 January 1912), looks back on his sojourn in Denmark in the eighties, he is generous in his remarks. He claims that he would not have been able to survive in Denmark without the help of the Brandes brothers. Edvard Brandes was always ready to assist him and his patience "was boundless." But the struggle against the conservative opinion in the press and in the Danish parliament had made him bitter. The differences of character were too great to allow any close familiarity between them. Edvard

Brandes was too skeptical for Strindberg's taste, and Strindberg in his turn seemed too much of a "romantic" to Brandes. In reality, Strindberg had more sympathy with Georg: "Men riktigt nära kom jag aldrig, ty det fanns ett hemligt program, problemdebatten, poesien som tjänare, icke som herre, Pegasus im Joche, m.m., vilket emellanåt steg upp som en mur emellan oss."[47]

Notes

1. Georg og Edvard Brandes, *Brevveksling med nordiske Forfattere og Videnskabsmænd*, 6 (Copenhagen: Gyldendal, 1939), p. 8. "Aren't they the same character applied to different arts?"
2. Ibid., pp. 4–5.
3. Ibid., p. 43. "You believe that we are a party here in this country. Oh, God help us. No, there are three or four of us who have managed to stay above water. There once existed a literary Left, which was antiromantic and antireligious—but that is all gone. There are only remnants of us left." The connections between Strindberg and Edvard Brandes have earlier been discussed by Harry Jacobsen in *Strindberg i Firsenes København* (Copenhagen, 1948), but Jacobsen is less interested in Edvard Brandes's purely literary judgment of Strindberg's writings.
4. Ibid., p. 51. "Finally: do me the favor of granting me your power of attorney in Denmark. That is, cancel all previous agreements and do not conclude any new ones except through me."
5. Ibid., p. 47. "If I should dramatize my newspaper article and call it a play and pretend that my abstractions are real human beings, what's the harm? What really matters is to find the best possible instruments for agitation and propaganda, for the dissemination of reason—I am equally delighted regardless of how that is done, once it meets with tolerable success."
6. Ibid., p. 52.
7. ". . . at once a doctor who wants to cure, a lawyer who wants to defend, an architect who wants to build, a provost marshal who wants to execute, a general who wants to lead."
8. Ibid., p. 55. "I intend to praise it (*Utopias*) with all energy, when it appears in Danish. We have common enemies, so we shall not quarrel."
9. Ibid., pp. 82–83. "It is an important and useful and profound and sincere book. I shall probably write an article about it tomorrow—I shall soon be in the habit of advertising for you."
10. ". . . a certain incoherence in the development."
11. Ibid., p. 93.
12. Ibid., p. 98–99.
13. Ibid., p. 132.
14. "We have far less reason to regard his [Strindberg's] latest plays as a reaction against Ibsen's or Bjørnson's plays, than as a *supplement* to them."
15. *August Strindbergs brev*, 6, ed. Torsten Eklund (Stockholm: Bonniers, 1958), p. 203.
16. Letter from Edvard Brandes to Oscar Levertin, The Royal Library, Stockholm. "Strindberg! The poor man, a deeply afflicted and hallucinatory human being, who desperately needs success, and for whom all roads are blocked. You cannot possibly imagine anything more tragicomical than his stay in Copenhagen."
17. Georg og Edvard Brandes, pp. 110–11.
18. ". . . an epitome of many religious controversies."
19. *August Strindbergs brev*, 6: 294.

20. Jacobsen, p. 50.
21. Letter from Edvard Brandes to Oscar Levertin, The Royal Library, Stockholm. "I never see a trace of Strindberg any more. He lives close by here in Lyngbye. But already from January on, he ceased to visit me when he was in Copenhagen." ". . . and obviously he prefers that kind of company—bad actors and corrupt clerks—to decent people. Partly he fears that we shall steal his ideas, partly, it seems, we look too critical and well dressed. . . . He is always equally absurd, brilliant, and pitiable."
22. "No doubt Carlsson is still alive."
23. *August Strindbergs brev,* 7: 233, 239–40.
24. Ibid., pp. 195–96.
25. Jacobsen, pp. 105, 134–35.
26. ". . . probably lacking a well-rehearsed team of actors."
27. Jacobsen, pp. 124–25.
28. *August Strindbergs brev,* 7: 265. "Edvard Brandes will probably denigrate the whole cast, because he has not been asked to rehearse you."
29. Georg og Edvard Brandes, p. 136.
30. "The audience must not be left speculating as to why a character speaks and acts the way he does."
31. "You can call *Pariah* a 'play' only with great reservations: it is a scene with two characters who are no more known to us than the cat."
32. "For ten minutes she keeps telling her mute acquaintance a lot of things in which the wholly unprepared audience could not feel the least interest. . . ." This demand for preparation returns in the reviews of *Printed and Unprinted I and II,* in which *Pariah, The Stronger,* and *Creditors* are printed (*Politiken* 10 March and 3 August 1890). Edvard Brandes inveighs against the view expressed by Strindberg in the essay "On Modern Drama and Modern Theater" in *Printed and Unprinted I.* According to Brandes, Antoine's theater performed two *quart d'heures.* They were not printed, in addition to which they failed on the stage (10 April 1890).
33. Letter from Ola Hansson to August Strindberg, *August Strindbergs och Ola Hanssons Brevväxling 1888–1892* (Stockholm, 1938), p. 32. ". . . his criticism is altogether peripheral." ". . . the ever changing play in this character [Tekla] of these two influences [Gustav and Adolf], with its light and shade and all the varied intermediate states between the two."
34. The article about *Fordringsägare* has been reprinted and translated into German in Knut Hamsun, *Etwas über Strindberg* (Munich, 1958), pp. 50ff.
35. Jacobsen, p. 143.
36. Georg og Edvard Brandes, p. 137.
37. "Perhaps Miss Julie is not of the same solid mold as the other two characters. . . ."
38. "One does not kill oneself when there is no imminent danger, and here there is no danger. Maybe in five months, but not this very night. The final scene is romanticism and a contrived end to the play by means of false effects."
39. *August Strindbergs brev,* 7: 192–93. "The suicide is correctly motivated: the disgust for her life, the wish to let the family end in the last corrupt individual, the aristocratic sense of shame at sexual intercourse with a lower species, more precisely: the mesmerizing effect of the blood of the bird, the presence of the razor, the fear that the theft will be discovered, and the command of a stronger will."
40. *En bok om Strindberg* (Karlstad, 1894), p. 86. ". . . a lackey-type drawn with matchless skill."
41. Ibid., p. 7. "In my view he is the most remarkable writer of his country, perhaps of his time; a superior talent, a brain on horseback, riding his own paths, leaving most other people far behind."
42. Ibid., p. 33. ". . . according to my opinion, Strindberg is the only writer in Scandinavia who has made serious attempts to forward modern psychology. In a number of dramatic works and small prose sketches written over the last few years, he

has added to literature psychological studies of no small value. . . . Strindberg perceives, perceives and understands the inadequacy of the currently prevailing psychology of character in depicting the divided and disharmonious self of modern man."

43. *August Strindbergs brev*, 7: 272. "Edv. B. is getting behind. . . . Your *Pariah* will run tonight! Surely he will not understand a thing."

44. *Dansk litteraturhistorie*, 3 (Copenhagen, 1966), 184.

45. Ibid., p. 188.

46. *August Strindbergs brev*, 7: 390. Shoemaker realism is a Swedish term from the eighties designating a narrowly conceived naturalism.

47. "Minnen från Danmark" in *Samlade Skrifter*, 53, ed. John Landquist (Stockholm: Bonniers, 1919), pp. 555–56. "But we never were really close, because there was always a secret program, the debate of problems, poetry as a servant, not as a master, Pegasus in yoke, etc., which at times shot up like a wall between us."

Strindberg and Diktonius: A Second Chapter

George C. Schoolfield

In his recent monograph,[1] Bill Romefors has analyzed the two portrait poems, collectively called "Strindberg," which Elmer Diktonius (1896–1961)—one of the North's major poets in the twentieth century—included in his volume *Taggiga lågor* (*Barbed Flames*) of 1926. Romefors is convinced that there is a "stor själsfrändskap mellan de båda temperamentsfulla författarna Diktonius och Strindberg," and that "båda har samma syn på tillvaron som fylld av rörelse och aktivitet. Strindberg har gett en viktig stimulans . . . för Diktonius." Romefors's opinion about the affinity between Strindberg and Diktonius would certainly seem to hold water; it might not even be untoward to suggest that the poet Diktonius learned a good deal from Strindberg's two books of verse, *Dikter* (*Poems*) (1883) and *Ordalek och småkonst* (*Word Play and Minor Art*) (1902, 1905), or at any rate, was vastly encouraged in his own leanings: in Strindberg, one finds the fondness for radical onomatopoeia, the frequent musical imagery, the intrusion of "unpoetical" words and slang, and the pervasive sentimentality that are Diktonius's hallmarks. Yet Romefors says that "det är svårt att exakt peka på direkta spår av Strindberg i Diktonius' litterära produktion. Man får emellertid antaga att Strindbergs sätt att tänka i bilder varit befruktande för Diktonius' eget bildtänkande."[2] Romefors can be gainsaid on the first of these points; a case exists where a remarkable image of Strindberg was borrowed by Diktonius—or rather, it served as the germ-cell of a Diktonius poem. The poem, though, does not come from the rambunctious, "expressionistic" poetry of the 1920s, but from a later, more relaxed, and, it may be, more resigned period of Diktonius's career.

In Elmer Diktonius's collection of verse from 1938, *Jordisk ömhet* (*Earthly Tenderness*), there is a suite of three poems with the general title *Kuokkala*. They are written in tribute to the place on the Karelian coast where the poet spent his summer vacations in 1937 and 1938;

"Villa Golicke" is the first poem of the set. As Tito Colliander explains in a memoir, "Villa Golicke"—the object, not the poem—was in fact three villas: "De låg tätt bredvid varandra på en strandremsa, inkilad mellan havet och landsvägen från Terijoki till Systerbäck och den stängda gränsen mot Ryssland."[3] Colliander goes on to say that the piece of property was one of the many in the district that had been owned before the Revolution by prosperous Saint Petersburgers; Robert von Golicke had been the director of a printing concern. In the 1930s these beach houses, lying just inside the Republic of Finland, became a popular resort for members of Finland-Swedish literary and artistic circles, and for promising young guests from Sweden, such as Erik Lindegren and Gunnar Ekelöf. Kuokkala had the mixed attractions of a sunny beach, of decaying summer places from a grander day, of a kind of eroticism, and of sheer danger. The summer guests—one might also say *Unruhige Gäste*, in the title of Wilhelm Raabe's novel about a perilous holiday spot—could well have the sense of dancing on the edge of a volcano; special permission was needed to enter the area at all.

The neighbors of the three Diktoniuses, Elmer, Leena, and little Silja, were a prominent lot. In a letter of 20 July 1937 to Kerstin Söderholm,[4] Diktonius tells how the Enckells, the poet Rabbe and his beautiful wife Heidi, a born Runeberg, live in the house next door, amidst "Baltic dirt," and how his particular friend, the artist Sven Grönvall, is just down the beach. It was Grönvall, by the way, who appears to have called the attention of the rest of the Grankulla coterie—for the summer guests, most of them, lived near one another in the winter too, in the pleasant community just outside Helsingfors—to the special charms and possibilities of Kuokkala. In that characteristic Finland-Swedish way, connections went along family lines: Ina Behrens, the wife of Tito Colliander, was Grönvall's cousin, and Ina's grandmother was Robert von Golicke's widow; Grönvall had then lured the Enckells, and eventually the Diktoniuses (poor as churchmice and thus something of an exception in Grankulla society) down to the balmy paradise in the southeast. Other members of the Grankulla-Kuokkala circle were the writer Ralf Parland and his first wife, the writer Eva Wichman; and, a little farther away, the actress and authoress Ragna Ljungdell with her fiancé, "a Swedish-American"; Gunnar Björling, wifeless of course, was a sometime visitor. Perhaps one can get some notion of the literary tone of the place (Edith Södergran's mother lived nearby in Raivola, and pilgrimages were made to Edith's grave) by means of quotations from a letter of Rabbe Enckell to Kerstin Söderholm from 28 July 1937, and one of Diktonius to the same addressee from 29 August 1938. Enckell wrote from "Suomen Riviera' som det kallas inte utan skäl."

De tomma villorna har sin speciella något makabra charm. Vi har Diktonius familjen, Ralf. P., och Sven Grönvall som grannar. Vi ses dock inte mycket, var och en går och grundar på sitt eget. Här finns också en rikssvensk Erik Lindegren som lär ha gett ut någon diktsamling och översätter någon bok av Faulkner. Jag har dock ej blivit närmare bekant med honom. Han lär vara Lawrence-adept. [Lorenz von] Numers är också här på ett par veckor, pratsam, nyter och uppfriskad av sin resa.[5]

The letter also has a postscript in Heidi Enckell's lovely hand: "Rabbe hjälper mig så snällt. . . . Han säger att jag är så lat att jag borde ha blivit en odalisk. Bäst trivs jag i vattnet."[6] Diktonius's letter tells still more about the literary industry that prevailed, save in Heidi's case: "I Häklis pensionat där vi tar middag sitter Gunnar Ekelöf och fullbordar sin nya diktsamling, och gubben Häkli sitter själv också nätterna i ända med näsan över någon översättning. Flit, fred, och frihet råder i bokstavsfabriken."[7]

But all was not peace, and Diktonius was keenly aware of Kuokkala's view, the view he had from the large glassed-in veranda where he sat with his typewriter. His descriptions of the place never fail to mention the immediate proximity of Finland's eastern frontier and of Kronstadt's guns. Early in the stay of 1938 (27 July), Diktonius could still render Kuokkala's atmosphere in disarmingly childlike terms to Kerstin Söderholm: "Och sjön går som en solig tjilivippan och ryska flottan säger bom och jag blåser mitt tara. Kattan heter Stalin och sköldpaddan Pack så det märks man bor nära Bolsjevikien."[8] But for other correspondents he provided details that were certainly more pungent and often more sinister. To Ulla Bjerne, he wrote on 4 August 1938: "Jävla bra ort med vinölkasino i skydd av Kronstadts kanoner. Detta är avstjälpningsplats för österns och västerns rester: en förfallen idyll mot havets starka bakgrund. Från denna grund steg Södergransdikt mot skyarna, och att den fick sådan hugskottsformer och färgpraktsbilder begriper man här i detta allt-möjligt-myller; i denna friska förruttnelse."[9] (And to Josef Kjellgren, on 10 August 1937: "Kuokkala, karelska näset, där jag vistats i tre veckor och hört på historier om ryska negerlik med ålar i byxorna. Allt annat i samma stil. Hav ända till öronen och Kronstadt mittför näsan."[10]) Then, to Eyvind Johnson on 2 September 1938: ". . . denna lilla vrå bland krigen i kattors doft, i rysskanoners gömma," thus paraphrasing the third poem of the Kuokkala suite;[11] the previous April he had invited Johnson to meet him "under Kronstadts kanoner på Kuokkalas sandstränder."[12] Elsewhere, Heidi Enckell reports on Rabbe's quite understandable timidity about approaching the demarcation line (they were divorced later on); whereas in a letter of September 1939 Sven Grönvall boasts to Diktonius of his "sun-and-beach promenade" right up to the Finnish border posts. As Diktonius said, poetically and prophetically (for the Winter War was in the immediate future), Kuokkala lay in "a small corner amid the wars," but the description was also literal: a short way along the beach, there were sentries and barbed wire; out to sea, there was the island of Kotlin, with Kronstadt; and there was the Soviet fleet, doing target practice.

***

Diktonius was particularly proud of the collection of poems he put together in the summer of 1938 at Kuokkala and mailed off to his editor Svedlin at Holger Schildt's publishing house. It was his first volume of more or less new verse since *Mull och moln* (*Earth and Clouds*) of 1934 (the book of 1936, *Gräs och granit* [*Grass and Granite*], contained poems culled from earlier collections, together with a few hitherto uncollected ones), and the poet, easily excited at any event, did not hesitate to praise his own work to Kerstin Söderholm: ". . . den nya diktsamlingen är ungefär den klokaste och vackraste jag hittils skrivit, så lugnom oss i denna lilla vrå bland krigen, där det bästa man kan göra kanske är att bombardera de argsinta kanonerna med lugnets blommor" (29 August 1938).[13] And again to Eyvind Johnson on 2 September: ". . . igår postades diktsamlingen Dikesdagg, höstens bästa om ej Runeberg deltar i leken, och Medborgarna åker snart i samma riktning, om Svedlin så vill. Förresten har man också simmat och tre (3) gånger unnat sig en ordentlig fylla."[14] (Diktonius liked to boast both about his verse and drinking ability.)

Diktonius's confidence about the quality of his new work may be, however, not just an expression of natural exuberance, but an attempt at self-persuasion or self-defense. After his difficulties at finding critical acceptance during the early 1920s, he had become something of a darling of established criticism during the 1930s (when his friends, the Enckell brothers, controlled the review columns of *Hufvudstadsbladet*); he had also become a familiar contributor, as music and literary critic, to the pages of the distinguished Finland-Swedish journal, *Nya Argus*. In the fall of 1937, however, the journal's editors had jolted him by refusing a poem that would then find its way into *Jordisk ömhet*. The poem was "Villa Golicke":

På vattnets vaxduk	On the water's oilcloth
Kronstadts smörgåsbord:	Kronstadt's buffet:

bastioners exkrement	bastions' excrement,
skorstenars nejonögon—	chimneys' lampreys—
på huvet stående	standing on their heads,
med bolm kring stjärten.	smoke-belch round their tails.
Och solil rispar horisont	And sun-gust scratches horizon
som blixtlås	like zipper.
Och havets blålustöppna mun	And the sea's blue mouth,
	open with desire,
med sandpuder på läppen.	sand powder on its lip.
Och innerst inne	And farthest within
måsens silverplomb.	the gull's silver filling.

We know something about the rejection from the letter that, in the epistolary remains of Diktonius, has landed in the correspondence with Hans Ruin, a member of the editorial board. But the letter, in fact, is not to Ruin but to another member of the staff of *Nya Argus*, the translator and novelist Bertel Kihlman: one may conjecture that Kihlman passed the complaint along to Ruin, who then preserved it, along with the letters he himself got from Diktonius. What the letter of 10 October 1937 has to say about the poem itself will be discussed presently; for the moment, it must suffice to report that Diktonius was annoyed at the board's "old gentlemen" for having taken umbrage at his use of "bastioners exkrement"—and that, conversely, he was surprised at their failure to object to the sudden appearance of the lampreys ("nejonögon") in his imagery. All the same, it appears from the letter that the editors were perplexed indeed on another point—the lustfully gaping mouth of the sea. A public criticism similar to the editor's private one was subsequently made by the conservative critic Agnes Langenskiöld in an otherwise very favorable review of *Jordisk ömhet* in *Finsk Tidskrift*. Miss Langenskiöld used the example of "Villa Golicke" to summarize all her objections to the book:

Från det pressade, sökta, som tidigare mött oss i naturliknelserna tycks diktaren alltmer växa bort. Några undantag kunna nämnas—t. ex. 'Villa Golicke.' där 'solil' liknas vid 'blixtlås,' och där det talas om 'havets blålustöppna mun—med sandpuder på läppen—Och innerst inne—måsens silverplomb'—vilket allt utan tvivel är mycket finurligt tänkt, men just därför föga tilltalande. Men sådant är undantag: mestadels är det något av spontant liv, som möter oss. . . .[15]

Now we must look for a few moments at the text that distressed the "old gentlemen" of *Nya Argus* and the competent critic, Langenskiöld. We are, of course, ready to swallow a great deal more in the way of difficult or bizarre or simply incomprehensible language than were our predecessors of the 1930s; on the other hand, it is possible that the editorial board and Miss Langenskiöld may have been right—or that they at least put us on the track of a valid criticism of the poem: its images, even for us, may be so clever that they get in the way of our comprehension of what the poem means to tell us. Yet it must be admitted at the outset that, however "confusing" the imagery, the poem's structure is simple in the extreme. It is comprised of two six-line sections, the first describing Kronstadt across the waters, and enclosed by the phrases that begin with "på," the second describing the sun-and-beach-and-sea world of Kuokkala, and made up of three phrases, each opening with the word "Och," in an extended anaphora. The poem depends very heavily on nouns, sometimes startling ones, for its effect: there are twenty nouns among the thirty-five words of the poem, as opposed to only one finite verb, "rispar" of line 7, and one present participle, "stående" of line 5; the nouns are distributed almost evenly between part one (eleven) and part two (nine); six of them (four in part one, two in part two) are used as genitives, and the reader is struck at the outset by the fourfold salvo of these double-noun constructions, "vattnets vaxduk / Kronstadts smörgåsbord / bastioners exkrement / skorstenars nejonögon." The poem has one adjective, another massive composite, "blålustöppen" of line 9; and it is all glued together with prepositions (six), conjunctions (four), and the double adverb "innerst inne" of the penultimate line. The first part of the poem is more abrupt, an asyndetic catalogue of descriptive phrases; the second (where all the conjunctions lie) has its joiners plainly displayed. In the first part, the punctuation, colon and dash, leads the reader along in fits and starts; in the second part, the three statements follow smoothly on one another. The turn, the *volta*, in the poem is marked very clearly, not just by the additional spacing in the printed text,[16] but also by the beginning of the series of "och" constructions, by the change in the nature of the images from grotesque to pleasant (summarily, we might say, from "stjärt" to "solil"), and by the sudden intrusion of movement with the violent verb, "rispar."

The poem's opening part has to do, plainly, with food and with digestive processes. At first, the food looks not unattractive: on the water's oilcloth, the waiting meal of the Russian fortress—a variegated spectacle of buildings some fifteen kilometers from Diktonius's beach. After the expectation aroused by the "smörgåsbord," however, our hopes are dashed, or our gorge raised, by the goody-table's transformation upon closer inspection (rather as the alluring lady of baroque poetry could turn abruptly into a worm-eaten corpse): the bastions look, we are told, like excrement; and then, without any intervening punctuation at all, which would let us catch our breath, we are confronted by the *aprosdoketon*, the unexpected appearance, of the lampreys. We understand well enough why there are smokestacks in Kronstadt's naval arsenal; but we are baffled at the lamprey-comparison. In order to grasp it, we must ask ourselves what sort of fish the lamprey is. For one thing, it is long and thin, like the eel. For another, it is unpleasant; it bores its rasping teeth into the flesh of other fish to suck their blood. Fishermen dislike it. However, it can and has been eaten, as a delicacy, although it is hard to digest: Henry I of England is supposed to have loved to eat lampreys, and died as a result of stuffing himself on them. Here—after the dash, which may give us just enough time to recover from our astonishment at finding them in the Kronstadt banquet at all—the lampreys stand upright, or rather, on their heads, puffs of smoke ("bolm") around their elevated tails. We may wonder if there is some association on Diktonius's part between "bolm" and "bom," the cannon sound of his letters: "ryska flottan säger bom," ("the Russian fleet says boom"). Indeed, the cannon-association—even though these brick cannons are pointed at the sky—forces itself upon us, as does a renewal of the association of food and excrement: the lamprey takes in the blood of other fish at one end and belches it out as excrement at the other. And, to paraphrase the letter of 29 August 1938 to Kerstin Söderholm, Diktonius himself is bombarding the military world across the water—the bastions, arsenal-chimneys, and "argsinta kanoner" ("ill-tempered cannons")—not with "lugnets blommor" ("the flowers of calm"), but with indignation's insult. Mankind is lured toward the "smörgåsbord" of Kronstadt, but it turns out to be a place of excrement—and a place too in which the aggressive lamprey, good to eat but dangerously indigestible, does something unnatural—stands on its head, straining, even as mankind does when it prepares for war.[17] What we have is a *laus Martis* in the best, ironic, seventeenth-century sense.[18]

The poem's second set of images erases those of the war-world. The second word of part two, "solil," has an air of movement, of fresh suddenness about it, that is put into contrast with—into contradiction of—"vattnets vaxduk," the flat, motionless water of the poem's beginning. "Solil" itself is a surprising word, on the analogy of "vind-il," "regn-il," "väder-il," and "snö-il"; it—this "sun-gust"— goes across the horizon (thus in counterdirection to the strained perpendicularity of the smokestacks), scratching like a zipper. The comparison, "solil" / "blixtlås," needs some examination. Both words have an air of abruptness about them; the first parts of both components are full, literally, of light ("sol," "blixt"), the second parts are alike in that the one may disturb or change a scene by its sudden coming, the other, "lås," may open or close. Diktonius leaves us guessing here as to whether the "zipper" is being opened or closed: closed, perhaps, in that the shift of illumination on the water's surface shuts out the easy and detailed view of Kronstadt, because of the different refraction of light from the ruffled sea; open, in that the viewer on the beach is made aware of another world, both more immediate and grander than the one he has just been looking at. And the amphiboly implicit in "blixtlås" is also present, has been prepared for, in "rispar": has the "solil" scratched the horizon of the viewer's mind, laid it open, letting him perceive a realm beyond Kronstadt? Or has it scratched a horizon-line that delimits his view, shutting Kronstadt out, making him concentrate on what is directly before his eyes? The presence of the two possibilities as it were expands the poem, which has been concerned in its first half with a single reality.

At any rate, a change, much for the better, has taken place. The sun-gust has blown one world away, throwing us into another. After all, why do we go to Kuokkala? Not primarily to enjoy the cheap thrill of being close to the cannon's maw, but to be by the beautiful sea; or as Heidi Enckell, the "odalisque," put it, "Bäst trivs jag i vattnet." We look out over the huge expanse, the world of water, and are aware of its healing and regenerative powers—aware, too, we suppose (although Diktonius was not a man for classical allusions, despite Bert Brecht's having called him "der finnische Horaz"[19]), of its being the element from which Venus emerged. The sea itself seems then to be a gigantic mouth of a still more gigantic bather, with sand stuck to its lips. The giant mouth opens, yawning or waiting in desire; and then, within it, we see—the silver filling, the sea gull. The reader of Diktonius's verse knows how the poet likes to engage in practical jokes (a trait he shares with his contemporary in American verse, William Carlos Williams); some other examples would be the poem "Orkester" in *Stenkol* (*Pit Coal*), the song of the lovesick tuba in *Gräs och granit*, or the intoxicated prose catalogue at the end of "Vårt land nummer 2:0" ("Our Country Number Two") in *Annorlunda*. The adduction of dental detail about the giant mouth at the conclusion of "Villa Golicke" could be nothing more than one of those guffaws in which Diktonius wants the reader to join: a request not to take the poem too seriously—which, in turn, plants the poem more firmly in the reader's memory, *prodesse et delectare*. But the lines and the image have other purposes: surely they make the reader more aware of the vast dimensions of that giant blue mouth, and the "innerst inne" shows how far the mouth stretches. But Diktonius does not say, "längst borta" ("farthest away"), he says "innerst inne" ("farthest or most inwardly within"), and, as he does so, gives a reminder of how all-encompassing and all-devouring the sea-mouth is. It is a mouth which can eat up the whole of the Kronstadt buffet without incurring more than a filling, and a handsome one at that. The giant mouth of life—putting it another way—can devour the little feast of death, including its small predators, the lampreys and their leftover excrement. The sea-mouth swallows all.

***

Surviving friends of Diktonius have remarked upon the fact that, for all his desire to shock (in literary, erotic, and political matters), he was a prudish man who in mixed company carefully avoided the obscene or the heavily scatological;[20] he maintained a decor in polite talk that would indeed have pleased his religious mother, to whom he was deeply devoted. The reader of his unpublished correspondence from the Grankulla years gets much the same impression; although he can boast again and again of his fondness for strong drink, and although he uses a language colorful in the extreme, he shies away from the prurient or even the simple erotic (as, in fact, he does from any clear expression of political views). In his verse, a hesitation to speak in detail about either the act of love or the act of revolution grows increasingly apparent in the poem collections of the 1930s and 1940s (although the guffaws remain). The pedophiliac hints of the "Rachel" suite in *Hårda sånger* (*Hard Songs*) (1922), the oral-genital imagery of "Kärleksfantasi till havet" ("Love Fantasy to the Sea") in *Taggiga lågor* (1924), and "Åländsk symfoni" in *Stark men mörk* (*Strong but Dark*) (1930):

Som regnbågen	Like the rainbow
sticker min själspets	my soul-tip sticks
sin tunga i havets sköte,	its tongue into the sea's womb,
bär på sin kullriga rygg	bears on its bellying back
i rytmiska stötar	in rhythmic thrusts
dess ursaft till mig. . . .	[the womb's] primal juice to me. . . .

have been muted, as has the use of scatological images and words. Diktonius has become a respectable man, husband and father, renter of a home in Grankulla, contributor to *Nya Argus*. Perhaps he was particularly annoyed at the rejection of "Villa Golicke" because he believed that he had already made concessions to accepted taste; perhaps he believed that he could have been coarser. At least this is what he argues to Kihlman in that complaining letter, to which we shall now return:

Dikten består av en stark synsyntes, innehåller alltså inga onödiga, måhända ens nödiga fraser. "Kronstadts smörgåsbord" är naturligtvis havets i stiltje flata och mattskenande yta, på vilken bastionerna simmar som torkade kolallor—så gör alla öar på långt håll, men jag var naturligtvis anständig och skrev "exkrement." Inte menade jag vad som flyter i land från dem, för jag är ingen realist—vad det beträffar vet alla vuxna mänskor att det karelska näsets berömda sandstränder är panelade med bolsjevikiska gummivaror, groteska att titta på i sin kolossala uppsvullenhet, och själv har jag sett ett väldigt negerlik med byxorna fulla av ålar. Kanske farbröderna mera gillat, om jag skrivit "bastionernas sockerkakor." Men för mig är kanoner fula ting och utspyr vidrigheter. (Undrar också, att de icke fastnat vid "nejonögon." Men i dallrande vatten blir döda tings avspeglingar levande och gudelov att jag inte såg binnikemaskar i dem).[21]

This is the first paragraph of his cömplaint and explication. Diktonius tells Kihlman what we already have deduced: that the war-world he sees from Kuokkala is a world of excrement, a world that he could have described more frankly, and colorfully, than he did: he could have said "kolallor," and he could have used parasites from within the intestines, "binnikemaskar," instead of his predator-fish. Here we could add that his alleged sense of decency has been bolstered by his poetic sense: lampreys are more frightening and, as delicacies, fit into the initial image of the table-spread, something that would not have been the case with his proposed tapeworms. And the omission of other details—the ballooned contraceptives and the bloated dead man, his trousers full of eels (shades of Günter Grass)—might also suggest that what Diktonius calls his decency has been, in fact, his instinct for the poetically effective. In June 1937 his friend Grönvall, describing the glories of Kuokkala for him, had made a point of bringing up the mixture of healthy weather and erotic flotsam that characterized Kuokkala's beaches, "glitterhav, åsksmällar, solsand, gummivaror från Nevans kloaker, splitternytt 'Kasino'—och Björling."[22] Diktonius, as we know, mentioned the stories about the "Russian corpses with eels in their trousers" to his Swedish sailor friend Kjellgren in turn, and hinted daintily of the same to Kerstin Söderholm, talking about "decay on the beach," and, to Ulla Bjerne, about the "fresh rottenness of the place." But the paraphernalia of love, the trousered dead, and the atmosphere of decay are left out of "Villa Golicke": their presence would distract the reader's attention from the poem's thrust, its attack upon a voracious war-world of the island fortress and its painting of a larger, all-embracing peace-world of the sea. Of course, there can be no question about the eroticism of that sea-mouth, open with desire, ready to receive; it can be conjectured too that the sea, the giant lover, *has* received the sexual forces implied by the contraceptives and swollen corpses of the letters—and "decently" omitted from the poem.

The letter concludes with a defense of the wide-open sea-mouth. Here, Diktonius makes no bones about its erotic connotation:

> Sedan var det den blålustöppna munnen med sandpuder. Jorden är ju en kropp, eller rygg, maanselkä, och havet en mun med spott i; man säger också "havets käftar," och man säger i allmänhet bra. Och i den stora lusten har man munnen öppen, och skriker—vanligast är man röd av lust, rödlust, men detta hände nu inte vid Röda havets stränder, och jag älskar fakta, både röda och blå. Läpparnas sandpuder är förstås—ja det begriper alla villiga barn.[23]

Despite Diktonius's verbal cadenzas, we can make out his meaning. He thinks of the earth as a giant body (he makes the analogy of Finnish "maanselkä," ["back or ridge of land"]) and the sea is its mouth. His claim that he loves facts is a joke made in earnest: the *fact* of the sea's giant blueness provides the basic element of the "visual synthesis" in the poem's second part. Then, as he says, any willing child can grasp the rest: the shore is the vast lip, the sand powder that lip's cosmetic, suggesting "ansiktspuder" and "läppstift." The giantess is adorned for love, a huge bathing beauty, as it were. In August 1938 Diktonius wrote a feuilleton for the newspaper *Hufvudstadsbladet* in which he pretended to interview himself at Kuokkala. There, after claiming that money, the training of young cats, and a good cigar (lighted with a thousand-mark note) were principal poetic stimuli for him, he went on to say that he worked "parodistically."[24]

***

Had he been a more serious sort of person, Diktonius could have called up a star witness in his defense against the old gentlemen of *Nya Argus*; they should have been obliged, one hopes, to accept an image that stems from Strindberg. The origin of the giant sea-mouth is to be found in a book that Diktonius had included (underlined) in his reading list for 1921;[25] evidently, the image had gone to seed in his mind, then to reemerge, transformed, in the beach poem of 1938. (It is altogether possible that Diktonius read the book again later on; the reading lists become desultory in the early 1920s and then cease altogether.) Near the beginning of the second chapter of *I havsbandet* (*By the Open Sea*) after the ichthyologist and dandy Axel Borg has made his perilous way to Österskär and has slept his exhausted sleep in Vestman's cottage, he looks out the window of his room at the calm sea: "Detta var havet, visserligen ingen nyhet för intendenten Borg, som sett åtskilliga kanter av världen, men det var det ödsliga havet och liksom sett i ett mellan-fyra-ögon. Det skrämde icke som skogen med dess dunkla gömmor, utan det verkade lugnt som ett öppet, stort, blått, trofast öga."[26] At the novel's end, it will be remembered, on "en stormig natt, under vilken han trott sig höra kanonskott och rop av människor," Borg goes to the beach, where he gathers flotsam from the wreck, dolls that had been on the way to Christmas market.[27] He then consigns himself, in that grandiose ending of which Strindberg was justly proud,[28] to "havet, allmodren, ur vars sköte livets första gnista tändes, fruktsamhetens, kärlekens outtömliga brunn, livets ursprung och livets fiende."[29] Diktonius took Strindberg's huge blue and calming eye, and changed it into a huge blue mouth, and a huge blue goddess.

Obviously, Strindberg's text did not lie before Diktonius as he wrote his poem at Kuokkala; he was on vacation, and he liked to travel light. The unforgettable details had stuck with him, and in this seaside place he remembered, or half-remembered, the sea of *I havsbandet*, "the atmosphere surrounding the memory of a landscape." And just as obviously, Diktonius used the image to his own pacificistic ends. Yet even in the visual techniques of the poem (as Diktonius then explained them to Bertil Kihlman) one may guess that a trace of *I havsbandet* remains; for the poem is built in part upon an awareness of the distortions that come about when objects are viewed over water—"that's the way all islands do at a distance." Every reader of *I havsbandet* will recall the use that Borg makes (in Chapters Seven and Eight) of his knowledge of such effects. Indeed, Strindberg makes a point of mentioning these maritime optical illusions at the opening of Chapter Two: "det [havet] reste sig som en lodrät vägg i stället för att sträcka ut sig som en vågrät yta, ty de långa dyningarne, fullt solbelysta, gåvo inga skuggor, av vilka ögat kunde bilda en perspektivisk bild."[30]

Finally, it should be added that Diktonius, in 1938, was a man ready to recall *I havsbandet*, where Borg, exhausted after his literally almost superhuman efforts, collapses and gives himself to the consolatory sea. In the idyllic verse of the prematurely aging Diktonius there is, as we all know, a strong sense of identification with earth, stone, sea, a wish to become part of them. There is even a desire for oblivion, probably to be connected with Diktonius's awareness of his physical and mental deterioration, the first symptoms of which appeared during the late 1930s. To be sure, in "Villa Golicke," written in the small corner amid the wars, there is still an urge to fight back with nature's aid against man-made destruction, rather than to fall exhausted into nature's bosom—or her mouth. With its images of food and excrement and huge amorousness, the poem is grotesque (may it be called a grotesque idyll?); but the images are used to make a pacific point of, likewise, huge importance.[31]

Notes

1. Bill Romefors, *Expressionisten Elmer Diktonius: En studie i hans lyrik 1921–1930* (Helsingfors: Svenska Litteratursällskapet i Finland, 1978), pp. 117–20: ". . . great affinity of spirit between the two authors, Diktonius and Strindberg," and that "both have the same view of existence—filled with movement and activity. Strindberg has provided an important stimulus . . . for Diktonius." (117).

2. Romefors, p. 202: "It is difficult to point to direct traces of Strindberg in Diktonius' literary production. However, one may assume that Strindberg's habit of thinking in images had a fertilizing effect upon Diktonius' own imagistic way of thought." (Note 80).

3. *Vaka* (Helsingfors: Schildts, 1969) p. 154. "They lay close to one another on a strip of beach, wedged in between the sea and the main road from Terijoki to Systerbäck and the Russian border, which was closed."

4. The correspondence of Diktonius is in the possession of the Swedish Literary Society in Finland (Svenska Litteratursällskapet i Finland, Helsingfors). The author wishes to thank the Society for allowing him to use it here.

5. ". . . the 'Riviera of Finland,' as it's called, and not without reason. The empty villas have their special, rather macabre charm, we have the Diktonius family, Ralf P., and Sven Grönvall as neighbors. Yet we don't see much of one another, each of us spends his time reflecting on his own concerns. There's a Swede from Sweden here too, Erik Lindegren, who's said to have published some collection of verse or other, and who's translating one of Faulkner's books. But I haven't got to know him very well. He's said to be a disciple of Lawrence. [Lorenz von] Numers is also here for a couple of weeks, garrulous, cheery, and refreshed by his trip."

6. "Rabbe helps me so nicely. . . . He says I'm so lazy that I ought to be an odalisque. I'm happiest in the water."

7. "In Häkli's boarding house, where we take our main meal, there sits Gunnar Ekelöf, finishing his new collection of poetry, and old Häkli himself sits there too for nights on end, with his nose stuck into a piece of translation. Perseverance, peace, and freedom prevail in the alphabet-factory."

8. "And the sea's going like a sunny teeter-totter, and the Russian fleet says boom, and I blow my fanfare. The cat's called Stalin and the tortoise is called Mob and so you can tell you're living near to Bolshevikia."

9. "Damned fine place with a wine-and-beer-casino in the shelter of Kronstadt's cannons. This is the dumping spot for the leftovers of east and west: a decayed idyll against the strong background of the sea. From this soil the poetry of Edith Södergran rose up toward the heavens, and the fact that it got such fanciful forms and images in splendid color can be understood here, in this welter where everything is possible, in this fresh rottenness."

10. "Kuokkala, Karelian isthmus, where I've stayed for three weeks and heard stories about black Russian corpses with eels in their trousers. Everything else in the same style. Sea up to my ears and Kronstadt right in front of my nose."

11. ". . . this small corner amid the wars, in smell of cats, in Russian cannons' cache." The poem, "Fredligt sällskap" ("Peaceful Company"), runs:

I kattors doft, i rysskanoners
   gömma
vår frid vi fann.
I denna lilla vrå bland krigen
blott blixtens myggsurr krusar
tankespegeln.
	In smell of cats, in Russian
	   cannons' cache
	we found our peace.
	In this small corner amid the wars
	only the lightning's gnat-hum ruffles
	thought's mirror.

Ej metargubbars slöfocksro av jagarvågor störs— disblå debussysk himlarand och poppelskuggors svalka.	Destroyer's waves do not disturb old anglers' drowsy rest— mist-blue Debussyan horizon and poplars-shadows' coolness.

Diktonius then quoted the poem near the conclusion of his depiction of the Kuokkala days in *Höstlig bastu* (*Autumn Sauna*) (Helsingfors: Schildts, 1943), pp. 81–88, where the third line of the poem is also used as the section's title. Here, too, as in "Villa Golicke" and "Fredligt sällskap," Diktonius mentions the reminders of the Russian military presence; at night, after parties at the Casino, the members of the coterie fell into bed, "och i de bäddarna väcks man sannerligen inte av kanondundret från Kronstadt eller ljuskastarnas strålknippen, som ogenerat gastar i ens sovkabyss för att visa ryssen hur finnen mår...." ("and in those beds one truly is not awakened by the thunder of cannons from Kronstadt or the bundle of beams from the searchlights, which unembarrassedly spook around in one's sleeping quarters to show the Russian how the Finn is getting along....") These recollections of Kuokkala have the penultimate sentence: "Men de där hejarna till kanoner, fankens fula bjässar, må för allan tid sjunka i havets djup." ("But may those pile-driver cannons, Old Nick's nasty brutes, sink for all eternity into the depths of the sea").

    12. "... under Kronstadt's cannons on Kuokkala's beaches."

    13. "... the new collection of poetry is about the wisest and most beautiful one I've written so far, so let us calm ourselves in this little corner amid the wars, where probably the best one can do is to bombard the ill-tempered cannons with flowers of calm." Diktonius was able to convince his colleague of the high quality of the book even before it came out; Gunnar Ekelöf told an interviewer that "Diktonius has written very fine poems this summer.... I believe that the new collection, together with ... *Stark men mörk* (*Strong but Dark*, 1930), will be his most outstanding book." Cf. Monsieur Coeur (ps.), "Gunnar Ekelöf prisar tre skalder," *Svenska Pressen* (Helsingfors, 24 November 1938). (The other poets praised by Ekelöf were Edith Södergran, whose grave he visited, and Rabbe Enckell.)

    14. "Yesterday the new collection *Dikesdagg* was mailed off, the best one of the autumn if Runeberg doesn't enter the competition, and *Medborgarna* (*The Citizens*) will soon set out in the same direction, if Svedlin so desires. Otherwise, we've gone swimming, too, and allowed ourselves a real drunk three (3) times." The collection's name was subsequently changed from *Dikesdagg* (*Ditch Dew*) to *Jordisk ömhet* at the suggestion of Svedlin, after a line in the poem that concludes the original section of the volume, "Det var en kväll. Mig mötte jordisk ömhet" ("It was one evening. Earthly tenderness met me"): the rest of the book was filled out with a set of translations which Diktonius had made from Finno-Ugric folksongs, dedicated to the academic poet and translator-into-Finnish, Otto Manninen. The second volume of Diktonius's novellas, *Medborgare [i republiken Finland]: Andra samlingen*, did not appear until 1940.

    15. "The poet seems to be growing away more and more from the strained and far-fetched quality that met us earlier in his nature metaphors. Some exceptions can be mentioned—e.g., 'Villa Golicke,' where 'sun-gust' is compared to 'zipper,' and where there is talk about 'the sea's blue mouth, open with desire—sand powder on its lip.— And farthest within—the gull's silver filling'—all of which is very cleverly thought out, no doubt, but rather unappealing just on that account. But such is the exception: for the most part, there is something of spontaneous life which confronts us...." Agnes

Langenskiöld, "Höstens lyriker," Finsk Tidskrift, 126-27 (1939), 1-2: 61-67, spec. 62. Other reviewers avoided the difficulties of the Kuokkala suite (Hagar Olsson in Hufvudstadsbladet, 26 October 1938, Eugène Napoleon Tigerstedt in Svenska Pressen, 29 October 1938, Atos Wirtanen in Arbetarbladet, 31 October 1938, Kerstin Söderholm, Nya Argus, 16 November 1938, Solveig von Schoultz in Astra, December 1938), although Söderholm does say that the Kuokkala verses are "snapshots" with a "more casual character than the other nature poems. . . . To some extent, they remind one of Diktonius's prose with its simple, genuine, and expressive turns of phrase."

16. That is, in the original printing. In Elmer Diktonius, Dikter 1912–1942 (Stockholm: Tiden, 1956), p. 303, the division into two "strophes" of equal length has disappeared.

17. In Höstlig bastu (p. 60), Diktonius wrote: "Hur kan du lilla mänska, . . . som mest lämnat efter dig exkrementer och kadaver—hur törs din belastade hjärna och ditt förhärdade hjärta alstra musik och umgås med toner?" ("How can you, little human being, . . . who have mostly left excrement and corpses in your wake—how dare your tainted brain and your hardened heart produce music and associate with tones?").

18. It may be worthwhile to remember that in the so-called Konfektlieder of the Thirty Years' War, the imagery of eating and food was employed to express hatred of an enemy, be he Protestant or Catholic, and to describe his rapacity. Cf. Werner Milch, Gustav Adolf in der deutschen und schwedischen Literatur (Breslau: M. & H. Marcus, 1928).

19. Bert Brecht, Arbeitsjournale (Frankfurt am Main: Suhrkamp, 1973), p. 122. (Entry of 30 June 1940). ". . . the Finnish Horace."

20. To be sure, the young Diktonius had a particular fondness for the scatological, richly demonstrated, for example, in Onnela: Finsk idyll (1925). Artur Lundkvist, who, together with Erik Asklund, visited Diktonius on Åland in the summer of 1930, has criticized the Finlander's "starkt primitivistisk[a] attityd. . . . Han försökte chockera oss med sin grovkornighet och höll sig till avföringsplanet med en envishet som kom oss att kalla honom för exkrementisten Diktonius i stället för expressionisten Diktonius" ("strongly primitivistic attitude. . . . He tried to shock us with his crudity and stuck to the realm of defecation with a doggedness that made us call him the excrementist Diktonius instead of the expressionist Diktonius"). Självporträtt av en drömmare med öppna ögon (Stockholm: Bonniers, 1966), p. 78.

21. "The poem consists of a strong visual synthesis, thus contains no unnecessary and perhaps even necessary phrases. 'Kronstadt's smörgåsbord' is naturally the surface of the sea in a calm, flat and dully shining, where the bastions swim like dried cow-flops—that's what all islands do, [seen] at a distance, but I was decent, naturally, and wrote 'excrement.' I didn't mean the stuff that is washed ashore from them, for I'm no realist—as far as that's concerned, every adult knows that the famed sandy beaches of the Karelian Isthmus are paneled with Bolshevik rubber articles, grotesque to behold in all their monstrous swollenness, and I myself have seen a huge black corpse with its trousers filled with eels. Maybe the old gentlemen would have liked it better if I had written 'the bastions' sponge cakes,' but, for me, cannons are ugly things, spewing out disgusting matter. (I wonder, too, about their not getting stuck on 'lampreys.' But in quivering water, the reflections of dead things become alive, and praise God I didn't see tapeworms in them.)"

22. ". . . glittering sea, thunderclaps, sunny sand, rubber articles from the sewers of the Neva, [a] brand new Casino—and Björling."

23. "Then there was that blue mouth, open with desire, and the sand powder. The earth, after all, is a body, or a back, maanselkä, and the sea a mouth with spit in it; one also says 'the jaws of the sea' and, in general, one says things well. And in that desire, one has his mouth open, and shrieks—most commonly, one grows red with desire, red desire, but this didn't happen on the shores of the Red Sea, and I love facts, both red and blue. The lips' sandpowder, of course, is—well, any willing child can understand that."

24. Elmer Diktonius, "Diktonius arbetar parodiskt," Hufvudstadsbladet (17 August

1938): "Om jag arbetar koncentrerat eller rapsodiskt? Nejdå, men parodiskt. Och om jag därvid först förnimmer diktens rytm eller det emotionella innehållet? Är det ej att ta väl grovt på saken? Viska hellre om atmosfären kring ett landskapsminne. . . ." ("Do I work concentratedly or rhapsodically? Of course not, but parodistically. And do I, in the process, first perceive the rhythm of the poem or the emotional content? Isn't that being quite heavy-handed in the matter? Whisper rather about the atmosphere surrounding the memory of a landscape. . . .")

25. In Folder 7, Diktonius Papers, Swedish Literary Society in Finland. Romefors (202) does not adduce *I havsbandet* among the works of Strindberg that Diktonius read: "Läslistan upplyser bl. a. följande: Röda rummet lästes 1916, 1920; Det nya riket, 1918, 1920, 1927; Inferno, 1919, 1920; Tal till svenska nationen, 1918, 1922; Dikter och Ordalek och småkonst 1918." ("The reading list gives information *i.a.* about the following: *The Red Room* was read in 1916 and 1920, *The New Kingdom* in 1918, 1920, and 1927, *Inferno* in 1919 and 1920, *Speeches to the Swedish Nation* in 1918 and 1922, *Poems* and *Word Play and Minor Art* in 1918."). (Note 79).

26. August Strindberg, *Samlade Skrifter*, 24, ed. John Landquist (Stockholm: Bonniers, 1914), p. 24. "This was the sea, no novelty to be sure for Superintendent Borg, who had seen various parts of the world, but this was the solitary sea, and beheld, as it were, tête-à-tête. It was not frightening, like the forest with its dark caches [*gömmor*], but it had a calming [*lugnande*] effect, like a huge, open, blue, faithful eye." In the translation by Ellie Schleussner, *By the Open Sea* (London: F. Palmer, 1913), p. 34, "a large, blue, candid gaze," weakens the image considerably; Elizabeth Clark Westergren's rendering, in *On the Seaboard: A Novel of the Baltic Islands* (Cincinnati: Stewart and Kidd, 1913), p. 24, is more felicitous: "an open, big, faithful, blue eye.") Is it of any importance that the two favorite words of Diktonius in the summers of 1937 and 1938, "lugnt" (see the letter to Kerstin Söderholm, note 13, with its "lugnom" and "lugnande") and "gömmor" (note 11: the word's appearance in conjunction with cannons, "kanoners gömma," is surprising), appear in the Strindberg passage?

27. *SS*, 24: 239. ". . . a stormy night in which he believed that he heard cannon shots and the cries of human beings." In Strindberg's novel, of course, the sounds are those of a shipwreck; the cannon fires a lifeline.

28. "Sista kapitlet är grandiost" ("the last chapter is grandiose") is what he wrote to Karl Otto Bonnier on 7 June 1890; cf. *Brev*, 8 (Stockholm: Bonniers, 1964), 54.

29. *SS*, 24: 243. ". . . the sea, the all-mother, from whose womb life's first spark was lit, the inexhaustible fountain of fertility and love, life's source and life's foe."

30. *SS*, 24: 22. "The sea raised itself up like a vertical wall, instead of stretching out like a horizontal surface, for the long swells, completely lighted by the sun, produced no shadows from which the eye could form an image with perspective."

31. Some of Diktonius's present-day admirers and exegetes will not want to admit it, but "Villa Golicke"—and much else that Diktonius wrote on the eve of the Winter War—shows that, for all his sympathy with the left, he could not blind himself to the identity of the disturbers of the peace.

Part II
Strindberg Abroad

Strindberg at the Opera
Raymond Jarvi

August Strindberg's influence as a theorist and shaper of drama is ubiquitous; he can be considered the playwrights' playwright of our century. His straining and breaking of the conventions of the late nineteenth-century stage has furnished impetus for virtually every aspect of the dramatic avant-garde during the last seven decades. Although his point of departure was the realistic theater of his time, he prepared the way for expressionistic drama; he contributed significantly to both the dream and the "supernaturalistic" play; he has also affected the development of modern symbolic, pageant, intimate, and historical drama. Has he had any impact at all on the operatic stage?

As far as the standard repertory goes, Strindbergian drama has not yet rendered an *Aïda*, *Bohème*, or *Carmen*. In the case of Ture Rangström's musical setting of *Kronbruden* (*The Crown Bride*) (1919), comparison can readily be made with the Maeterlinck-Debussy *Pelleas et Melisande* (1902) and the Wilde-Strauss *Salomé* (1905). Each composer has taken an already viable work for the stage and used its text as his libretto; each has produced a music-drama beyond the ken even of that crafty old wizard, Richard Wagner. The Rangström-Strindberg *Kronbruden* may well find a world audience among those who view Leos Janacek's *Jenufa* (1904) as a twentieth-century masterpiece (and their numbers are increasing); in any case, the annals of the operatic stage do record numerous other attempts that have been made to adapt or transcribe Strindbergian drama to its own ambience. During the 1920s, the German composer Julius Weismann produced operatic versions of *Svanevit* (*Swanwhite*), *Ett drömspel*, (*A Dream Play*), and *Spöksonaten* (*The Ghost Sonata*); his *Schwanenweiß* (1923), in particular, did receive fairly extensive production on the German lyric stage in its day. The American composer Ned Rorem's ill-fated version of *Miss Julie* (1965) might have fared better had its premiere at the New York City Opera not come in the aftermath of the company's first mounting of Prokofiev's *Flaming Angel*—nor just a few days before the famous metropolitan blackout that November. The Austrian-Yugoslavian composer Antonio Bibalo has, indeed, produced an intimate operatic version of *Miss Julie* (1975), which despite its obtrusive prologue—in which overdue attention is paid to the contrasting dreams of Julie and Jean—effectively adds a musical component to Strindberg's "naturalistic tragedy." Perhaps the most remarkable chamber opera based on a Strindberg text is the Australian composer Malcolm Williamson's *The Growing Castle*, premiered in a castle in Wales in 1968, subsequently produced in Göteborg and in the Spanish courtyard of the Caramoor mansion in New York state (July 1970). Influenced by Gustav Holst's *Savitri* (1916), Williamson has drastically reduced Strindberg's *Ett drömspel* so that four singers can perform all of its twenty-eight roles, and the accompaniment (piano, harpsichord, bells, and percussion) can all be managed by one musician. Reviewing the Caramoor performances, John W. Freeman commented: "Symbolism is perilous in opera, and some of the lines and images could be construed as jejune in another context, but somehow when Strindberg does it one doesn't laugh."[1] What might Strindberg have thought of such adaptations of his works? What was his relationship to, assessment of, and involvement with the lyric theater of his day?

During his teens and twenties, Strindberg occasionally attended operatic performances at Stockholm's Kungliga Teatern (The Royal Theater); in the 1870s, he enjoyed the friendship of such prominent members of the theater's ensemble as Pelle Janzon and Carl Fredrik Lundqvist ("Lunkan"). The premiere of *La belle Hélène* (*Beautiful Helen*) on the national lyric stage in 1865, Offenbach's official breakthrough in Sweden, made an indelible impression on an extremely serious sixteen-year-old Johan August, judging by the lengthy discussion of it that he included in the first volume of *Tjänstekvinnans son* (*The Son of a Servant*) (1886).[2] He considered Offenbach a latter-day Aristophanes whose works denoted the end of an era in a common European development, namely, two thousand years of Greco-Christian cultural hegemony. What Strindberg saw in 1865 as a veiled smile, assumed at length dimensions of a demonic leer, as his diatribe against these matters in *Öppna brev till Intima teatern* (*Open Letters to the Intimate Theater*) (1908) indicates.[3]

Less complex and more exclusively positive was the young Strindberg's enthusiastic response to Verdi's *Il Trovatore* (*The Troubadour*), premiered in Stockholm on 31 May 1860, to Mozart's *Don Giovanni*— that perennial enigma—and to what then was the rising star of Charles Gounod, whose *Faust* was a standard repertory piece at Kungliga Teatern from 1862 until the early 1950s and whose *Roméo et Juliette* was first performed in Stockholm on 11 June 1868, although it did not actually enter the repertory until the revival of 1884. Both of Gounod's world-wide successes, above all, *Roméo et Juliette*, were to retain an evocation of the dream of youth in Strindberg's memory and experience; well-worn piano reductions of both works are among the handful of operatic scores in the library that Strindberg collected after 1899, now in the archives of Nordiska Museet (The Nordic Museum).[4] In the case of *Faust*, however, the dream tarnished somewhat not only as Strindberg gained an appreciation of Goethe and his more faithful operatic disciple, Arrigo Boito,[5] but also when chance arranged things so that the Parisian premiere of *Fadren* (*The Father*) on 13 December 1894 necessarily had to compete for public attention with the gala 1,000th performance of Gounod's deathless triumph of the Victorian sensibility on 14 December 1894 at the Palais Garnier.[6]

The lyric stage remained, however, relatively low at best in the young Strindberg's scheme of priorities. Rousseauean idealist of a strongly Darwinian bent and son of a servant woman that he was, he found opera itself not only the epitome of the artificial but a bastion for the values and sensibilities of what he considered an oppressive and moribund elite, hence, an outmoded means of artistic expression doomed to extinction in the inevitable progress of natural selection. Remarks in a letter of 20 November 1885 to his brother Axel indicate Strindberg's characteristic pre-Inferno assessment: "Men Wagnerismen är bara en enskild persons fundering som nu är på modet. Operan kan ej utvecklas; den är onatur alltigenom och kan bara dö. Upplöses i operetten och slutar som Variété–teatern."[7]

Why then did Strindberg in the mid-1880s suggest that his Uppsala friend Eugène Fahlstedt adapt his short story "Odlad frukt" ("Cultivated Fruit") in *Svenska öden och äventyr* (*Swedish Destinies and Adventures*) (1882) as a libretto for the then prominent Swedish composer Andreas Hallén; or in his letter of 4 June 1891 to Fredrik Vult von Steijern roughly outline plans for an original libretto to an *opera seria* in the old number style on the subject of David and Saul? Economic necessity probably accounts for the first matter; Strindberg's almost lifelong, perilously uncertain financial base led him to plan infinitely more than even he—"Sveriges största eld" ("Sweden's greatest fire")—actually managed to produce. As far as the proposed *opera seria* goes, it would amount to repayment of a personal debt to Vult von Steijern, who from his position as editor-in-chief of *Dagens Nyheter* had gathered the economic means whereby Strindberg was able to fund his Swedish travels of 1890–1891. As one of Sweden's leading Wagnerians at the time, Vult von Steijern was keenly interested in the synthesis of drama and music. Neither project got any further than the indicated stages; Strindberg's commitment or motivation to pursue these matters evidently was not very strong.

An *opera seria* in the tradition of Händel and Mozart, entitled *Saul og David*, composed by the Danish symphonist Carl Nielsen between 1898 and 1901 and premiered at Copenhagen's Kongelige Theater (Royal Theater) on 28 November 1902 has decently maintained itself in that theater's repertory and traveled north to Göteborg (1928) and Stockholm (1931). The pre-Inferno Strindberg would probably have appreciated Nielsen's and his librettist Einar Christiansen's basic thesis: their treatment of Saul as a tragic hero, an intelligent and courageous individual who questions the accepted beliefs and superstitions of a primitive tribe, in conflict with the more conventional figure of David, who accepts the existing order, believes in it, and ultimately becomes the chosen king of Israel.

A shift in Strindberg's attitude toward the lyric stage can be detected in the early 1890s after his divorce from Siri von Essen and during his and his fellow expatriates' search for a new artistic synthesis—whatever the consequences might be—in the willed madness, among other assumed poses, of the "Zum schwarzen Ferkel" ("The Black Piglet") circle. He continued to dismiss Wagner and the Wagnerians as simply the cult of a given ego—of no real lasting significance. In the performances of *Die Walküre* (*The Valkyrie*) he attended in Berlin in 1893, he found neither music nor drama.[8] A wholly admirable work—and one that did not pretend to be a "music drama"—he now found in Bizet's *Carmen* (1875), which by the mid-1890s had firmly established itself in the European repertory, if it still was unsuitable for performance at L'Academie Nationale de Musique (The National Academy of Music). In Bizet, Strindberg obviously saw a fellow outsider—but one whose day had brilliantly arrived.[9] Georg Brandes had seen to it, moreover, that Strindberg got a copy of Nietzsche's *Der Fall Wagner* (*The Case of Wagner*) directly from the publisher in 1888.[10]

The work that now intrigued Strindberg, the theorist of the drama, was Pietro Mascagni's *Cavalleria Rusticana* (*Rustic Chivalry*), which first sizzled on the Roman lyric stage in 1890—the *Fröken Julie* (*Miss Julie*) (1888), roughly speaking, of the Italian veristic movement. Consider, for example, Strindberg's advice to the Finnish writer Adolf Paul, whose training had included music and who in 1894 wanted to make a libretto: "När Du nu gör operatext, har Du ej tänkt gå längre än Mascagni och Convaljen[11] och ta moderna kurrar i snygga gångkläder, utan folkkostym. Han, Hon, Den i redingoter och bord och stol. Hvad säger Du om Das Band? (Tänk de tolf nämdemännen kör för bariton och basar!) Hvilka körer, ensembler och Solon med Leitmotiv! Slå Mascagnis verldsrekord!"[12] Three people, two chairs, and a table: since the dissection of souls in *Fordringsägare* (*Creditors*) (1888) had been achieved with these extremely simple means, might they not also provide a new tack for the lyric stage—one that went further than Mascagni or Leoncavallo in confronting an audience with mirror images of the human condition? However far-fetched the idea might have seemed to Adolf Paul, a brace of twentieth-century composers from the Schoenberg of *Erwartung* (*Anticipation*) (1909; first performed 1924) to the Poulenc of *La Voix humaine* (*The Human Voice*) (1959) to the Hugo Weisgall of *The Stronger* (1952) have richly explored the possibilities of Strindberg's intuitive suggestion. And one may conjure indeed with *Bandet* (*The Bond*) (1892). Think of the twelve jurymen resounding from the deepest reaches of the male voice! Think of the Verdi of the king's closet scene in *Don Carlos* (1867), the *Dies Irae* movement of the *Requiem* (1874), or the revised council scene in *Simon Boccanegra* (1881) applying his heightened creative powers to these choruses, ensembles, and arias! Think of Strindberg's having been able to offer this text directly to Leos Janacek . . .

The Strindberg of "Kammarspelen" ("the chamber plays") (1907) devoted considerable thought to the shaping of "en kammaropera" ("a chamber opera") as his letters to his good friend, the conductor and violinist Tor Aulin, indicate. At the playwright's request, the latter had furnished the incidental music for the production of the verse *Mäster Olof* that inaugurated Dramaten's new "Vita huset" ("White House") on Nybroplan. The congenial results of that venture led Strindberg to write the following to Aulin on 20 January 1908:

När Du sist föreslog ett nytt samarbete . . . så frågar jag: Hvarför icke en opera? Men icke en svensk. Det blir antigen Den Bergtagna med C-dur och A-moll i oändlighet; och en visa är bara en liten detalj i operan. Eller Waldemarsskatten: en kombination af Skansen, Wagner och Waldteuffel.
På Ditt förslag föreslår jag: Drömspelet. Der har Du en text som pröfvat eldarne. Men den skall försäkras efter kompositörens behag; alla komiska moment utgå; personalen inskränkes, och orkestern indrages till Mozarts besättning (Din nuvarande). Och kort! Ett musikaliskt kammarspel, der all filosofencer utgå, och endast "scenerna" stå qvar. Alltså icke den sjungna romanen som i—Du minns den Franska på Svenska Teatern! Dramatisk—lyrisk musik men icke teatralisk—recitativ—resonerande.
Enkel men icke för enkel. Glück gerna (Orfeus), men fodrad med Beethoven, dock icke Beethoven helt![13]

A Strindberg-Aulin opera was never written: The former repeatedly brought the matter up in his letters of 1908–09, but the latter could only eat humble pie, so to speak, on his end of their correspondence because of the kind things the master was saying to him. Malcolm Williamson, however, has reduced *Ett drömspel*—dramatically to be sure—along the lines that Strindberg suggested to Aulin and thus has provided a version of the work for the modern intimate lyric stage. Williamson's music from the global village would probably elude the shade of Strindberg, were that happy ghost able to attend a current performance of *The Growing Castle*. The post-Inferno Strindberg's insistence that melody alone is the common denominator of all musical experience, his pointing Aulin back to Glück and Beethoven for models—one hopes that in his heart of hearts, even Strindberg realized it might be drudgery were it actually *this* simple.

A formidable Swedish composer did, however, appear at Strindberg's threshold in the early summer of 1909, the young Ture Rangström. Tor Aulin had, in fact, served as the go-between in arranging their first meeting. Rangström's calling card had been his recently published opus of *romanser* based on four poems from *Ordalek och småkonst* (*Word Play and Minor Art*) (1905),[14] legitimate expressions of the lyrics themselves, from Strindberg's point of view, but far too dependent as to their musicality on the Norwegian harmonies of Grieg, Sinding, and others of their school. Were Rangström to manifest the Swedish mode, said Strindberg, he was well advised to search for her secrets and nuances in his own musical folk drama *Kronbruden* (1901). The idea had already occurred to the young composer who replied to the playwright, all the same, that were he to pursue this Dalecarlian vein, the first four of Strindberg's six tableaux would be sufficient for his libretto. In them, the eye and ear of the musician could readily perceive the movement from sin to punishment to redemption that constitutes the essence of the crown bride Kersti's dream. "Ett ögonblicks tanke!" replied Strindberg. "Ni har rätt! Musiken har ibland en högre moral än dikten!"[15] The rest is—and will be on-going—operatic history.

Notes

1. *Opera News*, 35, No. 1 (5 September 1970), p. 22. Four operatic versions of Strindberg's *Ett drömspel* have thus far been produced. In addition to those by Weismann and Williamson, the Swiss composer Edward Staemfli made his debut on the lyric stage in 1943 with his setting of *Ein Traumspiel*. This text also furnished the libretto of the German composer Aribert Reimann's first opera *Traumspiel*, premiered in Kiel on 20 June 1965, and couched in a lyrically expressionistic modern idiom that tends towards shifting tonal foci. The Swedish composer Ingvar Lidholm is presently writing an opera on this intrinsically musical text.

2. August Strindberg, *Samlade Skrifter*, ed. John Landquist (Stockholm: Bonniers, 1912–1920), 18: 179–82 (hereafter *SS*).

3. *SS*, 50: 154ff.

4. The others are Auber's *La Muette de Portici*, Beethoven's *Fidelio*, Boito's *Mefistofele*, Flotow's *Martha*, Mozart's *Don Giovanni*, Spohr's *Jessonda*, and Weber's *Oberon*. In the stacks of sheet music that the library contains are also potpourris of Mascagni's *Cavalleria Rusticana*, Wagner's *Meistersinger*, *Parsifal*, and *Tristan*.

5. Kungliga Biblioteket, Stockholm: *Ockulta dagboken* MS, p. 110. See sup., also *Operan 200 år: Jubelboken* ed. Klas Ralf (Stockholm: Prisma, 1973), pp. 115–18.

6. *August Strindbergs brev*, ed. Torsten Eklund (Stockholm: Bonniers, 1947 to date), 10: 323 (hereafter *Brev*).

7. *Brev*, 5: 210. "But Wagnerism is only the speculation of a single person that is now in fashion. Opera cannot be developed; it is non-nature through and through and can only die. Decline into operetta and end as vaudeville."

8. Wetterhof-Asp, "Var Strindberg musikalisk?" *Nya Dagligt Allehanda*, 4 December 1927, p. 4ff.

9. Ibid.

10. *Brev*, 7: 127–28.

11. That is, Leoncavallo.

12. *Brev*, 10: 96. "Now that you are going to write the book for an opera, have you not thought of going farther than Mascagni and [Leoncavallo] and of taking modern chaps in stylish street clothes, *sans* folk costumes. He, She, a third person in formal wear and table and chairs. What do you say about *The Bond*? (Imagine the twelve jurymen as a chorus for baritones and basses!) What choruses, ensembles, and solos with Leitmotifs! Go one better than Mascagni's world record!"

13. August Strindberg, Letter to Tor Aulin, 20 January 1908, Nobelbiblioteket, Stockholm. "When you last suggested a new collaboration . . . I would ask: Why not an opera?

"But not a Swedish work. It would turn into either *Den bergtagna* with C major and A minor endlessly—and a song is only a small detail in an opera. Or *Waldemarsskatten*: a combination of Skansen, Wagner, and Waldteuffel.

"To your suggestion I would respond: *Drömspelet*. There you have a book that has tested the flames. But it will be assured as the composer sees fit; all comic material will be deleted: the *dramatis personae* will be reduced; and the orchestra will be limited to Mozart's instrumentation (your present usage). And brief! A musical chamber play in which all philosophizing is omitted and only the 'scenes' remain. Thus not a sung novel as in—you recall the French work at the Swedish Theater! Dramatic—lyrical music but not theatrical—recitative—discursive.

"Simple but not too simple. Glück by all means (*Orfeo*) but lined with Beethoven, yet not Beethoven entirely!"

14. Ture Rangström, *Visor* ("Mitt trollslott står i skogens bryn," "Sju rosor och sju eldar," "Semele," "Villemo") (Stockholm: Nordiska Musikförlaget, 1909), w.o.

15. Ture Rangström, "Strindberg och en musikant," *Nya Dagligt Allehanda*, 13 April 1942, pp. 4ff. "Let me think for a moment!" "You are right! Music sometimes has a higher morality than does poetry!"

Strindberg's *Ett drömspel* and Hofmannsthal's *Die Frau ohne Schatten*

Rochelle Wright

The central theme of both August Strindberg's *Ett drömspel* (*A Dream Play*, 1902, premiered 1907) and Hugo von Hofmannsthal's libretto to *Die Frau ohne Schatten* (*The Woman without a Shadow*, 1916, premiered 1919) is the quest for what is essentially human. The structural frameworks of the two theatrical pieces are correspondingly similar. In both the play and the opera, the character who is the central bearer of the theme, Indra's Daughter and The Empress respectively, is the daughter of a spirit-lord who descends to earth from a higher realm in order to experience earthly life and ultimately to form a judgment about it.[1] The main characters in both works are initiated and educated through suffering to come to the realization that true humanity and fulfillment of the self are achieved only through transcendence of the individual ego.

Since the most obvious difference between *Ett drömspel* and *Die Frau ohne Schatten* is the dimension of music—the latter work was of course set by Richard Strauss—it deserves initial mention that Strindberg intended his play to be performed to musical accompaniment, and such has often been the case. Although Strindberg's own musical suggestions, most of them excerpts from works by Beethoven,[2] generally have been ignored, the Göteborg production of 1916, for instance, featured music by the well-known Swedish composer Wilhelm Stenhammar.[3] Many commentators, beginning with the author, have remarked on the musical structure of the play itself.[4] Its various thematic strands function like a musical theme with variations, whereas Indra's Daughter's refrain, "Det är synd om människorna" ("human beings are to be pitied"), may be compared to a leitmotif. Furthermore, Strindberg's text has inspired not one, but *two* operas. Julius Weismann's *Ein Traumspiel*, in three acts with an orchestral prelude, was written in 1922–24 and premiered in Duisburg the year following its completion. Weismann also set two other Strindberg plays, *Svanevit* (*Schwanenweiß* or *Swanwhite*) and *Spöksonaten* (*Die Gespenstersonate* or *The Ghost Sonata*).[3] The contemporary Australian composer Malcolm Williamson borrowed Strindberg's central symbol for the title of his *The Growing Castle*. Premiered in Wales in 1968, the opera has been performed both in Sweden and the United States.[6] Although neither work shows sign of entering the standard operatic repertory, the prominent critic Walter Berendsohn has suggested that Weismann's Strindberg operas might succeed in the playwright's native land,[7] and Williamson's opera received generally favorable reviews, particularly in the United States.[8] A comparison of the interrelationship between text and music in the operas based on *Ett drömspel* with that of the Hofmannsthal-Strauss collaboration must, however, remain beyond the scope of this study.

Both Strindberg and Hofmannsthal drew their inspiration in part from Eastern tradition; the god Indra and Strindberg's fascination with the life-as-dream topos in *Ett drömspel* derive from Hinduism and Buddhism respectively, while Hofmannsthal wove many motifs from the *Thousand and One Nights* into his Oriental tapestry.[9] Yet neither author emphasizes the Eastern elements; for Strindberg they provide an overall structural framework, whereas for Hofmannsthal they serve to place the story in a kind of never-never land. Thus it is appropriate that the figures most directly associated with the East, the spirit-lords Indra and Kaikobad, remain absent from the stage and aloof from the main dramatic action. In *Ett drömspel*, only Indra's voice is heard, and that solely in the prologue to the play, added as a clarification for the premiere; Kaikobad in *Die Frau ohne Schatten* communicates his will through messengers and other-worldly voices. Indra and Kaikobad both serve as abstract, remote representations of absolute justice or moral law; it is left to the other characters to demonstrate the workings of such laws in the human sphere.

Through Indra's Daughter, *Ett drömspel* examines the human condition from virtually every possible perspective. The spirit-child is present in every scene of the play, but she is not merely a passive observer, nor does she, like Christ, descend to earth in order to save or transform it. Instead, it is her function to learn through experience and suffering as well as observation just how difficult life is. Variations on certain basic truths are presented over and over again in *Ett drömspel*. One such theme is the disparity between illusion and reality, between expectation and fulfillment. The Officer is perhaps more fortunate than the other figures in the play in that the real Victoria never appears to destroy his imaginative picture of her, while The Billboard Paster, in contrast, is disappointed that his fishnet is not the precise shade of green he had envisioned. Another related thematic strand is the near impossibility of harmonious relationships with other people, for no human act can satisfy everyone. As The Officer's Mother says: "Hu, detta livet! När man handlar vackert, så finns det alltid någon för vilken det är fult . . . gör man en gott, gör man en annan ont."[10] Or as Indra's Daughter phrases it later in the play: "Här äro mina barn! En och en äro de snälla, men bara de råka ihop, så kivas de och bli till dämoner."[11]

The key problem for human beings is thus the restraint of the individual ego to make possible communication and cooperation with others. The nightmarish scenes of married life between The Lawyer and Indra's Daughter, scenes that are strongly reminiscent of Strindberg's treatment of marriage in his earlier naturalistic plays, are the most crucial illustrations of this difficulty and of the disillusionment that so often is an intrinsic part of human relations. Although their union begins with high ideals and hopes, all too soon the harmony is shattered by harsh words. Whatever brings one partner pleasure gives the other pain. That there is no escape from this marital hell is represented by Kristin's incessant pasting. Clearly, Strindberg uses married life as a focal point in his presentation of human beings' dissatisfaction with earthly life. As she undergoes both the hardships and the less frequent joys of existence, Indra's Daughter expresses her verdict on the human condition in the phrase she repeats like a refrain throughout the play: "Det är synd om människorna."

Die Frau ohne Schatten does not present a panoramic picture of life on earth, as *Ett drömspel* does, yet certain scenes in the Hofmannsthal libretto show striking affinities to Strindberg's play and illustrate a similar perception of human existence. It is significant that both Indra's Daughter and The Empress, who are at home in a higher, spiritual realm, first experience the descent to earth in terms of physical oppressiveness and suffocation. Indra's Daughter says:

> Nu sjunker molnet, det blir kvavt, jag kvävs . . .
> Det är ej luft, men rök och vatten som jag andas . . .
> Så tungt, den drar mig nedåt, nedåt,
> och nu jag märker ren dess krängning,
> den tredje världen är dock ej den bästa . . .[12]

The Nurse, describing what awaits The Empress and herself in the third and lowest of the realms differentiated in *Die Frau ohne Schatten* (the others are that of The Emperor and Kaikobad's sphere), exclaims:

> Bei den Menschen!
> Grausts dich nicht?
> Menschendunst
> ist uns Todesluft! . . .
> Uns riecht ihre Reinheit
> nach rostigem Eisen
> und gestocktem Blut
> und nach alten Leichen![13]

Similarly, the next few lines of this speech could apply to Indra's Daughter's experiences on earth as well as to the initial perception of the Empress:

> Dich ihnen vermischen,
> hausen mit ihnen,
> handeln mit ihnen,
> Rede um Rede,
> Atem um Atem,
> erspähn ihr Belieben,
> ihrer Bosheit dich schmiegen,
> ihrer Dummheit dich bücken,
> ihnen dienen!
> Grausts dich nicht?[14]

The Empress' realization in Act II of mankind's suffering and disharmony—"Wehe, womit ist die Welt der Söhne Adams erfüllt!"[15]—is also a close echo of Indra's Daughter's refrain, "Det är synd om människorna."

Indra's Daughter learns both through direct experience and through observation of others that the fundamental dilemma of human existence is the conflict between egocentric demands and the desire for true harmony with others. The functions of observer and participant are to a large degree divided between two characters, The Empress and The Dyer's Wife, in *Die Frau ohne Schatten*, but both characters eventually come to the same conclusion that Indra's Daughter reaches. As in the Strindberg play, the treatment of marriage is of central importance in establishing this theme. The married life of The Dyer and his wife has many points of correspondence with that of The Lawyer and Indra's Daughter. Here is illustrated, once again, the difficulty of communication and the gap between expectation and fulfillment. Both Indra's Daughter and The Dyer's Wife feel chained to a life that is somehow beneath them and that prevents them from fulfilling their true selves. The Dyer's Wife sees her husband as an animal plodding about his daily tasks. She constantly repeats, "Verstehst du mich?," knowing that he does not, and laments that he cannot fathom "die Tiefe und das Geheimnis."[16] Although Indra's Daughter asks only for a touch of physical beauty to brighten her home and make life bearable, The Dyer's Wife demands nothing less than spiritual beauty and significance. She cannot understand her husband's simple, physical joy in providing for his family or his pride in his work, and because she is uncertain that life is worth living, she rejects the idea of bearing his children. Both The Lawyer in *Ett drömspel* and Barak in *Die Frau ohne Schatten* are in turn so preoccupied with the demands of the here-and-now that they fail to understand or sympathize with the yearnings of their wives for beauty and a higher meaning in life.

The important difference between the marriage in Strindberg's play and that of The Dyer and Dyer's Wife is that stagnation and sterility are doomed to continue eternally in the relationship of The Lawyer and Indra's Daughter, but Hofmannsthal's couple grows through catharsis to a new awareness of what each means to the other. In desperation, The Dyer's Wife threatens to sell her shadow, thus forever alienating her from the human race and dooming her to childlessness. Barak, in fury, tries to kill her, but is prevented from doing so by his brothers. Suddenly, The Wife sees her husband in a new light, that of mighty lord. By putting herself totally in his power and by transcending her egocentric demands, she makes possible a reconciliation. Barak too is filled with remorse. As Act III opens they sit, each unaware of the other's presence, in an underground prison, each avowing the new faith of love and tenderness they will bring to marriage if only they find each other again. When the Voice from Above tells them: "Auf, geh' nach oben / der Weg ist frei!"[17] the audience knows that they have endured their trial and passed the test.

The Empress too must be tested. Before she truly can become human, an act that is symbolically represented by the acquisition of a shadow, she must learn what it is that distinguishes true humanity from self-interest. Gradually she realizes that she cannot sacrifice another's happiness in order to attain her goal, and three times she refuses the shadow of The Dyer's Wife: "Ich will nicht den Schatten: / auf ihm ist Blut."[18]—even when it appears that only by taking it can she save The Emperor from being turned into stone. Thus, like Indra's Daughter, The Empress is educated through suffering, both her own and that of others, to reach an understanding of what true humanity entails. In both *Ett drömspel* and *Die Frau ohne Schatten* the implication is that happiness and beauty in life cannot be striven for directly but are achieved only through total self-abnegation.

The structural frameworks of *Ett drömspel* and *Die Frau ohne Schatten*, like their thematic content, are comparable in significant ways. As the title indicates, the unity in Strindberg's play lies in the dream image. In his famous introduction, two paragraphs that have always, since the first edition, been printed with the play, Strindberg explains this in detail. His technique is to string together a series of pictures, images that are connected only through association and imagination. Both the stage setting and the figures in the play contribute to the creation of a new reality based on dream consciousness. Images and situations melt into one another in *Ett drömspel* just as they do in a dream. Often, continuity is provided by the presence of a single stage prop that alters function as the scene changes. Thus a tree becomes a clothes hanger, the organ becomes Fingal's Cave, and the door with the four-leaf clover turns into a safe. Because dream logic permits inconsistencies, characters may enter and exit through walls, age prematurely and then grow young again, or carry on conversations with those already dead. Characters too lose their distinctive boundaries of personality and fade into one another; they frequently remain unnamed and are identified only by their functions or professions in order to stress their lack of individual contour. The three primary male characters, The Officer, The Lawyer, and The Poet, each of whom, together with Indra's Daughter, dominates the play, may thus be interpreted as representing three aspects of the same personality. As has been mentioned before, Indra's Daughter herself alternates between observing humanity and participating in life, moving without pause or explanation from one role to the other. The dream logic is not even always consistent with itself—the same character may be both a participant in a dream and a dreamer—but this is fully in keeping with Strindberg's introductory paragraphs if one assumes that the unifying consciousness is that of the author, or alternately, the reader/audience.

The roots of *Die Frau ohne Schatten* lie in the fairy tale; Hofmannsthal was in fact so captivated by the subject matter of the libretto that he wrote a *Märchen* version of the story. Significantly, a number of parallels may be drawn between what is permitted within the logic of a dream and within that of the fairy tale. In both, cause and effect are often suspended or distorted. Association replaces logic. The reader or audience willingly accepts magical events and transformations. Only in a fairy tale or a dream could jewels appear out of the air or a sword leap into the hand of the person who wishes to use it. Several times during the course of the opera, as in Strindberg's play, the setting miraculously is transformed: a bed appears for The Empress in The Dyer's home, the earth opens to swallow up The Dyer and his

Wife, walls disappear to reveal a cave, which vanishes in turn. Several of the supernatural beings can disappear or change shape at will, and The Emperor is nearly turned into stone. A more associative use of the shape-changing motif occurs when the fish The Dyer's Wife is frying suddenly become the voices of her unborn children. This is reminiscent of the song of the winds and the waves in *Ett drömspel*, where in a similar manner a human lament is voiced through a non-human agency.

In *Die Frau ohne Schatten*, moreover, the realm of the spirits, the magical world, is specifically identified by The Dyer's Wife with dream consciousness. When the image of The Youth is first made to appear before her by The Nurse, she realizes that her innermost thoughts have been given material form, and exclaims: "O Welt in der Welt! O Traum im Wachen!"[19] The Youth appears a second time when the Nurse persuades her to imagine him:

> . . . ein Knabe fast,
> der meiner nicht achtete— . . .
> mit hochmütigem Blick—
> und des ich gedachte
> heimlich, zuweilen,
> um Träumens willen![20]

The magic thus brings to life the previously unacknowledged unconscious desires of The Dyer's Wife, just as dreams may do.[21]

As in *Ett drömspel*, the characters in *Die Frau ohne Schatten*, with the exception of Barak, are unnamed, thus stressing their allegorical and symbolic function rather than their individuality. Just as The Officer, Lawyer, and Poet may be interpreted as facets of one personality, The Empress and Dyer's Wife (and to a lesser degree, The Emperor and Barak) may be seen as two sides of the same coin: both women must learn through suffering what true love and true humanity entail, and in the end both are rewarded with a shadow and the capacity to bear children. Hofmannsthal explained the function of this juxtaposition in a letter to Strauss, written in 1913 while work on the opera was in progress: "Es sind elf bedeutende, fast pantomimisch prägnante Situationen—durch ihre Verbindung aber—indem in ihnen zwei Welten, zwei Menschenpaare, zwei Konflikte einander wechselweise ablösen, einander spiegeln, einander steigern und schließlich einander aufheben—ist ein Ganzes hergestellt.[22]

In both *Ett drömspel* and *Die Frau ohne Schatten*, the dream or magic serves not only to provide structural unity or further the plot, but also to unite the work in a symbolic whole. In his post-Inferno period, Strindberg came more and more to believe that life itself is a dream from which the only awakening may be death. In *Ett drömspel*, dream, reality, and poetic creation ultimately blend together. In Fingal's Cave, Indra's Daughter wonders whether she has dreamed all her experiences on earth. The Poet replies:

> Det har jag diktat en gång!
> Dottern: Då vet du vad dikt är . . .
> Diktaren: Då vet jag vad dröm är . . . vad är dikt?
> Dottern: Ej verklighet, men mer än verklighet . . . ej dröm, men mer än drömmar . . .[23]

A later exchange illustrates the same sort of fusion between dream and reality:

> Diktaren: Mig tyckes att jag upplevat detta förr . . .
> Dottern: Mig även.
> Diktaren: Kanske jag drömt det?
> Dottern: Eller diktat det, kanske?
> Diktaren: Eller diktat det.
> Dottern: Då vet du vad dikt är.
> Diktaren: Då vet jag vad dröm är.
> Dottern: Mig tycks att vi stått någon annanstans och sagt dessa ord förr.
> Diktaren: Då kan du snart räkna ut vad verklighet är.
> Dottern: Eller dröm.
> Diktaren: Eller dikt![24]

It is within the context of this blurring of the distinctions between reality, dream, and poetic creation that one must examine the central theme of *Ett drömspel*, the apparently pessimistic theme that Indra's Daughter repeats like a refrain throughout the play: "Det är synd om människorna." This perception is further elaborated in The Poet's Lament to Indra:

> Jorden är icke ren,
> Jorden är icke ren,
> livet är icke gott,
> människorna icke onda,
> icke goda heller.
> De leva som de kunna,
> en dag om sänder.
> Stoftets söner i stoft vandra,
> av stoft födda
> till stoft varda de.
> Fötter att trampa fingo de,
> vingar icke.
> Dammiga bliva de,

är skulden deras
eller din?[25]

The apparent pessimism of Strindberg's theme is nevertheless tempered by a note of resignation, perhaps even of hope, through the symbolism of the play. Although much emphasis is placed on the misery of mankind, represented by the burden of guilt that The Lawyer and The Porteress, with her shawl, must shoulder, and although only emptiness lies behind the mysterious door that was alleged to hide the secret of life, the dominant symbol of *Ett drömspel* (other than Indra's Daughter herself) is the growing castle. It frames the play; it is present in the first scene, and Indra's Daughter returns to it at the end. The castle represents earthly life; it exists, as The Daughter tells The Officer in the first scene, so that one should long to escape from it. However, although the castle grows up from dung, it produces a beautiful golden chrysanthemum. When the castle is burned and earthly existence comes to an end, the chrysanthemum, symbolizing the soul, bursts into flower. Thus, in Strindberg's world view, release from the suffering of earthly life, from the confines of the individual ego, from the dream that we perhaps have created ourselves, comes only through death. Strindberg was not an orthodox Christian, but he clearly believed death to be the deliverer.

Hofmannsthal was preoccupied with the life-as-dream topos throughout his artistic career. In the early poems "Terzinen über Vergänglichkeit" ("Terze rime on Transitoriness") the third and final poem concludes: "Und drei sind Eins: ein Mensch, ein Ding, ein Traum."[26] His most complete expression of this concept is in *Der Turm* (*The Tower*), a reworking of Calderón's *La vida es sueño* (*Life is a Dream*), a work Strindberg also admired. In an essay from 1903 entitled "Die Bühne als Traumbild" ("The Stage as Dream Image"), Hofmannsthal called the stage "der Traum der Träume" ("the dream of dreams") and continued:

Wer das Bühnenbild aufbaut, muß wissen, wie, er muß daran glauben, vollgesogen muß er damit sein, daß es auf der Welt nichts Starres gibt, nichts was ohne Bezug ist, nichts was für sich allein lebt. Seine Träume müssen ihn das gelehrt haben, und er muß die Welt so sehen; die Kraft des Träumens muß groß in ihm sein und er muß ein Dichter unter den Dichtern sein. Sein Auge muß schöpferisch sein, wie das Auge des Träumenden, der nichts erblickt, was ohne Bedeutung wäre. . . . Wer die Bühne aufbauen wird, muß durchs Auge gelebt und gelitten haben. Tausendmal muß er sich geschworen haben, daß das Sichtbare allein existiert, und trausendmal muß er schaudernd sich gefragt haben, ob denn das Sichtbare nicht, vor allen Dingen, *nicht* existiert.[27]

Hofmannsthal thus explicitly connects the poet's ability to perceive the hidden significance of things with dream consciousness. Like Strindberg, he sees the interwovenness of the creative act, the dream, and reality, although he does not go so far as to fuse them completely, as Strindberg does. In fact, the symbolism of *Die Frau ohne Schatten* clearly differentiates reality, the purely human sphere, as being separate from and in some respects morally superior to the realm of the spirits, the world of magic and the dream. The relationship between The Empress and The Nurse illustrates this distinction. The Nurse belongs entirely to the spirit world, although she is only a servant there. In order to acquire a shadow for her mistress, she is willing to use any and all methods, showing no compassion for the suffering she causes mere human beings. In contrast, The Empress gradually rejects this amorality, and as she learns the true sympathy for others that will earn her the right to a shadow, she also distances herself more and more from The Nurse. As a sign of her full commitment to becoming human, she symbolically breaks off her ties with the world from which she came by telling The Nurse to leave her forever. It is important to remember, however, that The Nurse herself is being tested by Kaikobad and fails the test. Her lack of compassion is punished; she is doomed to wander forever in the world of men.

The Empress, like Indra's Daughter, has discovered that life among human beings can be full of hardship and disharmony, but she is also aware that it is rich and fraught with significance:

> Mit welchem Preis
> sie alles zahlen,
> aus schwerer Schuld
> sich wieder erneuen,
> dem Phönix gleich,
> aus ewigem Leben
> sich immer erhöhen—
> kaum ahnen sies selber—[28]

In *Ett drömspel*, it is death that leads to eternal life, and Indra's Daughter, freed from the confines of her mortal body, returns to the realm of the spirits from which she came. In *Die Frau ohne Schatten*, The Empress freely chooses permanently to become a member of the human race, and renewal is symbolized by the Unborn Children, the product of the love between husband and wife that becomes ". . . die Brücke überm Abgrund aufgespannt / auf der die Toten wiederum ins Leben gehn."[29] At the end of the opera The Dyer and Dyer's Wife stand on a golden bridge, a materialization of the image in the song of The Watchmen and a symbolic equivalent to the golden chrysanthemum in *Ett drömspel*, while The Emperor and Empress are near the waterfall that in like manner represents the self-renewing power of life. Both couples have risen to a new level of perception, of their own relationships but also of marriage and humanity in general, and they are justly rewarded.

Hofmannsthal was aware of Strindberg as early as 1893, when a letter from his friend Richard Beer-Hofmann mentions having attended a performance of *Gläubige* (*Fordringsägare* or *Creditors*).[30] There are brief, sporadic references to the Swedish writer in Hofmannsthal's correspondence over the ensuing decades. In "Aufzeichnungen zu Reden in Skandinavien" ("Notes for Speeches in Scandinavia") (1916) Hofmannsthal devotes a short paragraph to Strindberg before moving on to a more detailed discussion of the plays of Ibsen.[31] That the Austrian was specifically familiar with Strindberg's post-Inferno plays is indicated in a 1923 essay on Eugene O'Neill in which Hofmannsthal comments: "Und was Strindbergs Stücke zusammenhält, ist . . . nicht die erzählbare Anekdote, sondern ihre Atmosphäre zwischen Wirklichkeit und Traum."[32] The German premiere of *Ett drömspel* took place in Berlin in 1916, the same year the libretto version of Hofmannsthal's *Die Frau ohne Schatten* was published; Strindberg's play was not performed in Vienna until 1922;[33] however, Emil Schering's German translation of *Ett drömspel* (*Ein Traumspiel*) appeared simultaneously with its publication in Sweden. Considering Hofmannsthal's cosmopolitan orientation and his extensive knowledge of and wide readings in foreign literatures, together with his awareness of Strindberg's preeminent importance on the Swedish literary scene, it would be highly surprising had he not been familiar with the text of Strindberg's masterpiece when it first became available to the German reading public, in other words well before the idea for *Die Frau ohne Schatten* was conceived.

The parallels in overall framework, dramatic structure, characterization, and theme between *Ett drömspel* and *Die Frau ohne Schatten* nevertheless do not demonstrate direct influence so much as an affinity between the two authors and similarities in their approaches to writing for the stage. It is noteworthy that both Strindberg and Hofmannsthal were acutely aware of dramatic tradition. Both wrote morality plays following the medieval model—Strindberg's *Till Damaskus* (*To Damascus*) trilogy, Hofmannsthal's *Jedermann* (*Everyman*) and *Das Salzburger große Welttheater* (*The Salzburg World Theater*)—and Strindberg, like Hofmannsthal in *Die Frau ohne Schatten*, turned to the fairy tale for his inspiration in plays such as *Lycko-Pers resa* (*Lucky Per's Journey*) and *Svanevit*. Modern psychologists have often shown that both the dream and the fairy tale may reveal the inner significance of human experience by appealing to the unconscious rather than the conscious mind. Strindberg and Hofmannsthal seem to have reached the same conclusion intuitively, realizing that the truth about major philosophical and existential questions may best be approached through symbolism and allegory rather than strict realism, through synthesis rather than analysis. Both *Ett drömspel* and *Die Frau ohne Schatten* demonstrate that such metaphysical speculations may exert a timeless and universal appeal on the stage.

Notes

1. Walter Muschg, "Trakl und Hofmannsthal," *Von Trakl zu Brecht: Dichter des Expressionismus* (Munich: P. Piper & Co., 1961), p. 97. Muschg notes in passing this basic structural similarity, but does not pursue the Strindberg-Hofmannsthal comparison.
2. Strindberg's specifications concerning music to be performed with *Ett drömspel* have been printed in August Falck, *Fem år med Strindberg* (Stockholm: Wahlström & Widstrand, 1935), p. 274.
3. Gunnar Ollén, *Strindbergs dramatik* (Stockholm: Sveriges Radio, 1961), p. 407.
4. Kungliga Biblioteket, Stockholm: *Drömspelet: ett tryckt exemplar med Strindbergs tillägg till "En erinran" och om musiken*. Cited in Raymond Jarvi, "*Ett drömspel*: A Symphony for the Stage," *Scandinavian Studies*, 44, (1972), p. 31. Jarvi's study is the most detailed analysis in print of musical aspects of *Ett drömspel*.
5. Walter Berendsohn, "Strindbergsrenässansen i Tyskland," *Meddelanden från Strindbergssällskapet*, 20 (December 1956), 1–2.
6. Gunnar Ollén, "Strindbergspremiärer 1969–70," *Meddelanden från Strindbergssällskapet*, 45 (May 1970), 3.
7. Berendsohn, p. 2.
8. The American premiere at Caramoor, New York on 3 July 1970 was reviewed in *Opera News*, 35, No. 1 (5 September 1970), p. 22.
9. Cf. Wolfgang Köhler, "Die Frau ohne Schatten," *Hugo von Hofmannsthal und Tausendundeine Nacht*, Europäische Hochschulschriften, Series 1, Vol. 77 (Frankfurt am Main: Verlag Peter Lang, 1972), 126–53.
10. August Strindberg, *Samlade Skrifter*, 36, ed. John Landquist (Stockholm: Bonniers, 1916), p. 229 (hereafter *SS*). All translations are from *A Dream Play and Four Chamber Plays*, trans. Walter Johnson (Seattle: University of Washington Press, 1973). "This life! When you do something nice, there's always someone to whom it is ugly. . . . If you do something good for someone, you hurt someone else."
11. *SS*, p. 322. "These are my children! Each one by himself is good, but all you have to do to turn them into demons is to bring them together."
12. *SS*, p. 220. "The cloud is sinking . . . it's getting stifling . . . / I'm suffocating . . . / It isn't air but smoke and water I'm breathing . . . / so heavy, it pulls me down, down . . . / and now I already feel its sway . . . / the third world is not the best . . ."
13. Hugo von Hofmannsthal, *Dramen III* of *Gesammelte Werke* (Frankfurt am Main: S. Fischer, 1957), p. 159 (hereafter *Dramen III*). "Among human beings! / Don't you shudder? / The smell of human beings / is the breath of death to us! . . . / To us their purity smells / of rusty iron, / and stagnant blood, / and of old corpses!"
14. *Dramen III*, 159–60. "To mix with them / lodge with them, / deal with them / word for word, / breath for breath, / discover their pleasures, / conform to their evil, / bow to their stupidity, / serve them! / Don't you shudder?"
15. *Dramen III*, 204. "Woe, what kind of world do the sons of Adam inhabit!"
16. *Dramen III*, 199. "Do you understand me?" ". . . the depth and the secret."
17. *Dramen III*, 214. "Arise, ascend, / the way is free!"
18. *Dramen III*, 209–10. "I do not want the shadow: / there is blood on it."
19. *Dramen III*. 173. "O world within the world! O waking dream!"

20. *Dramen III*, 183ff. ". . . a boy almost, / who paid me no regard— . . . / with arrogant glance— / of whom I thought / secretly, occasionally, / for the sake of dreaming!"

21. Since dream or fairy-tale logic permits magical transformations to take place on stage, producing either *Ett drömspel* or *Die Frau ohne Schatten* calls for considerable imagination and ingenuity on the part of the director and set designer.

22. Letter from Hugo von Hofmannsthal to Richard Strauss, 20 January 1913, in *Richard Strauss-Hugo von Hofmannsthal: Briefwechsel*, ed. Willi Schuh (Zurich: Atlantis, 1952), p. 203. "There are eleven significant, almost pantomimically incisive situations—but it is their combination—in which two worlds, two pairs of beings, two interwoven conflicts, mutually alternate with each other, reflect each other, enhance each other, and eventually find their equilibrium—which gives unity to the whole work."

23. *SS*, p. 301. "Daughter: I've dreamed that . . . / Poet: I put it into poetry once . . . / Daughter: Then you know what poetry is . . . / Poet: Then I know what dreaming is . . . What is poetry? / Daughter: Not reality, but more than reality . . . not dreaming, but waking dreams."

24. *SS*, p. 311. "Poet: I seem to have lived through this before . . . / Daughter: I, too. / Poet: Perhaps I dreamt it? / Daughter: Or composed it, perhaps? / Poet: Or composed it. / Daughter: Then you know what poetry is. / Poet: Then I know what dreaming is. / Daughter: It seems to me we've stood elsewhere saying these words before. / Poet: Then you can soon determine what reality is! / Daughter: Or dreaming! / Poet: Or poetry!"

25. *SS*, pp. 298–99. "The earth is not clean, / life is not good, / human beings not evil, / nor are they good. / They live as they can, / one day at a time, / The sons of dust wander in dust, / born of dust / they return to dust. / They have feet to walk, / but not wings. / They become dusty. / Is the blame theirs / or yours?"

26. Hugo von Hofmannsthal, *Gedichte und Lyrische Dramen* in *Gesammelte Werke* (Stockholm: Bermann-Fischer, 1946), p. 19. "And three are one: a person, a thing, a dream."

27. Hugo von Hofmannsthal, *Prosa II* in *Gesammelte Werke* (Frankfurt am Main: S. Fischer, 1951), pp. 63, 66. "Whoever creates the setting for the stage must know how, he must believe in, must be completely absorbed by, the fact that there is nothing inflexible in the world, nothing that is without reference, nothing that lives for itself alone. His dreams must have taught him that and he must see the world in this way; the power of dreaming must be great in him and he must be a poet among poets. His eye must be creative, like the eye of a dreamer, which perceives nothing without meaning. . . . Whoever is to create for the stage must have lived and suffered through the eye. A thousand times must he have sworn that the visible alone exists, and a thousand times must he have asked himself, shuddering, whether the visible does not, above all, *not* exist."

28. *Dramen III*, 222. "At what price / they pay everything, / and again renew themselves, / out of deep guilt, / like the Phoenix, / from eternal life / they always rise— / hardly knowing it themselves—"

29. *Dramen III*, 180. ". . . the bridge spanned over the abyss / on which the dead once again return to life."

30. Letter from Richard Beer-Hofmann to Hugo von Hofmannsthal, 5 July 1893, in *Hugo von Hofmannsthal-Richard Beer-Hofmann: Briefwechsel*, ed. Eugene Weber (Frankfurt am Main: S. Fischer, 1972), p. 21.

31. Hugo von Hofmannsthal, *Prosa III* in *Gesammelte Werke* (Frankfurt am Main: S. Fischer, 1952), p. 350. In 1916 Hofmannsthal traveled to Scandinavia on a quasi-official lecture tour to promote cultural contact and general goodwill. While in Stockholm he attended a performance of his own *Elektra*, with Harriet Bosse, Strindberg's third wife, in the title role, and was much impressed with her skill as an actress. Although this occurred after the completion of the libretto version of *Die Frau ohne Schatten*, it is an interesting coincidence that Bosse was the model and inspiration for

Indra's Daughter in *Ett drömspel*. Cf. Algot Werin, "Hofmannsthal und Schweden," in *Nerthus III*, Nordisch-deutsche Beiträge, ed. Steffen Steffensen (Düsseldorf: Eugen Diederichs Verlag, 1972), p. 177.

32. Hugo von Hofmannsthal, *Prosa IV* in *Gesammelte Werke* (Frankfurt am Main: S. Fischer, 1955), p. 200. "And what holds Strindberg's plays together is . . . not the narrative tale, but rather their atmosphere between reality and dream."

33. Ollén, *Strindbergs dramatik*, pp. 416–18.

From *lilla helvetet* to the Boxing Ring: Strindberg and Dürrenmatt

Gerhard P. Knapp

I

Friedrich Dürrenmatt has, from the onset, demonstrated a very specific relationship to literary tradition, which has become even more pronounced in the past ten years. This attitude has been called indiscriminate, irreverent, even exploitive. Since the days of Brecht, however, terms like these are no longer justified, particularly in the light of a radically different concept of literary originality as witnessed since 1945. Literary and documentary materials are readily available to contemporary writers: the reading public and the theatergoer are well equipped to deal adequately with adaptations, quotations, and allusions. For the literary critic, established terms such as "influence," "effect,"[1] and "adaptation" call for new definitions;[2] the methods and orientation of thematology or "Stoffgeschichte" ("history of themes") need to be revaluated within the greater framework of a new methodology. A modified concept of literary *effect* will eventually replace the traditional trinity of "Stoff, Gehalt, Form,"[3] ("theme, content, form") and will loosen the unproportionally tight relationship between "author" on the one hand, "Geistesgeschichte" ("intellectual history") on the other. This concept will have to rest heavily on the changing potential for reception of a particular theme within different historical and societal situations, as well as its intended and/or actual reception under varying circumstances. In practical terms: the present study on Strindberg and Dürrenmatt will differentiate between *influence* (in the traditional sense of the word) and *effect*—which may ultimately express itself in form of a counterconception—as shown in the comparison of *Dödsdansen* (*The Dance of Death*) and *Play Strindberg*.[4]

II

Dürrenmatt's dramatic production spans the years from 1946 to the present with sixteen published plays—not counting numerous revisions of earlier texts and the radio plays. Although the author has never formally synthesized his views on the theater into a coherent theory, his essays, speeches and reflections on drama and stage fill two volumes thus far,[5] and must be regarded as an impressive contribution to contemporary dramaturgy. In the center of this heterogeneous, sometimes even contradictory theoretical complex, the author designs, in several stages, a complete revaluation of the concept of comedy. This may be distilled into a threefold redefinition of this dramatic form: only comedy, postulates Dürrenmatt, is suitable to come to grips with modern society, which he sees as devoid of metaphysical questions and answers. Only comedy can awaken its recipient to the confrontation with a world of total power concentration, of absolutely opaque and manipulative social structures. And only comedy as a last bastion of artistic autonomy can attempt to construe the causalities responsible for social and economic development.[6]

Tragedy, as opposed to this, presupposes the presence of an omnipotent—if not transcendent—*ordo*; and this belief must necessarily stand in contradiction to the chaotic nature of modern reality:

> Die Tragödie setzt Schuld, Not, Maß, Übersicht, Verantwortung voraus. In der Wurstelei unseres Jahrhunderts, in diesem Kehraus der weißen Rasse, gibt es keine Schuldigen und auch keine Verantwortlichen mehr. Alle können nichts dafür und haben es nicht gewollt. Es geht wirklich ohne jeden. Alles wird mitgerissen und bleibt in irgendeinem Rechen hängen. Wir sind zu kollektiv schuldig, zu kollektiv gebettet in die Sünden unserer Väter und Vorväter. Wir sind nur noch Kindeskinder. Das ist unser Pech, nicht unsere Schuld: Schuld gibt es nur noch als persönliche Leistung, als religiöse Tat. Uns kommt nur noch die Komödie bei.[7]

Though eliminating tragedy as a literary genre, Dürrenmatt does not refute the existence of the tragic as an inherent quality of life and, consequently, as one of the constituents of literature: "Doch ist das Tragische immer noch möglich, auch wenn die reine Tragödie nicht mehr möglich ist. Wir können das Tragische aus der Komödie heraus erzielen, hervorbringen als einen schrecklichen Moment, als einen sich öffnenden Abgrund, so sind ja schon viele Tragödien Shakespeares Komödien, aus denen heraus das Tragische aufsteigt."[8]

This distinction between *form* and *substance*, between literary genre and the epiphany of human experience, is essential to the understanding of Dürrenmatt's works. Comedy, as the only viable dramatic vehicle for modern audiences, must be capable of *revealing* tragic constellations, it must, to paraphrase the author, make allowance for the human element within the general framework of a dehumanized world.[9] It is plainly visible that Dürrenmatt operates with the reversed strategy of traditional tragedy: Strindberg's companion plays, for example, unfold in the pervading presence of a tragic constellation that allows only occasional glimpses of hope, remedy, or even humor. This basically unchanging tragic setting leaves little room for its *personae*—and equally, for its audience—to recognize themselves as victims of a situation that need not necessarily be as it is. Dürrenmatt, however, provides his recipient with the emancipatory insight that man's victimization is real, but by no means predetermined: "Denn der Mensch muß sich erst bewußt werden, daß er ein Opfer ist."[10] Only in light of this realization does comedy have its true *raison d'être*: in demonstrating whatever little room is left for modern man to opt for his own freedom, and not to capitulate in the face of circumstances seemingly beyond his control: "Auch die Opfer sind 'komisch,' weil es unmenschlich ist, Opfer sein zu müssen, weil die Opfer dadurch, daß sie Opfer sind, von dem getrennt sind, was sie sein könnten: Menschen. Darum gibt es heute vielleicht doch nur eine Dramaturgie: jene der Komödie. Leider."[11]

At this point, and after an altogether sketchy summary of Dürrenmatt's *Dramaturgie der Komödie* (*Dramaturgy of Comedy*), it seems necessary to recapitulate some of the more significant traces of Strindberg's influence on Dürrenmatt. In the early 1950s the latter wrote, admittedly for economic reasons, a sequence of theater critiques for the *Weltwoche* (Zurich). These brief critical essays may be regarded today as important stepping stones in his own development as a playwright and stage-theoretician. Among these texts we find a remarkable discussion of the "Kammerspiel" ("chamber play") performance of *Spöksonaten* (*The Ghost Sonata*). The author-critic, interestingly enough, rates it as the high point of the season. He criticizes a certain lack of action in the play, which he describes as "so much atmosphere and too little plot."[12] It fascinates him that this is one of Strindberg's plays written not only *for* the stage, but equally *with* the stage. The play, says Dürrenmatt, has its strongest impact in the mythical quality of its figures and their effect on the audience. Both Strindberg's ability to create highly "dramatic" plays that evoke the impression of improvisation even during actual performance, and his striving for *mythopoiesis* deeply impressed Dürrenmatt. Even if we do not have exact references for all of Dürrenmatt's literary sources, it can be safely assumed that several of his texts were influenced by Strindberg's dramas—in particular, if not exclusively, by *Fröken Julie* (*Miss*

Julie), Dödsdansen, and *Spöksonaten.* The main characters in his first major stage success, *Die Ehe des Herrn Mississippi (The Marriage of Mr. Mississippi)* (1950), for example, definitely have a Strindbergian flair. The protagonists, Florestan Mississippi and dame Anastasia, who have both poisoned their respective spouses, become locked into a deadly marriage struggle: "Um *uns* endlich foltern zu können. Unsere Ehe würde für beide Teile die Hölle bedeuten."[13] At the end of the play the bloodthirsty prosecutor and his nymphomaniac wife poison each other. It would be wrong, however, to call Dürrenmatt's *Mississippi* a strictly Strindbergian tragicomedy: despite clear similarities in characterization and setting, the basic thrust of the play is radically different. It could rightly be called a grotesque *danse macabre* of modern ideologies: a power struggle between divine, absolute justice (personified by the protagonist), social justice and communist thought (personified by Saint-Claude), and Christianity, which is represented by the sole survivor, Graf Bodo von Übelohe. The power struggle ends in all-around defeat, and thus leads the recipient to the conclusion that a cure for the evils of our time is not to be found in any given ideology. Already here, Dürrenmatt in effect adapts the kinetic structure of *Dödsdansen*—which he complicates considerably—but for a radically different purpose. The *circulus vitiosus* of an inescapable marriage-hell is, again, encircled by the larger ring of the equally deadly, analogously vicious merry-go-round of ideologies locked in endless battle. In *Die Ehe des Herrn Mississippi,* the playwright reshapes elements of literary tradition to the purpose of a biting criticism of ideology and in doing so unfolds for the first time his extremely complex relationship to this tradition.

The motif of the *danse macabre* can be found once more in Dürrenmatt's successful tragicomedy *Der Meteor (The Meteor)* (1966). Here, the protagonist Wolfgang Schwitter has already died before the play begins. He arises from the dead and, in the course of the play, dies and resurrects a second time. His inability to die instills in him both a disgust for life and a cruelty toward others that is matched only by his son's outcry: "Dann stirb endlich!"[14] Schwitter, however, never fully resigns himself to his immortality: "Wann krepiere ich denn endlich!"[15] Dürrenmatt attempts to illustrate the unbelievable by means of comedy, to illuminate a "real" world of chaos and corruption through a mythical, "meteoritic" force—but his dramaturgical strategy is pressed very hard in this text. In fact, Schwitter, the "meteor" and violator of physical laws, ultimately personifies nothing more or less than immortalized human brutality.[16]

Similarly, the Strindbergian marriage, a ritual of mutual torment, could be identified as a recurring element in Dürrenmatt's works. It is, among other texts, explored to perfection in *Frank der Fünfte* (*Frank the Fifth*), an opera with music by Paul Burkhard (1958). One can, incidentally, safely exclude any biographical significance in this recurring situation—Dürrenmatt himself has been happily married for more than thirty years. On the contrary: it should be seen as characteristic of the author's social criticism, which frequently concentrates on marriage as the smallest of all social cells.

The later 1960s show a decisive reorientation in Dürrenmatt's work, both as an author and as a stage director. In a series of essayistic writings he establishes a new and more engaged sociopolitical position,[17] and during his tenure as artistic advisor of the *Basler Bühnen* (Basel Theaters) he turns to adaptations of "classical" plays for the contemporary stage. The reworking of his own first play *Es steht geschrieben* (*It Is Written*) (1946) under the title of *Die Wiedertäufer* (*The Anabaptists*) (1967) provides a demarcation line between the "old" and the "new" Dürrenmatt, and indicates the general direction of his new dramaturgy: "What was a scream of horror uttered by a young idealist reared during the holocaust of World War II was turned into a skeptical and weary statement by a middle-aged practitioner of the theater with grotesque effects as his most characteristic mannerism, with no belief left in a reasonable world order."[18]

In fact, a pronounced skepticism provides a plausible common denominator for all of Dürrenmatt's later works, from *König Johann* (1968) (after Shakespeare's *King John*) and *Play Strindberg* of the following year to his adaptations of *Urfaust* (1970), Shakespeare's *Titus Andronicus* (1970), and Büchner's *Woyzeck* (1972). There is, however, more to this "new" Dürrenmatt than disillusionment and resignation. His modified stance toward stage and audience must be seen against the background of the political and intellectual unrest of the late 1960s: the *Züricher Literaturstreit* (Zurich Literary Controversy), the awakening of a social consciousness from Berkeley to Berlin, and the rapidly changing self-definition of the theater that originated in France, in particular through the works of Antonin Artaud.[19] During these years, several authors tried their hands at rearranging classical pieces, such as Heiner Müller, who wrote adaptations of *Philoktet* (*Philoctetes*) (1965) and *Oedipus Tyrann* (*Oedipus Tyrannus*) (1967), and others.

Dürrenmatt's adaptations of traditional stage "classics" are radically different from these. For him, a *linear* adaptation of any tragedy is out of the question. Nor does he attempt to "modernize" previous literary accomplishments by employing the techniques of standard literary parody, that is, comical exaggeration or distortion on a one-to-one basis. His Shakespeare and Strindberg adaptations, in fact, are not primarily directed against the texts themselves, rather they parodize the *effect* of the given text on its audience. Consequently, Dürrenmatt alters the strategy of the adapted text according to his own dramaturgical principles *and* to the expectations of his audience. His adaptation of *King John*, a first attempt to establish a counterconception to a stage classic, evokes a fundamentally different response from its audience than did the original: "Aus einer dramatisierten Chronik wird ein Gleichnis: Die Komödie der Politik, einer bestimmten Politik."[20] The inherent power struggles in Shakespeare's play are refracted against a decisively "modern" constellation: "Es [sc. *König Johann*] zeigt die Maschinerie der Politik, das Zustandekommen ihrer Abkommen und ihrer Unglücksfälle, doch ist es ein Spiel unter Mördern, nicht unter Opfern."[21]

III

In *Play Strindberg*, Dürrenmatt concentrates on the victims. He had first seen *Totentanz* performed in Basel in 1948. His recollection in the following years was not of the play itself and its substance, but rather of the actors, particularly of Maria Fein and Rudolf Forster. His own adaptation, which in reality represents a full-fledged counterconcept,[22] was written in 1968: at the peak of the international student revolts and at a time when Dürrenmatt's own political convictions took a decisively antibourgeois turn. In order to do justice to both the original and the adaptation—Dürrenmatt's most successful play of the past decade—we must now briefly turn to Strindberg's impact on the German-speaking theater.

Strindberg established, for the modern stage, the basis of what was to be called "subjective" dramaturgy, the drama of the "I."[23] The production of the years from 1887 (*Fadren* [*The Father*]) to 1909 (*Stora landsvägen* [*The Great Highway*]), during the development of the "master dramatist" Strindberg from psychological naturalism to a pre-Expressionist technique,[24] made a strong impact on Imperial Germany. Several of his plays were premiered along with German Naturalist plays, with great success. The most kindred talent among German writers of the era, and at the same time the one influenced most strongly by Strindberg, is Frank Wedekind. Wedekind's and Frida Strindberg's paths crossed in 1896, and Wedekind's Lulu incorporates more of Strindberg's thoughts than any other literary figure of the time (apart, of course, from the blatantly Freudian undertones in Lulu, which are missing in Strindberg's writings).

Dödsdansen was first performed in September 1905 at the *Kölner*

Residenztheater (Cologne Court Theater). Successful stagings of either one or both parts followed in Berlin, Vienna, Mannheim, Hamburg, and Bremen—all prior to the Swedish premiere at the Stockholm Intimate Theater on 8 September 1909. By that time the play had already conquered the German-speaking stages, a victory that was to culminate in Max Reinhardt's memorable production at the *Berliner Deutsches Theater* (Berlin German Theater) in 1912. Since then, many attempts have been made to "modernize" *Dödsdansen*, mostly by implementing more or less severe cuts, up to the point of outright mutilations such as those staged at the New York Ritz Theatre by Paul Avila Mayer in 1971 or by A. J. Antoon at the Vivian Beaumont Theatre in 1974. The fact remains, though, that Strindberg's plays still reach large audiences, and that his successor playwrights such as Eugene O'Neill, Edward Albee, Tennessee Williams, or even Antonin Artaud have not surpassed the depth and penetration of his probing into the human soul.

The *effect* of Strindberg's plays on German audiences was predetermined, from the very beginning, by several factors: by the broader context of prewar Wilhelminian social structures on the one hand, and by a strong sense of alienation within this society experienced by many members of the bourgeoisie on the other. Notably, Strindberg has always been performed and received in Germany in deadly earnest. Translations of the time attest to this,[25] and those used for stage productions reflect ". . . the prevalent image of these [sc. Scandinavian] authors," namely, that of "profound and unsmiling bores, brooding at their desks in the middle of a dark Arctic winter night, with the wind blowing, snow falling, and with their thoughts circling around the consoling notion of happy and peaceful suicide."[26] According to this general concept, most traces of humor that exist in the original were eliminated in German renditions throughout the decades. Equally (and this applies both to *Dödsdansen* and *Spöksonaten*, which are certainly the most successful of all Strindberg plays on German stages) any potentially *objective* qualities of the texts have been consistently underplayed. In fact, Strindberg's tragedies reveal many more supraindividual, societal, and class-related phenomena than most recipients realize. *Dödsdansen* in particular may be read as a pathography of the Swedish bourgeoisie around the turn of the century, by virtue of its protagonists: it is not without significance that Alice is a has-been actress and Edgar a member of the impoverished but socially influential officer caste. And the play has, not without reason, made its strongest impact throughout the decades on bourgeois audiences, who understood it primarily as a "bürgerliche Ehetragödie."[27]

Dürrenmatt, whether he realizes it or not, seems to fall prey to this aura of a strictly humorless and obsessively tragic Strindberg.[28] The intent of his counterconception is obvious: he strives to eliminate all "literary" qualities of the original. By doing so, he most certainly "cuts away a dimension of depth,"[29] of psychological poignancy and atmosphere; but not without replacing it by the distinctively "objective" strategy typical of Dürrenmatt's comedies. Dürrenmatt is, after Brecht—one of his masters—among the most "objective" playwrights of our time, and his approach may at first glance seem ill-suited to a play as "subjective" as *Dödsdansen*. But this is not necessarily true, as will be shown by the details of the following comparison.

IV

The title *Play Strindberg* alludes to jazz improvisations on Bach's scores that were popular in the 1960s, and it implies a certain playful lack of reverence in dealing with the original. It requires, however, further explanation. Dürrenmatt's rescoring of *Dödsdansen* stays absolutely in character with his concept of comedy: this is illustrated already by the setting. As opposed to Strindberg, who requires, for Part I, a rather elaborate stage portraying the interior of a round tower in a granite fortress, as well as many props, and for Part II an ornate living room against the background of seashore batteries, Dürrenmatt uses an almost Beckettian stage. A round boxing arena contains four clusters of requisites: in the foreground a sitting area, to the left the piano, the daybed to the right, and in the background the telegraph and barometer. All other props have to be carried on and off stage by the actors themselves. The play now belongs exclusively to the actor, who is the performer of a total abbreviation.

Dürrenmatt utilizes primarily Part I of *Dödsdansen*, though he does, particularly in the final pages, incorporate material from Part II. Structurally, he abandons Strindberg's traditional sequence of acts and scenes: his division of twelve "rounds" corresponds to the boxing-ring stage setting and is even more revealing than the title *Play Strindberg*. The different "rounds" are called out by the actors in turn, as are their respective subtitles: 1. Unterhaltung vor dem Abendessen; 2. Endlich Besuch; 3. Ohnmachtsanfälle; 4. Am Krankenlager; 5. Hausmusik; 6. Einsames Abendessen; 7. Eine Stunde später; 8. Unterhaltung vor dem Abendessen; 9. Alice philosophiert; 10. Krankenpflege; 11. Kurt gesteht; 12. Abschied. Every round is initiated and concluded by a gong. These structural changes are indeed vital. Not only do they, as Dürrenmatt intended, underscore the impromptu character of the play,[30] they also heavily stress its circular, ringlike movement, which has been recognized by some critics,[31] and which, in fact, is a skeletal reminiscence of Strindberg's ornate dance-of-death setting. Moreover, the ring-versus-spectator setting suggests an important strategic move on the author's part: by delegating the roles of "boxers" to the actors, he implies that their struggle is at once ritualistic *and* senseless. And by projecting his audience into the passive situation of sportshall spectators, he attempts to provoke them to reflect on their own roles, that is to say, he makes clear to the viewer that he along with the actor on stage has a "role" in the play. Apart from this important effect, Dürrenmatt clearly utilizes the techniques of epic theater, in that he lets his actors "direct their own play." This gives them an autonomy and authority that, in Strindberg's play, were held by the tragic constellation itself.[32] In doing so, Dürrenmatt, in keeping with the tenets of epic theater, relies on and encourages the audience's willingness to intellectualize the contents of a play, to avoid any emotional entanglement or even identification with the events on stage.

In his striving toward didactic objectification, Dürrenmatt virtually eliminates everything in the original that might contribute to an affirmative reception through a bourgeois audience: he strips it of what he calls "Plüsch x Unendlichkeit."[33] This includes the tragic quality of Strindberg's characters, which is rooted primarily in their potential for change toward "personal and social good"[34] (even if, as in the case of *Dödsdansen*, it is doomed to fail from the beginning), as well as any outbursts of grotesque humor. The latter he replaces by an ever-present and biting, if occasionally limp, sarcasm. Just as he deprives the setting of its island-garrison flair, he removes any individual *and* class-specific traits from his actors. These combatants are no longer in need of their own *"lilla helvete* ("little hell"): the intrapersonal configuration alone suffices. As in Brecht's early play *Im Dickicht der Städte* (*In the Swamp*) (which was undoubtedly influenced by Strindberg), the fight itself is at the core of the dramatic conception. Whereas Strindberg's protagonists are at times touching, even humorous in their grotesque helplessness—be it only snide or outrightly vicious—Dürrenmatt's actors are performing an almost bloodless but vitriolic ritual that is, even in its language, reduced to convey only the bare "essentials" of their antagonism. The following exchange between Edgar and Alice sets the tone of Strindberg's play:

Kapten. Kära Alice, eländigt har det varit, men vi ha haft roligt, stundtals!
    Och man får begagna den korta tiden, ty sen är det slut!
Alice. Är det slut? Om så väl vore![35]

Whenever one of the characters becomes acutely aware, as does Edgar in the above scene, of the passing of time or, more specifically, of his and his partner's mortality, a glimpse can be gained at the human potential of these figures. Invariably, however, this moment of realization is curtailed by the partner's cutting and basically grotesque response. In Dürrenmatt's adaptation, the same exchange reads as follows:

E: Wir müssen unsere silberne Hochzeit feiern.
A: Unser fünfundzwanzigjähriges Elend brauchen wir nicht zu feiern.
E: Wir hatten es machmal nett miteinander.
A: Das bildest du dir bloß ein.[36]

Dürrenmatt reduces and depersonalizes the roles of Alice and Edgar, his sparring opponents, to the "typically" female and male essentials: that of the tormentor and that of the occasionally combatant, occasionally cunning or placating tormented. Both figures are identified with their respective musical pieces, which are used leitmotivically throughout the play:

A: Soll ich dir nicht doch was vorspielen?
E: Wenn du mir nicht mit deiner ewigen Solveig kommst.
A: Dann nicht.
E: Dann frag nicht.
A: Die einzige Musik, die du liebst, ist dein unmöglicher Einzug der Bojaren.[37]

Already at the end of the first round, it becomes apparent that their struggle is basically absurd, Beckettian in its aimlessness:

A: Wir sind erledigt.
E: Wir hängen uns am besten auf.[38]

The suicide motif (which is, as in absurdist plays, typically discarded as pointless) is augmented by Alice's repeated order to the Captain to die: "Stirb endlich, du mickriger Bojare, aufs Gartenbeet mit dir!"[39] Edgar is unable to die, even if he should want to: "Ich muß leben, auch wenn ich nicht mehr will."[40] The ritualistic nature of this sadomasochistic relationship is verbalized under Kurt's questioning:

K: Warum haßt ihr euch eigentlich?
A: Keine Ahnung.
K: Es muß doch einen Grund geben.
A: Wir sind verheiratet.[41]

Dürrenmatt's irony is obviously double edged: his *non sequitur* questions the logic behind the equation marriage = hatred, precisely because this was the cornerstone of Strindberg's tragic conception, and because it may still hold occasional truth in present-day society. Here, the playwright lets his audience catch a glimpse of man's futile but adamant victimization through institutions such as marriage.

Shortly after "half-time" (in round seven) the Captain summarizes the situation, now in his own words, in the form of an attack against Kurt:

> E: Eine glückliche Ehe. Wir waren glücklich zusammen, Alice und ich, bevor du gekommen bist. Wir lebten zusammen, spielten Karten, schwatzten was, sie spielte Solveigs Lied, und ich tanzte den Einzug der Bojaren.
> K: Du wolltest sie ermorden.
> E: Und? Ich wollte sie öfters ermorden. Eine jede Ehe züchtet Mordgedanken. . . .[42]

The repetitions in Dürrenmatt's text lend it certain affinities with a musical score; at the same time they cement the impression of an inescapable *circulus vitiosus*: everything has been said before and will, in all probability, be said again.[43] As opposed to Strindberg's texts, in which the "male characters are rendered speechless by the bottomless villainy of their female antagonists,"[44] and the Captain, in this particular case, repeatedly collapses after his wild emotional outbursts and then remains comatose, Dürrenmatt's Edgar cunningly manipulates his fainting spells. He is present on stage, and most certainly conscious, when Alice lures Kurt into the bedroom, using him as an instrument for her ultimate revenge. When Edgar then, in round seven, after having humiliated Kurt and Alice, becomes seriously afflicted and appears to be dying on the daybed, his attack is not taken seriously. At this point, however, the thoroughly playful make-up of Dürrenmatt's comedy suddenly changes. Until the end of the seventh round, none of the actors seems genuinely to suffer; nor do they experience the profound self-pity so characteristic of Strindberg's players. Both the playfulness of the action and its ritualistic dimension are constantly underlined by language, repetition, even by actual games such as cards ("Kartenspielszenen" ["card-playing scenes"]), music and dancing, philosophizing ("Philosophieszenen" ["philosophy scenes"]), or leafing through the family photo album ("Fotoalbumszenen" ["photo album scenes"]). These "Gesellschaftsspiele" ("parlor games") are just as essential to the causal nexus of the play as are literary tradition and the exposition of Alice's and Edgar's senseless power struggle. With Edgar's paralyzation—as becomes apparent in round eight—the aspect of "parlor games" is eliminated from the causal nexus. A new dimension enters the play in its place: the Captain experiences real suffering for the first time, as grotesque as this may seem. Alice then becomes his spokeswoman in her further exchanges with Kurt. As is so often the case in his plays, Dürrenmatt utilizes the principle of an *Einfall*,[45] a sudden change from the comical to the threatening that leaves his audience baffled. The play takes on a new and more somber mood. Edgar, immobilized and speechless, is reduced to total passivity. By overstepping the invisible limits of the battle, by plotting with Kurt, an outsider, against her intimate opponent, Alice has destroyed the Captain and, even though this was her declared goal, has thereby lost her only purpose in life. Thus, the comic struggle unexpectedly reveals a tragic quality.

Edgar's "knockout" (to stay within Dürrenmatt's boxing-ring terminology) arouses a certain tenderness in Alice: she assures Kurt of Edgar's splendid health and his remaining hearing powers; she even tries her hand at a needlepoint project as a gift for him on the occasion of their silver wedding anniversary. She maintains, as if speaking about a dead person: "Ich habe ihn immer geliebt."[46] At this point, *Play Strindberg* in fact becomes strongly reminiscent of the conclusion of *Dödsdansen II*. There, the Captain dies and Alice bemoans in no uncertain terms the departure of her husband-enemy: ". . . Men nu, då han är död, känner jag en underlig benägenhet att tala väl om honom!"[47] The key to this transformation is provided by Edgar's last words, a quotation from Luke: "förlåt dem, ty de veta icke vad de göra" ("Forgive them, for they know not what they do").[48] And at the very end, Alice confesses her love for Edgar, which now stands side by side with her hatred: "Min make, min ungdoms kärlek—ja, skratta?—han *var* en god och en ädel man—likafullt! . . . Jag måtte ha älskat den mannen![49] Whereas Strindberg's ending implies both the proximity of opposed emotions and the inevitability of a tragic outcome, however, Dürrenmatt once more asserts the absurdity of the struggle: a struggle in which both proponents are victimized and, after their last round, completely destroyed.

Ironically, but typically for Dürrenmatt's plays, there is a victor as well. Rounds eleven and twelve now hold one more surprise, in the form of Kurt's triumph. Having been instrumental during the play both as a not quite impartial referee and as an *agent provocateur* who contributes to the defeat of the fighters, he now drops the pose of the petty swindler and turns out to be the representative of big business and organized crime. During his stay with Alice and Edgar, he has gained some new insights:

K: . . . Die drei Tage, die ich bei dir und Edgar verbringen durfte, haben mir innerlich geholfen. . . . Ich durfte in eure kleine Welt hineinsehen. In der großen Welt, in der ich lebe, geht es in keiner Weise schlechter zu: Nur die Dimensionen sind anders.[50]

At the end, Alice asks Kurt, although not very convincingly, to take her with him. Kurt declines: she belongs to Edgar, and their bond is even stronger now. Further, there is no room for people like Alice in Kurt's world of monstrous gangsterism. Whereas she realizes, finally, that the world is not a decent place, Kurt takes pride in further ruining it:

A: Kurt, die Welt ist unanständig.
K: Leute meines Schlages ruinieren sie wenigstens.[51]

V

The question remains whether Dürrenmatt's counterconception indeed "hardly stands comparison with the original."[52] Critics have stated that it "failed to bring out the essential elements in the Swedish master of the stage," that it is starkly monothematic, at best a theatrical experience that is "intellectually stimulating, emotionally trite."[53] By the standards of conventional adaptation, "modernization," or even parody of the original, all this may be true. Dürrenmatt's intent, however, included none of these, nor the possibility that his *Play Strindberg* should actually replace *Dödsdansen* on stage. His text, like any given epic play, has to be understood primarily as a suggestion, as an intellectual stimulus that in part modifies, in part contradicts the original. Dürrenmatt's concept, although not completely severing the ties to its artistic predecessor, nevertheless challenges its statement and arrives at a quite different result.

A comparison of the dramatic nexus reveals the difference as well as the dependency:[54] for Strindberg, the suffering of his protagonists is a tragic necessity. His play illuminates the causes for this suffering and the powerful drives of the characters. Even beyond physical incapacitation, the essential hatred remains: Edgar, already crippled and speechless, spits in Alice's face, she slaps his face and pulls his beard. Only death can break the spell, but not solve the "riddle." Dürrenmatt, however, abandons all secrets, and by presenting merely the fact of a violent but illogical struggle he raises the fundamental question *if this struggle must be.* This question is supported by the boxing-ring setting, as well as by Dürrenmatt's reliance on epic elements. By depriving the dramatic action of any apparent motivation—in fact approximating it to absurdist plays in this respect—he forces his audience to confront the question why individuals torture each other. Any individualization of his *personae*, any specific atmospheric or psychological traits would, as in Brecht's *Lehrstücke* (*Didactic Pieces*) and parabolic plays, only obstruct the path toward a valid generalization. The answer to the question posed is, typically, not given in the text. It may, however, be found in Dürrenmatt's later play *Der Mitmacher* (*The Accomplice*) (unsuccessfully premiered in 1973), where "Doc" explains his criminal behavior as follows:

> Warum? Weil ich an der Gesellschaft zugrunde ging? Weil ich es der Welt noch einmal zeigen wollte? Weil ich mich selbst verachtete? Aus Haß? Aus Verbitterung? Alles große Worte. Vielleicht bloß aus Gedankenlosigkeit . . .[55]

When he discards any possible individual motivation as "große Worte," Dürrenmatt indicates that the real *radix malorum* is often mere thoughtlessness, failure to take a stand as an individual. Precisely through the absence of responsible causalities, his play reveals that human victimization and mutual destruction often have no logical *raison d'être*, that they are as ludicrous and pitiful as the spectacle of boxers mutilating each other in the arena. (The acute observer might add that even the financial incentive—a motivation for real boxers—is lacking in such domestic struggles.)

But this quintessence alone is not enough to satisfy Dürrenmatt. In addition, he introduces, at the play's end, a different kind of nexus. By promoting Kurt to the position of an unscrupulous industrial magnate who gains satisfaction from the insight that the "small world" of marital life is no better than his own snake pit, Dürrenmatt retroactively puts the play into perspective. On a much larger scale, he indicts the *homo homini lupus* as acted out by Edgar and Alice, who are victims of a power struggle they will never even begin to comprehend. Kurt, a typical protagonist of the "new" Dürrenmatt, is the amoral master criminal who represents the last stage in a long chain of corruption and degeneration. He, who will preside over a new order—once humanity has given up all resistance and willingly submits to the dictates of the conglomerates—leaves the battlefield for greater and better horizons: the sole victor.

In conclusion, we may ask if Dürrenmatt's strategy is successful, that is, if his play might actually provoke its audience to pose the question *why* "there is no love left."[56] We doubt it. First, the witty setting and stage artistry are in acute danger of being taken at face value, thus obliterating the text's critical qualities. The success of the play on stage thus far attests to this. But even more important: the predominant fatalism of the comedy, and particularly of its ending, may seduce many theatergoers to affirm human capitulation in the face of an all-pervading manipulation, to accept it as a *fait accompli*. Should this be the case, Dürrenmatt would have overshot his goal. Where there is a glimmer of hope left at the end of *Dödsdansen* in the future of Allan and Judith (even if it is purely irrational), Dürrenmatt leaves his audience with a strictly rational, double-edged alternative: either to resist and learn from the implications of his tragicomic model, or to accept it as a confirmation of inevitable reality. Many might prefer to take the easier course.

Notes

1. Horst Rüdiger, "Comparative Literature in Germany," *Yearbook of Comparative and General Literature*, 20 (1971), 15–20; for the purposes of the following study, Rüdiger's definition of "effect" seems to be most suitable: "Effects are, indeed, created by vital energy, and reception as well is a product of such energy, which reshapes themes, motifs, style, metaphors, topoi, symbols, quotations, etc., in a manner peculiar to itself." (Ibid., p. 19).

2. Cf. Raymond Trousson, "Plaidoyer pour la Stoffgeschichte," *Revue de littérature comparée*, 38 (1964), 101–114; Manfred Beller, "Von der Stoffgeschichte zur Thematologie. Ein Beitrag zur komparatistischen Methodenlehre," *Arcadia*, 5 (1970), 1–38; Adam John Bisanz, "Zwischen Stoffgeschichte und Thematologie. Betrachtungen zu einem literaturtheoretischen Dilemma," *Deutsche Vierteljahrsschrift*, 47 (1973), 148–66; Jean Burgos, "Thématique et Hermeneutiques ou le thématicien contre les interprètes," *Revue des langues vivantes*, 43 (1977), 522–34.

3. Bisanz, p. 152.

4. August Strindberg, *Samlade Skrifter*, 34, ed. John Landquist, (Stockholm: Bonniers, 1916). Hereafter SS. The English translations are from Walter Johnson's *Dramas of Testimony* (Seattle: University of Washington Press, 1975). Friedrich Dürrenmatt, *Play Strindberg. Totentanz nach August Strindberg*, in Friedrich Dürrenmatt, *Komödien III* (Zurich: Arche, 1966ff). Hereafter PS.

5. *Theater-Schriften und Reden* (Zurich: Arche, 1966). Hereafter Th; and *Dramaturgisches und Kritisches. Theater-Schriften und Reden II* (Zurich: Arche, 1972). Hereafter Th II.

6. Cf. especially "Theaterprobleme," in Th, pp. 92–131.

7. Ibid., p. 122. "Tragedy presupposes guilt, suffering, moderation, global vision, responsibility. In the routine muddle of our century, in this last dance of the white race there are no longer any guilty people nor any responsible ones either. Nobody can do anything about it and nobody wanted it to happen. Things can really happen without anybody. Everything is dragged along and gets caught in some sort of rake. We are too collectively guilty, too collectively embedded in the sins of fathers and forefathers. We are only grandchildren now. That is our bad luck, not our guilt: guilt only exists now as a personal accomplishment, as a religious act. Only comedy can still get at us."

8. Ibid., pp. 122–23. "However, the tragic element is still possible, even if pure tragedy is no longer possible. We can extract the tragic from comedy, bring it forward as a terrible moment, as a chasm beginning to open; in this way, indeed, many tragedies of Shakespeare are already comedies from which the tragic factor rises up."

9. Th II, 129. "Das Tragische ist das Menschliche, das Komische das Unmenschliche."

10. Th II. 130–31. "For man must first become conscious of the fact that he is a victim."

11. Ibid., p. 131. "Also the victims are 'comic' because it is inhuman to have to be a victim, because victims by being victims are separated from that which they should be: human beings. Therefore there is today perhaps but one dramaturgy: that of comedy. Unfortunately." Interestingly enough, even the young Dürrenmatt, as opposed to both

the Expressionists and many of his contemporaries, was never influenced by the *Damaskus* trilogy. The alternative *dream versus reality* (which plays an important role in the early texts of his countryman Max Frisch) has been replaced by the alternative *reality versus comedy*.

12. *Th*, p. 340. "*Die Gespenstersonate* ist nicht eigentlich eine Handlung, mehr eine Stimmung, so sehr Stimmung, daß die Handlung dazu nicht ausreicht, daß zwei Handlungen, zwei Ideen miteinander verwoben sind. . . ." ("*The Ghost Sonata* does not actually have a plot, it is more an atmosphere, so much atmosphere that the plot is not sufficient to interweave two plots, two ideas with each other. . . .")

13. Quoted from the 1964 version: *Komödien I* (Zurich: Arche, 1957), p. 103. "In order finally to be able to torture ourselves. Our marriage would mean hell for both parties."

14. *Komödien III*, 40. "Well, die then!"

15. Ibid., p. 75. "When will I finally kick the bucket!"

16. For an excellent interpretation of *Der Meteor*, see Peter Spycher, "Friedrich Dürrenmatts *Meteor*. Analyse und Dokumentation," in *Friedrich Dürrenmatt. Studien zu seinem Werk*, ed. Gerhard P. Knapp (Heidelberg: Stiehm, 1976), pp. 145–87.

17. Cf. Mona Knapp and Gerhard P. Knapp., "Recht—Gerechtigkeit—Politik. Zur Genese der Begriffe im Werk Friedrich Dürrenmatts," *Text + Kritik*, 56 (1977), 23–40.

18. Timo Tiusanen, *Dürrenmatt. A Study in Plays, Prose, Theory* (Princeton: Princeton University Press, 1977), p. 320. See too his article "Strindmatt or Dürrenberg? Dürrenmatt's *Play Strindberg*" in *Strindberg and the Modern Theatre* (Stockholm: Strindbergssällskapet, 1975), pp. 43–56, which is the basis for the chapter in the book dealing with the Strindberg question.

19. For a more detailed clarification of Dürrenmatt's more recent positions, see Jan Knopf, *Friedrich Dürrenmatt* (Munich: Beck, 1976), pp. 120ff.

20. "Prinzipien der Bearbeitung," in *Komödien III*, 281. "Out of a dramatized chronicle, there develops an analogy: the comedy of politics, of specific politics."

21. Ibid., p. 283. "It [King John] demonstrates the workings of politics, the phenomenon of its treaties and its casualties, yet it is a drama of murderers, not of victims."

22. Cf. Walter Hinck's careful assessment: "So ist *Play Strindberg* . . . mehr der Gegenentwurf zu Strindbergs *Totentanz* als dessen Bearbeitung." W. H., *Das moderne Drama in Deutschland* (Göttingen: Vandenhoeck, 1973), p. 183.

23. Peter Szondi, *Theorie des modernen Dramas (1880–1950)* (8th ed.; Frankfurt: Suhrkamp, 1971), p. 40. "Mit Strindberg hebt an, was später den Namen 'Ich-Dramatik' trägt und das Bild der dramatischen Literatur Jahrzehnte hindurch bestimmt."

24. Cf. Walter Johnson, *August Strindberg* (New York: Twayne, 1976), pp. 138–73.

25. For example the two widely used translations by Heinrich Goebel, *August Strindberg. Der Totentanz* (Berlin: Osterheld, 1919), and *August Strindberg: Gespenstersonate* (Berlin: Osterheld, 1919). Both parts of the ubiquitous *Der Bühnen-Strindberg* were still used for stage productions after 1945.

26. Tiusanen, p. 327.

27. ". . . bourgeois marriage tragedy." Dürrenmatt in his "Bericht," *PS*, p. 349.

28. Tiusanen, p. 327. "Dürrenmatt seems to have been blind to the light shed by Strindberg's sense of the comic."

29. Ibid., p. 324.

30. "1. Conversation before Dinner. 2. Company at Last. 3. Dead Faint. 4. At the Sickbed. 5. A Little Home Music. 6. Dinner Alone. 7. One Hour Later. 8. Conversation before Dinner. 9. Alice Philosophizes. 10. Tending the Sick. 11. Kurt Tells All. 12. Farewell." Cf. "Bericht," p. 349. In an interview with Fritz Rumler in *Der Spiegel*, 23, No. 6 (1969), p. 120, he proclaims his intention "den Schreibtisch auf die Bühne zu stellen."

31. Tiusanen, pp. 325ff.

32. Szondi (pp. 47–57) maintains that in later Strindberg plays such as *Ett drömspel* (*A Dream Play*) a nucleus of an "epic" presence can be found. This is not the place to dis-

cuss such a theory, but it may be suggested that even in *Dödsdansen* a certain epification exists in the form of the frequent reflections of the *personae* on their own fates (e.g., at the end of Part I) that are directed *ad spectatores* as well as toward each other. If this epification were carried through, however, the inherently tragic quality of the play would collapse: the "blindness" would be lifted from the personae and the vicious spell broken.

33. "Bericht," p. 349. "Plush x Infinity."
34. Walter Johnson, "Introduction to *The Dance of Death I and II*," p. 6.
35. *SS*, p. 237. "The Captain: Alice, dear, it has been miserable, but we've had fun . . . at times. And we'd better use what little time we have left—afterward it will be all over. / Alice: All over? If it only were!"
36. *PS*, p. 291. "E: We have to celebrate our silver wedding anniversary. / A: There's no call for us to celebrate our twenty-fifth year of hell. / E: We sometimes got on well together. / A: You're imagining things."
37. *PS*, p. 298. "A: Shall I play you something? / E: As long as it's not your everlasting Solveig. / A: Then I won't. / E: Then why do you ask? / A: The only music you like is your insufferable Entry of the Boyars." Remarkably, the more sentimental of the two pieces, Solveig's Song, is attributed to the brash Alice, while the grotesquely triumphant "Entry of the Boyars" is associated, as in *Dödsdansen*, with The Captain.
38. *PS*, p. 299. "A: We're done for. / E: We might as well hang ourselves." Cf. Germaine Brée, ed., *En attendant Godot* (Toronto: Macmillan, 1963), p. 19: "Si on se pendait?" or p. 108: "Et si on se pendait?"
39. *PS*, pp. 316, 324. "Go on, die then, you miserable Boyar, under the soil with you!"
40. *PS*, p. 323. "I must live, even if I no longer want to."
41. *PS*, p. 320. "K: Why do you really hate each other so much? / A: No idea. / K: But there must be some reason. / A: We are married."
42. *PS*, pp. 329–30. "E: A happy marriage. We were happy together, Alice and I, before you showed up. We lived together, played cards, chatted a bit; she used to play Solveig's Song, and I danced to the Entry of the Boyars. / K: You wanted to murder her. / E: So? I frequently wanted to murder her. Every marriage begets murderous impulses. . . ."
43. Tiusanen (p. 325) errs in his assumption that they "create an atmosphere of secrecy." On the contrary: the play's intent is to rob the actors of any resort to private secrets.
44. Børge Gedsø Madsen, *Strindberg's Naturalistic Theater. Its Relation to French Naturalism* (Seattle: University of Washington Press, 1962), p. 66.
45. Cf. Knopf, pp. 153ff.; also Everett M. Ellestad, "Das 'Entweder-Oder' der 'Mausefalle.' Strukturtechnik und Situation in Dürrenmatts Dramen," in *Friedrich Dürrenmatt. Studien zu seinem Werk*, ed. by Gerhard P. Knapp (see note 17), pp. 69–79.
46. *PS*, p. 344. "I have always loved him."
47. *SS*, p. 209. ". . . But now, when he is dead, I feel a strange need to speak well of him!"
48. *SS*, p. 210.
49. *SS*, p. 210. "My husband, the man I loved when I was young—laugh, if you will—he was a good and a noble man—all the same. . . . I must have loved that man!"
50 *PS*, p. 347. "The three days I spent with you and Edgar gave me inner strength. . . . I needed this glimpse into your little world. In the great world in which I operate, life goes on just as it does here: only the dimensions are different."
51. *PS*, p. 348. "A: Kurt, the world is indecent. / K: People like myself at least contribute to ruining it."
52. Tiusanen, p. 334.
53. Ibid.

54. The term is used in accordance with Adolf Beiss, "Nexus und Motive. Beitrag zur Theorie des Dramas," *Deutsche Vierteljahrsschrift*, 36 (1962), 248–76.

55. *Der Mitmacher. Ein Komplex.* . . . (Zurich: Arche, 1976), p. 48. "Why? Because I was ruined by society? Because I once again wanted to show the world? Because I despised myself? Because of hate? Because of bitterness? All big words. Perhaps just because of thoughtlessness. . . ."

56. Tiusanen, p. 335.

Some Notes on Strindberg and Péladan
Örjan Lindberger

I

At the end of the description of his religious crisis in *Inferno*, Strindberg writes: "Den 1 maj läste jag för första gången Sâr Péladans bok Comment on devient mage. Sâr Péladan, dittills okänd för mig, kommer som en stormvind, en uppenbarelse av Nietzsches 'övermänniska,' och med honom håller katolicismen sitt högtidliga och triumferande intåg i mitt liv."[1]

Joséphin Péladan (1859–1918), who called himself Sâr Péladan, was one of the major proponents of French *fin de siècle* mysticism. Together with Papus and Guaita, he reinstituted the *Ordre de la Rose-Croix* (*Order of the Rosicrucians*) in 1888; in May 1890 he proclaimed himself Grand Master of this order. He combined religious aspirations with much real literary talent: his prolific writings include a number of programs, a great cycle of novels depicting contemporary life in France, several dramas, and numerous essays in art criticism. As a prose writer, he is best known for his shrewd perspicacity; as a dramatist for his blending of fluid dialogue and lyric intensity.

It seems that Strindberg continued reading Péladan for the rest of his life. His last library contains eight of Péladan's works, most of them bearing signs of having been read with pen in hand. At least nine more titles are mentioned in his own books or in his letters. Strindberg's favorite among Péladan's novels was *L'Initiation sentimentale* (*The Sentimental Initiation*), a splendidly bound copy of which we find in his library. But he thought highly of Péladan as a dramatist too and on 14 February 1901 he wrote to his painter friend, Richard Bergh:

Mitt hus är nu fullt af Maeterlinck och Péladan. Péladan är en Gigant! Han har författat de saknade delarne I, III af Æschylos Prometheus och öfversatt

II eller det qvarvarande midtelstycket. Han har öfverträffat mästaren! En fräckhet som lyckets! Huru sällsynt!
Tre dramer af honom har jag; det är lejonmat, och borde läsas af Per Hallström o. fl.
En roman har jag också! och väntar flera.
Péladan och Maeterlinck äro af samma rot: Pariser–Ockultismen deriverad från Balzac' Séraphita, Ursule Mirouet o fl, samt Barbey d'Aurevilly (Les Diaboliques)—Alltså: respekt för Maeterlinck! plats för Sâr Péladan.[2]

It is worthy of note that Péladan stands, in Strindberg's view, at least on the same level as Maeterlinck. The influences from Maeterlinck's plays upon Strindberg's works have been duly noted; but possible influences from Péladan seem not to have been given much attention. I propose to discuss this question with regard to several of the dramas from 1901, a year that may well be the most prolific and artistically profound of Strindberg's entire life; especially the plays *Svanevit* (*Swanwhite*), *Kristina* (*Queen Christina*), and *Ett drömspel* (*A Dream Play*) will be considered.

Strindberg's conclusive assessment of Péladan is given in *Götiska rummen* (*Gothic Rooms*), in which Strindberg maintains that the prophet of youth for the French 1880s is not Zola, but rather Péladan:

Redan 1884, alltså när Zola endast nått fram till Au bonheur des Dames, börjar Peladans verksamhet med första volymen av hans cykel La Décadence latine—kallad Le Vice Suprême.
Under de tjugo åren, som sedan dess förflutit, har han utgivit fjorton romaner, förutom dramer och filosofiska arbeten, sammanlagt trettiåtta volymer. De fjorton romanerna gå parallellt med Zolas, men under det denne i Rougoncykeln skildrar andra kejsardömet, målar Péladan sin samtid, tredje republiken. Finis Latinorum är hans motto, och han tror att latinarne skola förgås; han förutsäger deras undergång, skildrar som en Juvenalis allt elände i det moderna Paris; med samma oförskräckthet som Zola och med lika naiv oblyghet. Hans materiel av upplevat och sett är oerhört, men hans stil brinnande av nitälskan; han dyker ner i gyttjan, men kommer alltid upp igen, klipper med vingarne och höjer sig mot skyn.
Hans mest lysande roman är L'initiation sentimentale, en bok om kärleken i alla arter, tonarter, och avarter, där han lyfter av taken på alla slags hus och visar innanmätet av Paris. Det är en fruktansvärd bok, rik, stor, och skön trots allt det fula han visar fram.
Samme man har vågat ett storverk och lyckats! Han har tilldiktat till Äschylos' Prometheus de två delar av trilogin, som förkommit; och om de icke fullt stå i ton, så beror det av deras rikare och djupare innehåll, åtminstone synes det så för den som icke tror på antikens oupphinnelighet. Det vore ju bedrövligt om icke världen gått framåt och fört tankeliv och uttrycksmedel med sig framåt.
Péladan är ingen nationalist eller revanche-man; han är världsborgare och

har i Frankrike infört Wagner trots patrioternas motstånd; och knappast har någon tysk fått sin Wagner så gigantisk som Péladan sin.

För den moderna konsten har han strävat genom sina utställningar, och allt vad symbolism heter har han startat.[3]

Strindberg concludes by saying that Péladan's influence is immeasurably great, but that it works indirectly through his disciples. One does not quote him, but one nourishes oneself at his table. It is, of course, highly plausible that Strindberg took his share of intellectual sustenance from this figure and it develops that this is indeed the case. Péladan's first published work, a short story in Le Foyer (1881) was entitled "Le Chemin de Damas" ("The Road to Damascus") and, although it seems unlikely that Strindberg ever had an opportunity to read it, he may well have read about it and recollected the title when he christened his own drama Till Damaskus in 1898.

II

Early in 1901 Strindberg fell in love with the young actress Harriet Bosse and his notes in Ockulta dagboken (The Occult Diary) register his oscillation between a growing, irresistible attraction and a reluctance to enter into a new marriage. The diary reveals that during this time he read and reread Péladan, whom he considered to be an authority on love. Moreover, he had found that Péladan's opinions as to "the essence of woman" coincided with his own.[4]

In Péladan there is a strong obsession with the sexual aspect of love and at the same time a will to sublimate and transform love into something spiritual and ethereal. In a letter to Emil Kleen of 2 September 1898 Strindberg enthusiastically remarks: "Läser Péladan med stigande beundran men icke oblandade känslor. En urliderlig moralist! En paradox! som castigerar sin sinnlighet, men njuter af flagelleringen."[5] Strindberg's reactions to Harriet Bosse revealed, however, much of the same pattern. He desired her carnally but reproached himself for his desire, and her for arousing his desire. He wanted her to be childlike, good, and absolutely pure, dreaming as he did of a love free of physicality.

Péladan tries to unite his conflicting inclinations by means of the concept of the androgyne. In his play Le Prince de Byzance (The Prince of Byzantium) (1896), the heroine Antonia is a princess who has been educated in a convent as though she were a boy, Antonio. She meets a courtier and warrior named Giorgio Cavalcanti, whom she identifies with Saint George. He thinks initially that she is a prince, the heir to the realm of Tarent, and tries to help her in regaining her royal position. Their efforts are, however, in vain, and in the end they are both killed. Gradually, love has arisen between them and on their deathbed they are married. But the vital point here is that the marriage is never consummated, despite the sensuous coloring of the last love scene. Antonio-Antonia remains an androgyne and proclaims at the end of the play: "Quelle gloire d'avoir connu l'amour en plénitude, amant sans Péché et sans la chair, époux."[6]

This is one of the passages that is underlined in Strindberg's copy of the play. Another is a discussion in the first act between Cavalcanti and The Prior, in which the courtier says: "je ne crois plus aux femmes, ce sont des êtres vains." The Prior adds: "Mais si vous rencontriez un vrai coeur, vierge et haut sous les traits d'une princesse, un coeur qui n'eût jamais battu, un androgyne, un ange et pour qui il faudrait accomplir des prodiges!" And Cavalcanti replies: "Ah— croire en un être et se dévouer tout fanatiquement devant l'idole, . . . pourvu que le doute jamais ne vienne. . . . Si je trouvais cela, Prieur, je bénirais la vie!"[7]

Strindberg sent his copy of *Le Prince de Byzance* to Harriet Bosse in February 1901, an action that only bewildered her. Strindberg responded to her query:

Hvarför jag sänt Er den bizarra Le Prince de Byzance? Det är en mycket lång historia, som skulle börja med Eleonoras slägting, Balzacs Séraphita— Séraphitus, Engeln, för hvilken jordisk kärlek icke finnes på den grund att hon-han är l'époux et l'épouse de l'humanité. Symbol af den högsta, fullkomligaste menniskotyp, hvilken spökar mycket i den modernaste litteraturen och antages af några befinna sig på vägen hit ner till oss. Begär nu ingen förklaring men behåll ordet i minnet.[8]

Harriet Bosse had been given Eleonora's part in the first Swedish performance of *Påsk* (*Easter*), and evidently in Strindberg's mind there existed some kind of identification between Balzac's Séraphita, Péladan's Antonia, Eleonora, and Harriet Bosse. In Strindberg's dreams Bosse occasionally appeared as an androgyne and we read in his diary for the night between 26 and 27 January 1901: "Drömde om B.: hon spelade på teatern. Derpå såg jag B. klädd som en pojke, sittande hopkrupen, och jag förvånades hon var så liten."[9]

The diary mentions "signs" that make Strindberg suspicious of Harriet's character: on 11 February, however, he writes:

Hela dagen ensam och i en stilla stämning; läsande Péladan och tänkande på B. bedjande henne om förlåtelse för mina onda tankar. På aftonen föll en grön ljusstrimma från lampan på mitt bröst och följde mig hvart jag gick. Skall nu ljuset ändtligen komma? Sedan Bs besök har jag inträdt i ett nytt skede i mitt lif. Längtar till renhet, skönhet och harmoni. 2: a akten af Damaskus III är influerad af B som nu inträdt i mitt lif.[10]

It would seem that reading Péladan contributed toward making Strindberg's feelings towards Harriet Bosse more harmonious, a tendency that is reflected in his conception of *Svanevit*. On 26 February Strindberg writes in his diary: "Lefde i ett rus hela dagen af conceptionen till *Svanevit*."[11] This play takes its themes from medieval ballads and its form is influenced by Maeterlinck's *La Princesse Maleine*, a fact that has already been noted by Martin Lamm and repeated by later scholars.[12] One cannot doubt the authenticity of this source but to accept it does not disallow the possibility of other sources of inspiration as well. The erotic scenes of *La Princesse Maleine* are cool and the general atmosphere of the play is somewhat pale, whereas in *Svanevit* there is that same mixture of sensuousness and chastity that one finds in Péladan's *Le Prince de Byzance*. The growing love between Swanwhite and the Prince culminates in a scene where they join on the bridal bed, separated, however, by a sword.

This scene has its precedent in an exchange of words in *Till Damaskus III*. The Lady says to The Stranger: "Så illa tänkte du om mig! Märkte du ej att jag fällde en slöja mellan mig och dig, riddarens svärd i brudbädden. . . ."[13] The view of women and love in *Till Damaskus III* is much more tolerant than that presented in the earlier parts of the trilogy. Strindberg, as we have seen, ascribed this change to Harriet Bosse's influence and, in order to maintain this attitude, Strindberg tries to avoid the earthly ramifications of love. His first plan for *Svanevit* was to append to the play a tragic ending with the death of the Prince. This is highly reminiscent of the ending of *Le Prince de Byzance*—the pure ectasy of love will never be soiled. Ultimately he changed his mind and revived the Prince, but the lofty intensity of the dialogue in the love scene still suggests Péladan.

The most important of Péladan's dramas is surely *La Prométhéide* (1895). Its mighty verse brings Claudel to mind, as R. L. Doyon has noted.[14] Péladan has introduced Christian ideas of suffering and propitiation into his reconstruction of the trilogy, an interpretation that, along with the play's treatment of the Pandora myth, Strindberg found particularly attractive. On 13 February Strindberg notes his impressions in his diary:

Läste Joséphin Péladan's Prométhéide; der han har författat de saknade 1ª och 3ᵉ Delen af Æschylus samt öfversatt Æschylus Prometheus 2ª. Det är gigantiskt!
    Dagen har varit ljusare än i går. Febern borta—
    På aftonen sände jag B ett bref och ett påskris samt en påsklilja.
    . . .

I Péladans Prométhéide skildras Pandora, Grekernas Eva, först såsom sänd af Zeus (hvilken skrattade när han släppte ner henne) för att plåga menniskorna; men Prometheus förvandlade henne till menniskornas välsignelse i modern, makan. . . . Hvad skall nu ske?[15]

In his copy of the play Strindberg has underlined Prometheus's words when he sees Pandora, adding on his own the word *femme*:

> C'est donc toi, [femme] le vivant stratagème qu'ont
> machiné les Dieux!
> Toi, qu'on envoie, en place de tonnerre,
> toi, qui dois abolir la justice, abrutir l'homme,
> et ruinera, en un moment, tout le génie de Prométhée!
> . . .
> Quels yeux reconnaîtraient, en toi,
> une oeuvre de mort et de haine?[16]

Prometheus's countermove, the deed for which he will be punished by Zeus, is his giving to Pandora his own love for mankind and marrying her to Epimetheus:

> On t'envoie pour nuire à la terre
> Mais tu déjoueras les desseins de ces parents dénaturés,
> tu aimeras les hommes![17]

These words are underlined by Strindberg, as is also Prometheus's great incantation to Pandora:

> Viens régner, viens aimer, viens consoler, viens enfanter
> Toi qui sera le foyer, la famille
> Toi qui sera la douce vierge, et puis, le mère auguste
> Toi qui incarnera le dévouement et la bonté
> . . .
> viens créer l'homme, une seconde fois,
> selon la douceur et la joie infinies![18]

The central theme of Péladan's trilogy is Prometheus's compassion for mankind:

> Mon coeur plein de pitié, mon coeur plein de tendresse,
> mon coeur saignant des maux d'autrui[19]

and:

> La douleur! la douleur! Voilà donc le mystère
> et l'unique rapport entre la créature et l'Incréé;
> Comme elle nous élève, comme elle explique tout!
> . . .

Je comprends, je comprends mon supplice!
J'ai assumé sur moi les mille ans de détresse
d'affreux tâtonnements, d'impuissante faiblesse
que devait au Destin la triste humanité!
. . .
    seul, j'ai souffert pour tous.[20]

And finally, Strindberg has also underlined: "le plus sage est celui qui a le plus souffert."[21]

In Strindberg's historical play *Kristina*, from the autumn of 1901, there are a number of puzzling elements, the clue to which lies in *La Prométhéide*. The man whom Kristina really loves is Klas Tott, but he loves her in a platonically ecstatic way, maintaining that she is the daughter of the gods, whom they have sent down to earth. Kristina tries to cool his mystical ardor: "Barn lilla, håll dig nere vid marken. . . . Kerstin kan inte flyga! . . . Ve! jag kommer att bringa dig olycka . . . Epimetheus!" Tott answers: "Pandora! Du som givit mig första aningen om att sällhet finns . . . Du, den rena, den snövita, ty det är du längst in i själen, om dock. . . ."[22] Evidently Strindberg sees the relationship between Kristina and Tott in light of the interpretation of the Pandora myth given by Péladan. His diary, furthermore, shows that he associates Péladan's Pandora with Harriet Bosse; and, as we know, Kristina's part was written for Harriet Bosse.

The daughter of the gods, whom they have sent down to earth, returns as the central theme of *Ett drömspel*, written in late autumn 1901. Here she is called Indra's Daughter, obviously based in Indian mythology. But a story of Indra's Daughter descending to earth is not to be found there. The explanation for this discrepancy seems to lie in the assumption that Strindberg has further extrapolated on Péladan's Pandora myth. The Daughter, like Pandora, is going to experience love, to be a wife and a mother. She is going to partake of man's numerous sufferings and to discover that the essence of human life is pain. At the end of the play, she says: "Jag har lidit alla Edra lidanden, men hundrafalt, ty mina förnimmelser voro finare. . . ."[23] Her suffering is, like that of Péladan's Prometheus or that of Christ, vicarious. Her character has taken on essential traits also from Prometheus, particularly his compassion for mankind, and her experience of earthly life makes her exclaim over and over again: "Det är synd om människorna."[24]

In late summer and early autumn of 1901, Strindberg's marriage with Harriet Bosse was very discordant and she left their home for six weeks but returned in October to live with him and await the birth of their child. During this period Strindberg wrote *Ett drömspel*. His diary for September tells of his brooding on this marital conflict and on the thirteenth of that month, he compares himself to Prometheus: "I fyra månader hade hon [Bosse] hackat på min lefver."[25] But his mood changes and on 20 September he writes, "Harriet har ingen skuld! Hennes uppträdande i mitt lif var som hon säger en 'uppgift'. . . . När jag såg Harriets skönhet, som ibland kunde vara 'överjordisk' så bäfvade jag. Och då rubbades min äldre tro på qvinnan såsom en mellanlänk mellan man och barn. Då sade jag mig, att qvinnan är af högre ursprung, men djupare fallen än mannen."[26] In his efforts to interpret his fate, Strindberg goes on utilizing the concept of the suffering Prometheus and the woman descended from heaven. He moves within the sphere of ideas that he had imposed upon Harriet Bosse, after having read Péladan during the decisive weeks of their infatuation in early spring 1901.

Notes

1. August Strindberg, *Samlade Skrifter*, 28, ed. John Landquist (Stockholm: Bonniers, 1919), p. 201 (hereafter *SS*). "On May 1, I read for the first time Sâr Péladan's book *On Becoming a Magus*. Sâr Péladan, previously unknown to me, arrives like a whole gale, a revelation of Nietzsche's 'superman,' and with him Catholicism makes its solemn and triumphant entry into my life." This statement is in accordance with Strindberg's remark in a letter to his daughter Kerstin 4 May 1887: "Sâr Péladan ist der Reformierende Katolische Ockultist und sein Buch Comment on devient mage ist das grösste und schönste was ein Katholik lesen kann." (*August Strindbergs brev*, ed. Torsten Eklund [Stockholm: Bonniers, 1947], 12: 107) (hereafter *Brev*).

2. *Brev*, 14: 25. "My house is now full of Maeterlinck and Péladan. Péladan is a Giant! He has composed the missing parts I, III of Aeschylus' *Prometheus*, and translated II, or the still existing middle part. He has surpassed the master! An insolence that has succeeded! How rare!

"I own three of his plays; it is food for a lion and ought to be read by Per Hallström and others.

"I have one novel too and I expect more.

"Péladan and Maeterlinck are of the same root: the Parisian occultism, derived from Balzac's Séraphita, Ursule Mirouet and others, and Barbey d'Aureville (The Fiends)—

"Consequently: respect to Maeterlinck! make way for Péladan."

3. *SS*, 40: 110–12. Strindberg allowed Schering to use this text as an introduction to his translation of Péladan, *Das allmächtige Gold* (1911). As Torsten Eklund has observed (*Brev*, 12: 344), the view expressed in *Götiska rummen* is foreshadowed in a letter of July 1898.

"Already in 1884, when Zola had only arrived at *For M'Lady's Pleasure*, Péladan's activity had commenced with the first volume of his cycle *La Décadence latine*—called *Le Vice suprême*.

"During the twenty years that have transpired since then, he has published fourteen novels, as well as dramas and philosophical works, in all thirty-eight volumes. The fourteen novels are parallel to those by Zola, but whereas the latter in the Rougon cycle depicts the Second Empire, Péladan is painting his own time, the Third Republic. *Finis Latinorum* is his motto, and he believes that the Latin peoples are doomed; he predicts their ruin, describes like a Juvenal all the misery of modern Paris; with the same undauntedness as Zola and the same naive immodesty. His experience is immense, but his style burns with zeal; he dives into the mud, but he always comes up again, clipping his wings and rising to the sky.

"His most splendid novel is *The Sentimental Initiation*, a book about love of every kind and ilk, where he lifts off the roofs from all kinds of Parisian houses and shows the very soul of Paris. It is a terrible book, rich, great, and beautiful in spite of all the ugliness he shows.

"This man has embarked upon a great achievement and succeeded! He has added the two lost parts to the *Prometheus* by Aeschylus; and if they do not strike exactly the right note, it is because of their richer and deeper contents—at least so it seems if one is not a believer in unrivaled Classical Antiquity. It were indeed a pity if the world had not advanced thought and form in some way. Péladan is no nationalist or man of revenge; he is a citizen of the world, and has introduced Wagner into France despite the patriots' resistance; and hardly has any German made his Wagner so gigantic as Péladan has made his.

"Through his exhibitions, he has struggled for modern art and he has alone started everything that we call symbolism."

4. *Brev*, 7: 344 (22 July 1898).

5. *Brev*, 7: 5. "Am reading Péladan with increasing admiration but not unmixed feelings. A terribly lewd moralist! A paradox! who castigates his sensuousness, but enjoys the flagellation."

6. *Le Prince de Byzance*, p. 135 (hereafter *PB*). "What glory to have known the plenitude of love, immaculate lover and disincarnate, spouse." [Editor's translation.]

7. *PB*, pp. 19–20. Cavalcanti says: "I no longer believe in women: they are vain beings." The Prior adds: "But if you were to meet a true heart, virginal and proud beneath the features of a princess, a heart that had never throbbed, an androgyne, an angel and for whom one should have to accomplish prodigious acts!" And Cavalcanti replies: "Ah—to believe in a being and to devote oneself fanatically to this idol, to make oneself an angel's demon, to fight, to bleed, to die, provided that doubt would never arise. . . . If I were to find that, Prior. I would bless life!"

8. *Brev*, 14: 34. "Why did I send you the bizarre Prince de Byzance? It is a long story beginning with Eleonora's relative, Balzac's Séraphita–Séraphitus, the Angel, to whom earthly love does not exist because he–she is *l'époux et l'épouse de l'humanité* ('the husband and wife of mankind'). Symbol of the highest, most perfect type of man, who reappears many places in the most modern literature and is supposed by some to be on its way down to us. Do not ask for an explanation but keep this word in your memory."

9. "Dreamed of B: she was acting onstage. Then, I saw B dressed like a boy, sitting crouched up, and I was astonished that she was so small."

10. "The whole day, alone and in a quiet mood: reading Péladan and thinking of B, asking her forgiveness for my evil thoughts. In the afternoon a green streak of light fell upon my chest and followed me wherever I went. Is the light going to come at last? Since B's visit, I have entered upon a new phase of my life. Long for purity, beauty, and harmony. The 2nd act of Damascus III is influenced by B, who has now entered into my life."

11. "Lived in an ecstasy the whole day about the conception of *Svanevit*."

12. Martin Lamm, *Strindbergs dramer II* (Stockholm, 1926), 273–79.

13. *SS*, 29: 275. "You had evil thoughts of me! Did you notice that I lowered a veil between me and you, the knight's sword in the bridal bed. . . ." This and all other translations from Strindberg's plays are from Walter Johnson, *A Dreamplay and Four Chamber Plays* and *Queen Christina, Charles XII, and Gustav III* (Seattle: University of Washington Press, 1973, 1955).

14. R. L. Doyon, *La douloreuse aventure de Péladan* (Paris, 1946), p. 146.

15. "Read Joséphin Péladan's *Prométhéide*; where he has composed the missing first and third parts of Aeschylus and translated Aeschylus' *Prometheus*, part two. It is gigantic!

"The day has been lighter than yesterday. The fever gone—

"In the afternoon I sent B a letter and some twigs with cock's feathers and a daffodil. . . .

In Péladan's *Prométhéide* Pandora, the Eve of the Greeks, is depicted as first sent by Zeus (who laughed when he let her fall) in order to torment mankind; but Prometheus transformed her to the blessing of mankind in the mother, the spouse. . . . What is going to happen now?"

16. *PB*, p. 42. "It is, however, you [Woman], the living strategy / whom the gods have provided! / You, who have been sent in place of thunder, / You, who must abolish jus-

tice, brutalize man, / and will, in a moment, ruin all the genius of Prometheus! / . . . / What eyes would recognize in you / a work of death and of hatred?"

17. PB, p. 49. "You have been sent to harm the earth / but you will thwart the designs of those unnatural parents, / you will love men!"

18. PB, pp. 46–47. "Come to reign, come to love, come to console, come to bear children, / You who will be the hearth, the family, / You who will be the sweet virgin and then the august mother, / You who will incarnate goodness and devotion / . . . / Come, create man a second time, / according to the precepts of infinite sweetness and joy!"

19. PB, p. 17. "My heart full of compassion, my heart full of tenderness / My heart bleeding from the wrong-doings of others."

20. PB, p. 109. "Ah sorrow! ah sorrow! Here is the mystery / and the unique rapport between creature and uncreated; / As she instructs us, she explains all! / . . . / I understand, I understand my agony! / I have taken onto myself a thousand years of grief / of frightful gropings, of impotent weakness / that unhappy humanity owes to Destiny! / . . . / alone I have suffered for all."

21. PB, p. 138. ". . . the wisest is he who has suffered the most."

22. SS, 29: 19. "Stay on earth, little child. . . . Kerstin cannot fly! . . . Woe! I am going to bring thee misfortune . . . Epimetheus!"—Tott: "Pandora! Thou who gavest me the first notion of the existence of bliss . . . Thou pure, thou snow-white, for such thou art at the bottom of thy soul, notwithstanding. . . ." Later in the play (242ff.), Kristina performs a scene from her ballet *Pandora*, acting herself in Pandora's part, while Tott plays Prometheus.

23. SS, 36: 325. "I have suffered all your sufferings, but hundredfold, for my perceptions are finer. . . ."

24. "Mankind is to be pitied."

25. "For four months she [Bosse] had hacked at my liver."

26. "Harriet is not guilty. Her appearance in my life was, as she says, a 'mission'. . . . When I saw Harriet's beauty, which sometimes could be celestial, I trembled. Then my older faith in woman as an intermediate link, between man and child was shaken. Then I told myself that woman is of a higher origin, but has fallen farther than man."

August Strindberg in America, 1963–1979: A Bibliographical Assessment

Birgitta Steene

From the very beginning, Strindberg's reputation in America has rested on a somewhat ambivalent interest in his dramatic works among playwrights, theater directors, and drama critics alike. In a doctoral dissertation from 1959 dealing with Broadway productions of Strindberg's plays, Ralph Haugen lists thirty productions of twelve of Strindberg's works between 1912 and 1956.[1] Not very many of these seem to have been first-rate stagings and the critical reception, especially of the earlier ones, was mostly negative: Strindberg was considered crude, pessimistic, and archaic. Yet his plays obviously had an impact on a number of American playwrights. John Gassner, in an article on the influence of Strindberg in the United States, has pointed out that: "in one way or another, American playwrights were bound to become aware of Strindberg's work, which was too powerful to be ignored despite the dearth of adequate productions of his plays in this country."[2]

Gassner saw Strindberg as the father of the modern psychological drama and as an important catalyst in the American theater. His impact was not only technical but above all one of dramatic temperament. His boldness, intensity, and integrity of feeling account, according to Gassner, for his lasting interest to such American playwrights as O'Neill, Tennessee Williams, William Inge, and Edward Albee. As several of the articles and dissertations in this bibliography indicate, critics have become well aware of the parallels between Strindberg's stagecraft and the works of twentieth-century American playwrights.

Egil Törnqvist has noted that during the period 1893–1909 only eleven articles had been written in the United States about Strindberg.[3] But the playwright's death in 1912 resulted in an upsurge of interest so that by 1919 one hundred and fifty articles had appeared on the Swedish dramatist in America. Translations of his works increased during the same period, the first sizable edition being that of Scribner from 1912 to 1916 with Edwin Björkman as the translator of the eighteen plays.[4] From the beginning, then, Strindberg's reception in the United States reflects an interest in his work in both academic and theatrical circles. Today the volume of Strindberg scholarship published in the United States continues to grow. New translations of his works are still forthcoming. Productions of his plays, although not overwhelming in number, nevertheless indicate that he is securely ensconced among the group of modern classics whose works are a challenge to the living theater.

In 1962, to mark the fifty years since Strindberg's death, the Swedish playwright became the first continental dramatist to be honored by a special issue of the journal *Modern Drama*. The occasion emphasized once more that in America (as elsewhere outside Sweden) Strindberg is primarily known as a writer for the stage. This is reflected in translations of his works, where his plays outnumber many times his novels, and in the concentration of scholarly articles dealing with his literary production.

One of the most talked about early productions of a Strindberg play was the Provincetown Theatre rendering of *The Spook Sonata* (*The Ghost Sonata*) in 1924. In the years to follow, however, it was almost entirely Strindberg's naturalistic dramas that were performed in the United States, especially *The Father*, *Miss Julie*, *Creditors*, and *The Dance of Death*. A look at the production list for the period covered by this bibliography (1963–79) would indicate that these are still the plays that dominate the Strindberg repertory in America. A notable exception is the 1977 production of *The Ghost Sonata* at the Yale Repertory Theater, which elicited very favorable reviews from such leading drama critics as Harold Clurman and Jack Kroll.[5] Perhaps American theaters will soon follow the trend among recent Strindberg scholars in the United States and center more of their attention on Strindberg's post-Inferno plays. Most dominant are those studies that examine the cultural and intellectual background of these dramas, and articles that trace motifs and themes in one or more of Strindberg's works. Numerous references are also made to Strindberg's impact on the Theater of the Absurd, noting the importance of his dramatic language and symbolistic stagecraft.

The bibliography that follows is intended to bring up to date the American part of the excellent bibliographies of Esther H. Rapp and Jackson R. Bryer from 1951 and 1962 respectively.[6] For the most part, only books and articles either originally published in the United States or written by Americans in other English-language publications have been included. The listings fall into four major categories: Translations, Books, Articles, and Dissertations.

A. Translations

A great many translations of Strindberg's works were done in the 1950s and early 1960s, among them Walter Johnson's pioneer translations of several of the historical plays; Arvid Paulson's edition of Strindberg's letters to Harriet Bosse; and Elizabeth Sprigge's Doubleday edition of six plays. The current list includes only new translations (not reprints), published after 1963.

1. *The Cloister* (*Klostret*). Translated by Mary Sandbach. New York: Hill and Wang, 1969.
2. *The Dance of Death* (*Dödsdansen*). Translated by Norman Ginsburg. Minneapolis: Tyrone Guthrie Theatre editions, Cornelius Publications, 1965.
3. *The Dance of Death*. Translated by Arvid Paulson. New York: Norton, 1976.
4. *Days of Loneliness* (*Ensam*). Translated by Arvid Paulson. New York: Phaedra, 1971.
5. *Dramas of Testimony*, (*The Dance of Death I and II, Advent, Easter, There Are Crimes and Crimes*). Translations and introductions by Walter Johnson. Seattle: University of Washington Press, 1975.
6. *A Dream Play* (*Ett drömspel*) and *The Ghost Sonata* (*Spöksonaten*). Translation by Richard Mueller. San Francisco: Chandler, 1966.
7. *A Dream Play*. Translated by Evert Sprinchorn. New York: Avon Books, 1974.
8. *A Dream Play and Four Chamber Plays* (*A Dream Play, Stormy Weather, The House That Burned, The Ghost Sonata, The Pelican*). Translations and introductions by Walter Johnson. Seattle: University of Washington Press, 1973.
9. *The Dutchman* (*Holländarn*), *A Fragment*. Translated by John L. Greenway. *The Malahat Review*, 5 (Jan. 1968), 5–37.
10. *Eight Expressionistic Plays* (*Lucky Per's Journey, The Keys to Heaven, To Damascus I, II, III, A Dream Play, The Great Highway, The Ghost Sonata*). Translated by Arvid Paulson. New York: Bantam, 1965.
11. *From an Occult Diary: Marriage with Harriet Bosse* (*Ockulta dagboken*). Translated by Mary Sandbach. Edited by Torsten Eklund. New York: Hill and Wang, 1965.
12. *Getting Married* (*Giftas*). Edited and introduced by Mary Sandbach. New York: Viking, 1972.
13. *Hercules*. Translated by Harry G. Carlson. *Scandinavian Review*, 64 (Sept. 1976), pp. 25–26.
14. *Inferno, Alone and Other Writings* ("The New Arts, or The Role of Chance

Strindberg in America, 1963–1979   259

in Artistic Creation," "Graveyard Reveries," "Jacob Wrestles"). Edited and introduced by Evert Sprinchorn. Garden City: Doubleday, 1968.
15. *A Madman's Defense (En dåres försvarstal)*. Translation based on Ellie Scheussner's 1912 translation (Confessions of a Fool) and introduction by Evert Sprinchorn. New York: Doubleday, 1967.
16. *A Madman's Manifesto*. Translated by Anthony Swerling. University, Ala.: University of Alabama Press, 1971.
17. *Open Letters to the Intimate Theater (Öppna brev till intima teatern)*. Translated by Walter Johnson. Seattle: University of Washington Press, 1966.
18. *The Plays of Strindberg*. Translated by Michael Meyer. New York: Random House, 1976. British English.
   Contents: *The Father, Miss Julie, Creditors, The Stronger, Playing with Fire, Erik the Fourteenth, Storm, The Ghost Sonata*.
19. *Pre-Inferno Plays (The Father, Lady Julie, Creditors, The Stronger, The Bond)*. Translations and introductions by Walter Johnson. Seattle: University of Washington Press, 1971.
20. "Psychic Murder (Apropos *Rosmersholm*)," ("Om Själamord"). Translated by Walter Johnson. *Tulane Drama Review*, 13: 2, pp. 113–18.
21. *The Red Room (Röda rummet)*. New translation by Elizabeth Sprigge. New York: Dutton, 1967.
22. *The Son of a Servant*, Vol. 1. (*Tjänstekvinnans son*) Translated by Evert Sprinchorn. Garden City, N.Y.: Doubleday, 1966.
23. *The Strindberg Reader*. Edited and translated by Arvid Paulson. New York: Phaedra, 1968.
   Contents: Short Stories; Essays; Poetry; Plays: *Dance of Death, Swanwhite, Stormclouds, The Black Glove*; Excerpts from Novels: *The Natives of Hemsö* and *The Scapegoat*. Commentaries. *The Natives of Hemsö* and *The Scapegoat* published as separate volumes. New York: P. S. Eriksson, 1965 and 1967.
24. *Strindberg. Three Experimental Plays*. Translated by F. R. Southerington, Charlottesville: University Press of Virginia, 1975. (*Miss Julie, The Stronger, A Dream Play*).
25. *Strindberg's One-Act Plays*. Translated by Arvid Paulson. New York: Washington Square, 1969.
26. *The Vasa Trilogy: Master Olof, Gustav Vasa, Erik XIV*. Translated by Walter Johnson. Seattle: University of Washington Press, 1966.
27. *World Historical Plays (The Nightingale of Wittenberg, Through Deserts to Ancestral Lands, Hellas,* and *The Lamb and the Beast*). Translated by Arvid Paulson. New York: American-Scandinavian Foundation, 1970.

B. Books

28. Blau, Herbert. *The Impossible Theatre*. New York: Macmillan, 1964, pp. 258–61.

A discussion of *The Dance of Death* as a play that breaks the boundaries of naturalistic theater and anticipates the grotesque and absurdist elements in contemporary drama.

29. Carlson, Harry G. *Strindberg och myterna*. Translated by Sven Erik Täckmark. Stockholm: Författarförlaget, 1979, 286 pp.

    An archetypal approach to Strindberg's work, in which Carlson investigates eight plays from both the early and late Strindberg according to their mythological sources.

30. Freedman, Morris. *The Moral Impulse: Modern Drama from Ibsen to the Present*. Carbondale: Southern Illinois University Press, 1967, pp. 19–30.

    See entry no. 68.

31. *The Genius of Scandinavian Theater*. Edited by Evert Sprinchorn. New York: New American Library, 1964.

    Contains the following articles on Strindberg: Gunnar Brandell's "Toward a New Art Form"; Eric Bentley's "The Ironic Strindberg"; Pär Lagerkvist's "Modern Theater: Points of View and Attack"; and Evert Sprinchorn's introduction, "Strindberg."

32. Glicksberg, Charles J. *The Self in Modern Literature*. University Park: Pennsylvania State University Press, 1963, pp. 27–35, 67–68.

    Brief discussions of *To Damascus*.

33. Grant, Vernon W. *Great Abnormals: The Pathological Genius of Kafka, van Gogh, Strindberg and Poe*. New York: Hawthorne Books, 1968, pp. 127–80.

    A psychological study of Strindberg as an individual who never matured emotionally. The core motive behind his actions was an intense drive toward recognition to alleviate a deep-rooted sense of insecurity.

34. Hoy, Cyrus. *The Hyacinth Room: An Investigation into the Nature of Comedy, Tragedy and Tragicomedy*. New York: Knopf, 1964, pp. 290–94.

    A brief discussion of the comic mode in *Easter*, *A Dream Play* and *The Ghost Sonata*.

35. Johannesson, Eric O. *The Novels of August Strindberg. A Study in Theme and Structure*. Berkeley: University of California Press, 1968, 317 pp.

    The first full length English study of Strindberg's prose fiction.

36. Johnson, Walter. *August Strindberg*. Boston: Twayne (TWAS No. 410), 1978, 221 pp.

    A chronological survey of the entire Strindberg canon by one of the leading American translators of Strindberg's work.

37. ———. *Strindberg and the Historical Drama*. Seattle: University of Washington Press, 1963, 326 pp.

    A pioneer study in English of Strindberg's history plays.

38. Klaf, Franklin S. *Strindberg. The Origin of Psychology in Modern Drama*. New York: The Citadel Press, 1963, 192 pp.

    Regards Strindberg as a schizophrenic who successfully translated his personal tragedy into stage characters that serve as symbols

of universal misery. Religion became a means of assuaging schizophrenic hatred.
39. *Masterpieces of the Modern Scandinavian Theatre.* Edited by Robert W. Corrigan. New York: Macmillan, 1967.

　　Contains brief introductions by Robert W. Corrigan and reprints of *Miss Julie, The Ghost Sonata, Notes to the Members of the Intimate Theatre.* (Sprinchorn translation).
40. Matthews, Honor. *The Primal Curse. The Myth of Cain and Abel in the Theater.* New York: Schocken Books, 1967, pp. 123–36.

　　Chapter 4, entitled "August Strindberg: The Appearance of Eastern Mythology," discusses the strife of opposites as an "obsessive motif in Strindberg's work," and relates it to the myth of the warring brothers in Zurvanism and to the Manichaean hostility to body and sex.
41. *Miss Julie.* Critical Material Selected and Introduced by Henry Popkin. New York: The Avon Theater Library, 1965, 160 pp.

　　Contains (in addition to Sprigge's translation of the play) material from Vernon Young's "The History of Miss Julie," F. L. Lucas's *Ibsen and Strindberg*, Robert Brustein's *The Theater of Revolt* and Børge G. Madsen's *Strindberg's Naturalistic Theatre.*
42. Steene, Birgitta. *The Greatest Fire: A Study of August Strindberg.* Carbondale: Southern Illinois University Press, 1972, 178 pp.

　　A thematic overview of Strindberg's major prose and dramas. Sees Strindberg as a conscious artist engaged in objectifying his personal experiences.
43. *Strindberg. A Collection of Critical Essays.* Edited by Otto Reinert. Englewood Cliffs, N.J.: Prentice-Hall, 1971.

　　Contains reprints of the following articles: Robert Brustein's "August Strindberg"; Raymond Williams's "Private Tragedy: Strindberg"; R. J. Kaufman's "Strindberg: The Absence of Irony"; Victor Svanberg's "The Strindberg Cult"; Maurice Gravier's "The Character and the Soul"; Pär Lagerkvist's "Strindberg and the Theater of Tomorrow"; Eric Bentley's "Strindberg, The One and Many"; Martin Lamm's discussion of *Miss Julie*; Walter Johnson's "Strindberg and the Dance Macabre"; Birgitta Steene's "Shakespearian Elements in Historical Plays of Strindberg"; Evert Sprinchorn's "The Logic of *A Dream Play*"; Brian Rothwell's "The Chamber Plays."
44. *The Unknown Strindberg.* Edited by Harry G. Carlson. Strindberg issue. *Scandinavian Review*, 64 (Sept. 1976).

　　See also items nos. 60, 61, 79, 83, and 116.
45. Valency, Maurice. *The Flower and the Castle.* New York: Macmillan, 1963, pp. 326–42.

　　Strindberg section of book is an overview of Strindberg's work, seeing it as an ingenious recreation again and again of the same neurotic situation, making "the subject matter of his plays . . . almost invariably the same."

46. Weinstock, John M. and Robert T. Rovinsky, eds. *The Hero in Scandinavian Literature from Peer Gynt to the Present*. Austin: University of Texas Press, 1975.

   Contains two articles on Strindberg by visiting Swedish scholars Lars Gustafsson and Ingvar Holm: the incisive "Strindberg as a Forerunner of Scandinavian Modernism" (pp. 125–42) and the less discerning "Strindberg and the Theater" (pp. 143–56).

C. Articles

47. Alin, Hans. "August Strindberg: Reminiscences of a Protégé." *Modern Drama*, 5 (1962), 276–77.

   Personal recollections of Strindberg by the editor of the *Swedish-American Tribune* who made Strindberg's acquaintance in 1908 as a 16-year-old playwright.

48. Allen, James L., Jr. "Symbol and Meaning in Strindberg's *Crime and Crime*." *Modern Drama*, 9 (1966), 62–63.

   Claims that Strindberg's *Crime and Crime* (Brott och brott) can only be understood through study of certain major symbolic motifs, such as the concept of original sin and the *felix culpa* (the fortunate fall). The title refers to two kinds of crime: (1) those never repented and (2) those atoned for through penance.

49. Bandy, Stephen C. "Strindberg's Biblical Sources for *The Ghost Sonata*." *Scandinavian Studies*, 40 (1968), 200–209.

   Sees the structure of *The Ghost Sonata* as a series of tightly interlocking allusions to incidents recorded in the Bible and relates the Milkmaid, Hummel, and the Student to specific episodes and people in the Bible.

50. Bentson, Alice N. "From Naturalism to the *Dream Play*: A Study of the Evolution of Strindberg's Unique Theatrical Form." *Modern Drama*, 7 (1965), 382–98.

   Argues that Strindberg's naturalistic plays, which were patterned upon traditional drama, lack universality since their reference is to the rational world and their conflict based on particular personal experiences, the interpretation of which can be refined by the audience. Only in his dream-plays did Strindberg find an artistic form that completely merges with his message.

   See also entry no. 127.

51. Bentley, Eric. "The Ironic Strindberg." In Sprinchorn, Evert, ed. *The Genius of the Scandinavian Theater*. New York: New American Library, 1964, pp. 599–603.

   A brief discussion of *Crimes and Crimes* as a "fake melodrama" and of Strindberg as a playwright representing a later cultural phase than Ibsen.

52. Bergeron, David M. "Strindberg's *Easter*: A Musical Play." *University Review* (Kansas City, University of Missouri), 33 (1967), pp. 219-22.

Discusses the relationship between Haydn's oratorio *The Seven Last Words of Christ* and the point-counterpoint structure of Strindberg's play, with specific reference to thematic development and arrangement of characters.

53. Bergholz, Harry. "Strindberg's Anthologies of American Humorists, Bibliographically Identified." *Scandinavian Studies*, 43 (1971), 335-43.

Examines briefly Strindberg's 2-volume translations of Artemus Ward, Mark Twain, Charles Dudley Warner, Bret Harte, Thomas Bailey Aldrich, and James M. Bailey.

54. Block, Haskell. "Strindberg and the Symbolist Drama." *Modern Drama*, 5 (1962), 314-22.

Argues that Strindberg's symbolist affinities in the 1890s were religious rather than literary in origin. A symbolist playwright like Maeterlinck "was not so much a model for Strindberg as an incitement to continued exploration of his own occultism."

55. Borland, Harold H. "The Dramatic Quality of Strindberg's Novels." *Modern Drama*, 5 (1962), 299-305.

A study of the dramatic quality of *The Red Room*, *The People of Hemsö*, and *By the Open Sea*. Although no common denominator can be found for Strindberg's three novels, all of them display a strong dramatic sense, a view of life as conflict and encounter.

56. Boyd, Ursel D. "Friedrich Dürrenmatt und sein Drama *Play Strindberg*." *Germanic Notes*, 3:3 (1972), pp. 18-21.

Discusses Dürrenmatt's "adaptation" of Strindberg's *Dance of Death* in terms of theatrical motifs, plot and mise-en-scène.

57. Bronsen, David. "*The Dance of Death* and the Possibility of Laughter." *Drama Survey*, 6 (1967), 31-44.

Sees the *Dance of Death* as a macabre tragedy, grotesque mime, and farce. These modes complement each other and create a drama of uneasy tension.

58. Carlson, Harry G. "Ambiguity and Archetypes in Strindberg's *Romantic Organist*." *Scandinavian Studies*, 48 (1976), 256-71.

Sees the complex archetype of the Great Mother as a possible unifying element in the novella *The Romantic Organist*. Suggests that the lighthouse keeper's daughter, whom the organist marries, is another figment of his imagination.

59. _____. "Problems in Play Translation." *Educational Theatre Journal*, 16 (1964), 55-58.

A comparison between Elizabeth Sprigge's and Arvid Paulson's translations of *The Father*, arguing that the basic criteria for play translations are "speakability" and duration of speeches.

60. _____. "Several Unknown Strindbergs." *Scandinavian Review*, 64:3 (Sept. 1976), pp. 5-6.

Introduction to special Strindberg issue, edited by Harry G. Carlson. A challenge to the biographical approach to the Swedish playwright.

See also entry no. 79.

61. _____. "The Unknown Painter of Myth." *Scandinavian Review*, 64:3 (Sept. 1976), pp. 32–38.

    Presentation of Strindberg as a graphic artist. Sees his paintings as further examples of his mythopoeic artistry, which "used resonances from ancient myths to give his work universal relevance."

62. Corrigan, Robert W. "Strindberg and the Abyss." Introduction to *A Dream Play* and *The Ghost Sonata*. San Francisco: Chandler, 1966.

    Brief introduction to Strindberg's post-Inferno production.

63. Dear, Irving. "Strindberg's Dream Vision: Prelude to Film." *Criticism*, 14 (1972), 253–65.

    A discussion of Strindberg's "dream mode" as a filmic conception of experience, expressing itself in his concern with objectifying subject states and in his emphasis on objects and actions in themselves.

64. DePaul, Brother C.F.X. "Bergman and Strindberg: Two Philosophies of Suffering." *College English*, 26 (1965), 620–30.

    Mostly an analysis of Bergman but with reference to such "Strindbergian" themes as suffering, atonement, and estrangement.

65. Dukore, Bernard. "Strindberg: The Real and the Surreal." *Modern Drama*, 5 (1962), 331–34.

    A brief discussion of two California productions of Strindberg's *The Dance of Death* and *Creditors*, which leads the author to advocate the creation of "a uniquely Strindbergian style . . . wherein would exist a mutual transformation of the real and the surreal."

66. Flaxman, Seymour L. "The Debt of Williams and Miller to Ibsen and Strindberg." *Comparative Literature Studies* (Special Advance Issue, 1963), pp. 51–60.

    Traces the dramaturgy of Williams back to Strindberg's major plays.

67. Fletcher, John. "Bergman and Strindberg." *Journal of Modern Literature*, 3 (1973), 173–90.

    Singles out such parallels between Strindberg's and Bergman's work as the blurring of dream and reality, of past and present; the preoccupation with Christian morality; and the black-and-white mood. Sees Bergman as a disciplined artist, Strindberg as a diffuse and unfocused one. Bergman is a late modernist, Strindberg a late Romantic.

68. Freedman, Morris. "Strindberg's Positive Nihilism." In Freedman, Morris, ed. *Essays in the Modern Drama*. (Boston: Heath, 1964), pp. 56–63. Reprinted from *Drama Survey*, 2 (1963), 288–96.

    A brief discussion of *The Father*, *Miss Julie*, *Easter*, and *A Dream Play* to show the development from characters who are "unable to yield to the requirements of reality" to those who can bind their nature and accept resignation. The development is one from destructive despair to positive nihilism.

69. Goodman, Randolph. "Playwriting with a Third Eye: Fun and Games with Albee, Ibsen and Strindberg." *Columbia University Forum*, 10: 1 (Spring 1967), pp. 18–22.

    Suggests Ibsen's *Hedda Gabler* as a model for Albee's *Who's Afraid of Virginia Woolf?* but argues that Strindberg's life and work inspired Ibsen's drama.

70. Grabowski, Simon. "Unreality in Plays of Ibsen, Strindberg and Hamsun." *Mosaic*, 4:2 (Winter 1972), 63–76.

    Discusses briefly *A Dream Play* as a journey from cosmic reality to material earth-dream. The dreamer is "a supra-personal, supra-objective eye with a claim to total planetary awareness."

71. Hamilton, Mary G. "Strindberg's Alchemical Way of the Cross." *Mosaic*, 7:4 (Summer 1974), pp. 139–53.

    Demonstrates how alchemy contributes to the major themes, images, structural technique and character development of *To Damascus*.

72. Hartman, Murray. "Strindberg and O'Neill." *Educational Theatre Journal*, 18:3 (Oct. 1966), pp. 216–31.

    Defines certain parallels in Strindberg's and O'Neill's lives: an Oedipal obsession, misogyny, rebelliousness against middle-class complacency. Both playwrights were restless experimenters with dramatic technique.

73. Hauptman, Ira. "Strindberg's Realistic Plays." *Yale Theatre*, 5:2 (1974), pp. 87–94.

    A discussion of *The Father* and *Miss Julie* as a gradual shrinking of Strindberg's dramatic universe, with nothing objective over which to fight, and no sense of an objectified society in which victory can have more than purely personal implications.

74. Hayes, Stephen G. and Jules Zentner. "Strindberg's *Miss Julie*: Lilacs and Beer." *Scandinavian Studies*, 45 (1973), 59–64.

    Flora and alcohol are seen as important intoxicants in bringing out the social and sexual battle between Jean and Julie. After the seduction, the floral and alcoholic symbolism is maintained and culminates in Miss Julie's Lake Como fantasy.

75. Hildeman, Karl-Ivar. "Strindberg, *The Dance of Death* and Revenge." *Scandinavian Studies*, 25 (1963), 267–94.

    A discussion of Strindberg's dependence for source material upon his personal interpretation of the marriage between his sister, Anna, and Hugo Philp, a school superintendent and former friend of Strindberg's from his Uppsala days.

76. Holtan, Orley I. "The Absurd World of Strindberg's *The Dance of Death*." *Comparative Drama*, 1 (1967), 199–206.

    Identifies a number of themes in *The Dance of Death*: isolation, imprisonment, boredom, gratuitous cruelty, the meaninglessness of existence and sees the play as a grotesque combination of the comic and the tragic.

77. Jarvi, Raymond. "Strindberg's *The Ghost Sonata* and Sonata Form." *Mosaic*, 5:4 (Summer 1972), pp. 69–84.

A detailed analysis of the musical (sonata) structure of Strindberg's drama, concluding that *The Ghost Sonata* might be placed between the first and second movements of Beethoven's D-minor Piano Sonata.

78. ———. "Ett drömspel: A Symphony for the Stage." *Scandinavian Studies*, 44 (1972), 28–42.

    Considers *A Dreamplay* a symphony for dramatic ensemble and an analogy to a sonata for orchestra, i.e., an extensive composition that treats the full orchestra as a single dynamic instrument.

    See also entry no. 138.

79. ——— and Harry G. Carlson. "Strindberg: Alive in the Blue Tower." *Scandinavian Review*, 64:3 (Sept. 1976), pp. 7–10.

    A presentation of the Strindberg museum in Stockholm, lodged in the same locale where Strindberg spent the last four years of his life.

80. Johannesson, Eric O. "*Syndabocken*: Strindberg's Last Novel." *Scandinavian Studies*, 35 (1963), 1–28.

    Considers Strindberg's best fiction to be the short novels *The Romantic Organist*, *Alone*, *The Roof-Raising* [Roofing] *Feast*, and *The Scapegoat*, in which he could maintain a consistent tone and sense of atmosphere. His characters are modern in their shifting identities and propensity for wearing psychological masks.

81. ———. "*Taklagsöl*: An Early Experiment in the Psychological Novel." *Scandinavian Studies*, 35 (1963), 223–38.

    Like the previous entry, an excerpt from author's book *The Novels of August Strindberg*. Sees *The Roof-Raising Feast* as Strindberg's most experimental work of fiction.

    See also entry no. 35.

82. Johns, Marilyn. "Journey into Autumn: *Oväder* and *Smultronstället*." *Scandinavian Studies*, 50 (1978), 133–49.

    A comparison between Strindberg's play *Oväder* and Bergman's film *Smultronstället* in terms of theme, characterization and visual technique.

    See also entry no. 139.

83. ———. "Kindred Spirits: Strindberg and Bergman." *Scandinavian Review*, 64:3 (Sept. 1978), p. 16.

    A brief account of the affinities between the two artists that led to Bergman's subsequent dependence on Strindberg.

84. ———. "Dream Reality in August Strindberg's *A Dreamplay* and Ingmar Bergman's *Wild Strawberries*: A Study in Structure." *Proceedings of the Pacific Northwest Council on Foreign Languages*, 27, Part 1 (1976), pp. 122–25.

    Traces the use of dream consciousness, logic, and distortion as it effects the depersonalization of character and organic scene structure. Also discusses four individual scenes from the film that are directly derivative of the play.

85. ———. "Strindberg's *Folkungasagan* and Bergman's *Det sjunde inseglet*: Medieval Epic and Psychological Drama." *Scandinavica* 27:1 (May 1979), pp. 21–34.

Postulates a fundamental tension in both works between the "epic" and the "psychological" and investigates the ways in which this tension permeates setting, character, plot, visual motifs, and music.

86. Johnson, Walter. "*Creditors* Reexamined," *Modern Drama*, 5 (1962), 278–90.

    Challenges the Swedish biographical approach to Strindberg's drama and analyzes the play as a psychological ménage à trois, a marriage drama of universal interest.

87. ———. "*Gustaf Adolf* Revised." *Scandinavian Studies for Henry Goddard Leach*. Seattle: University of Washington Press, 1965, pp. 236–46.

    Discusses the cuts and changes suggested by Strindberg to make his long historical drama *Gustaf Adolf* more stage-worthy.

88. Kaufman, K. J. "Strindberg: The Absence of Irony." *Drama Survey*, 3 (1964), 463–76.

    Argues that in Strindberg, the normal boundaries between thought and act, interior and exterior reality, past and present are blurred or denied. He wrote gripping but incomplete plays, based on "a devastated vision of an absurd, divinely abandoned world."

89. Kaufman, Michael W. "Strindberg's Historical Imagination: Erik XIV." *Comparative Drama*, 9 (1975–76), 318–31.

    A reading of *Erik XIV*, not as a historical drama but "as a drama about history," revealing Strindberg's view of the past as "discontinuous, fragmented, and chaotic, where the only principles of order inhere in the mind of the individual perceiver.

90. Lapisardi, Frederick S. "The Same Enemies: Notes in Certain Similarities between Yeats and Strindberg." *Modern Drama*, 12 (1969), 146–54.

    Among the similarities noted are: a desire to found an intimate theater; the use of national "sagas" as bases for plays; an influence from the Orient and the occult; their interest in the drama of Maeterlinck.

91. Lawson, Stephen R. "Strindberg's *Dream Play* and *Ghost Sonata*." *Yale Theatre*, 5:2 (1974), pp. 95–102.

    A brief discussion of two of Strindberg's post-Inferno plays in which an omnipresent dualism is noted; like Keats, Strindberg has an oxymoronic vision of life.

92. Lewis, Leta Jane. "Alchemy and the Orient in Strindberg's *Dream Play*," *Scandinavian Studies*, 35 (1963), 208–22.

    Analysis of a *Dream Play* with emphasis on concepts and symbols originating in Strindberg's enthusiasm for alchemy and the Orient.

93. Lide, Barbara. "Strindberg and Molière: Parallels, Influence, Image." *Molière and the Commonwealth of Letters: Patrimony and Posterity*. Jackson: Mississippi University Press, 1975.

    A comparison between Molière's *Tartuffe* and Strindberg's *Creditors* as comedies, and a brief description of the possible impact of *Tartuffe* on *Gustav Vasa*.

    See also entry no. 142.

94. Lyons, Charles R. "The Archetypal Action of Male Submission in Strindberg's *The Father*." *Scandinavian Studies*, 36 (1964), 218–32.

    Traces the archetypal images in *The Father* of the demonic female and the apocalyptic male who succumbs to a demonic vision of the world and is destroyed by it.

95. McNamara, Brooks. "Scene Design: 1876–1965. Ibsen, Chekhov, Strindberg." *Tulane Drama Review*, 13:2 (T42), (Winter 1968), pp. 77–91.

    Illustrated discussion of productions of [There Are] *Crimes and Crimes*, *The Father*, *Mother[ly] Love*, and *Miss Julie*.

96. Madsen, Børge Gedsø. "Naturalism in Transition: Strindberg's 'Cynical' Tragedy *The Bond*." *Modern Drama*, 5 (1962), 291–98.

    Discusses Strindberg's drama from 1892 as a work too subjective and one-sided to gratify entirely as a naturalistic drama. In addition its anthropomorphic references link *The Bond* with the post-Inferno period.

97. Mays, Milton A. "Strindberg's *Ghost Sonata*: Parodied Fairy Tale on Original Sin." *Modern Drama*, 10 (1967), 189–94.

    Argues that *The Ghost Sonata* takes as its main structural mode the fairy tale, but is a parody of this literary genre in that Strindberg demonstrates the inevitable consequences of original sin.

98. Milton, John. "A Restless Pilgrim: Strindberg in *The Inferno*." *Modern Drama*, 5 (1962), 306–313.

    Sees Strindberg in *Inferno* "as Everyman in a world of duality." Strindberg makes conscious use of his personal experience to build a fable of modern man whose life is governed by the metaphor of coincidence. Swedenborg's spiritualism comes to his aid but Strindberg is caught between two methods of structure—the logical and the nonlogical, frustrations Strindberg turns into art. *Inferno* is a record of the conditions of the artist.

99. Oster, Rose-Marie. "Hamm and Hummel: Beckett and Strindberg on Human Condition." *Scandinavian Studies*, 41 (1969), 330–43.

    A comparison between Beckett's and Strindberg's view of man as a tormented and tormenting creature in a shabby world, summed up in images of mud and enclosures.

100. Parker, Gerald. "The Spectator Seized by the Theatre: Strindberg's *The Ghost Sonata*." *Modern Drama*, 15 (1972), 373–86.

    Contends that in *The Ghost Sonata* language becomes a spectacle in itself, designed to act "physically" upon the spectator, rather than a means of rational discourse. In this sense Strindberg anticipates the drama of Ionesco.

101. Paulson, Arvid. "*The Father*: A Survey of Critical Opinion of August Strindberg's Tragedy and Leading American Performances of it During the Past Half Century." *The Strindberg Reader*. Translated and edited by Arvid Paulson. New York: Phaedra, 1968, pp. 437–49. First published in *Scandinavian Studies for Henry Goddard Leach*. Seattle: University of Washington Press, 1965, pp. 247–59.

    Discusses five productions of Strindberg's play in America from 1912 to 1962, when the Royal Dramatic Theatre of Stockholm gave a guest performance in New York.

102. _____. "Probing Strindberg's Psyche." *The Strindberg Reader*, pp. 429–36. Cf. entry no. 101.

   Argues against interpretations of Strindberg as a paranoid schizophrenic and maintains that Strindberg was always in control of his mind.

103. Plasberg, Elaine. "Strindberg and the New Poetics." *Modern Drama*, 15 (1972), 1–14.

   A discussion of *The Dance of Death* as "a mixture of hornpipes and funerals," i.e., as an example of an impure dramatic genre, with special focus on the difficulties this creates for a director. Sees the play as "a caricature of tragedy," representing the modern theater's perspective on incongruity.

104. Raphael, Robert. "Strindberg and Wagner." *Scandinavian Studies for Henry Goddard Leach*. Seattle: University of Washington Press, 1965, pp. 260–68.

   Focuses attention on Wagnerian features in *Swanwhite* and points out stylistic and thematic (Caritas or Love through Empathy) similarities between Wagner's and Strindberg's works.

105. Reinert, Otto. Introduction to *Strindberg: A Collection of Critical Essays*. Englewood Cliffs: Prentice-Hall, 1971.

   See item no. 43.

106. Scanlan, David. "*The Road to Damascus, Part One*: A Skeptic's Everyman." *Modern Drama*, 5 (1962), 343–51.

   A textual analysis of the first part of the *To Damascus* trilogy, focusing on The Stranger's experiences as a series of crises, all of which are altered after his visit to the convent.

   See also item no. 148.

107. Scobbie, Irene. "Strindberg and Lagerkvist." *Modern Drama*, 7 (1964), 126–34.

   A comparison between Strindberg's *To Damascus* and Lagerkvist's *Sista mänskan*, both of which employ a supernatural force as the antagonist, an emphasis on mood rather than analysis, and abstracted characters."

108. Sehmsdorf, Henning K. "August Strindberg's *Swanwhite* and Scandinavian Folk Poetry: Idea and Form." *The Barat Review*, 1:2 (June 1966), pp. 98–104.

   Argues that the basic characteristic of Strindberg's stylistic method in *Swanwhite* is the transformation of certain formal traits of the folktale (scenery, plot, imagery) into forms functioning as symbols which serve to put forth the main idea of the play, Caritas, the Great Love.

109. Senelick, Laurence. "Strindberg, Antoine and Lugné-Poë: A Study in Cross Purposes." *Modern Drama*, 15 (1973), 391–402.

   An analysis of Strindberg's reception on the Parisian stage. Although produced by the leading theater experimenters in the French capital, Strindberg never became a widely discussed playwright in Paris.

110. Sharp, Corona. "Dürrenmatt's *Play Strindberg*." *Modern Drama*, 13 (1970), 276–83.

    A discussion of Dürrenmatt's version of Strindberg's *The Dance of Death*. Strindberg explores the motivation of marital warfare. Dürrenmatt studies only the battle tactics themselves.

111. Sprinchorn, Evert. "The Logic of *A Dreamplay*." *Modern Drama*, 5 (1962), 352–65.

    A Freudian reading of *A Dreamplay* that sees the veiled sexual imagery, such as the castle and Fingal's cave, as a unifying structural force in the drama.

112. _____. "Strindberg and the Greater Naturalism." *Tulane Drama Review*, 13:2 (Winter 1968), pp. 119–29.

    Discusses Strindberg's reaction against "lesser" or photographic Naturalism as presented in the essay "The Battle of the Brains" and calls him "a renewer of synthetic decor" and symbolic sets.

113. _____. "Winning an Audience for Strindberg." *American Swedish Historical Foundation Yearbook* (Philadelphia: American Swedish Historical Society, 1972), pp. 23–30.

    Calls for a less ponderous approach to the staging of Strindberg and a revision of him as a mad and melacholy Swede. Suggests that one way to save Strindberg in the theater would be to let glamorous actresses and handsome actors play the leading roles.

114. _____. "The Zola of the Occult: Strindberg's Experimental Method." *Modern Drama*, 17 (1974), 250–66.

    Examines Strindberg's intention of becoming "a Zola of the occult" after his Inferno period. The method he used was to examine his so-called hidden or subliminal self, thereby allowing us to follow step by step the process of his conversion. Emphasizes the importance of Kierkegaardian and Swedenborgian concepts.

115. _____. "Hell and Purgatory in Strindberg." *Scandinavian Studies*, 50 (1978), 371–80.

    Maintains that Swedenborg's concept of *devastation*, i.e., a process where our external state is stripped and our internal self made visible, provides Strindberg with a dramatic device, whereby he can depict *conversion* on the stage.

    See also entry nos. 7, 14, 15, 22, 31.

116. Steene, Birgitta. "The Ambiguous Feminist." *Scandinavian Review*, 64:3 (Sept. 1976), pp. 27–31.

    Discusses Strindberg's conflict-ridden view of women as mothers, madonnas, child bearers, and parasites.

117. Stockenström, Göran. "The Journey from the Isle of Life to the Isle of the Dead: The Idea of Reconciliation in *The Ghost Sonata*." *Scandinavian Studies*, 50 (1978), 133–49.

    Argues that *The Ghost Sonata* is representative of the whole body of chamber plays in maintaining an outer movement from reality to unreality, which has its thematic analogue in the dramatization of

three spiritual stages: illusion, unmasking and resignation, all of which are part of a process of *reconciliation*.
118. Syndergaard, Larry E. "The *Skogsrå* of Folklore and Strindberg's *The Crown Bride.*" *Comparative Drama*, 6 (1972–73), 310–22.

    Discusses the organic function of the *skogsrå*—midwife figure in Strindberg's drama. It is a psychologically more complex figure than the *skogsrå* of folklore and affects four principal aspects of the play: plot, character, expressionist technique, and theme.
119. Taylor, Marion A. "A Note on Strindberg's *The Dance of Death* and Albee's *Who's Afraid of Virginia Woolf?*" *Papers on Language and Literature*, 2 (1966), 187–88.

    A brief comparison between the marital/sexual conflict in Strindberg's and Albee's plays.
120. Törnqvist, Egil. "Strindberg's *The Stronger.*" *Scandinavian Studies*, 42 (1970), 297–308.

    A discussion of the problem of power in *The Stronger*. Argues that, contrary to conventional opinion, Mlle. Y (the silent woman) is the stronger at the end of the play. Törnqvist supports this with reference to Strindberg's biography.
121. _____. "Miss Julie and O'Neill." *Modern Drama*, 19 (1976), 351–64.

    Both the drama *Miss Julie* and Strindberg's preface had an impact on O'Neill's work, especially his Electra trilogy. Points out similarities between the two playwrights' concept of fate, their dramatic techniques and their use of symbolism.
122. Vincentia, Sister, M.O.P. "Wagnerism in *Road to Damascus.*" *Modern Drama*, 5 (1962), 335–43.

    Argues that *To Damascus* shows analogies with the Wagnerian *Gesamtkunstwerk* and displays a frequent borrowing from both music and dance. Other Wagnerian features are a symbolic use of folklore; a rhythmic use of language; and an emphasis on mise-en-scène in evoking a mood.
123. Vowles, Richard B. "A Cook's Tour of Strindberg Scholarship." *Modern Drama*, 5 (1962), 256–68.

    An introduction to *Modern Drama*'s commemorative issue in December 1962.
124. _____. "Strindberg's Isle of the Dead." *Modern Drama*, 5 (1962), 366–78.

    A presentation of four dramatic fragments left by Strindberg and a translation of one of them.
125. White, Kenneth S. "Visions of a Transfigured Humanity: Strindberg and Lenormand." *Modern Drama*, 5 (1962), 323–30.

    A comparison between Strindberg's *Easter* and *La Maison des Remparts* by Lenormand, French vanguard playwright of the twenties. Both playwrights believed that life was a nightmare illuminated now and then "by lightning flashes of regained purity."
126. Zenter, Jules. See entry no. 74.

D. Dissertations

127. Bentson, A. N. "Theatricality in Contemporary Drama." Emory University, 1963 (*DA* 24:04, p. 2026).

    Discusses Strindberg's search for new dramatic forms and for new ideas in *The Father, Miss Julie, There Are Crimes and Crimes, A Dream Play,* and *The Ghost Sonata.*

128. Dawson, William Meredith. "The Female Characters of August Strindberg, Eugene O'Neill, and Tennessee Williams." University of Wisconsin, 1964 (*DA* 25:04, p. 2663).

    Examines the childhood and adolescent experiences of the three playwrights and shows how similarities in relationship to parents, school, and social conditions developed a distrust and fear of women.

129. Denton, Frankie Belle. "Hamsun, Strindberg, Rilke: The Limits of the Naturalistic Narrative." University of Texas, 1977 (*DA* 38:12, p. 7356–A).

    Examines the themes and narrative technique of three works that represent a development beyond the limits of naturalism between 1890 and 1910, namely Hamsun's *Sult,* Strindberg's *Inferno,* and Rilke's *Malte Laurids Brigge.*

130. Dittmann, Reidar. "Strindberg and Munch: Parallelisms and Mutual Influences, 1883–1897." University of Washington, 1976 (*DA* 37:05, p. 2460–A).

    A study of the social and moral climate that led Munch and Strindberg into voluntary exile, and an account of their friendship in Berlin and Paris.

131. Eaton, Winnifred Kittredge. "Contrasts in the Representation of Death by Sophocles, Webster, and Strindberg." Syracuse University, 1965 (*DA* 26:10, p. 6020).

    Traces the treatment of death as a psychological but actual event in *The Father, Miss Julie* and *Creditors,* and as a psychological and religious experience in the post-Inferno dramas, with the history plays forming a transition.

132. Friou, Kenneth A. "Non-Naturalist Elements in Strindberg's Principal Naturalist Plays: *Miss Julie* and *The Father.*" University of Wisconsin, 1972 (*DA* 33:08, p. 4577–A).

    Maintains the thesis that Strindberg's naturalistic dramas contain many features that foreshadow the later expressionistic plays.

133. Harper, Glenn Alan. "Strindberg's Fictional Life-Worlds: A Study of the Confessional Novels from the Point of View of the Sociology of Knowledge." Florida State University, 1976 (*DA* 37:10, p. 6491–A).

    Defends the thesis that the confessional novels of Strindberg (*The Son of a Servant, A Madman's Defense, Inferno,* and *Legends*) are composed of fictional life-worlds, which exhibit the formative influence of contemporary social institution.

134. Heard, William III. "Strindberg and Williams: A Study in Affinities." University of Washington, 1975 (*DA* 37:2, p. 698–A).

A comparative study of Strindberg's and Williams's personal and social background and an analysis of the moral world that each playwright discovered during periods of stress.

135. Howard, Gordon S. "Strindberg's Use of Irony in his Post-Inferno Dramas." University of Minnesota, 1969 (*DA* 29:10, p. 3714).

    Concludes that Strindberg's view of life was at times ironic and that this is reflected in his use of ironic contrasts in the dramatic content of the post-Inferno plays.

136. Jacobs, Barry. "Strindberg and the Problem of Suffering." Harvard University, 1964.

    A study of guilt, suffering, and redemption in Strindberg's oeuvre from *Miss Julie* to *The Great Highway*. Twelve plays and prose works are treated.

137. Jarvi, Raymond R. A. "Strindberg's Post-Inferno Dramas and Music." University of Washington, 1970 (*DA* 31:10, p. 5566–A).

    A study of Strindberg's 34 completed post-Inferno dramas in terms of their musical content and the influence of musical form on the dramatic structure.

138. Jensen, Howard J. "Swedenborgian and other Religious Influences upon Strindberg's Dramatic Expressionism." Wayne State University, 1972 (*DA* 33:11, p. 6500–A).

    Examines the use of Swedenborgian correspondences (symbols) in five of Strindberg's expressionistic plays (*To Damascus I–III, Crime and Crime, A Dream Play, The Ghost Sonata* and *The Great Highway*).

139. Johns, Marilyn E. "Strindberg's Influence on Bergman's *Det sjunde inseglet, Smultronstället,* and *Persona*." University of Washington, 1976 (*DA* 38:03, p. 1401–A).

    A textual and visual analysis of Strindberg's *The Saga of the Folkungs, A Dream Play, To Damascus,* and *Storm* as these plays relate to Ingmar Bergman's films *The Seventh Seal, Wild Strawberries,* and *Persona*.

140. Kirk, John W. "Dramatism and the Theatre: An Application of Kenneth Burke's Critical Methods to the Analysis of Two Plays." University of Florida, 1962 (*DA*, 23:06, p. 3027).

    Examines Strindberg's *To Damascus* in the light of the Burkean *Pentad* construct (act, scene, agent, agency, and purpose).

141. Lane, Harold. "The Continuity of Strindberg's *Damascus* Cycle." University of Toronto, 1978 (*DA* 39:04, p. 2257–A).

    Examines the three "Damascus" plays as a unity and discusses their continuity with earlier and later Strindberg plays in terms of theme and dramaturgy.

142. Lide, Barbara A. B. "Strindberg's Comic Spirit: A Study of August Strindberg's Comedies and Their Relationship to the Comic Tradition." University of Illinois, 1975 (*DA* 36:09, p. 6107–A).

    Examines those plays that Strindberg designated as "comedies" or "tragi-comedies." Divides them into two categories: marital and religious comedies.

143. Mattson, Margareta F. "Strindberg's *Miss Julie* in English: Problems

of Translation." Case Western Reserve University. 1974 (*DA* 36:04, p. 2199–A).

An examination of 13 English translations of *Miss Julie*.

144. Pampel, Brigitte C. G. "The Relationship of the Sexes in the Works of Strindberg, Wedekind, and O'Neill." Northwestern University, 1972 (*DA* 33:06, p. 2946–A).

Sees vacillation between hatred and praise for women as characteristic for Strindberg, who deemed women the source of evil in his earlier works but later declared both men and women victims of forces of nature.

145. Passerini, Edward M. "Strindberg's Absurdist Plays: An Examination of the Expressionistic, Surrealistic, and Absurd Elements in Strindberg's Drama." University of Virginia, 1971 (*DA* 32:08, p. 4628–A).

Lists 27 separate elements of absurdism in Strindberg's dramatic production from the epilogue to *Master Olof* to *The Great Highway*. Central work to the study is *To Damascus*.

146. Reinhardt, Nancy Simonds. "Visual Meaning in Strindberg's Theatre." Cornell University, 1975 (*DA* 36:06, p. 3224–A).

Examines the central visual motifs and composition in Strindberg's nonverbal imagination (paintings, photographs) and applies these to the action and dialogue of three groups of Strindberg plays: domestic dramas, wander plays, and histories.

147. Roth, Marc Allen. "Role-Playing in Historical Drama and the Changing Visions of History: A Study of Shakespeare, Schiller, Büchner, and Strindberg." University of California, Berkeley, 1976 (*DA* 37:09, p. 5806–A).

A study of historical dramas that focus on the crisis of the protagonist as he faces his public and private self. Examines Strindberg's *Erik XIV*, *Charles XII*, and *Gustav III*.

148. Scanlan, David E. "Traditional Comic Form in Strindberg's Naturalistic Plays." University of Minnesota, 1970 (*DA* 31:07, p. 3637–A).

Argues that many of Strindberg's Naturalistic dramas make use of traditional comic form and share traditional comedy's concern with the establishment of domestic happiness as a primary social value.

149. Schmidt, Verne V. "Strindberg's Impact on Kafka." University of Texas, 1966 (*DA* 27:08, p. 2545–A).

Considers Strindberg a seminal influence on Kafka, especially his use of dream structures, his themes of metamorphosis, and his satire on bureaucracy. Claims that Kafka must be understood through Strindberg.

150. Steiner, Donald Lee. "August Strindberg and Edward Albee: *The Dance of Death*." Northwestern University, 1972 (*DA* 33:02, p. 766).

In Albee and Strindberg the *dance macabre* is a painful but positive rebirth of consciousness. Compares *The Dance of Death* and *Who's Afraid of Virginia Woolf?*; *Pariah* and *The Zoo Story*; *The Ghost Sonata* and *Tiny Alice*.

151. Thompson, Carol Lee. "Problems of Adaptation: Strindberg's *Miss Julie*." Carnegie-Mellon University, 1972 (*DA* 32:12, p. 7124–A).

Presents author's adaptation of Strindberg's play, in which the setting is changed to modern New York City and Jean and Julie are black. Argues that the sexual and social freedom of contemporary society makes the downfall of Strindberg's Julie obsolete and ludicrous. Racial conflict replaces Strindbergian class conflict.

Notes

1. Ralph Haugen, "American Drama Critic's Reactions to Productions of August Strindberg," (diss., University of Minnesota, 1959). (*DA* 20:04, 1481–82).
2. John Gassner, "The Influence of Strindberg in the United States," *World Theatre*, 11 (Spring 1962), 21–29.
3. Egil Törnqvist, "Strindberg and O'Neill," *Modern Drama*, 19 (1976), 351–64.
4. At this time (1916) twenty-six of Strindberg's plays had appeared in English translation. See Törnqvist, p. 353.
5. See *Nation* (5 November 1977), 466–67 and *Newsweek* (24 October 1977), 85–86.
6. Esther H. Rapp, "Strindberg's Reception in England and America," *Scandinavian Studies*, 23 (1951), 1–22; 23 (1951), 49–59; 23 (1951), 109–37. Jackson R. Bryer, "Strindberg 1951–62: A Bibliography." *Modern Drama*, 5 (1962), 269–75.

Strindberg and O'Neill
Egil Törnqvist

Strindberg's importance for Eugene O'Neill has often been pointed out, but perhaps O'Neill's best known statement on the matter is his Nobel Prize speech in 1936, approximately half of which was devoted to Strindberg:

It was reading his plays when I first started to write back in the winter of 1913–14 that, above all else, first gave me the vision of what modern drama could be, and first inspired me with the urge to write for the theater myself. If there is anything of lasting worth in my work, it is due to that original impulse from him, which has continued as my inspiration down all the years since then—to the ambition I received then to follow in the footsteps of his genius as worthily as my talent might permit, and with the same integrity of purpose.

Of course, it will be no news to you in Sweden that my work owes much to the influence of Strindberg. That influence runs clearly through more than a few of my plays and is plain for everyone to see. Neither will it be news for anyone who has ever known me, for I have always stressed it myself. . . .

No, I am only too proud of my debt to Strindberg, only too happy to have this opportunity of proclaiming him to his people. For me, he remains, as Nietzsche remains in his sphere, the Master, still to this day more modern than any of us, still our leader. And it is my pride to imagine that perhaps his spirit, musing over this year's Nobel award for literature, may smile with a little satisfaction, and find the follower not too unworthy of his Master.[1]

Before the speech was sent away to Stockholm, O'Neill read it to his friend, the critic Sophus Keith Winther. As he was reading, he suddenly interrupted himself with the comment: "I wish immortality were a fact, for then some day I would meet Strindberg." When Winther replied that "that would scarcely be enough to justify immortality," O'Neill answered quickly and firmly: "It would be enough for me."[2]

Already in the mid-twenties O'Neill had lauded the Swedish playwright in a program note for the Provincetown Players' production of *The Spook Sonata*:

Strindberg still remains among the most modern of moderns, the greatest interpreter in the theater of the characteristic spiritual conflicts which constitute the drama—the blood—of our lives today. He carried Naturalism to a logical attainment of such poignant intensity that, if the work of any other playwright is to be called "naturalism," we must classify a play like *The Dance of Death* as "super-naturalism," and place it in a class by itself, exclusively Strindberg's since no one before or after him has had the genius to qualify.

Strindberg knew and suffered with our struggle years before many of us were born. He expressed it by intensifying the method of his time and by foreshadowing both in content and form the methods to come. All that is enduring in what we loosely call "Expressionism"—all that is artistically valid and sound theater—can be clearly traced back through Wedekind to Strindberg's *The Dream Play, There Are Crimes and Crimes, The Spook Sonata,* etc.

Hence, *The Spook Sonata* at our Playhouse. One of the most difficult of Strindberg's "behind-life" (if I may coin the term) plays to interpret with insight and distinction—but the difficult is properly our special task, or we have no good reason for existing.[3]

At about the same time he told a newspaper reporter that he considered Strindberg "the last undeniably great playwright."[4]

His first acquaintance with Strindberg's work took place in the spring of 1913.[5] O'Neill was then a patient at the Gaylord sanatorium in Connecticut. The six months he spent there meant, he has said, a spiritual awakening.[6] It was either during this stay or shortly thereafter that he composed his first play, *A Wife for a Life*, which does not, however, show any traces of his reading of Strindberg. It was apparently when he stayed with a certain Rippin family in New London— from September 1913 to March 1914—that O'Neill seriously began to devote himself to the Swedish dramatist; about his time with the Rippins he has said: "I read about everything I could lay hands on: the Greeks, the Elizabethans—practically all the classics—and of course all the moderns. Ibsen and Strindberg, especially Strindberg."[7]

Strindberg's death in May 1912 (strangely enough he died the very month and year O'Neill tried to commit suicide) resulted in a marked increase in the attention bestowed on him all over the world, including America. During the period 1893–1909 only eleven articles had been written in the U.S. about the man whom Huneker already in 1905 called "the Shakespeare of Sweden."[8] The period 1910–19 gave rise to no fewer than 150 articles on Strindberg,[9] and a glance at the number of translations confirms Strindberg's prominence during this period.

O'Neill has himself pointed out that he read the plays "as they came out in the original Scribner . . . edition—four volumes, twelve plays or so, as I remember."[10] O'Neill here refers to the five (!) volumes with the common title *Plays by August Strindberg*, published 1912–16 in Edwin Björkman's translation. As a matter of fact, the five volumes include not twelve but twenty-four Strindberg plays. It is probable also that O'Neill was familiar with some other translations.[11]

O'Neill's second wife, Agnes Boulton, has reported how strong Strindberg's impact was on her husband around 1920:

> Gene considered the author of *A Dream Play* and *The Dance of Death* a greater and much more profound playwright than Ibsen, whom he liked to belittle as being conventional and idealistic. . . .
>
> Gene was impressed by Strindberg's anguished personal life as it was shown in his novels (*The Son of a Servant* and others, all autobiographical); particularly of his tortured relationship with the women who always seemed to be taking advantage of him. . . . These novels Gene kept by him for many years, reading them even more frequently than the plays. I don't know—but I imagine he had the same feeling of identification with the great tortured Swede up to the time of his death.
>
> I knew nothing about this great playwright, but when one night, a little drunk, he read *Miss Julie* aloud, losing himself in the sound of the words and their haunted meaning, I was able to understand what Gene meant. He read passages from *The Confession of a Fool*, smiling with sarcastic sympathy. . . .
>
> Nietzsche, Strindberg—he kept these always with him, discussed them and quoted from them.[12]

O'Neill's third wife, Carlotta Monterey, has informed Karl Ragnar Gierow that shortly after her marriage to O'Neill in 1929, her husband was extremely delighted when he found that "his wife, just like himself, possessed everything by Strindberg in English."[13] What other dramatists had written he did not care much about, Carlotta also told Gierow, but before Strindberg he would kneel.[14]

That O'Neill read Strindberg in anything but English—for example, in Schering's German translation—is highly unlikely. Judging by his library, one must assume he read all foreign literature in English translation. Nor do we have any proof that O'Neill ever saw a production of a play by Strindberg. This may seem surprising but becomes less so when we remember that O'Neill, except for a few years in his youth, rarely went to the theater—even when his own plays were being produced. His familiarity with Strindberg's plays was therefore that of the reader, not the spectator.

Although Strindberg's novels, as Boulton suggests, may have influenced O'Neill as much as the plays, only the genre that the two writers have in common, the drama, will be considered here. With one exception—*To Damascus*, appearing in English in 1913—the Strindberg plays will be quoted from the Scribner edition with which O'Neill was familiar.

The first Strindberg play that seems to have left certain traces in O'Neill's work is *The Comrades*. The professional rivalry between Axel and his wife Bertha, both artists, is echoed in the rivalry between the couple in *Welded* (1923): Michael Cape, a playwright, and his wife Eleanor, an actress. Usually, however, *Welded* is regarded as an "analysis of love after the manner of Strindberg's *Dance of Death*,"[15] O'Neill's favorite play.

Much more obvious is the impact of Strindberg's next play, *The Father*. Thus the idea that "the child bound us together, but the bond became a chain," as The Captain puts it, is dramatized in *Beyond the Horizon* (1918) in a scene that bears certain similarities to the lamp-flinging scene of Strindberg's play; Ruth has just told her husband Robert that she is in love with his brother Andy:

RUTH: . . . So go! Go if you want to!
ROBERT: (*throwing her away from him. She staggers back against the table—thickly*) You—you slut! (*He stands glaring at her as she leans back, supporting herself by the table, gasping for breath. A loud frightened whimper sounds from the awakened child in the bedroom. It continues. The man and woman stand looking at one another in horror, the extent of their terrible quarrel suddenly brought home to them.*)

Similarly, The Captain's comparison of the relationship between husband and wife to "race-hatred" is dramatized in the marriage between a Negro and a white woman in *All God's Chillun Got Wings* (1923). More striking, perhaps, is the correspondence between Strindberg's Captain and O'Neill's Emperor in *The Emperor Jones* (1920), both of them fighting a losing battle against powers they cannot fathom. Indicative of Adolf's decline is his change of costume: his initial uniform, suggesting masculinity and power, is finally replaced by a straitjacket, symbol of his powerlessness. In *The Emperor Jones* we likewise witness how Jones is gradually stripped of his uniform. But in his case the costume carries negative connotations of cultural make-up from which he must liberate himself: "Damn dis heah coat! Like a straitjacket!"

To demonstrate Laura's double morals, Strindberg at one point has his Swedish Captain allude to the American Civil War: "You women, who were so tender-hearted about freeing black slaves, kept the white ones. I have slaved for you, for your child, your mother, your servants." A little later he adds: "I—in the army the one to command —became at home the one to obey. . . . And when at last I woke to the realization that I had lost my integrity, I wanted to blot out my humiliation by some heroic action. . . . I wanted to go to war, but I couldn't." What Strindberg here could only hint at, O'Neill could dramatize in *Mourning Becomes Electra* (1931), where the setting is New England at the time of the Civil War. Brigadier General Ezra Mannon is a stern, somewhat unimaginative variation on Strindberg's Captain. His fighting against the slavery of the South mirrors in the last instance his own struggle for freedom. Although both Strindberg and O'Neill are indebted to Aeschylus, it seems reasonable to assume that *The Father* intrigued O'Neill when he was penning his trilogy. After all, here was another attempt to embody a play with "a modern psychological approximation of the Greek sense of fate,"[16] another *Agamemnon* set in roughly the same period as *Mourning Becomes Electra*.

At the end of *The Father* the Captain suffers a stroke that, by implication, turns him into a mental and/or physical invalid. His last words are significantly directed not to the wife but to the old nurse:

CAPTAIN: . . . Let me put my head on your lap. Ah, that's warmer! Lean over me so I can feel your breast. Oh how sweet it is to sleep upon a woman's breast, be she mother or mistress! But sweetest of all a mother's.
NURSE. Listen! He's praying to God.
CAPTAIN. No, to you, to put me to sleep. I'm tired, so tired. Goodnight, Margaret. "Blessed art thou among women."

The pietà group visualized here is not unlike the more explicit one created by O'Neill at the end of *A Moon for the Misbegotten* (1943), where James Tyrone hides his face on the firm, large bosom of the maternal Josie Hogan: "*The two make a strangely tragic picture in the wan dawn light—this big sorrowful woman hugging a haggard-faced middle-aged drunkard against her breast, as if he were a sick child.*" Like the Captain's, Jim Tyrone's days are numbered: figuratively speaking, they are both dead when the final curtain drops.

Even more evident is the influence of *Miss Julie* on O'Neill's work.[17] One of his earliest, and worst, pieces, *Recklessness* (1913), is in fact little more than a rewriting of Strindberg's play. This one-act drama deals with an affair between Fred Burgess, a young chauffeur, and Mildred Baldwin, the wife of his employer. The affair comes to a sudden end when the maid, Gene, whom Fred has earlier courted and promised to marry, reports what is going on to the master of the house. Pretending that his wife is seriously ill, Baldwin makes Fred drive away with the car whose steering mechanism he knows does not work. Fred is killed, and when Mildred discovers what has happened she shoots herself. The plot in this very melodramatic piece, it will be seen, has obvious similarities to that of *Miss Julie*. In both cases we deal with mésalliances, and in both cases they concern women who have love affairs with their servants. Jean and Julie are worried about the return of the Count, just as Fred and Mildred are worried about the return of the husband. Both couples plan to escape, but both find that they lack money. Julie steals money from her father, Mildred says that she can take with her the jewels her husband has given her. Jean's relations with Christine compare with Fred's connection with Gene. And finally both dramas end with the off-stage suicide of the heroine.

Jean's ambition to climb the social ladder is clearly echoed in Fred's lines:

FRED: I worked my way this far and I don't intend to stop here. As soon as I've passed those engineering examinations—and I will pass them—we'll go away together. I won't be anybody's servant then. (*He glances down at his livery in disgust.*)

MRS. BALDWIN: (*Pleading tearfully*) Fred dearest, please take me away now—tonight—before he comes. What difference does the money make as long as I have you?

FRED: (*With a harsh laugh*) You don't know what you're talking about. You'd never stand it. Being poor doesn't mean anything to you. You've never been poor. Well, I have, and I know. It's hell, that's what it is.

The name of the maid, Gene, relates both to *Miss Julie* and to O'Neill, for it is a homonym of Jean pronounced in English and O'Neill was always called Gene by his friends. Even the title may have been borrowed from Strindberg. Thinking of their sexual encounter and the unwelcome consequences this may have, Jean philosophizes: "Once on the wrong path, one wants to keep on, as the harm is done anyhow. Then one grows more and more reckless—and at last it all comes out." Well aware of Fred's role as his wife's lover, Baldwin sarcastically tells Mildred: "Fred is very careless—very, very careless in some things. I shall have to teach him a lesson. He is absolutely reckless . . . , especially with other people's property."

Julie's suicide is made possible through Jean's hypnotic power over her:

JULIE: (*Ecstatically*) I am asleep already—there is nothing in the whole room but a lot of smoke—and you look like a stove—that looks like a man in black clothes and a high hat—and your eyes glow like coals when the fire is going out—and your face is a lump of ashes.

In O'Neill's *Bound East for Cardiff* (1914) the dying Yank experiences something similar: "How'd all the fog git in here? . . . Everything looks misty." The resemblance is striking, although Yank's hallucinatory experience, admittedly, is realistically motivated: what he takes to be fog is tobacco smoke; moreover, his eyesight is impaired as a consequence of his death struggle. Shortly before he dies, however, he has a hallucination very similar to that of Miss Julie: he imagines that he sees "a pretty lady dressed in black."

A more obvious example of how the suggestion (or self-hypnosis) scene at the end of Miss Julie has inspired O'Neill is found in the ending of Diff'rent (1920). "Go now, while it is light—to the barn—and—," Jean whispers to Julie, and before the curtain falls we see her go *"firmly out through the door."* "Wait, Caleb, I'm going down to the barn," Emma Crosby whisperingly says in the closing speech of Diff'rent. She has just learned that Caleb, who has remained faithful to her for thirty years, has hanged himself in the barn after realizing that she has thrown herself away to a reckless good-for-nothing. As the curtain falls she *"moves like a sleepwalker toward the door in the rear"* on her way to the barn where she is to share Caleb's fate.[18]

An echo of the end of Miss Julie is also found in Before Breakfast (1916). In Strindberg's play we find the following stage direction: *"JEAN is seen in the right wing, sharpening his razor on a strop which he holds between his teeth and his left hand; he listens to the talk with a pleased mien and nods approval now and then."* In Before Breakfast, similarly, we see only the hand of Alfred Rowland, who is off stage in a room to the right, shaving: *"From the inner room comes the sound of a razor being stropped."* Finally, Alfred, the rich boy who had to marry a simple seamstress after he had made her pregnant, commits suicide with the help of the razor.

Like Jean, O'Neill's Brutus Jones of The Emperor Jones has worked his way up from a miserable existence. Jean dreams of buying himself a count's title in Rumania; Jones has already bought himself an emperor's title and all that goes with it.

As a head waiter and servant Jean has learned the manners of high society: "I have listened to the talk of better-class people, and from that I have learned most of all. . . . And I have heard a lot, too, when I was on the box of the carriage, or rowing the boat." From the nature of these conversations Jean has concluded that the upper classes are just as crude and vulgar as the lower ones. Jones has had the same possibility to listen to so-called better-class people, and he has arrived at an even more radical conclusion concerning the pillars of society: "For de little stealin' dey gits you in jail soon or late. For de big stealin' dey makes you Emperor and puts you in de Hall o' Fame when you croaks. (*Reminiscently*) If dey's one thing I learns in ten years on de Pullman ca's listenin' to de white quality talk, it's dat same fact."

When Jean plans the escape he does it with calculating exactness: "We'll be in Malmö at 6:30; in Hamburg at 8:40 tomorrow morning; in Frankfurt and Basel a day later. And to reach Como by way of the St. Gotthard it will take us—let me see—three days." Jones is even more foreseeing; his escape has been planned long in advance: "I'll be 'cross de plain to de edge of de forest by time dark comes. Once in de woods in de night, dey got a swell chance o' findin' dis baby! Dawn tomorrow I'll be out at de oder side and on de coast whar dat French gunboat is stayin'. She picks me up, takes me to Martinique when she go dar. . . ."

When Strindberg, in the foreword, describes his characters as "conglomerates, made up of past and present stages of civilization," he is touching on an idea that O'Neill has taken to heart in *The Emperor Jones*, where he lets Jones reexperience past stages of civilization, both those that belong to his own past and those that belong to the past of his race.

In *Miss Julie* Strindberg touches on the idea of a psychological family fate when he has Julie say that "now it is my mother's turn to revenge herself again, through me." This thought is expressed visually in *Mourning Becomes Electra*, where Lavinia in the third part has become a kind of reincarnation of the dead mother—a circumstance that Orin draws attention to when he tells her: "you're Mother."

There are, in fact, several resemblances between Julie and Lavinia. They are both of about the same age: Julie is twenty-five, Lavinia twenty-three. They both come from venerable families on their father's side and they have both been brought up in manor houses in the latter part of the nineteenth century. Julie has been brought up like a boy by her father, and Lavinia is also, when we first meet her, very boyish in appearance: she is flat-chested, keeps her hair *"pulled tightly back, as if to conceal its natural curliness,"* and moves in a stiff, military way—an illustration of how she has suppressed all femininity. In Part III she is completely changed; she now resembles the mother with her *"voluptuous figure"* and *"flowing animal grace."* Toward the very end, however, she returns to her wooden, Puritan, Mannon self. Even more clearly than Strindberg, O'Neill in this way illustrates his heroine's vacillation between her father and mother: Julie's self-characterization "half woman and half man" fits Lavinia.

In his "Working Notes" O'Neill points out that, unlike the Attic tragedians, he wishes to give his Electra (i.e., Lavinia) a tragic end "worthy of her character."[19] In *Miss Julie* he could find a figure who fulfilled the demands he made, a woman who, as Strindberg says in the foreword, "would take vengeance upon herself" and who "would be moved to it by that innate or acquired sense of honor which the upper classes inherit—whence?" The fact that she is the last member of her family makes the ending seem even more definite: it is not only an individual who dies, it is a whole social class and the evaluations that go with it.

The same could be said about Lavinia. She is, in an even more literal sense than Julie, the last member of her family. After all, Julie's father survives her, but no one survives Lavinia.[20] Like Julie, Lavinia punishes herself. The end of Strindberg's tragedy shows us how Julie with firm steps walks out through the door on her way to death. The end of O'Neill's trilogy shows us how Lavinia woodenly marches into the Mannon house, the Mannon "tomb," to bury herself alive in its eternal darkness. Both endings are truly worthy of the heroines of the plays.

Strindberg's amorous couple also has a counterpart in O'Neill's trilogy. Christine's affair with Adam Brant, this "son of a servant," as he is called, is a kind of mésalliance. Like Jean and Julie, they plan to escape. Their goal is the South Sea islands, which Adam describes in even more romantic terms than Jean bestows on the Italian lakes. In both cases we deal with a paradise lost and never regained.

As has often been pointed out, the earlier mentioned *Before Breakfast* is structurally modeled after Strindberg's *The Stronger*. In a letter O'Neill has himself characterized the play as "thoroughly Strindbergian."[21] *Before Breakfast* represents a more restricted and subjective variant of the Strindbergian monodrama, for by placing the mute character off stage, out of sight, O'Neill prevents us from getting a direct impression of Alfred. This does not mean that we see him through the eyes of his wife other than in a technical sense. Her evaluation is certainly not ours. Like Mrs. X, Mrs. Rowland has a tendency to ascribe to the person addressed feelings and motives that actually fit herself. In his monodrama *Hughie* (1941), O'Neill has created a worthier counterpart of *The Stronger* and one technically closer to Strindberg's little masterpiece, for Hughie, the almost mute night clerk, is visible throughout the play.

Strindberg's *Pariah* deals with the confrontation of two criminals. Whereas Mr. X has kept his crime hidden and consequently never been punished for it, Mr. Y has spent some time in an American prison. The two men and their struggle to dominate each other find their counterpart in the first scene of *The Emperor Jones*, where the white trader, Smithers, forms both a parallel and a contrast to the black emperor Jones.

SMITHERS: Well, blimey, I give yer a start, didn't I?—when no one else would. I wasn't afraid to 'ire you like the rest was—'count of the story about your breakin' jail back in the States.
JONES: No, you didn't have no s'cuse to look down on me fo' dat. You been in jail you'self more'n once.

SMITHERS: (*furiously*) It's a lie! (*Then trying to pass it off by an attempt at scorn*) Garn! Who told yer that fairy tale?
JONES: Dey's some tings I ain't got to be tole. I kin see 'em in folk's eyes.

Like Mr. X, Jones appears to be a psychological detective of almost superhuman stature; there is something impressive about both of them. But the cowardly Smithers, like Mr. Y, has the succumbing nature of a pariah.

With its circular composition, *The Emperor Jones* also bears a certain kinship to *To Damascus I*, often considered the first expressionistic drama. As such, Strindberg's play can be considered essentially one long dramatic monologue. This is literally true about the major part of *The Emperor Jones*, where the escaping black is the only speaker. As Clara Blackburn has pointed out, the characters who function as reminders of the Stranger's past guilt in *To Damascus I* correspond to the phantoms that Jones has to face in the jungle.[22]

Alternatively, the characters surrounding the Stranger in Strindberg's play can be seen as conflicting selves within the protagonist. As such, they resemble the two selves constituting the man John Loving in *Days without End* (1933). Thus, Doris Falk regards the Stranger, the Beggar, and the Doctor in *To Damascus I* as a conglomerate character comparable to John, "while the Tempter is the voice of rationality and experience—Loving. There is even an all-knowing 'Confessor,' comparable to Father Baird in *Days without End*."[23] In Act III John tells his "Confessor" about the end of the story he is working on. The hero, actually his alter ego, "realizes he can never believe in his lost faith again. He walks out of the church—without love forever now—but daring to face his eternal loss and hopelessness, to accept it as his fate and go on with life." In the last scene of the play we find John Loving in "an old church." Confronted with the symbol of Love, Loving is forced to surrender:

He slumps forward to the floor and rolls over on his back, dead, his head beneath the foot of the Cross, his arms outflung so that his body forms another cross. JOHN *rises from his knees and stands with arms stretched up and out, so that he, too, is like a cross. While this is happening the light of the dawn on the stained-glass windows swiftly rises to a brilliant intensity of crimson and green and gold, as if the sun had risen. The gray walls of the church, particularly the wall where the Cross is, and the face of the Christ shine with this radiance.*

In the first scene of *To Damascus I* we see "*a small Gothic church*," which The Lady enters. When she leaves it, "the sun comes out and lights up the stained-glass rose window over the portal." In the second scene, "By the sea," the three Golgotha crosses are evoked in the form of the masts of a wrecked ship. At the end of the play we are back by the little church. But this time The Stranger is prepared to enter it together with The Lady: *Das Ewig-Weibliche zieht uns hinan.* Just as in *Days without End* the hero returns to his old belief in a benevolent God. Or rather we might say that whereas Strindberg implies this and reserves a definite ending for the last part of his trilogy, O'Neill is rhetorically explicit when he has John and Loving in unison —as a sign of ultimate integration—express their *gloria in excelsis deo*: "Life laughs with God's love again!"

The Dance of Death, we have already noted, bears a definite thematic kinship to *Welded*. But it is a misconception to believe that O'Neill's play title should primarily be understood in a negative, so-called Strindbergian sense. In the draft version Michael draws attention to the positive, platonic meaning when he says: "Welded, not bound by a tie! We've realized the ideal, we conceived of our marriage."[24]

Barrett Clark has observed that Nina in *Strange Interlude* (1927) is a Strindbergian "beast of prey,"[25] and Clara Blackburn finds her reminiscent of Alice in *The Dance of Death* as a representative of "Woman engaged in the eternal war of the sexes."[26] Yet Alice, it seems to me, remains very much an individual and the war between the sexes can hardly be considered a central issue of O'Neill's play. The thought asides used in *Strange Interlude* and *Dynamo* (1928) represent a technique never adopted by Strindberg; yet they seem a logical consequence of the idea expressed in *The Pelican* that people talk just to hide their thoughts.

Much more convincing is Blackburn's comparison of *A Dream Play* to *The Hairy Ape* (1921).[27] In Strindberg's play Indra's Daughter descends to Earth to share the lot of mankind. Similarly, in *The Hairy Ape* Mildred Douglas, daughter of the President of the Steel Trust, dressed in white like an angel, descends from her first-class cabin to the dark, hot and murky stokehole, from "heaven" to "hell": Strindberg's metaphysical contrast has been translated into social opposition. But the social perspective is not altogether lacking in *A Dream Play*. Notably in the scene by the Mediterranean the antithesis between the rich and the poor is emphasized. Blackburn has interestingly demonstrated how closely O'Neill's forecastle and stokehole scenes resemble this part of *A Dream Play*; for example:

A Dream Play	*The Hairy Ape*
To the right a huge pile of coal and two wheelbarrows . . . two coalheavers, naked to the waist, their faces, hands,	*The stokehole . . . murky air laden with coal dust. . . . A line of men stripped to the waist. . . . One or two are*

and bodies blackened by coal dust, are seated on the wheelbarrows. Their expressions show intense despair. . . .

. . .

FIRST COALHEAVER. This is hell.

. . .

FIRST HEAVER. What have we done? We have been born of poor and perhaps not very good parents.

. . .

SECOND HEAVER. Yes, the unpunished hang out in the Casino up there and dine on eight courses with wine. . . .

. . .

FIRST HEAVER. And yet we are the foundations of society.

arranging the coal behind them. . . . The others can be dimly made out leaning on their shovels in relaxed attitudes of exhaustion.

. . .

LONG. This is 'ell. We lives in 'ell.

. . .

And who's ter blame, I arsks yer? We ain't. . . .

. . .

Hit's them's ter blame—the damned Capitalist clarss!

. . .

YANK. We run de whole woiks.

In the posthumously published, uncompleted *More Stately Mansions* (written 1939–41), finally, there is a counterpart of the enigmatic door of *A Dream Play*. Both doors are visualized on the stage—one as part of a theater corridor, the other of a summer house; both are related to childhood memories; both function as suspense-evoking elements. But whereas Strindberg refrains from commenting explicitly on the significance of the door and what is behind it—since the riddle of life is insoluble, O'Neill, whose concern here is psychological rather than metaphysical, provides a complicated, explicit (and sentimental) interpretation.

"Strindberg," it has been said, "was more than a literary kindred spirit to O'Neill; . . . he became in some ways a pattern for O'Neill's life."[28] And another commentator states; "In the history of the theater perhaps only Strindberg . . . told as much about himself," adding: "Perhaps the most important thing he [O'Neill] took from Strindberg was the courage to explore in his writings the darkest corners of his own character."[29]

In Strindberg's depiction of family relations O'Neill could often recognize his own situation. A few examples may illustrate this point. Strindberg's feeling that he was an unwanted child is frequently expressed in his work; in *The Father*, for example, the Captain complains: "My mother did not want me to come into the world because birth would give her pain." As *Long Day's Journey Into Night* (1941) testifies, O'Neill always felt that he was merely a substitute for the brother who died as an infant, in the play significantly named Eugene. After his mother's death O'Neill told a friend that as a semirecluse she had reminded him of the Mummy in *The Ghost Sonata*, the old lady who lives in a cupboard.[30] *The Dance of Death*, the Gelbs claim, "struck an overwhelmingly responsive chord" because it "put into words what . . . O'Neill had for a long time recognized as one of the motivating forces of his parents' relationship with each other and the resultant effects upon him."[31] O'Neill's remark to his second wife that "what he wanted in a woman was mistress, wife, mother, and valet"[32] has a Strindbergian flavor. In a letter to her, probably from the late twenties, he states: "if, at this so crucial moment of our union, we cannot keep petty hate from creeping into our souls like the condemned couples in a Strindberg play . . . then we are lost; . . ."[33]

But O'Neill's profound concern with Strindberg must also be sought in the Swedish playwright's power to deal with modern psychological problems in a dramatically convincing and arresting way. The Strindbergian method, George Jean Nathan once remarked, is "the intensification of the dramatic action, of which O'Neill was so fond. If he stems from anyone, he stems from Strindberg."[34] Strindberg's conglomerate characters must have seemed extremely truthful to O'Neill, the proof of which is to be found in his own *dramatis personae*. In the art of depicting people fighting themselves, torn between contrasting loyalties, vacillating between hatred and self-hatred, driven by impulses and desires that they cannot restrain or of which they are not aware—in all this Strindberg is, as O'Neill put it in 1924, "the most modern of moderns," "foreshadowing both in content and form the methods to come." And in this, Eugene O'Neill is clearly the Master's true disciple.

Notes

1. Horst Frenz, ed., *American Playwrights on Drama* (New York: Hill and Wang, 1965), pp. 41–42.
2. Sophus K. Winther, "Strindberg and O'Neill: A Study in Influence," *Scandinavian Studies*, 31 (1959), 103.
3. "Strindberg and Our Theatre," *Provincetown Playbill*, Season 1923–24, No. 1, p. 1.
4. Arthur and Barbara Gelb, *O'Neill* (New York, 1962), p. 585.
5. Crosswell Bowen, *The Curse of the Misbegotten: A Tale of the House of O'Neill* (New York: Harper, 1959), p. 52.
6. Barrett H. Clark, *Eugene O'Neill: The Man and His Plays* (New York: Dover, 1947), p. 21.
7. Clark, p. 25.
8. James Huneker, *Iconoclasts: A Book of Dramatists* (London: Scribners, 1905), p. 139.
9. Murray Hartman, "Strindberg and O'Neill: A Study in Influence," (unpublished dissertation, New York University, 1960), p. 17.
10. "Letter to M. T. Bacon," April 1940, quoted in Bacon's unpublished master's thesis, "The Influence of August Strindberg on Eugene O'Neill" (New York University, 1940), p. 12.
11. In the part of O'Neill's library now at C. W. Post College on Long Island, I have come across *Lucky Pehr* in V. S. Howard's translation from 1912. There are several other Strindberg editions in the O'Neill library at C. W. Post, including *Lucky Peter's Travels and Other Plays* (London, 1930), dated "Le Plessis '30."
12. Agnes Boulton, *Part of a Long Story* (New York: Doubleday, 1958), p. 76.
13. Karl Ragnar Gierow, *Introduktioner till O'Neills dramatik* (Stockholm: Bonniers, 1958), p. 10.
14. Karl Ragnar Gierow, "Ett teaterprogram," *Svenska dagbladet*, 15 September 1958.
15. George Jean Nathan, *The American Mercury*, May 1924. Quoted from the reprint in Alan Downer, *American Drama and Its Critics* (Chicago: University of Chicago Press, 1965), p. 81.
16. Eugene O'Neill, "Working Notes and Extracts from a Fragmentary Diary" for *Mourning Becomes Electra*, first working note, Spring 1926.
17. The impact of this drama on O'Neill's work has earlier been discussed in E. Törnqvist's "Fröken Julie och O'Neill," *Meddelanden från Strindbergssällskapet*, May 1969, pp. 5–16.
18. Cf. Doris Alexander, *The Tempering of Eugene O'Neill* (New York: Harcourt, Brace, and World, 1962), p. 183. The combination of suggestion and suicide appears in several O'Neill plays. Cf., for instance, Brutus Jones in *The Emperor Jones*, who just before he dies—a symbolic suicide—moves with *"a strange deliberation like a sleepwalker or one in a trance,"* and Pompeia in *Lazarus Laughed* (1926), who *"like a sleep-walker"* approaches the fire that is to burn her body to ashes.
19. Frenz, p. 3.
20. Autobiographical circumstances have undoubtedly also played a part here. When O'Neill composed his trilogy he was, as he himself points out in a letter, "the only

O'Neill of our branch left" (to Mary Clark, 28 May 1924, in the O'Neill Collection at the Yale University Library).

21. Bacon, p. 12.
22. Clara Blackburn, "Continental Influences on Eugene O'Neill's Expressionistic Drama," *American Literature*, 13 (May 1941), 115–16.
23. Doris Falk, *Eugene O'Neill and the Tragic Tension: An Interpretive Study of the Plays* (New Brunswick: Rutgers University Press, 1965), p. 153.
24. The longhand draft of *Welded* belongs to the O'Neill Collection of Princeton University Library.
25. Clark, p. 115.
26. Blackburn, p. 128.
27. Ibid., pp. 119ff.
28. Gelb, p. 234.
29. Louis Sheaffer, *O'Neill: Son and Playwright* (Boston: Little, Brown, and Co., 1968), pp. 79, 254.
30. Ibid., p. 317.
31. Gelb, p. 233.
32. Boulton, p. 63.
33. The letter is to be found in the O'Neill Collection of Harvard University Library.
34. Gelb, p. 731.

III
Bibliography of the Scholarship of Professor Walter Johnson, 1933–1979

Compiled by Raymond Jarvi

BOOKS AND MONOGRAPHS

James Thomson's Influence on Swedish Literature in the Eighteenth Century. Urbana: University of Illinois Press, 1936. Reprint. Folcroft, Pa.: Folcroft Library Editions, 1973.

Beginning Swedish. Preliminary ed. Minneapolis: Burgess Publishing Company, 1936. First ed. Rock Island: Augustana Book Concern, 1939. Rev. ed., 1952. Rev. ed. Rock Island: Augustana Press, 1961.

Continuing Swedish. Minneapolis: Burgess Publishing Company, 1938.

A Handbook of English (with Charles W. Roberts and Jesse W. Harris). New York: Oxford University Press, 1944.

Strindberg and the Historical Drama. Seattle: University of Washington Press, 1963.

Four Plays by Hjalmar Bergman (ed.). Seattle: University of Washington Press, and New York: American-Scandinavian Foundation, 1968.

August Strindberg, Boston: Twayne Publishers, 1976.

THE WASHINGTON STRINDBERG
(TRANSLATIONS AND INTRODUCTIONS)

Queen Christina, Charles XII, Gustav III. Seattle: University of Washington Press, and New York: American-Scandinavian Foundation, 1955.

The Last of the Knights, The Regent, Earl Birger of Bjälbo. Seattle: University of Washington Press, 1956.

Gustav Adolf. Seattle: University of Washington Press, and New York: American-Scandinavian Foundation, 1957.

The Vasa Trilogy: Master Olof, Gustav Vasa, Erik XIV. Seattle: University of Washington Press, 1959.

The Saga of the Folkungs, Engelbrekt. Seattle: University of Washington Press, 1959.

Open Letters to the Intimate Theater. Seattle: University of Washington Press, 1966.

Pre-Inferno Plays: The Father, Lady Julie, Creditors, The Stronger, The Bond. Seattle: University of Washington Press, 1970. Reprint. New York: The Norton Library, 1976.

A Dream Play and Four Chamber Plays: Stormy Weather, The House That Burned, The Ghost Sonata, The Pelican. Seattle: University of Washington Press, 1973. Reprint. New York: The Norton Library, 1975.

Dramas of Testimony: The Dance of Death I and II, Advent, Easter, There Are Crimes and Crimes. Seattle: University of Washington Press, 1975.

Plays of Confession and Therapy: To Damascus, I; To Damascus, II; To Damascus, III. Seattle: University of Washington Press, 1979.

ARTICLES

"A Swedish Imitator of Thomson." *Scandinavian Studies and Notes,* 12:8 (1933), pp. 113–27.

"Encouraging Freshmen to Read." *College and Research Libraries,* 11 (1941), pp. 124–26.

"American Loanwords in American Swedish." *Scandinavian Studies Presented to George T. Flom by Colleagues and Friends,* "Illinois Studies in Language and Literature," 29. Urbana: University of Illinois Press, 1942, pp. 79–91.

"High School English." *IEB,* 30 (1942), 1–12.

Webster's Biographical Dictionary (consultant for Swedish). Springfield, Mass.: The Merriam Company, 1943.

"Errors Most Frequently Checked" (co-author). *IEB,* 31 (1943), 1–15.

"Skriften om Paradis and Milton." *JEGP,* 44 (1945), pp. 163–69.

"The University of Illinois Experimental Writing Clinic: A Report and a Plan." *IEB,* 33 (1946), 9–13.

"Fröding and the Dramatic Monologue." *SS,* 24 (1952), 141–48.

"Moberg's Emigrants and the Naturalistic Tradition." *SS,* 25 (1953), 134–46.

"Strindberg's Gustav Adolf and Lessing." *SS,* 28 (1956), 1–8.

"Theater in Stockholm." *MD,* 1 (1958), 125–29.

"A Theater That Is National." *MD,* 1 (1958), 192–95.

"Fifty Years: 1911–1960." *SS,* 32 (1960), 1–6.

"Strindberg and the Danse Macabre." *MD,* 3 (1960), 8–15. Reprint. *Strindberg: A Collection of Critical Essays.* Englewood Cliffs, N.J.: Prentice-Hall, 1971, pp. 117–24.

"Creditors Re-examined." *MD,* 5 (1962), 281–90.

"Gustav Adolf Revised." *Scandinavian Studies: Essays Presented to Dr. Henry Goddard Leach on the Occasion of His Eighty-fifth Birthday.* Seattle: University of Washington Press, and New York: American-Scandinavian Foundation, 1965, pp. 236–46.

"Strindberg and the Swedes: Past and Present." *Essays on Strindberg*. Stockholm: The Strindberg Society, 1966, pp. 75–86.
"Mobergs utvandrarsvit och den naturalistiska traditionen." *Emigrationer: En bok till Vilhelm Moberg 20.8.1968*. Stockholm: Bonniers, 1968, pp. 230–40.
"The Recording of American Swedish." *Studies in Scandinavian-American Interrelations. Dedicated to Einar Haugen,"* "Americana Norvegica," III. Oslo: Universitetsforlaget, 1971, pp. 64–73.
"A Dream Play: Plans and Fulfillment," *Scan*, 10:2 (1971), pp. 103–111.
"Strindberg and the American University Audience." *Strindberg and Modern Theatre*. Stockholm: The Strindberg Society, 1975, pp. 56–72.

BIBLIOGRAPHIES

"The Romantic Movement: A Selective and Critical Bibliography for the Year 1938" (contr.). *JELH*, 6:1 (1939), pp. 1–34.
"The Romantic Movement: A Selective and Critical Bibliography for the Year 1939" (contr.). *JELH*, 7:1 (1940), pp. 1–35.
"The Romantic Movement: A Selective and Critical Bibliography for the Year 1940" (contr.), *JELH*, 8:1 (1941), pp. 1–40.
"The Romantic Movement: A Selective and Critical Bibliography for the Year 1941" (contr.). *JELH*, 9:1 (1942), pp. 1–35.
"The Romantic Movement: A Selective and Critical Bibliography for the Year 1943" (contr.) *JELH*, 11:1 (1944), pp. 1–37.
"American Scandinavian Bibliography for 1947" (ed.). *SS*, 20 (1948), 229–38.
"American Scandinavian Bibliography for 1948" (ed.). *SS*, 21 (1949), 101–119.
"American Scandinavian Bibliography for 1949" (ed.). *SS*, 22 (1950), 57–77.
"American Scandinavian Bibliography for 1950" (ed.). *SS*, 23 (1951), 73–96.
"American Scandinavian Bibliography for 1951" (ed.). *SS*, 24 (1952), 59–79.
"American Scandinavian Bibliography for 1952" (ed.). *SS*, 25 (1953), 52–74.
"American Scandinavian Bibliography for 1953" (ed.). *SS*, 26 (1954), 70–94.
"American Scandinavian Bibliography for 1954" (ed.). *SS*, 27 (1955), 70–99.
"American Scandinavian Bibliography for 1955" (ed.). *SS*, 28 (1956), 48–80.
"American Scandinavian Bibliography for 1956" (ed.). *SS*, 29 (1957), 59–93.
"American Scandinavian Bibliography for 1957" (ed.). *SS*, 30 (1958), 53–84.
"American Scandinavian Bibliography for 1958" (ed.). *SS*, 31 (1959), 73–93.
"American Scandinavian Bibliography for 1959" (ed.). *SS*, 32 (1960), 89–112.
"American Scandinavian Bibliography for 1960" (ed.). *SS*, 33 (1961), 82–105.
"American Scandinavian Bibliography for 1961" (ed.). *SS*, 34 (1962), 120–38.
"American Scandinavian Bibliography for 1962" (ed.). *SS*, 35 (1963), 132–56.
"American Scandinavian Bibliography for 1963" (ed.). *SS*, 36 (1964), 127–51.
"American Scandinavian Bibliography for 1964" (ed.). *SS*, 37 (1965), 168–92.
"American Scandinavian Bibliography for 1965" (ed.). *SS*, 38 (1966), 131–54.
"American Scandinavian Bibliography for 1966" (ed.). *SS*, 39 (1967), 155–81.
"American Scandinavian Bibliography for 1967" (contr.). *SS*, 40 (1968), 133–58.
"American Scandinavian Bibliography for 1968" (contr.). *SS*, 41 (1969), 160–97.

REVIEWS

G. A. Campbell, "Strindberg." *JEGP*, 34 (1935), 288–89.
Einar Haugen, "Norwegian Word Studies." *JEGP*, 41 (1942), 542–43.
Alrik Gustafson (ed.), "Scandinavian Plays of the Twentieth Century." *JEGP*, 42 (1943), 334–36.
"Webster's Dictionary of Synonyms." *IEB*, 32:1 (1944), pp. 10–12.
"Anthology of Norwegian Lyrics," "Icelandic Poems and Stories," "The Vatndaler's Saga." *PQ*, 24 (1945), 286–87.
Stefán Einarsson, "Icelandic Grammar." *PQ*, 24 (1945), 381–83.
Martin Söderbäck, "Elementary Spoken Swedish," "Advanced Spoken Swedish," *SS*, 20 (1948), 53–54.
Andrew Hilen, "Longfellow and Scandinavia: A Study of the Poet's Relationship with the Northern Languages and Literature." *SS*, 20 (1948), 102–105.
"The Will to Succeed: Stories of Swedish Pioneers." *SS*, 21 (1949), 56–58.
Torsten Eklund (ed.), "August Strindbergs brev, I; 1858–1876." *SS*, 21 (1949), 128–30.
Bergliot Ibsen, "De tre: Erindringer om Henrik Ibsen, Suzannah Ibsen, Sigurd Ibsen." *SS*, 21 (1949), 159–61.
Aasta Stene, "English Loanwords in Modern Norwegian." *JEGP*, 49 (1950), 135–36.
Martin Lamm, "Det moderna dramat." *SS*, 22 (1950), 23–24.
Elizabeth Sprigge, "The Strange Life of August Strindberg." *SS*, 22 (1950), 27–28.
Gunnar Ollén, "Strindbergs dramatik: En handbok." *SS*, 22 (1950), 28–30.
"Swedish Songs and Ballads." *SS*, 22 (1950), 191.
Stig Hellsten, "Kyrklig och radikal äktenskapsuppfattning i striden kring C. J. L. Almqvists Det går an." *SS*, 23 (1951), 200–02.
Vilhelm Moberg. "The Emigrants," Gustaf Lannestock (trans.). *SS*, 24 (1952), 23–25.
"Nobel: The Man and His Prizes." *SS*, 24 (1952), 86–87.
G. E. Kidder Smith, "Sweden Builds: Its Modern Architecture and Land Policy, Background, Development, and Contribution." *SS*, 24 (1952), 90–91.
Charlton Laird (ed.), "The World Through Literature." *SS*, 24 (1952), 131–33.
Adolph Burnett Benson, "American-Scandinavian Studies." *SS*, 24 (1952), 175–77.
Bergliot Ibsen, "The Three Ibsens: Memories of Henrik Ibsen, Suzannah Ibsen and Sigurd Ibsen," Gerik Schjelderup (trans.). J. P. Jacobsen, "Marie Grubbe," Hanna Astrup Larsen (trans.). *SS*, 25 (1953), 80–82.
Martin Lamm, "Modern Drama," Karin Elliott (trans.). *SS*, 26 (1954), 98–99.
Einar Haugen, "The Norwegian Language in America: A Study in Bilingual Behavior." *SS*, 26 (1954), 186–90.
Gustaf af Geijerstam, "Mina pojkar," Arthur Wald (ed.). *SS*, 27 (1955), 41.
Signe Rooth, "Seeress of the Northland: Fredrika Bremer's American Journey, 1849–1851." *SS*, 28 (1956), 31–32.

Harold H. Borland, "Nietzsche's Influence on Swedish Literature." *MLQ*, 19 (1959), 355-56.
Arvid Paulson (trans.), "Letters of Strindberg to Harriet Bosse." *SPHQ*, 10 (1959), 147-48.
Stellan Ahlström (ed.), "Ögonvittnen: August Strindberg: Ungdom och mannaår." *SS*, 32 (1960), 171-72.
"Learn Swedish: Swedish Reader for Beginners." *SS*, 32 (1960), 229.
Adolph Burnett Benson, "Farm, Forge, and Philosophy: From a Swedish Immigrant's Life in America." *SS*, 33 (1961), 260.
"American Swedish Handbook, VI." *SS*, 34 (1962), 149.
Børge Gedsø Madsen, "Strindberg's Naturalistic Theatre: Its Relationship to French Naturalism." *SS*, 35 (1963), 86-87.
Alrik Gustafson, "Den svenska litteraturens historia," Nils Holmberg (trans.). *MP*, 61 (1963), 43-45.
Franklin Scott, "Wertmuller: Artist and Immigrant Farmer." *SPHQ*, 15 (1964), 88-89.
Lilly Lorenzen, "Of Swedish Ways." *SS*, 37 (1965), 207.
Ingvar Gullberg, "Svensk-engelsk fackordbok för näringsliv, förvaltning, undervisning och forskning." *SS*, 37 (1965), 285-86.
Maurice Valency, "The Flower and the Castle: An Introduction to Modern Drama." *SS*, 37 (1965), 384-86.
Carl Reinhold Smedmark (ed.), "Strindbergs dramer, I, II, III." *SS*, 38 (1966), 76-77.
Lennart Josephson, "Strindbergs drama Fröken Julie." *SS*, 38 (1966), 354-55.
Paul Britten Austin, "The Life and Songs of Carl Michael Bellman: Genius of the Swedish Rococo." *SS*, 40 (1968), 338-40.
Erland Lagerroth, "Svensk berättarkonst." *Scan*, 8 (1969), 145-47.
Bure Holmbäck, "Det lekfulla allvaret: Studier över erotiska och polemiska motiv i Hjalmar Söderbergs roman Den allvarsamma leken mot bakgrund av hans tidigare författarskap," *SS*, 42 (1970), 221-22.
Albin Widen, "Amandus Johnson, svenskamerikan: En levnadsteckning." *SS*, 42 (1970), 449-50.
James W. McFarlane (ed.), "The Oxford Ibsen, I." *MD*, 14 (1971), 360-61.
Maria Bergom-Larsson, "Diktarens demaskering: En monografi över Hjalmar Bergmans roman Herr von Hancken," Karin Petherick, "Stilimitation i tre av Hjalmar Bergmans romaner: En undersökning av den roll pastisch, parodi och citat spelar i Knutmässo marknad, En döds memoarer och Herr von Hancken," *Scan*, 10:1 (1971), 55-57.
Henry Olsson, "Vinlövsranka och hagtornkrans: En bok om Fröding." *SS*, 43 (1971), 302-304.
Torsten Eklund (ed.), "August Strindbergs brev, XII; december 1896-augusti 1898." *SS*, 43 (1971), 453-55.
Martin Lamm, "August Strindberg," Harry G. Carlson (trans.). *JEGP*, 71 (1972), 104-106.
Peter Cassirer, "Deskriptiv stilistik: En begrepps-och metoddiskussion," "Stilen i Hjalmar Söderbergs Historietter." *SS*, 44 (1972), 148-50.

Anthony Swerling, "In Quest of Strindberg." *MD*, 15 (1972), 334.
Ulf Boethius, "Strindberg och kvinnofrågan till och med Giftas I." *SS*, 44 (1972), 571-72.
Ulf Beijbom, "Swedes in Chicago: A Demographic and Social Study of the 1846-1880 Immigration." *SS*, 45 (1973), 159-60.
Göran Stockenström, "Ismael i öknen: Strindberg som mystiker." *SS*, 45 (1973), 271-73.
Carl L. Anderson, "Poe in Northlight: The Scandinavian Response to His Life and Work." *SS*, 45 (1973), 395-97.
Gunnar Brandell, "Strindberg in Inferno," Barry Jacobs (trans.). *SS*, 47 (1975), 261-63.
Gunnar Eidevall, "Vilhelm Mobergs emigrantepos: Studier i verkets tillkomsthistoria, dokumentära bakgrund och konstnärliga gestaltning." *Scan*, 14:1 (1975), pp. 65-66.
Arvid Ernvik, "Att resa i Värmland: *SPHQ*, 26 (1975), 274-76.
George C. Schoolfield (trans.), "Swedo-Finnish Short Stories." *SS*, 47 (1975), 520-21.
Emory Linquist, "An Immigrant's American Odyssey: A Biography of Ernst Skarstedt." *PNQ*, 67 (1976), 179-80.
Tell G. Dahllöf, "I utvandrarnas spår." *SPHQ*, 27 (1976), 76-77.
Emory Lindquist, "Bethany in Kansas." *SPHQ*, 27 (1976), 139-40.
Sven G. Johansson, "Historical Review of the Vasa Order of America, 1897-1971." *SPHQ*, 27 (1976), 290-91.
H. Arnold Barton (ed.), "Letters from the Promised Land." *PNQ*, 68 (1977), 57-58.
Marc Pachter (ed.), "Abroad in America: Visitors to the New Nation, 1776-1914." *SPHQ*, 28 (1977), 73-75.
Alvin Holmes, "Swedish Homesteads in Idaho on the Minidoka Irrigation Project." *SPHQ*, 28 (1977), 137-38.
Gunnar Eidevall, "Berättaren Vilhelm Moberg." *SPHQ*, 28 (1977), 220-22.
"An Early Look at Chisago County." Holger O. Warner, "District 33: A Complete History of Chisago County School District 33, Fish Lake Township, Minnesota from 1874 to 1976," *SPHQ*, 28 (1977), 298-300.
Gustaf Lannestock, "Vilhelm Moberg i Amerika." *SPHQ*, 29 (1978), 148-49.
Ragna Ahlbäck *et al.*, "Amerika trunken: Emigranter berätta om sig själva." *SPHQ*, 29 (1978), 222-23.
Arvid Ernvik (ed.), "Beskrivning över Värmland." *SPHQ*, 29 (1978), 296-97.
Gösta Lext, "Studier rörande svensk emigration till Nordamerika." *SPHQ*, 30 (1979), 74-75.
Magnus von Platen, "Den unge Vilhelm Moberg: En levnadsteckning." *SPHQ*, 30 (1979), 151-52.

TRANSLATIONS

Lars Ahlin's "Polluted Zone," in *The Literary Review* 9 (1965), 221–36. Reprinted in *Stories from The Literary Review*, 1969, pp. 248–69.

Hjalmar Bergman's *Mr. Sleeman Is Coming*, in *Four Plays of Hjalmar Bergman*. Seattle: University of Washington Press, and New York: American-Scandinavian Foundation, 1968, pp. 273–98.

August Strindberg's "Psychic Murder," in *The Drama Review*, 13 (1968), 113–18.

Abbreviations of Periodicals

IEB	*Illinois English Bulletin*
JEGP	*Journal of English and Germanic Philology*
JELH	*Journal of English Literary History*
MD	*Modern Drama*
MLQ	*Modern Language Quarterly*
MP	*Modern Philology*
PNQ	*Pacific Northwest Quarterly*
PQ	*Philological Quarterly*
SS	*Scandinavian Studies*
Scan	*Scandinavica*
SPHQ	*Swedish Pioneer Historical Quarterly*

Index of Titles and Names

This index is organized according to Library of Congress alphabetization and not that of the national languages. All works except those by Strindberg are cited in the original but are cross-referenced in English if they have been translated. An exception are those works whose original titles are so close to their English translations that an English rendering is unnecessary (e.g., *Legionärerna, The Legionnaires*). Strindberg's works, however, including those which have not been translated, are all cross-referenced. The two bibliographies in this volume are not indexed, for such material would be overwhelmingly repetitious.

A
Abell, Kjeld, 159
Aeschylus, 245, 246, 249, 281
Ahlin, Lars, 71
Albee, Edward, 232, 256
Almqvist, C. J. L. A., 7, 71
Andersson, Nils, 31
Artaud, Antonin, 232
Asch, Max, 103
Atterbom, P. D. A., 7, 14

B
Balzac, Honoré de, 7, 10–12, 16, 122, 246, 248
   Louis Lambert, 12, 16
   Séraphita, 11–12, 16, 246, 248
Bang, Herman, 153, 155
   Haabløse Slægter, 153
Baudelaire, C. P., 7, 22
Beethoven, Ludwig van, 131, 207, 211
Bergh, Richard, 95, 245
Bergman, Ingmar, 49–64, 71
   Cries and Whispers. See *Viskningar och rop*
   Nattvardsgästerna, 49–58
   Persona, 55, 61
   Såsom genom en spegel, 49–58
   The Seventh Seal. See *Det sjunde inseglet*
   The Silence. See *Tystnaden*
   Det sjunde inseglet, 61
   Smultronstället, 61
   Through a Glass Darkly. See *Såsom genom en spegel*
   Tystnaden, 49–58
   Viskningar och rop, 61
   Winter Light. See *Nattvardsgästerna*

Bibalo, Antonio, 204
Bizet, A. C., 206
Björling, Gunnar, 184
Bjørnson, Bjørnstjerne, 121–22, 128, 166–67, 170, 172
   En Hanske, 166–67, 170
Blake, William, 112
Blawatzki, Mme., 5
Bojer, Johan, 123
Bosse, Harriet, 40, 157, 247–49, 251–52
Brandes, Edvard, 153, 155–57, 165–82
Brandes, Georg, 107, 122–23, 128, 155, 157, 165–67, 169–72, 177–79, 206
Branner, H. C., 161
Brecht, Bertolt, 190, 234
Büchner, Georg, 230

C
Calderón de la Barca, Pedro, 219
Camus, Albert, 71
Cappelen, Peder W., 137–50
   Sverre. Berget og Ordet, 137–50
Chekhov, Anton, 80–81
Christensen, Inger, 161
Collet, Camilla, 170

D
Dagerman, Stig, 65, 71
Dahl, Christian, 100
Dahlgren, C. F., 39, 45
Dante, 87
Dauthendey, Max, 103
David, Marie, 72
Debussy, C. A., 203
Dehmel, Richard, 103
Delius, Frederick, 111
Diktonius, Elmer, 183–99

Index

Gräs och granit, 186
Hårda sånger, 191
Jordisk ömhet, 183, 187
Kuokkala suite, 183
Mull och moln, 186
Stark men mörk, 191
Taggiga lågor, 183, 191
Dostoevsky, Fyodor, 132
Drachmann, Holger, 103, 166, 172
Dürrenmatt, Friedrich, 226–44
   Dramaturgie der Komödie, 228
   Die Ehe des Herrn Mississippi, 229
   Frank der Fünfte, 230
   König Johann, 230–31
   Der Meteor, 229
   Play Strindberg, 226–44
   Urfaust, 230
Dumas, *père et fils*, 175

E
Edelfelt, Albert, 124–25
Ekelöf, Gunnar, 184–85
Ekelund, Vilhelm, 7
Emerson, Ralph Waldo, 7, 31
Enckell, Raabe, 184–86
Enquist, Per Olov, 65–78
   Chez Nous, 67
   Färdvägen, 68–69
   Hess, 67, 69
   Kristallögat, 68
   Legionärerna, 67, 69
   Magnetisörens femte vinter, 67, 69
   Mannen på trottoaren, 76
   Musikanternas uttåg, 71, 76
   Sekonden, 67, 70
   Tribadernas natt, 65, 67, 69–76
Essen, Siri von, 72, 101, 156, 174, 206

F
Falck, August, 157, 159
Flaubert, Gustave, 122
Fröding, Gustaf, 38, 41, 42

G
Gallén-Kallela, Axel, 103
Garborg, Arne, 121, 170
Goethe, J. W., 7, 31
Grönvall, Sven, 184–85
Gyllensten, Lars, 7, 71

H
Händel, G. F., 206
Hamsun, Knut, 103, 121–36, 175–77
   "America," 126, 130–31
   Fra det moderne Amerikas Aandsliv, 123, 126
   "Fra det ubevidste sjæleliv," 129
   Growth of the Soil. See *Markens Grøde*
   Hunger. See *Sult*
   Konerne ved Vandposten, 132
   Markens Grøde, 131
   Mysterier, 103, 123
   Ny Jord, 123
   On Overgrown Paths. See *Paa gjengrodde Stier*
   Paa gjengrodde Stier, 132
   Pan, 130
   Redaktør Lynge, 123
   Shallow Soil. See *Ny Jord*
   Sult, 103, 123, 155
   En Vandrer spiller med Sordin, 131
   The Women at the Pump. See *Konerne ved Vandposten*
Hansson, Lars, 83
Hansson, Ola, 101, 157, 175–78
Hartleben, Otto Erich, 103
Hartmann, Eduard von, 127
Hedlund, Torsten, 12–14
Heiberg, Gunnar, 103
Heidenstam, Verner von, 38, 40–43
Hemingway, Ernest, 68, 71
Herrlin, Axel, 14, 15, 20
Hoffman, Kai, 157
Hofmannsthal, Hugo von, 211–25
   Die Frau ohne Schatten, 211–25
   Jedermann, 221
   Das Salzburger große Welttheater, 221
   Der Turm, 219
Holberg, Ludvig, 159, 162

I
Ibsen, Henrik, 79–81, 85–87, 89, 100, 113, 121–22, 161, 168, 170, 172, 175, 278
   A Doll's House. See *Et dukkehjem*
   Et dukkehjem, 170
   An Enemy of the People. See *En folkefiende*
   En folkefiende, 100
   Fruen fra havet, 122, 175
   Gengangere, 80–81, 85–87, 89, 155
   Ghosts. See *Gengangere*
   The Lady from the Sea. See *Fruen fra havet*
   Peer Gynt, 113
Inge, William, 256

J
Jacobsen, J. P., 165, 166
Jørgensen, Johannes, 157
Johnson, Eyvind, 185–86
Jonsson, Thorsten, 71
Juell, Dagny, 107–10, 112

K
Kant, Immanuel, 10
Karlfeldt, Erik Axel, 38–48
    Fridolins lustgård, 38, 46
    Fridolins visor, 38
Kielland, Alexander, 122, 165–66, 172
Klemming, Gustaf Edvard, 3, 9, 10, 14
Klinger, Max, 105
Krohg, Christian, 92–93, 103

L
Lagerkvist, Pär, 7, 71
Lagerlöf, Selma, 37
Lange, Sven, 124–25
Larsen, Nathalia, 155–56
Larsson, Carl, 93, 115
Levertin, Oscar, 38, 40–42
Lidforss, Bengt, 107–8, 110
Lie, Jonas, 122, 124–25, 127, 166
Lindegren, Erik, 184–85
Linné, Carl von, 3–4
    Nemesis Divina, 4
Luther, Martin, 5

M
Maeterlinck, Maurice, 31, 203, 245–46, 249
    La Princesse Maleine, 249
Mann, Thomas, 68, 132
Mascagni, Pietro, 206–7
Michaelis, Sophus, 157
Mill, John Stuart, 128
Mozart, W. A., 204, 206
Munch, Edvard, 92–120, 131
    Absurdity. See Galematias
    Aften på Karl Johansgate, 93, 99, 100
    Aftenstemning, 97, 104
    Dagen derpå, 98, 104, 109
    The Dance of Life. See Livsdansen
    The Day Thereafter. See Dagen derpå
    Death. See Døden
    Death and the Girl. See Døden og pike
    Death in the Sickroom. See Døden i sykeværelset
    The Death of Marat. See Marats død
    Despair. See Fortvivelse
    Døden, 105
    Døden i sykeværelset, 105
    Døden og piken, 105, 115
    Early Morning. See På morgenkvisten
    Erotisch, 105
    Evening at Karl Johansgate. See Aften på Karl Johansgate
    Evening Mood. See Aftenstemning
    Feber, 105
    Fever. See Feber
    Fortvivelse, 97
    Galematias, 99
    The Hands. See Hendene
    Hendene, 109
    Jealousy. See Sjalusi
    The Kiss. See Kysset
    Kvinnen i tre stadier, 115
    Kysset, 104
    Liebe und Schmerz, 105
    Livsdansen, 115
    Love and Pain. See Liebe und Schmerz
    Løsrivelse, 112
    Madonna, 109
    Marats død, 115
    Melankoli, 93
    På morgenkvisten, 92
    Pubertet, 98, 104, 106, 109
    The Rising Sun. See Soloppgang
    Separation. See Løsrivelse
    The Shriek. See Skriket
    Sick Girl. See Syk pike
    Sjalusi, 108, 112, 115
    Skriket, 106
    Soloppgang, 115
    Springtime. See Vår
    Syk pike, 93, 103–4
    Vår, 93, 103–4
    The Vampire. See Vampyren
    Vampyren, 105, 112
    Woman in Three Stages. See Kvinnen i tre stadier
Munk, Kaj, 159

N
Nietzsche, Friedrich, 11, 128, 131–32, 178, 206, 279
Nilsen, Jappe, 108
Nordström, Karl, 95
Normann, Adelsteen, 98

O
Oehlenschläger, Adam, 171
Østerlind, Allan, 124
O'Neill, Eugene, 232, 256, 277–91
    All God's Chillun Got Wings, 280
    Before Breakfast, 283, 285
    Beyond the Horizon, 280
    Bound East for Cardiff, 282
    Days without End, 286–87
    Diff'rent, 283
    Dynamo, 287
    The Emperor Jones, 280, 283–84, 285–86
    The Hairy Ape, 287
    Hughie, 285
    Long Day's Journey into Night, 288
    A Moon for the Misbegotten, 281
    More Stately Mansions, 288

Index

Mourning Becomes Electra, 281, 284
Recklessness, 281
Strange Interlude, 287
Welded, 280, 287
A Wife for a Life, 278
Origen, 12–13

P
Paul, Adolf 101–2, 123
Péladan, Sâr, 245–55
   L'Initiation sentimentale, 245
   Le Prince du Byzance, 247–49
   La Prométhéide, 249–52
Pontoppidan, Henrik, 153, 155, 170, 173
Prokofiev, Sergei, 203
Przybyszewski, Stanislaus, 102, 105, 108, 110, 112–13
Pythagoras, 12–13

R
Raabe, Wilhelm, 184
Rangström, Ture, 203, 208
Rorem, Ned, 203
Rousseau, Jean-Jacques, 71, 130
Runeberg, J. L., 186
Rydberg, Viktor, 30

S
Sartre, Jean-Paul, 71
Schelling, F. W. J. von, 7
Schering, Emil, 114, 221, 279
Schleich, Carl Ludwig, 103
Schlittgen, Hermann, 103, 106
Schopenhauer, Arthur, 13, 138
Segelcke, Severin, 103
Shakespeare, William, 159, 162, 230–31
Snoilsky, Carl, 43, 152
Södergran, Edith, 184
Soya, 159
Strauss, Richard, 203, 211–12
Stravinsky, Igor, 56
Strindberg, August
  Paintings, 96–97
  Plays
    Bandet, 157, 161, 178, 206–7
    The Bond. See *Bandet*
    Brända tomten, 49–58, 161
    Brott och brott, 278
    The Burned House. See *Brända tomten*
    Carl XII, 3, 28, 31
    Charles XII. See *Carl XII*
    Comrades. See *Kamraterna*
    Creditors. See *Fordringsägare*
    Crimes and Crimes. See *Brott och brott*
    The Crown Bride. See *Kronbruden*
    The Dance of Death. See *Dödsdansen*
    Debet och kredit, 178
    Debit and Credit. See *Debet och kredit*
    Dödsdansen, 87–88, 90, 158, 226–44, 257, 278–79, 287, 289
    A Dream Play. See *Ett drömspel*
    Ett drömspel, 28, 54, 84, 89, 115, 159–61, 203–4, 207–8, 211–25, 246, 251, 278–79, 287–88
    The Dutchman. See *Holländaren*
    Easter. See *Påsk*
    Erik XIV, 156, 161
    Facing Death. See *Inför döden*
    Fadren, 71, 90, 93, 95, 153, 157, 159, 171, 173–74, 176, 205, 231, 257, 280–81, 288
    The Father. See *Fadren*
    The First Warning. See *Första varningen*
    Första varningen, 178
    Folkungasagan, 45–46, 156
    Fordringsägare, 173–77, 221, 257
    Fröken Julie, 66, 71, 79, 81–82, 87, 93, 95, 101, 121–22, 126–27, 129, 154–55, 159–61, 167, 173–74, 176–77, 203–4, 228, 257, 279, 281–85
    The Ghost Sonata. See *Spöksonaten*
    Gillets hemlighet, 152, 155, 178
    The Great Highway. See *Stora landsvägen*
    Gustav III, 158, 161
    Gustav Adolf, 31
    Gustav Vasa, 156
    Herr Bengts hustru, 155, 178
    Holländaren, 53
    Inför döden, 178
    Kamraterna, 170–74, 177, 280
    Kristina, 161, 246, 251
    Kronbruden, 203, 208
    Leka med elden, 160, 161, 178
    Lucky Per's Journey. See *Lycko-Pers resa*
    Lycko-Pers resa, 22, 153, 157, 221
    Mäster Olof, 73, 87, 152, 154, 155, 158, 166, 178, 207
      Efterspelet (The Epilogue), 11
    Maradörer, 161, 170–71
    Marauders. See *Maradörer*
    Miss Julie. See *Fröken Julie*
    Moderkärlek, 178
    Motherlove. See *Moderkärlek*
    Oväder, 49–58, 158, 160
    Påsk, 158–61
    Paria, 155, 175, 285–86
    The Pelican. See *Pelikanen*
    Pelikanen, 49–58, 287
    Playing with Fire. See *Leka med elden*
    The Saga of the Folkungs. See *Folkungasagan*
    The Secret of the Guild. See *Gillets hemlighet*

Index

Sir Bengt's Wife. See Herr Bengts hustru
Spöksonaten, 49–58, 76, 80–90, 115, 158, 203, 212, 228–29, 232, 257, 277–78, 289
Den starkare, 75–76, 160–61, 175, 285
Stora landsvägen, 40, 231
Stormy Weather. See Oväder
The Stronger. See Den starkare
Svanevit, 159, 203, 212, 246, 249
Swanwhite. See Svanevit
Till Damaskus, 22, 25–30, 68, 115, 126, 132, 144, 221, 247, 249, 279, 286
To Damascus. See Till Damaskus
Poetry
  Dikter, 183
  Ordalek och småkonst, 43, 183, 208
  Poems. See Dikter
  Word Play and Minor Art. See Ordalek och småkonst
Prose
  Among French Farmers. See Bland franska bönder
  En blå bok, 4–6, 9, 15, 22, 80, 82–83, 90, 160
  Black Banners. See Svarta fanor
  Bland franska bönder, 126
  Blomstermålningar, 128, 130
  A Blue Book. See En blå bok
  By the Open Sea. See I havsbandet
  The Cloister. See Klostret
  En dåres försvarstal, 178, 279
  Flower Paintings. See Blomstermålningar
  Giftas, 18, 126, 130, 153, 159, 167–70
  Götiska rummen, 3, 21, 246
  Gothic Rooms. See Götiska rummen
  I havsbandet, 95, 121, 156, 193–94
  Hemsöborna, 66, 71–72, 93, 132, 172
  I röda rummet, 126
  In the Red Room. See I röda rummet
  Inferno, 3, 5, 11, 19, 111–12, 156–57, 245
  Jäsningstiden. See Time of Ferment
  Jacob Wrestles. See Jakob brottas
  Jakob brottas, 5
  Klostret, 106–7, 109
  Legender, 5
  Life in the Skerries. See Skärkarlsliv
  Lilla katakes för underklassen, 130
  A Madman's Defense. See En dåres försvarstal
  Married. See Giftas
  The Natives of Hemsö. See Hemsöborna
  The New Kingdom. See Det nya riket
  Det nya riket, 166
  Occult Diary. See Ockulta dagboken
  Ockulta dagboken, 3, 5, 9, 12, 14–15, 20, 90, 247
  Öppna brev till Intima teatern, 55, 204
  Open Letters to the Intimate Theater. See Öppna brev till Intima teatern
  Printed and Unprinted. See Tryckt och otryckt
  The Red Room. See Röda rummet
  Röda rummet, 152–53, 159, 165
  "The Romantic Sacristan on Rånö." See "Den romantiska klockaren på Rånö"
  "Den romantiska klockaren på Rånö," 126, 173
  Skärkarlsliv, 153, 172–73
  Sleepwalking Nights. See Sömngångarnätter
  Sömngångarnätter, 121, 126–27
  Son of a Servant. See Tjänstekvinnans son
  Svarta fanor, 39–40
  Svenska folket i helg och socken, 66
  Svenska öden och äventyr, 66, 153–54, 205
  Swedish Destinies and Adventures. See Svenska öden och äventyr
  Swedish People on Holy Day and Every Day. See Svenska folket i helg och socken
  The Time of Ferment. See Jäsningstiden
  Tjänstekvinnans son, 71, 94–95, 127–29, 169, 204, 279
  Tryckt och otryckt, 175
  Tschandala, 154
  Utopier i verkligheten, 70, 126, 168
  Vivisektioner, 171
Sudermann, Hermann, 102, 106
Swedenborg, Emanuel, 3, 37
  Arcana coelestia, 14, 21
  Apocalypsis revelata, 14
  De amore conjugiali, 14
  De coelo et ejus mirabilibus, 14
  De cultu et amore dei, 17, 31
  De telluribus in mundo nostri solari, 14, 17
  Diarium spirituale, 4, 31
  Swedenborgs drömmar 1744, 9, 14, 16
  Tankar och syner i andliga ämnen, 8
  Vera religio christiana, 8, 30–31

T
Thousand and One Nights, 212
Twain, Mark, 128

U
Uhl, Frida, 20, 106–10, 125
Uhl, Marie, 12, 16

V
Verdi, Giuseppe, 204, 207

W
Wagner, Richard, 203, 205–6, 247
Weismann, Julius, 203, 211
Wied, Gustav, 155–56
Wilde, Oscar, 203
Williams, Tennessee, 232, 256
Williams, William Carlos, 190
Williamson, Malcolm, 204, 208

Willumsen, J. F., 99
Wirsén, Carl David af, 38, 41, 43
Wrangel, F. U., 10, 124

Y
Yeats, W. B., 7

Z
Zola, Emile, 71, 73, 124, 246
Zorn, Anders, 124